The Making of the Luso-Asian World

Nalanda-Sriwijaya Series

General Editors: Tansen Sen and Geoff Wade

The Nalanda-Sriwijaya Series, established under the publications program of the Institute of Southeast Asian Studies, Singapore, has been created as a publications avenue for the Nalanda-Sriwijaya Centre. The Centre focuses on the ways in which Asian polities and societies have interacted over time. To this end, the series invites submissions which engage with Asian historical connectivities. Such works might examine political relations between states; the trading, financial and other networks which connected regions; cultural, linguistic and intellectual interactions between societies; or religious links across and between large parts of Asia.

1. *Nagapattinam to Suvarnadwipa: Reflections on the Chola Naval Expeditions to Southeast Asia*, edited by Hermann Kulke, K. Kesavapany and Vijay Sakhuja
2. *Early Interactions between South and Southeast Asia: Reflections on Cross-Cultural Exchange*, edited by Pierre-Yves Manguin, A. Mani and Geoff Wade
3. *Anthony Reid and the Study of the Southeast Asian Past*, edited by Geoff Wade and Li Tana
4. *Hardships and Downfall of Buddhism in India*, by Giovanni Verardi

The Institute of Southeast Asian Studies (ISEAS) was established as an autonomous organization in 1968. It is a regional centre dedicated to the study of socio-political, security and economic trends and developments in Southeast Asia and its wider geostrategic and economic environment. The Institute's research programmes are the Regional Economic Studies (RES, including ASEAN and APEC), Regional Strategic and Political Studies (RSPS), and Regional Social and Cultural Studies (RSCS).

ISEAS Publishing, an established academic press, has issued more than 2,000 books and journals. It is the largest scholarly publisher of research about Southeast Asia from within the region. ISEAS Publishing works with many other academic and trade publishers and distributors to disseminate important research and analyses from and about Southeast Asia to the rest of the world.

PORTUGUESE AND LUSO-ASIAN LEGACIES IN SOUTHEAST ASIA, 1511-2011
VOLUME 1

The Making of the Luso-Asian World

Intricacies of Engagement

EDITED BY
LAURA JARNAGIN

ISEAS
INSTITUTE OF SOUTHEAST ASIAN STUDIES
Singapore

First published in Singapore in 2011 by
Institute of Southeast Asian Studies
30 Heng Mui Keng Terrace
Pasir Panjang
Singapore 119614

E-mail: publish@iseas.edu.sg
Website: <http://bookshop.iseas.edu.sg>

ISEAS Library Cataloguing-in-Publication Data

Portuguese and Luso-Asian legacies in Southeast Asia, 1511–2011. Volume 1, The making of the Luso-Asian world : intricacies of engagement / edited by Laura Jarnagin.
Most papers in the volume were originally presented to a Conference on Portuguese and Luso-Asian Legacies in Southeast Asia 1511–2011, Singapore, 28–30 September 2010.
1. Portuguese—Southeast Asia—History—Congresses.
2. Portuguese—Asia—History—Congresses.
3. Southeast Asia—Civilization—Portuguese influences—Congresses.
4. Asia—Civilization—Portuguese influences—Congresses.
5. Portuguese—Southeast Asia—Ethnic identity—Congresses.
6. Portuguese—Asia—Ethnic identity—Congresses.
I. Jarnagin, Laura.
II. Institute of Southeast Asian Studies.
II. Conference on Portuguese and Luso-Asian Legacies in Southeast Asia 1511–2011 (2010 : Singapore)
III. Title: Making of the Luso-Asian world : intricacies of engagement
DS523.4 P81P85 2011

ISBN 978-981-4345-25-5 (soft cover)
ISBN 978-981-4345-26-2 (E-book PDF)

Cover photo: Close-up of a green parrot's feathers. The green parrot, or *papagaio verde*, is an enduring, centuries-old folk motif found throughout the Lusophone world. Photo © Audrey R. Smith, 2011.

Typeset by Superskill Graphics Pte Ltd
Printed in Singapore by Mainland Press Pte Ltd

CONTENTS

LIST OF CHARTS, FIGURES AND TABLES

Charts

Figures

Tables

A TRIBUTE TO GLENN JOSEPH AMES

Timothy D. Walker

Professor Glenn Ames of the University of Toledo had planned to attend the "Portuguese and Luso-Asian Legacies in Southeast Asia, 1511–2011" conference in Singapore and Malacca in late September 2010. Many of us, his long-time colleagues, were looking forward to seeing him again, and to hearing his scheduled contribution, a paper entitled "A Tale of Two Cities: The Creation and Role of 'Creole' Power Groups in Goa and Malacca, *circa* 1510–1683". Because Glenn had not burdened us with the knowledge, we were unaware that he was ill; so, it was puzzling — and very unlike Glenn — when he simply did not appear. Two weeks later, his friends were shocked to learn the true reason behind his absence: Glenn Ames passed away on 14 October 2010, after struggling for months against a relapse of melanoma cancer. He was fifty-five years old.

In his relatively brief career, Glenn Ames distinguished himself as a leading scholar of the Lusophone world and European expansion in Asia. It is therefore particularly fitting that the conference participants and organizers have decided to dedicate this publication to his memory as an historian and friend.

Glenn earned his Ph.D. in history from the University of Minnesota in 1987; his concentration fields were early modern Europe, French history and the history of European expansion. He spent a postdoctoral year at the University of Bristol (United Kingdom) as a Leverhulme Fellow. For twenty-two years, he was a member of the history faculty at the University of Toledo (USA). Glenn accumulated many academic awards and honours over the years, including a Fulbright grant and fellowships from the American Institute of Indian Studies, the Portuguese Ministry of Education and the Calouste Gulbenkian Foundation of Lisbon. In 2002, he was a Union Pacific Visiting Professor at the Center for Early Modern Europe at the University of Minnesota.

A keen and assiduous archival researcher, Glenn had worked on documentary collections in France, England, the Netherlands, Portugal and India, often for very extended periods of time. He was also a prolific author, with some six books to his credit, numerous journal articles and book chapters in edited volumes. Most recently, he was the progenitor and general editor of the European Expansion and Indigenous Response Series (Brill Academic Publishers, the Netherlands), which published a number of important new works of scholarship (including a primary source journal of Vasco da Gama's 1497–99 voyage, which Glenn himself translated and edited).

Glenn was a generous colleague and mentor; he gave liberally of his time and expertise to his many students, and he typically answered colleagues' queries with uncommon attention and detail. Those of us who had the privilege to know him will miss the stimulating conversation that we enjoyed with him at conferences and in far-flung archives, or visiting him at his home in Toledo, Ohio. Glenn's nimble wit and passion for the events he studied emerged in his engaging lecture style, making him exceptionally popular with undergraduate students, who frequently described Glenn as their all-time favourite history teacher. Similarly, his graduate advisees appreciated his broad knowledge and dedication to their progress, recognizing their good fortune in receiving his enthusiastic support — and, if necessary, firm direction — as they worked through their theses and dissertations.

My best personal memories of Glenn come from winter 2005, when I crossed paths with him and his family in western India. We spent several days visiting historic sites together in Goa, including climbing up to the seventeenth-century Portuguese Chapora Fortress in northern Bardez province. One day, after working alongside him in the Historical Archive of Goa, we were drinking a beer on the terrace of the Panjim Inn. Glenn began to recount, with obvious relish and respect, stories of his conversations with Professor Charles Boxer in the UK while Glenn was a young postdoc. Clearly, these encounters had made an enormous impression on Glenn as a scholar, and he was good enough to share some anecdotes highlighting the celebrated Boxer mystique with me, so I could enjoy them vicariously.

Despite his rigorous work commitments, Glenn took enormous and obvious pleasure in spending time with his children, Miranda and Ethan. During summer term courses, Glenn occasionally brought his son and daughter to sit in on lectures — and he sometimes called on them to answer questions that his students could not. (This was a bit of lighthearted classroom theatre; Glenn liked a joke, so he supplied his kids with the answers in advance!) He delighted in taking them along with him on research trips to Portugal and India, too, sharing with them in ways few parents can some of the extraordinary places he had come to know through his studies.

Glenn Ames's remarkable scholarly output has influenced a generation of researchers and students of European expansion, and will continue to do so. His books include *The Globe Encompassed: The Age of European Discovery, 1500–1700* (2007); *Vasco da Gama: Renaissance Crusader* (2005); *Distant Lands and Diverse Cultures: The French Experience in Asia, 1600–1700* (co-edited with Ronald S. Love, 2003); *Renascent Empire? The House of Braganza and the Quest for Stability in Portuguese Monsoon Asia, ca. 1640–1683* (2000); and *Colbert, Mercantilism and the French Quest for Asian Trade* (1996).

We are far richer for Glenn Ames's scholarship and friendship. He will be deeply missed.

Timothy Walker
Lisbon, Portugal
15 January 2011

PREFACE

This book, the first of two volumes, is the outgrowth of an international, interdisciplinary conference entitled "Portuguese and Luso-Asian Legacies in Southeast Asia, 1511–2011" that was held in Singapore and Malacca on 28–30 September 2010, co-sponsored by the Institute of Southeast Asian Studies (ISEAS), Singapore and the Universiti Teknologi MARA (UiTM), Bandaraya Campus, Malacca, Malaysia. Major financial support for the conference came from ISEAS as well as from the Comemorações Portugal/Asia programme of the Government of Portugal, for which we extend our sincerest appreciation.

This event was the brainchild of Ambassador K. Kesavapany, director of ISEAS, who has an abiding commitment to promoting deeper historical and contemporary understandings across societies everywhere, and particularly those that comprise the dense and complex cultural cum geographical nexus that is today's Southeast Asia. The coming of the Portuguese by sea into Southeast Asia half a millennium ago marked the opening of a major shift in relations between Asians and Europeans, one that would have a profound impact not only on this region and its peoples, but also on the course of world history. I am especially indebted to Ambassador Kesavapany for bestowing this challenging and rewarding project on me, and for the confidence he has placed in this Brazilianist to make enough of an intellectual transition from the Lusophone Atlantic world to that of the Luso-*present* Indian and Pacific oceans in order to do justice to this undertaking.

Special thanks for the many and varied contributions to this conference are hereby extended to Ambassador Jaime Leitão, head of the diplomatic mission to Singapore, Embassy of Portugal in Singapore, for his unwavering enthusiasm, dedication and assistance; to Ambassador Dato Dr Mohd Yusof Ahmad, director of the Institute of ASEAN Studies and Global Affairs (INSPAG), Faculty of Adminstrative Science and Policy Studies (FSPPP),

Universiti Teknologi MARA (UiTM), Shah Alam Campus, Malaysia, who orchestrated the Malacca portion of the event with his customary unruffled aplomb and attentiveness; to Dr Mizan Hitam, dean of the UiTM, Malacca Campus, for committing his university's resources to this event; to Dr Roaimah Omar, Faculty of Business Administration, UiTM, Malacca Campus, who coordinated the Malacca portion of the conference; to Dr Peter Borschberg, Department of History, National University of Singapore, for his intellectual guidance, wisdom and wit at many critical junctures; to Dr Tansen Sen, head of the Nalanda-Sriwijaya Centre at ISEAS for helping to define the scope of the conference; to Dr Geoffrey Wade, also of the Nalanda-Sriwijaya Centre, for serving on the panel selection committee and as a session chair, and for his expansive knowledge of this region and his unvarnished candor in all matters; to Dr Ivo Carneiro, vice-rector of the University of Saint Joseph in Macao, who served as our keynote speaker and proffered many valuable observations about the importance of the contributions made by the scholars whose works appear herein; in Macao, to Father Luís Manuel Fernandes Sequeira, SJ, vice-rector of the Macao Ricci Institute, and to Manuel Carvalho, consul general of Portugal to Macao and Hong Kong, both of whom employed their good offices in the furtherance of this event in the fine tradition of Portuguese finessing; to Mr William Jansen, president of the Eurasian Association of Singapore, along with his gracious staff and many associates who hosted a memorable dinner in the unique and special surroundings of the Eurasian Community House; to Mrs Y. L. Lee, head of administration at ISEAS, along with Ms May Wong and Mr Loh Joo Yong of her staff, all of whom bring an exceptional and devoted level of professionalism to project planning and execution; to two Singaporean scholars who chaired panel sessions, Dr Goh Beng Lan (associate professor and head of the Department of Southeast Asian Studies, National University of Singapore) and Dr Sim Yong Huei (lecturer in Humanities and Social Studies Education at Nanyang Technological University); to Drs Christopher Larkosh, Ricardo Roque and Timothy Walker, all contributors to this volume, for special insights and advice that went into putting this volume together; and to Dr Eul-Soo Pang, visiting professorial fellow at ISEAS, my husband, and my colleague, whose counsel, expertise and assistance are always invaluable.

Above all, I would like to express my gratefulness to the conference participants, who hail from a dozen different nationalities, for making this event an exceptional success. Most of them travelled from great distances to attend, and all of them cheerfully endured three long days of intense activity. Their enthusiasm for the interdisciplinary nature of the conference was palpable and infectious, and their individual commitment to making it a success with their contributions was uncharacteristically high, as academic conferences go. It was especially rewarding to know that many individuals were able to meet some of their intellectual counterparts and scholars whom they admire for the first time (in one instance, capping a thirty-year correspondence). Along with the warm afterglow of this conference, however, we will always carry a deep sense of loss. Dr Glenn Ames, who was the first to submit a proposal, was unexpectedly unable to attend and passed away a few days after our meeting. Befittingly, we open this work with a tribute to him and the lasting contributions he made to the history of the Portuguese and their legatees in Asia; heartfelt thanks go to Dr Timothy Walker for authoring this remembrance.

Finally, a brief word is in order regarding Portuguese orthography, quotations and translations used throughout this work. For the reader's convenience, most proper names and proper nouns have been converted to the current orthography in the text (for instance, "Afonso de Albuquerque", not the original "Affonso d'Albuquerque"), with a few "judgement call" exceptions. Inevitably, though, given the distinct creole communities and languages that evolved from the Portuguese presence in Asia, it would not be appropriate to modernize the spellings of the names of individuals associated with these groups, although it is not always obvious to know where to "draw the line". Thus, for instance, "Frank Correa" of mid-twentieth-century Macao appears as such in the text, and not as "Frank Correia". In a similar vein, cities and other geographic entites that have current, commonly used English variations are spelled as such; hence, "Lisbon" instead of "Lisboa", "Macao" instead of "Macau", and so forth. However, original spellings of all words in all languages have been retained in quotations and citations. Translations into English of all passages originally in another language have been done by the individual authors themselves, unless stated otherwise.

Laura Jarnagin
The Editor

LIST OF CONTRIBUTORS

Paolo Aranha originally pursued political studies and international relations at Sapienza Università di Roma but later turned his scholarly interests towards the history of the early modern Catholic missions to India. In 2004 he defended his master's thesis on the history of Latin Christianity in India during the sixteenth century, subsequently published as *Il Cristianesimo Latino in India nel XVI secolo* (2006). He is completing his doctorate in the Department of History and Civilization at the European University Institute of Florence. His dissertation is entitled "Malabar Rites: An Eighteenth-Century Conflict on Social and Cultural Accommodation in the Jesuit Missions of South India". As of 2011, he is a Marie Curie Intra-European Fellow at the Warburg Institute in London, researching the early modern Catholic representations of Hinduism. He has presented papers in several international conferences and published articles on various aspects of the history of early modern Portuguese India.

Ujjayan Bhattacharya is a Calcutta-based historian who teaches at Vidyasagar University, Midnapore, where he teaches Indian and European history of the early modern period. He obtained his Ph.D. from Jawaharlal Nehru University, New Delhi, in 1985. In 1991, he joined Goa University, Panjim, where he taught for twelve years. While in Goa, his interest in Portuguese studies matured, intensified and subsequently translated into an investigation of the Portuguese presence in Bengal. His research interests include the social and economic history of Eastern India.

John Byrne is a Singapore-born Eurasian whose background reflects the diversity of the European expansion into Asia. He traces his lineage, on his mother's maternal side, to some of the early Portuguese Eurasian families in Malacca, Malaysia. His mother's paternal side is Luso-Indian, originally from Goa. His father's ancestry is also Eurasian, with several generations of British-Asian and Dutch-Asian heritages. Having left Singapore for New Zealand in 1967, John was part of the Eurasian exodus to the West, which he describes as the "second dispersion" in his chapter. He is a graduate of the University of Auckland with a degree in anthropology and sociology and is passionate about Luso-Asian history and the Luso-Asian people. He has been doing research over many years and is currently writing a book on the Eurasian communities. John is an independent researcher and a practising financial planner in Auckland.

Anthony Disney, who specializes in the history of the Portuguese in maritime Asia in the late sixteenth and early seventeenth centuries, is a scholar emeritus at La Trobe University in Melbourne. His main published works are *Twilight of the Pepper Empire* (originally published in 1978; a slightly revised second edition was published in 2010), *A History of Portugal and the Portuguese Empire: From Beginnings to 1807* (two volumes, 2009) and *The Portuguese in India and Other Studies, 1500–1700* (2009). He is now working on a biography of Dom Miguel de Noronha, fourth Conde de Linhares and viceroy at Goa in 1629–36. Dr Disney has an MA from Oxford and a Ph.D. from Harvard.

K. David Jackson is professor of Portuguese at Yale University. He specializes in Portuguese and Brazilian literatures, modernist movements in literature and other arts, Portuguese literature and culture in Asia, poetry, music and ethnography. His publications include a photograph album, *A Hidden Presence: 500 Years of Portuguese Culture in India and Sri Lanka* (1995); a study of creole folk verse in Asia, *Sing without Shame* (1990); *Builders of the Oceans* (1998); three CDs in the series *The Journey of Sounds* (1998); two volumes on the Brazilian and Portuguese avant-garde movments, *A Vanguarda Literária no Brasil* (1998) and *As Primeiras Vanguardas em Portugal* (2003); a CD-ROM, "Luís de Camões and the First Edition of *The Lusiads*, 1572"; and a book on the literature of empire, *De Chaul a Batticaloa: As Marcas do Império Marítimo Português na Índia e no Sri Lanka* (2005). Professor Jackson recently edited *Haroldo de Campos: A Dialogue with the Brazilian Concrete Poet* (2005) and the *Oxford Anthology of the Brazilian Short Story* (2006). He is the author of a new interpretation of Fernando Pessoa in English, *Adverse Genres in Fernando Pessoa* (2010).

Laura Jarnagin (Pang) is a visiting professorial fellow at the Institute of Southeast Asian Studies in Singapore and an associate professor emerita in the Division of Liberal Arts and International Studies at Colorado School of Mines (Golden, Colorado) where she served as its director for five years and was a co-founder of its Master of International Political Economy of Resources programme. She is the author of *A Confluence of Transatlantic Networks: Elites, Capitalism, and Confederate Migration to Brazil* (2008). Her current research interests include late eighteenth- and nineteenth-century transatlantic merchant networks and the application of complexity theory to understanding their dynamics. She holds a doctorate in Brazilian history from Vanderbilt University.

Christopher Larkosh is an assistant professor of Portuguese in the Luso-Afro-Brazilian Studies and Theory Program at the University of Massachusetts Dartmouth, while concurrently serving as director of the UMass Dartmouth Summer Program in Portuguese. He has published numerous articles on five continents as part of a long-standing commitment to a broad global and multilingual approach to Lusophone and comparative literary and cultural studies, both in collected volumes and in journals such as *Translation Studies, TTR, Portuguese Literary and Cultural Studies, Social Dynamics, Contemporary French and Francophone Studies/Sites, Annali d'italianistica, TOPIA* and *The Translator.* He has recently edited a volume of articles entitled *Re-Engendering Translation: Transcultural Practice, Gender/Sexuality and the Politics of Alterity*, to be published by St. Jerome in 2011, and is currently writing a book on Lusophone transnational diasporas, as well as co-editing a volume on German-Brazilian intercultural encounters.

Everton V. Machado is a postdoctoral researcher at the Centre for Comparative Studies of the School of Humanities at the University of Lisbon (Centro de Estudos Comparatistas, Faculdade de Letras, Universidade de Lisboa). He earned his doctorate in comparative literature from the Université Paris – Sorbonne (Paris IV) and has taught Portuguese, literature and Brazilian cultures at the Université Lumière Lyon 2. He is the co-author of *Joaquim Heliodoro da Cunha Rivara, 1809–1879* (2009) and has chapters in *Don Juans insolites* (edited with Pierre Brunel, 2008) and *Insurgent Sepoys: Europe Views the Revolt of 1857* (edited with Shaswati Mazumdar, 2011). He is currently preparing a critical edition of the first Indian novel written in the Portuguese language, *Os Brahamanes* (1866) by Goan Francisco Luís Gomes, for Classiques Garnier, the French version of which was serialized in 1870.

Paulo Teodoro de Matos holds a master's degree in history from the Universidade Nova de Lisboa and a doctorate in historical demography from the Universidade do Minho. He has taught Portuguese history at the Instituto

Superior. Currently, he is a full-time member of the Centro de História de Além-Mar of the Universidade Nova de Lisboa – Universidade dos Açores in Lisbon where he holds the position of affiliated researcher (Programa Ciência 2008). He is also an assistant visiting professor of the Universidade Católica Portuguesa. While he was a postdoctoral fellow, he developed a joint project of the Universidade Católica Portuguesa and the University of Goa entitled "Goa do Antigo Regime ao Liberalismo: Demografia, família e herança (1718–1830)" [Goa from the Old Regime to Liberalism: Demography, Family and Heritage (1718–1830)] and later another one entitled "A Demografia do Atlântico Português: Gentes, grupos populacionais e dinâmicas populacionais em perspectiva comparada (1770–1820)" [The Demography of the Portuguese Atlantic: Peoples, Population Groups and Population Dynamics in Comparative Perspective (1770–1820)], co-sponsored by the Universidade Nova de Lisboa and The Johns Hopkins University. His current research interests centre on social history, history of the family, historical demography and Portuguese overseas expansion.

Isabel Maria da Costa Morais is an associate professor and vice-rector for Student Affairs at the University of Saint Joseph in Macao. She has a doctorate degree in comparative literature from the University of Hong Kong, and her research interests include comparative and transcultural studies, diasporic memory, gender/ethnicity and human rights. She is also the Coordinator of the Center of Heritage and History Studies (CHERISH) and has published in different journals, including *Mare Liberum: Revista de História dos Mares* (Portugal), the *Journal of Social Sciences* (Guangdong), the *Chinese Heritage Centre Bulletin* (Singapore), *Chinese Cross Currents* (Macau Ricci Institute), *Review of Culture* (Macao) and *Transtext(e)s Transcultures: Journal of Global Cultural Studies* (University of Jean Moulin Lyon 3, Lyon, France). More recent work is included in the collection of essays *Gendering the Fairs: Histories of Women and Gender at World Fairs* (2010) and *Americans, Macau and China 1784–1950: Historical Relations, Interactions and Connections* (2011).

Stefan Halikowski Smith is a senior lecturer in the Department of History at Swansea University, where he specializes in early modern Portuguese overseas history. He has just finished a book entitled *Creolization and Diaspora in the Portuguese Indies: The Social World of Ayutthaya* (2011) and is completing an edited collection of essays entitled *Reinterpreting the Indian Ocean World: Essays in Honour of Professor Kirti N. Chaudhuri* (2011).

Timothy Walker is an associate professor of history at the University of Massachusetts Dartmouth. He is an affiliated researcher of the Centro de História de Além-Mar (CHAM), Universidade Nova de Lisboa, Portugal. He was a visiting professor at the Universidade Aberta in Lisbon (1994–2003), and a visiting professor at Brown University (2010). Walker is the recipient of a Fulbright dissertation fellowship to Portugal (1996–97), a doctoral research fellowship from the Portuguese Camões Institute (1995–96), and an NEH-funded American Institute for Indian Studies Professional Development Grant for postdoctoral work in India (2000–02). Teaching fields include early modern Europe, the Atlantic World, the Portuguese and their empire, maritime history and European global colonial expansion. Current research topics focus on the seventeenth and eighteenth centuries, and include the adoption of colonial indigenous medicines by European science during the Enlightenment as well as slave trading in the Atlantic and Indian oceans. He is the author of *Doctors, Folk Medicine and the Inquisition: The Repression of Magical Healing in Portugal during the Enlightenment* (2005).

Felicia Yap is a fellow in international history at the London School of Economics and an affiliated lecturer at the University of Cambridge. Her research work centres on the Japanese occupation of East and Southeast Asia during the Second World War. She has written widely for a number of publications and institutions, such as *The Economist*, the U.K. Parliament, *Asia!*, *Asian Geographic* and the *Business Times*.

GLOSSARY

Definitions of the words and terms in this glossary are followed either by the language of origin or a location where the word or term is or was used with reference to the subject matter covered in this book. Most nouns are given in both their singular and plural spellings, as is relevant to their usage in this work. Plurals formed by the simple addition of an *s* are indicated parenthetically at the end of the singular, such as *casa(s)*; more complex spellings of plurals are shown separately, as in *balão*; pl. *balões*.

agente de negócios	Business agent. (Portuguese)
águas	Literally, "waters"; in the context of this work, waters that have healing properties. (Portuguese)
alfândega	Custom house. (Portuguese)
alferes	An ensign; in the context of this work, second in command. (Portuguese)
aloes	*Aloe* (botanical name). (Portuguese)
altea	*Althea* (botanical name). (Portuguese)
alvadar	A local Mughal governor. (India)
Angélica	*Angelica*, a genus of about sixty species of plants in the Apiaceae family. (Botany)
arzees	A petition. (India)
ashrafi	A gold or silver coin minted in Goa and other western parts of maritime Asia worth 300 *reis*, or standard money of account to the same value, in the context of this work. Also known in Portuguese as *xerafim* (pl. *xerafins*). (Persian)
azebre	*Aloe* (botanical name). (Portuguese)

azulejos	Decorative tile panels. (Portuguese)
balão; pl. *balões*	Richly decorated ceremonial Siamese barges. (Portuguese)
balon; pl. balons	Richly decorated ceremonial Siamese barges. (Spanish; also an anglicized version of *balão*)
bangue	*Cannabis* (botanical name). (Portuguese)
banian	A Hindu merchant or shopkeeper. The corrupt term *banyan* or *banian* was used in Bengal to designate the native who managed the money concerns of a European, and sometimes served him as an interpreter. Same as *dubash* of Madras. (derived from Sanskrit)
bantim; pl. *bantins*	Banteen(s), a type of small Malay sailing vessel. (Portuguese)
batcar	A landowner. (India)
bebinca	A traditional Luso-Asian layer cake made with flour, sugar, ghee and coconut milk. Variants of this dessert are found not only in Goa, but also in Macao and Timor. (Portuguese)
bhang	*Cannabis* (botanical name). (Several Indian languages)
bigha(s)	A land measure equal to about one-third of an acre, but varying in different Indian provinces. (India)
bodki	A Hindu widow. (India)
bom rei	Good king; obsolete orthography: *bom rey*. (Portuguese)
botica	Pharmacy. (Portuguese)
branhô	A kind of party in which men, women and children take part and compete with each other in singing folk stanzas; common on wedding days, birthdays and the like throughout Luso-Asian communities. (Portuguese)
broas	A sweet made with eggs, rice and bread of maize. (Portuguese)
butua	A vine; also known as *pareira brava* or *pereira brava*. (Portuguese, as *pereira brava*; apparently a corrupted form of Portuguese otherwise)
câmara	A local governing council. (Portuguese)
campo	Literally, a field or grounds; also, in the context of this work, a compound. (Portuguese)

canarim; pl. *canarins*	Native(s) (meaning non-white) Christian(s). (Portuguese)
cancioneiro(s)	Songbook(s). (Portuguese)
cantiga	A popular seven-syllable quatrain or verse. (Portuguese)
capitão-môr	A local commander appointed by the crown. (Portuguese)
cardamomo	Cardamom. (Portuguese)
carta de crença	A letter or charter of credence or credibility. (Portuguese)
cartaz; pl. *cartazes*	A maritime passport issued by the Portuguese authorities. (Portuguese)
casa	A house. (Portuguese)
casaco(s)	Coat(s). (Portuguese)
casado(s)	Married Portuguese man/men. (Portuguese)
castiços	Broadly, those born in Asia of Portuguese parentage. More specifically, Portuguese immigrants and Eurasians born in Malacca or elsewhere in maritime Asia, such as India, who had effectively become permanent settlers and Lusitanized Asians. (Portuguese)
chikotie	A fast dance style among Portuguese Burghers. (Sri Lanka)
chowkie(s)	The station(s) of a guard or watchman. Place(s) where an officer is stationed to receive tolls and customs. (India)
chunam	Lime. (India)
cirurgião-môr	Chief surgeon. (Portuguese)
concentimento	Consent or permission. (Portuguese)
condrin(s)	Candareen(s). A traditional measurement of weight in East Asia, approximately 378 milligrams. (Malay: *kandūri*)
cowle	A written lease or grant. (India)
cristão(s)	Christian(s); obsolete orthography: *christão(s)*. (Portuguese)
cruzado(s)	A Portuguese monetary unit. (Portuguese)
curumbin(s)	Member(s) of a Christian caste of rural workers. (India)
cutcherry	The public office where rents are paid and other revenue collection-related business is transacted; also a court of justice. (India)

descendentes	Literally, "descendants". In particular, a term used in Goa to designate those inhabitants of Goa directly descended from Portuguese colonists. (Portuguese)
divan	A council. (India)
donzelas sem pergaminhos	Damsels without pedigrees. (Portuguese)
droga	A drug. (Portuguese)
dusun	A small rural property on the fringes of the forests. (Malaya)
especiaria(s)	Spice(s). (Portuguese)
farmān	An order or mandate; a royal decree or charter. In Portuguese, *formão;* in English, *firman.* (originally Persian; used in India)
faujdar	Under the Mughal government, a magistrate of the police with control over a large district who took cognizance of all criminal matters within his jurisdiction and sometimes was employed as receiver-general of the revenues. (India)
feni	Cashew wine. (Konkani [Goa])
feringhee(s)	Foreigner(s); also spelt *firinghee(s).* (India)
fidalgo(s)	Individual(s) with a Portuguese nobility title. (Portuguese)
filho atrás da porta	Literally, "son behind the door", a euphemism for an illegitimate son. (Portuguese)
firinghee(s)	See *feringhee(s).*
físico d'el Rei	A physician named by the king. (Portuguese)
físico-môr	A chief physician. (Portuguese)
galeota(s)	Small, fast sailing vessel(s) propelled by oars and sails; originally used in the Mediterranean world. (Portuguese)
ganvti vokot	Medicine of the land. (India)
gãocares	Community leaders. (India)
genro-comensal; pl. *genros-comensais*	Son(s)-in-law who is/are the head of a family in which there are only female siblings. (Portuguese)
gente Kristang	Christian people. (Portuguese/Kristang)
geragok	A type of local small shrimp. (Malacca)
geragok(s)	A somewhat derogatory term meaning "shrimp-eater(s)" for Malaccans descended from Portuguese. (Malacca)

geragok-people	The first Portuguese Eurasians from Malacca. (Macao)
gingebre	Ginger. (Portuguese)
gomastas	Generally, a commissioned factor or agent; derived from the Persian word *gumastan*, meaning to send forth upon any particular matter of business. (India)
grago	Traditional Malaccan Portuguese-descended shrimp fishermen; also *gragoh*. (Kristang)
horta(s)	Vegetable garden(s). (Portuguese)
jagir	A grant of territory to an individual for a temporary period of time (from three years to a lifetime), originally in recognition of military service. The *jagirdar*, or holder of the grant, effectively ruled that region and realized income from the taxes it produced. Although such grants reverted to the ruler upon the grantee's death, they could and usually were re-granted to heirs and successors. Also *jakeer*, a corruption of *jagir*. (India)
jagirdar	One who holds a *jagir*. (India)
jaina	A follower of Jainism; concerning the Indic religion of Jainism. (India)
jakeer	See *jagir*.
jália	A small galley-type of ship common in Southeast Asian waters and the Bay of Bengal. (Indian Ocean, Straits of Malacca and elsewhere in Southeast Asian waters)
juíz dos órfãos	Judge for orphans. (Portuguese)
khalsa	An office of government in which the business of the revenue department is transacted; the exchequer. (India)
kruisvaarders	Crusaders. (Dutch)
limey(s)	A derogatory term for a British person. (English)
logie	The Dutch trading factory. (Dutch)
lorcha(s)	A hybrid type of sailing vessel common in Macao. (Portuguese)
Luso-descendente(s)	Individual(s) of partial Portuguese ancestry. (Portuguese)

mahal(s)	Place(s) or source(s) that yield(s) revenue, particularly of a territorial nature; lands. (India)
mahāmaṇḍaleśvara	A provincial governor. (India)
mahattaran	Lands given to "respectable", non-Brahmin people; also *motran*. (India)
mapa(s)	Statistical table(s); in this work, census or population charts.
materia medica	The body of collected knowledge about the therapeutic properties of any substance used for healing. (Latin)
médico(s)	Physician(s).
mestiço(s)	Individual(s) of mixed race; in this work, those born of mixed Portuguese and Asian parentage; more properly, *Luso-descendentes*. (Portuguese)
morador; pl. *moradores*	Resident(s).
mordexi	A variety of cobra wood. (Portuguese)
motran	A corruption of the word *mahattaran*. (India)
mui-tsai	Literally, "little younger sister". In this case, a system whereby girls were sold to perform household or other work, or to be a prostitute, often for many years or even decades. The system lasted until the twentieth century in South China, mainly in Macao and Hong Kong. (Cantonese).
namban	Literally, "southern barbarian". In this case, a Japanese screen depicting the arrival of the Portuguese. Such screens were produced in sixteenth- and seventeenth-century Japan. (Japanese)
navio(s)	Ship(s). (Portuguese)
nawāb	A governor. (India)
nhonha(s)	Married woman/women. (Macao and elsewhere in the Luso-Asian world)
nirguna	A term used in Hindu philosophy to discuss whether the Supreme Being, Brahman, should be conceptualized as either having attributes (*saguna*, "with qualities") or, in this case, not (*nirguna*, "no qualities"). In essence, a deity that is formless. (Sanskrit)

nona(s)	Daughter(s) of a European man and a Chinese woman. (Macao and elsewhere in the Luso-Asian world)
opperhoofd	Head of the Dutch trading factory or *logie*. (Dutch)
ouvidor	A judge. (Portuguese)
paclé	The Portuguese. (India)
palmos	Literally, "palms", in the sense of a unit of measure equivalent to a hand span. (Portuguese)
papagaio(s)	Parrot(s).
papagaio berde	A green parrot, wherein *berde* is a creolization of the Portuguese *verde*, meaning "green". (Portuguese creole)
papagaio verde	A green parrot. (Portuguese)
pardo(s)	The offspring of Portuguese and black Africans. (Portuguese)
pargana(s)	Small district(s) consisting of several villages, being a subdivision of a larger district. (India)
parvāna	See *parwana*.
parwana	A decree; a written warrant issued by an authority to summon or arrest. (India)
passarinho	A small bird. (Portuguese)
patta	A lease granted to the cultivators on the part of the government, either written on paper or engraved with a style on a leaf. (India)
pau cobra	Cobra wood. (Portuguese)
pau de cobra	The same as *pau cobra*.
pareira brava	A type of vine; apparently a spelling corruption over time of the Portuguese *pereira brava*.
pereira brava	A type of vine. (Portuguese)
pinheiro	A pine tree. (Portuguese)
pom(s)	A derogatory term for a British person(s), especially recent immigrants to Australia or New Zealand. (English)
pooneah	Rent day. (India)
portista	A supporter of the Portuguese soccer (*futebol*) team FC Porto (Futebol Clube de Porto), based in the city of Porto. FC Porto's team colours are blue and white, and its mascot is the dragon. (Portuguese)

pragana(s)	District(s). (India)
praja	See *ryot(s).*
quinta(s)	Farm(s). (Portuguese)
quintal	A plant nursery. (Portuguese)
raíz de cobra	Snake root. (Portuguese)
regimento	Governing by-laws. (Portuguese)
reino(s)	Kingdom(s).
reinol; pl. *reinóis*	Individual(s) born in Portugal.
real; pl. *réis*	A former Portuguese monetary unit, also used elsewhere in the Lusophone world. (Portuguese)
rooinek(s)	A derogatory term for a British person. (Afrikaans)
ryot(s)	A peasant cultivator of land or tenant of a house; synonymous with *praja*. (India)
sagoate	Gifts or presents; also *segoate* and *seguate*. (Siam)
saguna	A term used in Hindu philosophy to discuss whether the Supreme Being, Brahman, should be conceptualized as either having attributes, as in this case (*saguna*: "with qualities"), or not (*nirguna*: "no qualities"). In essence, a deity possessing an identifiable form. (Sanskrit)
śaivite	A temple of the Śaivism branch of Hinduism; in honour of the god Śiva. (Sanskrit/English)
sanad	An official term used in Mughal administration expressing the authority, original or delegated, to confer a privilege, make a grant, give a diploma and issue a charter or a patent; a state-recognized document granting an individual or institution titles, offices or privileges. (India)
sangrador; pl. *sangradores*	Phlebotomist(s). (Portuguese)
sarkar mutsuddie	An accountant or clerk in a public office. (India)
sarkas	Literally, a head of affairs of the state or government; also a large division of a province. (India)
sarsaparilha	Sarsaparilla. (Portuguese)
shāhbandar	A harbourmaster, tax collector and arbitrator; also *xabandar*. (India)

sida	*Sida* (botanical name), a genus of the Mallow family; a marsh mallow. (Portuguese)
soldado(s)	Soldier(s). (Portuguese)
solteirona(s)	Spinster(s). (Portuguese)
tamarindo	Tamarind. (Portuguese)
tanga(s)	A Portuguese Indian silver coin struck at Goa and originally worth sixty *réis*. (Portuguese)
tefolán(s)	The João Lopes pine tree(s) (Konkani, the language of Goa)
terço	The equivalent of an infantry regiment. (Portuguese)
tonelada(s)	Tonne(s); originally the equivalent of fifty-four *arrobas*, or roughly 1,800 pounds. (Portuguese)
topass; pl. *topasses*	Also *topaze(s)*. Variously: (a) a Portuguese Timorese *mestiço* group; from volume 1 of this work; (b) the offspring of Portuguese men and South Asian women; (c) the descendants of Portuguese mestizos who married native Sinhalese and Tamil women of Sri Lanka (Ceylon); and (d) possibly, an interpreter, in a Tamil derivation. *Topasses* were also referred to as "black Christians", and the men often became professional soldiers, leading to the additional meaning of a "hat-wearing mercenary soldier". (Southeast Asia; South Asia)
topaze(s)	See *topass/topasses*.
trikalam	Literally, three times, in reference to the past, the present and the future. (India)
tumenggung	An official responsible for law and order. (Malacca, possibly of Javanese origin)
tumengó(s)	Ancient title(s), possibly of Javanese origin, based on the term *tumenggung*.
vaidya(s)	Indigenous Goan healer(s). (India)
vaiṣṇavite	A temple of the Vishnu branch of Hinduism; in honour of the god Viṣṇu. (Sanskrit/English)
vinho de caju	Cashew wine. (Portuguese)
visitador	An external or outside official appointed to conduct a review. (Portuguese)
xerafim; pl. *xerafins*	A gold or silver coin minted in Goa and other western parts of maritime Asia worth 300 *réis*. See also *ashrafi*. (Portuguese)

zamindar	Landholder or land-keeper in Muslim government who was charged with the superintendence of the lands of a district. The appointment was generally continuous as long as the *zamindar* conducted himself to the satisfaction of the ruling power, and even continued to his heirs. (India)
zamindarry	The office or jurisdiction of a *zamindar.* (India)
zedoária	*Curcuma zedoaria* (botanical name).

INTRODUCTION: TOWARDS CLARITY THROUGH COMPLEXITY

Laura Jarnagin

At the opening of the twenty-first century, statistical evidence indicates that European dominance of shipping and maritime traffic in Southeast Asia is now — slowly, glacially — coming to an end.[1] This means that, for the first time in history, Westerners no longer account for majority ownership of the global maritime trade in and out of the region, a global seaborne commerce whose origins are five centuries old. The initiation of oceanic trade between the western extremities of the Eurasian landmass and its southeastern and eastern extremities (including insular and archipelagic appendages) dates to the early sixteenth century, and was first undertaken by the modest but scientifically advanced Western European state of Portugal and underwritten by capital from the Italian city-state of Genoa. On a grander scale, accessing Asia by sea in combination with the concurrent (re)discovery of the Western Hemisphere on the part of the Europeans changed the dynamic of humankind's interactions for all time and set in motion the makings of the globalized world we now know. Today, the Straits of Malacca, where the Portuguese arrived in 1511, continue to be the "shipping superhighway between the Indian and Pacific Oceans".[2]

From the very late fifteenth century until the mid-sixteenth century, the Portuguese installed themselves in strategic interstices throughout maritime Asia, especially at locations in the Indian Ocean and South China Sea, where an active seaborne trade linking southern Chinese, Southeast Asian and South Asian ports already existed. At the nexus of these two bodies of water, mingled in narrow straits, was the cosmopolitan emporium of Malacca, where Gujarati, Arab, Chinese and European merchants, among others, traded at this commercial hub. As one of Portugal's explorers in Asia, Tomé Pires, observed, "whoever is lord of Malacca has his hand on the throat of Venice",

Genoa's principal rival in the incipient capitalist economy then emerging in Western Europe.

In 1511, Afonso de Albuquerque established a commanding Portuguese presence at Malacca and thus "pierced the archipelago's chief commercial ganglion", leaving this trading zone fragmented into more specialized components.[3] Over time, the Portuguese "empire" or "network" (depending on whose nuanced academic terminology one prefers) became overextended and largely supplanted by other European interlopers in Asia: the Dutch, the French (to a lesser degree) and the English.[4] Yet, the relatively fractured, tenuous and diasporic Portuguese presence in the region, in both formal and informal senses, remains discernible today in a variety of manifestations. It is upon the occasion of the quincentenary of the Portuguese seaborne arrival in Southeast Asia that the Institute of Southeast Asian Studies in Singapore, in conjunction with the Universiti Teknologi MARA in Malacca chose to reflect on Portuguese, Luso-Asian and Asian actions, reactions and interactions over the past five centuries at a conference held in September 2010, and to ask what the legacies of those dynamics have been and continue to be.

Two issues merit comment at this juncture: the choice of an anniversary date around which to organize a conference, and the use of the term "legacy".

First, in purely objective terms, there is nothing inherently special about reflecting upon a watershed occurrence in an anniversary year with a nice round number attached to it relative to any other date, other than it conjures a kind of comforting numerical orderliness in an otherwise busy and usually disorderly world. It is also convenient mnemonically. More importantly, however, such dates serve as a reminder that it behoves us to stop and reflect on the impact of the past in terms of how it has shaped our present and how it is likely to affect our future. In turn, a better understanding of that past as well as of the present contributes to making more informed decisions and choices — political, economic, social, cultural. Further, when addressing as sensitive an issue as this one — the forceful assumption of one polity's power by another and the attendant centuries-long era of colonization it ushered in — we do not seek to "commemorate", we do not seek to "celebrate", and we do not seek to attach value judgements to what has transpired.

Instead, we seek to reflect, reassess and reconsider afresh when we acknowledge such anniversary dates. Since the late 1980s, as the many quincentenaries in the pantheon of initial explorations in Portugal's global oceanic expansion have approached, we have witnessed an attendant, broad range of revisionist thinking on this subject in the academic world. Notably receding from the discourse are works whose rhetorical overlay either gratuitously glorifies or vilifies the past and its legacies.[5] The themes that are the grist of current scholarly enquiry into the Portuguese and Luso-Asian experience across many disciplines include hybridity, transformation, accommodation, reciprocity, conflict, collaboration and integration — all of which have variously engaged the contributors in the two volumes that comprise this work. Collectively, their work adds to our knowledge of a half-millennium-long process that has wrought the long-term transfer, adaptation and fusion of cultures from a geographically broad and culturally diverse spectrum of perspectives.

Second, the choice of the term "legacy" as an overriding theme of the conference deserves comment and clarification. In its legal sense, of course, a legacy is a grant of personal property or money made in a will and bequeathed to another — that is, something consciously set aside by one person to be a gift to another after the former's demise. Clearly, this definition is not what our use of the word seeks to convey. Rather, we opt for a more open and inclusive sense of "legacy" as something that has been left, in this case, by an abstract predecessor — the Portuguese and subsequently Luso-Asian peoples in Asia — and that continued for some time or still continues to survive, to be observable and influential at some level of being, well beyond the lifetime of its original agent, albeit with modifications along the way. Or, perhaps more broadly still, we refer to something that remains perceptible and active that has its roots in the past and can be traced along some common pathway, even though the evolutionary process itself has been and continues to be a stochastic one — that is, one in which there is a degree of indeterminacy in the path an evolutionary process will take, although some paths are more likely than others.

That there is something still to be transmitted over the *longue durée* is far more the result of informal processes and structures than formal ones. The five-centuries perspective delivered in this work allows the reader to accompany what some would term a "self-standing hybrid" culture that has emerged over time, through accommodation and insertion into larger Asian communities, although individuals belonging to these groups often struggle with their own identities. The chapters in this work address different facets of this culture creation — insertion, survival and, in some cases, even dissipation.

Given the aim of the conference, to explore as broad a theme as Portuguese and Luso-Asian legacies, it was obvious that no single academic discipline would be able to capture the many facets of the phenomenon that would be relevant to the discussion; hence, the interdisciplinary composition of the content, with papers variously based in history, anthropology, linguistics, ethnomusicology, literature, culture studies and architecture. The conference also benefited from a mix of professional levels of expertise, ranging from senior scholars in the field to rising stars, doctoral candidates and even a few independent researchers. This mélange of disciplines and talent created a thought-provoking environment that prompted a cross-fertilization of ideas and stimulated participants to consider other ways of looking at information and issues — an experience that we trust will find expression in future scholarly endeavours. Similarly, we encourage readers of this work to venture off their usual disciplinary paths and travel along the others contained herein as a way of expanding their own thinking and perspectives.

By virtue of the interdisciplinary nature of this undertaking and the five-centuries-long time frame, no attempt was made to advance the discussion of any one theory or concept, nor was the conference designed to focus on the current polemics within any one discipline. However, one theme does surface in many of the works presented herein, namely, that of the *complexity* of the phenomena under investigation. In recent times, academia in general has been moving away from a long tradition of viewing subject matter in predominantly dichotomous or dualistic terms and towards acknowledging, seeking, conceptualizing, theorizing and analysing complexity, whether in the natural world or in the human condition and what humankind has wrought. In this regard, it is not surprising that one of the main themes of postcolonial discourse, hybridity (itself originally a term describing the results of combining two organic things), is found by some to be a useful and apropos concept for their work, while others find it wanting — perhaps as yet too underdeveloped to adequately account for what they observe, or perhaps simply inappropriate as an all-embracing conceptual tool for dealing with certain manifestations of complexity.[6] The works comprising these two volumes contribute to our store of empirical knowledge of this phenomenon and as such move us further along a continuum to greater clarity in our understanding of it.

The chapters contained in this work look at various dimensions of Portuguese and Luso-Asian legacies through microscopic lenses for the most part, but with macroscopic implications. Volume 1 treats the making of the Luso-Asian world, exploring how significantly different cultures, polities and societies interacted with one another within the South, Southeast and East Asian theatres. Although this work privileges the date of the Portuguese arrival in Southeast Asia — 1511 — as its organizing principle, it would have made little sense to limit the scope of enquiry to this subregion alone: the Portuguese and Luso-Asian communities of Asia were inextricably interconnected with one another, both formally and informally in political, economic, social, cultural and religious terms, in part reinforced by frequent migrations and dispersions of these peoples across time and space throughout the East.

Volume 1, "The Making of the Luso-Asian World: Intricacies of Engagement", is organized into three thematic parts: "Adaptations and Transitions in the South and Southeast Asian Theatres, Sixteenth through Eighteenth Centuries"; "Dispersion, Mobility and Demography from the Sixteenth into the Twenty-first Centuries"; and "Mixed Legacies: The Portuguese and Luso-Asians in the Twentieth and Twenty-first Centuries". Within each of these parts, chapters are arranged in roughly chronological order, and although there is some temporal overlap from one part to the next, the volume's overall trajectory is also a chronological one. Although the volume obviously makes no attempt to cover these themes along a seamless continuum of 500 years, the reader will at least be aware that an adumbration of the evolutionary flow of trends and processes can be discerned if one reads the material in this order.

Volume 2, "Culture and Identity in the Luso-Asian World: Tenacities and Plasticities", is a collection of case studies that allow the reader to delve into what might best be termed the "living spirit" of a broad spectrum of Portuguese and Luso-Asian communities in South, Southeast and East Asia at various points in time across half a millennium of existence. It is organized around three themes: "Crafting Identity in the Luso-Asian World", "Cultural Components: Language, Architecture and Music", and "Adversity and Accommodation".

Part One of this volume, "Adaptations and Transitions in the South and Southeast Asian Theatres, Sixteenth through Eighteenth Centuries", examines aspects of the evolution of the Portuguese and Luso-Asian presence through the lens of a variety of "ground-level" settings: a royal medicinal garden in Goa; a viceroy's frustrated attempts to secure Malacca; a Coromandel community's stubborn retention of its Portuguese identity; the Macanese senate's bid to square its relationship with regime change in Siam; and the effects of British rule on the life of a Luso-Indian community.

In Chapter 1, Timothy Walker's "Supplying Simples for the Royal Hospital: An Indo-Portuguese Medicinal Garden in Goa (1520–1830)" gives us a view of three centuries' worth of both adaptation and transition in a rather prosaic but highly specialized sphere of endeavour. The Royal Military Hospital at Goa was the largest facility of its kind in Portuguese Asia, attending not only to locals, but also collecting plants with medicinal properties from throughout the colonial Lusophone world for cultivation in its garden. It also was tasked with developing knowledge of and producing drugs for dissemination throughout that same world (in itself, a kind of *feitoria* or factory, the quintessential expression of Portuguese colonialism). In this unique physical and cultural space, concepts about healing from Europe, Africa, South

America and China were blended with a strong dose of the highly regarded Indian cosmology of pharmacological and medical knowledge.

As Goa's attractiveness as a destination for migrating Portuguese physicians waned in step with the declining fortunes of the Estado da Índia as a whole,[7] the staffing of the facility segued increasingly and eventually exclusively to the Christian Indo-Portuguese. Run by Jesuits for most of its existence until their expulsion in the later eighteenth century, the garden languished thereafter, albeit with a brief attempt at revitalization in the late eighteenth and early nineteenth centuries. At several turns, Walker's study, based in extensive archival material, especially from Goa, makes it clear that the undertakings in the medicinal garden were of a pragmatic and syncretistic nature. Whereas Europeans defined the form, function and purpose of the space and effectively commercialized its produce on a global scale, South Asians executed the plan and dominated the intellectual healing cosmology with "resilient subaltern sensibility".

Walker finds the term "hybridized" an appropriate one for capturing the essence of this "exceptional multicultural space", whether in reference to its specific parts (the mix of the plants cultivated, the personnel, its organizational principles and, perhaps most importantly, the applied scientific and botanical knowledge it generated) or to the totality thereof. His work also provides us with an all-too-rare glimpse at how one geographic corner of the Portuguese colonial system was actively engaged, to varying degrees, with other parts of its far-flung dominion. This aspect of his work suggests that we could arrive at a deeper understanding of how a sense of "Portugueseness" may have been transmitted and either enhanced, maintained or diminished by examining some of the more pedestrian features of empire that nevertheless lent themselves to global thinking and administration.

From a three-century time frame to a much tighter one of only a few years, Chapter 2, "Malacca in the Era of Viceroy Linhares (1629–35)" by Anthony Disney, examines a critical period of transition for the Estado da Índia, marked most visibly and sharply by the loss of Malacca to the Dutch in 1641. Ahead of that pivotal event, however, slippage in Malacca's military and commercial integrity was already occurring. The Estado da Índia would soon relinquish its offensive stance in Asia as "a widespread maritime entity controlling and managing commercial networks" in favour of a defensive one as "a small, more coherent landed empire". By examining the administration of the fourth Conde de Linhares, an intelligent and dedicated viceroy, over a five-year period in the decade preceding the loss of Malacca, Disney demonstrates that other factors were already in play that ultimately undermined the city's viability in terms of Portuguese administration and control, notwithstanding capable leadership.

Although Linhares's term began on a high note (when the sultan of Aceh's effort to capture Malacca was successfully thwarted by the Portuguese in collaboration with the sultan of Johor), two exceptionally adept military commanders died during the viceroy's term. Meanwhile, unrest elsewhere (mostly notably in Ceylon, but also at Mombasa and Hugli) resulted in diversions of resources to those flashpoints, a significant portion of which Linhares had initially earmarked for bolstering the Portuguese presence at Malacca, in light of increasing Dutch activity in the region. Despite the growing intensity of this maritime commercial competition, the ultimately short-lived Portuguese India Company in Lisbon proposed a new China-Goa trade initiative in which Malacca would play a key role. An apparently better informed treasury council nixed the plan, however, perhaps in light of the declining customs revenues accruing to the Portuguese crown from Malacca, even before Linhares assumed his post — a trend that accelerated precipitously throughout his term and beyond.

In addition to this cascade of imperial misfortunes, Malacca's own liabilities came to stand out in even greater relief from the end of Linhares's term to the Dutch takeover. Its hinterland offered virtually no prospects for expansion. Its food came mainly from elsewhere on the peninsula as well as from Java and Siam. It had no shipyard and produced no military or naval supplies. Already in Linhares's time, private Portuguese traders were leaving in growing numbers for more promising locales, notably Makassar. In short, ahead of the final capitulation of the city to the Dutch, Malacca was already irretrievably compromised. Nevertheless, to this day, Malacca remains the site of one of the few identifiable concentrations, albeit small, of Luso-Asians in the whole of Asia, despite numerous outward migrations and dispersions over the centuries. Several chapters in this volume and the next examine this phenomenon and the persistence of this legacy from a variety of angles.

In Chapter 3, "From Meliapor to Mylapore, 1662–1749: The Portuguese Presence in São Tomé between the Quṭb Shāhī Conquest and Its Incorporation into British Madras" by Paolo Aranha, our focus shifts to the Coromandel coast in the period after Portugal's posture in Asia had become more defensive. One of many small outposts along the Indian subcontinent's eastern edge, what became the autonomous community of São Tomé de Meliapor was of paramount interest to the Christian Portuguese, given that it was believed to be the burial site of Saint Thomas. This chapter presents the initial results of a research project investigating the "strategies of resilience" that translated into São Tomé's persistent identification with "being Portuguese". Indeed, the inextricable connection between this sacred site and "being Portuguese" may go a long way towards explaining the endurance of this feisty town, often embroiled in its own internal conflicts, through a time of major political transformation on the Indian subcontinent. This modest outpost of the "shadow empire" was variously conquered by Muslim Golconda (1662), the French (1672–74), Golconda again with assistance from the Dutch (1674), the Mughal Empire — at the behest of the Portuguese viceroy, as conveyed by an Augustinian friar (1687) — and eventually the British (1749).

After conquest by Golconda, much of the Portuguese community left for nearby British Madras, which had been siphoning off local talent (both Portuguese and the much larger Christianized Indian population) anyway — a scenario not unlike the times preceding and following the fall of Malacca, when significant numbers of Portuguese relocated to Makassar. Over subsequent years, both internal and external tensions characterized life in São Tomé: confiscated properties were not returned as promised; Portuguese wanting to return to the town in calmer times were rebuffed by those who had stayed; for decades, no support was forthcoming from the Catholic Church; local inhabitants were often seriously at odds with the viceroys; and poorly devised diplomatic strategies for improving relations with the Mughal empire failed.

In 1749, São Tomé was incorporated into British Madras in order to keep it out of French hands. Protestations by Portugal were brushed aside with the observation that no revenue from the port had accrued to its king over the preceding fifty years. Yet, as Aranha concludes, São Tomé continued to see itself as "Portuguese", albeit "more in terms of desire and imagination than in concrete ways". Based in archival research in Goa, Lisbon and Rome, Aranha's findings reveal a town's complex history that "shows the inadequacy of a simple dichotomy between absolute hegemony and a fate of stagnation and decline", and hence fertile ground for ongoing enquiry and analysis.

In Chapter 4, "Eighteenth-Century Diplomatic Relations between Portuguese Macao and Ayutthaya: The 1721 Debt Repayment Embassy from Macao", Stefan Halikowski Smith examines relations between Siam and Macao during an era in which some scholars see the former as a "hermit kingdom", following its transitional "National Revolution" of 1688 that ousted French influence and forces. Other historians counter this characterization by pointing to Siam's active engagement with various regional polities. Smith's study adds weight to the latter reading of the times and is accompanied by an appendix of four primary Portuguese documents that appear in English translation for the first time herein.

The debt to Siam dated from 1667, when the then king granted the Macanese a large loan. Relations between Portugal and Siam extended back to the early sixteenth century and were built upon Ayutthaya's sovereignty over Malacca and other Malay areas from the fifteenth century onwards.

The ensuing political stability created a propitious environment for trade, which first attracted Chinese merchants and later the Portuguese. In time, the international commerce conducted in Ayutthaya "was almost all in the hands of successfully established shipowners from Macao", a state of affairs underscored by a Siamese concession of commercial privileges to the Portuguese in 1616, even though that trade was generally on a modest scale. By the later 1600s, however, the "Portuguese" community in Siam mostly comprised Luso-Asians who had suffered "repeated displacements" from elsewhere in Southeast Asia. Most held no allegiance to Portugal and thus have been described as a "rootless 'tribe' of individuals".

The Macanese were disposed to secure their commercial footing with the new regime in Siam, but were financially incapable of doing so until 1721. Decades of political and economic uncertainty in Macao were finally reversed, however — a 1717 Chinese ban on international trade (except with Japan) launched a cosy commercial relationship between Macao and Canton, and a new, skilled governor of Macao was installed in 1718. With prosperity restored, the Noble Senate of Macao was able to complete the loan repayment.

The 1721 Macanese embassy generally went well, but its presentation at court in Ayutthaya was lacklustre, owing to a perceived deficiency in the accompanying gifts to the king. Meanwhile, a concurrent and more robust representation by the Spanish from Manila netted them a choice commercial treaty, but that ultimately foundered due to changing political fortunes in the Philippines. However, the Siamese king indicated his willingness to extend yet another loan to Macao, if it so desired, and in the long run, "Macao remained considerably more important to Siam than the Philippines". Ultimately, this event demonstrates how two regional polities found ways to rekindle reciprocal long-standing commercial ties that transcended changing political realities.

Chapter 5, "Continuities in Bengal's Contact with the Portuguese and Its Legacy: A Community's Future Entangled with the Past", completes the case studies of adaptation and transition involving Portuguese and Portuguese-derived communities during the first two centuries of Portugal's presence in South, Southeast and East Asian waters. In it, Ujjayan Bhattacharya puts forth the hypothesis that vibrant and vigorous interactions *across* cultures and even transcultural syntheses were possible while Portugal was still a dynamic maritime colonial power in Asia, but that interactions *within* cultures found greater intensity as that formal power diminished. His chapter, based in extensive archival research in West Bengal, engages these communities midstream in an evolutionary process in which the survival of Portuguese identity eventually translated into acute cultural insecurity by the early twentieth century. Bhattacharya characterizes this process as "the parochialisation of an erstwhile imperial culture". The underlying mechanics of that process are the focus of this work and have been gleaned from the records of such entities as the Board of Customs, the Board of Revenue, the Governor-General in Council and the Calcutta Provincial Council of Revenue and involve such commonplace transactions as sales and acquisitions of property.

By the eighteenth century, British control of Madras (today's Tamil Nadu state) and Calcutta (Kolkata) created demand for a host of "settled professions": registrars in custom houses; linguists; functionaries in revenue departments and courts; skilled workers; and various occupations associated with internal trade and trading networks throughout the Indian Ocean. As a consequence, there was a general trend towards the dispersal of the Portuguese, Luso-Indians and other Luso-Asians from Hugli and Bandel towards nearby Calcutta. Within this internal migratory trend, Bhattacharya also documents the case of two elite Indo-Portuguese merchants, Joseph Barretto and Luís da Costa — among the last of their breed — and their commercial collaboration with British counterparts.

In the nineteenth century, class differences began to emerge within the Luso-Indian communities. Those elites who had realized significant success in Calcutta increasingly lived apart from the others. Despite their social standing, however, the Luso-Indian elites of Calcutta had to reconcile their Portuguese lineage with their status as British subjects. The Portuguese-derived communities of West Bengal had, over time, first been part of one hegemonic colonial power, then adapted many traits of the indigenous dominant culture while retaining a separate identity. They later found it difficult to define and reconcile their identities as subjects of another hegemonic European colonial power.

Part Two of this volume, "Dispersion, Mobility, and Demography from the Sixteenth into the Twenty-first Centuries", examines aspects of population dynamics and interconnectedness, ranging from an overview of the main Luso-Asian communities and various waves of dispersion across five hundred years, to a demographic profile of the Estado da Índia from the mid-eighteenth to the early nineteenth century, and an enduring folkloric motif that provided a common cultural denominator to diffused pockets of Portuguese and Luso-descendant populations.

In Chapter 6, "The Luso-Asians and Other Eurasians: Their Domestic and Diasporic Identities", John Byrne provides a succinct, sweeping review of these communities in terms of their founding and flux over 500 years. As such, he provides the reader with a convenient source of basic information that complements the many references to these groups found throughout this volume and the next. Byrne's special contribution, however, lies in the statistical data he has compiled from several national censuses that track the global dispersions of these various communities from the post-World War II era and into the early twenty-first century.

The chapter summarizes the many Luso-Asian communities founded between 1510 and 1558 throughout Asia: the Luso-Indians; the Portuguese burghers of Sri Lanka; the Kristang of Malacca; the Macanese of Macao; the Larantuqueiros of the Nusa Tenggara province of Indonesia; and the Mestizos of East Timor. It also identifies other communities that were subsequently incorporated into larger ethnicities: the Bayingyis of Myanmar; the Luso-Siamese of Thailand; the mestizos of the Spice Islands, the Batavian Portuguese, and the Mardijkers, all of Indonesia. The "non-Luso" ethnicities of these groups included Goans, Bengalis, North Indians, Dravidian Indians, Sinhalese, Tamil Sri Lankans, Malays, Indonesians, Papuan Timorese, Chinese, Japanese and Africans.

Perhaps the most dramatic changes in the nature of the Luso-descendant communities in Asia came with their dispersion throughout the nineteenth-century British colonial world. Luso-Asians filled intermediary colonial administration roles in such British Asian and African locales as Calcutta (see Chapter 5), Bombay, Karachi, Pune, Ceylon, Penang, Singapore, Hong Kong, Shanghai, Kenya, Tanganyika, Uganda and Zanzibar. As a consequence, class differences began to emerge, along with a trend towards the Anglicization of identities. A second wave of dispersion occurred between the early 1950s and the early 1970s in the aftermath of World War II and the ensuing decolonization of much of Asia and Africa. In this migration, language appears to have been a major factor in the choice of destination. Luso-Asians who had acquired English-language skills or for whom it was now a mother tongue favoured English-speaking countries: the United Kingdom, Australia, New Zealand, the United States and Canada. Migrating Luso-Asians who spoke a Portuguese-derived patois, on the other hand, usually chose other parts of the Portuguese-speaking world for their new homes.

Today, as Byrne demonstrates, it is increasingly difficult to trace the geographic whereabouts of what he estimates to be some 463,000 Luso-Asians and other Eurasians (see Chapter 6 for an important explanation of how this latter term is used) living outside of Asia, due to different census categories from one country to the next, as well as the various ways that individuals are allowed to identify themselves in these population counts. Nevertheless, his research provides a statistical platform for continuing to follow these legatees of a Portuguese colonial past.

In Chapter 7, "The Population of the Portuguese Estado da Índia, 1750–1820: Sources and Demographic Trends", Paulo Matos deepens our demographic knowledge about the scope and composition of the Estado's population. The time frame extends from when Portugal first employed the principles of "political arithmetic" (which European states used to try to quantify social and economic realities and potentials) to the introduction of a new methodology for gathering demographic statistics that coincided with the rise of liberalism.

Between these chronological bookends, "an impressive corpus of population *mapas*", or statistical tables, can be found in the Arquivo Histórico Ultramarino in Lisbon and the Historical Archives of Goa in Panaji, in addition to Brazil's Biblioteca Nacional in Rio de Janeiro, all of which form the basis of this study. Goa, Daman, Diu, Macao and Timor are covered by these *mapas*, although the data for Timor and Macao are comparatively scarce, sometimes contradictory and "fragile". Nine analytical tables and charts are included in the chapter, and an accompanying appendix lists population maps dating from 1720 to 1820.

Matos first discusses these little-known sources in terms of their normative schemes, information typologies and relative reliability. During this time frame, categories changed. From 1776 to 1796, religion formed the sole criterion for classification: one was either a Christian or a "gentile", that is, a Hindu or a Muslim. These categories then furcated in the period from 1797 to 1825, splitting the population into "white Christians", "natural Christians" (meaning non-white), "negros" (meaning slaves), "pardos" (meaning someone of African and non-African descent but not necessarily a slave) and "gentiles and Muslims" (whereas before "gentiles" had included both Hindus *and* Muslims).

The second part of the chapter presents a comparative analysis of the demographic structures of various territories, especially between the predominantly Christian "Old Conquests" of Goa and Daman and the insubstantially Christian "New Conquests" of Diu and Macao. Matos's more salient findings include strong asymmetries in social and religious composition from one locale to another; a concentration of the white population in Goa, whose numbers were becoming "vanishingly low"; a small slave population in constant flux; a shrinkage of urban centres in and outmigration from Goa; evidence of epidemics and food crises; and proportionately greater growth in the Hindu population in all Indian locales. During this time, "Portuguese Asia" posted an overall moderate population growth but represented only 10 per cent of the Portuguese overseas population, the vast majority by then residing in Brazil. Even so, as Matos observes, "the Estado da Índia stood out as the area with the most complexity and the greatest disparity in social terms".

In Chapter 8, K. David Jackson traces one gene in the cultural DNA of the Luso-Asians that has transmitted an element of Portuguese culture across vast extents of time and space but also mutated to adapt to changing local environments along the way. He follows the mythical flight path of the *papagaio verde* — the green parrot — as it has taken wing throughout the Lusophone world for centuries with a mobility that rivals that of the humans it entertains.

The green parrot's intelligence, wit and proclivity to tell the truth, however inconvenient, are conveyed through seven-syllable quatrains or *cantigas*. Jackson's chapter includes some sixty examples of these *cantigas*, collected by linguists, folklorists and ethnologists from locations throughout Portugal and South, Southeast and East Asia, written variously in Portuguese and several Portuguese creoles.

Examples from India (Mangalore, Cochin, Daman, Diu and other northern enclaves) and Sri Lanka demonstrate a shared legacy of traditional melodies and lyrics that "functioned as essential components of social life, festivities, ceremonies, and rituals". Courtship and marriage, private desires and social concerns are voiced in these examples. In Malacca, *cantigas* "function as a mirror of the popular culture of Portuguese descendants", often focusing on female love laments, satire and personal insults. In a community noted for its metaphor-laden modes of expression, Malacca's *passarinho berde* is integrated into local popular beliefs and superstitions. In Macao, the parrot identifies Macanese by calling out their Portuguese nicknames, challenging one hypothesis that these sobriquets originated in the language of Chinese nursemaids.

"Papagaio Verde" is one of the oldest songs of maritime Portugal, transmitting a cultural legacy in Asia that has coursed through five centuries and continues to be a part of popular culture in Luso-Asian communities. The fact that the green parrot is always understood to be mobile, not local, has enhanced the motif's ability to make communities feel connected across oceans and across time. In short, as a purveyor of shared popular culture, the green parrot has been a catalyst for the informal, intergenerational and social transmission of culture throughout the Luso-Asian world.

Part Three, "Mixed Legacies: The Portuguese and Luso-Asians in the Twentieth and Twenty-first Centuries", reveals the many complex dimensions of identity that emerged with changing political, economic and social realities, especially as a result of twentieth-century conflicts. The four chapters comprising this section reveal the little-known history of these communities in Southeast and East Asia during the Japanese occupation of World War II; the search for identity as transmitted through the medium of literature by authors from Goa, Macao and Singapore; and a critical assessment of the literary and artistic shortcomings that suggest we have yet to grasp the full scope of Luso-Asian identities.

In Chapter 9, "Portuguese Communities in Southeast and East Asia during the Japanese Occupation", Felicia Yap examines the experience of Portuguese-derived communities during the understudied period of the Japanese occupation of British Asia during World War II. In particular, she focuses on Hong Kong and Macao and, to a lesser extent, Malaya and Singapore. The Portuguese colony of Macao remained unoccupied by the Japanese, given Portugal's officially neutral position during the conflict. As discussed in Chapter 6, the post-war era saw significant outmigration by Luso-Asians to other countries, especially English-speaking ones. This study, which makes extensive use of primary material in London's Imperial War Museum, transcripts of interviews from the Hong Kong Heritage Project, and the Hong Kong Public Records Office, among other archival sources, augments our understanding of this watershed event that left these communities "irretrievably altered".

The wartime experiences of these communities were "vastly different" from those of other European civilians: most Europeans were sent to internment camps, while civilians of Portuguese background were categorized as "third nationals", given Portugal's (tenuously) neutral stance. (In Singapore and Malaya, the same designation was often disregarded by Japanese officials, resulting in many deaths.) Despite their officially privileged standing, though, hundreds of "Hong Kong Portuguese" felt uneasy enough to flee to Macao.

For about a century before the war, these individuals, whose ancestors came mostly from Macao, had been working for the British colonial office and for British banks, trading companies and other firms as clerks, bookkeepers and interpreters (many then could speak Cantonese), similar to the Luso-Indian communities discussed in Chapter 5. Over time, they came to hold loyalties to Hong Kong and "formed a distinct and recognisable community of their own with clearly defined social, religious, and cultural institutions". By the 1920s, English was their primary language, admixed with some Macanese Patuá, but by then they were "completely illiterate in Chinese".

During the war, a number assisted with organized Allied resistance movements in both Hong Kong and Macao (where the British maintained a consulate). In particular, they facilitated escape conduits through which Allied workers, refugees and recruits were dispatched from Macao to China. They were also vitally instrumental in keeping clandestine banking operations going (especially for the Hongkong and Shanghai Banking Corporation), which proved invaluable when the British retook Hong Kong in 1945.

Several Hong Kong Portuguese played key roles in post-war reconstruction, and some rose to prominent positions. But many chose to leave, especially for the United States, Canada, Australia, New Zealand and Brazil. Some racially motivated disturbances against them, in addition to the Communist takeover of China, prompted further outmigration. Once again, in the long history of the Portuguese and Luso-Asians, conflict proved to be a powerful catalyst for relocation, especially to countries beyond Asia.

In Chapter 10, "Indo-Portuguese Literature and the Goa of Its Writers", Everton V. Machado delves into literary representations of Goan culture in his search for a satisfying characterization of this unique culture. However, he finds that these authors — natives of what was once the epicentre of the Portuguese colonial presence in Asia — have been unable to reconcile their own confused identities, and thus have yet to accurately depict Goa's "cultural specificity". Machado examines this complex legacy of confused identity that has precipitated out over the centuries, from a Christian European environment on the one hand and the Indian caste system *cum* Hindu ancestral universe on the other.

Machado examines the works of Goa's most prominent writers from the late nineteenth century to the present, including Orlando da Costa, Vimala Devi, Francisco Luís Gomes, Leopoldo da Rocha and Gip, all native Goans raised in a "Catholic and Portuguese-like environment". Within this medium, however, the caste system was maintained as a result of the conversion of large segments of the Hindu population (see the demographic data presented in Chapter 7), "albeit with important differences relative to the original system, whether in their constitution or in their social implications". It is this "rupture" or "divide", underscored by socio-economic as well as religious differences, that appears to be unbridgeable for these authors, especially those writing since Goa's independence in 1961 and its subsequent incorporation into India.

Late nineteenth-century writers portrayed Goa variously as "a repository of noble Christian and Portuguese ideas", especially when contrasted with the British colonial presence in India (Gomes), or as a society dominated by Portuguese Catholic Goans who were superficial, lacking purpose in life and highly subservient to European culture (Gip). In the 1930s, Rocha lamented "the Christianization of Goans as a 'confusion' in the life of the natives, but specifically in terms of sexual matters" ("sinful" versus the Hindu view of sex as the "natural way"). By the 1960s, Devi — perhaps the most qualified author to write authoritatively about both the Portuguese and Hindu worlds — characterized Goa as "a communion of monasteries and pagodas", but nonetheless of two different worlds. In the 1980s, Costa's Christian protagonist has a Hindu friend who is like a twin brother, but his awareness of the barrier between them induces existential doubts.

Machado concludes that Goa's authors may have created their own "imagined community", in Benedict Anderson's definition of the term, but have been unable to "constitute in fact a nation apart from either India or Portugal, as many have wished". Instead, they have been hobbled by the "depth of the historical inequalities and exploitation of the colonial legacy", so that the uniqueness and essence of Goa's culture still elude literary capture.

Other Luso-Asian authors who have created "imagined communities" are treated in Chapter 11, "Binding Ties of Miscegenation and Identity: The Narratives of Henrique Senna Fernandes (Macao) and Rex Shelley (Singapore)" by Isabel Maria da Costa Morais. Whereas Machado found that Indo-Portuguese Goan writers had yet to accurately express the uniqueness of Goan culture, Morais reveals that these two prominent contemporary authors invoke a nuanced Lusotropicalism in the style of Brazil's Gilberto Freyre that projects a "peculiar miscegenated tropical identity" as a way of defining the distinctness of the Luso-Asian or "Luso-Eurasian" communities they chronicle.

Morais's analysis discloses overlooked interconnectivities and commonalities employed by both authors. She demonstrates that their novels "contain unexpected and similar references to Portuguese culture and history, myths, cuisine, linguistic hybridity, and shared Portuguese heritage legacies associated with the old and emblematic cities of Macao and Malacca". Shelley and Senna Fernandes were the first Eurasian authors to have written about "a sense of belonging to a wilfully self-contained and distinctive community", especially with reference to the "realities and dilemmas faced by their Eurasian female subjects".

Rex Anthony Shelley (1930–2009) wrote novels that occur mostly from the World War II Japanese occupation of the Malay Peninsula through the postcolonial era (Malaysia was founded in 1957; subsequently, Singapore became a separate republic in 1965). The recipient of several major Singaporean book awards (*The Shrimp People*, 1991; *The People of the Pear Tree*, 1993; and *Island in the Centre*, 1995), Shelley's works treat such ideological and political issues as nationalism, independence, racial discrimination, clandestine armed struggle and espionage.

Also the winner of literary awards, Henrique Senna Fernandes (1923–2010) is regarded as the premier author of Lusophone Macanese literature. His works focus on exposing the cultural and social contradictions and ambivalence in Macanese society primarily from the time of World War II to when Macao reverted to China in 1999. Such works as *Amor e Dedinhos de Pé* (*Love and Little Toes*, 1986) and *Trança Feiticeira* (*The Bewitching Braid*, 1992) also explore the reasons behind Macanese outmigration and above all disclose "the values of a patriarchal society on the verge of disintegration due to rapid sociopolitical changes".

Both Shelley and Senna Fernandes construct and reconstruct "Luso-Eurasianness" by depicting communities that retain distinct creolized identities relative to "others", whether Chinese, Portuguese, Europeans in general or indigenous Asian populations. The resulting collective identity is one of Eurasian minority communities that have forged and maintain separate identities by devising complex responses to the challenges posed by changing political, social and cultural realities in their "beloved countries of birth", into which societies they have sought to integrate without disappearing. Part of that composite identity, however, continues to reside in a pride associated with a distant and mythical Portuguese past characterized by a capacity for miscegenation and adaptation.

Part Three's review of the mixed legacies of the Portuguese and Luso-Asians in the twentieth and early twenty-first centuries is brought to a conclusion with Chapter 12, "Portuguese Past, Still Imperfect: Revisiting Asia in Luso-diasporic Writing", Christopher Larkosh's essay on the ways that Asian and Lusophone or Luso-diasporic cultures interact today, but not solely in the sense of interactions between the Portuguese metropolis and its former colonies. Larkosh examines the works of two contemporary authors, José Eduardo Agualusa (variously of Luanda, Rio de Janeiro and Lisbon) and Frank X. Gaspar, a "bi-coastal" Portuguese-American (with roots in New England and residence in California). Although neither is from Asia, both have experienced and written about it.

Agualusa travelled to Goa in 1998 on a Fundação Oriente/Cotovia creative-writing travel grant and subsequently published *Um Estranho em Goa* (*A Stranger in Goa*) in 2000, which offers "a more complex vision of contemporary Goa than one might expect". While many characters in this novel long for the "good old days" of Portuguese colonial rule, other aspects of the narrative, "however unwittingly", undermine the nostalgia and "even provide alternatives or exit strategies from this all-too-recurrent cultural perspective". While some critics view the work as a "halfway point between different cultures", Larkosh is not so inclined and instead sees it as being entrenched in the symbols of the Portuguese world, that is, a unidirectional cultural flow. In particular, he argues that Eastern religious traditions are not as deeply understood by the novel's narrator as one would like.

Gaspar's introduction to Asia came with his service in the Vietnam War and travel to locales that were also part of the Portuguese presence in Asia: Hong Kong, Malaysia and Japan (near Nagasaki). Following these experiences, Gaspar began to read deeply in classical texts from a variety of Eastern religions and cultural traditions. In Gaspar's *Field Guide to the Heavens* (1999) and *Night of a Thousand Blossoms* (2004), Larkosh discerns a "divergent model for remapping a cultural dialogue between East and West, one in which Portuguese-American culture, for example, is as irreversibly shaped by other points in the universe, whether in Asia or somewhere in the rest of the cosmos, as by Portugal, the U.S., or the Western tradition".

In essence, Larkosh would like to see "an expanded cultural politics for literary and artistic interaction" that "relies as much on translation between multilingual spaces as it does on *multidirectional* cultural exchange". While a "critical mass" of multilingual, intercultural scholars would be necessary to bring about such a new era in our understanding of the Luso-Asian world, for the time being, even though we close out this volume with his chapter, we should recognize that we "conclude" nothing. The complex legacies as well as historical and contemporary processes wrought by the Portuguese presence in Asia to this point in time are but part of an ongoing, imperfect evolutionary process.

When considered as a whole, the chapters in this volume and the next illustrate the value of academic perspectives packaged together in a way that departs from the usual focus of edited scholarly works, not in the sense of being better, but of provoking fresh takes on the subject at hand. In this case, our objective was achieved by combining a long time frame with perspectives from multiple disciplines and, perhaps most importantly, an international mix of individuals who were otherwise unlikely to cross paths. The work they have produced reveals complexities on a wide variety of levels: local, global, individual, community, formal, informal. Taken together, these "venues" have all contributed in one form or another to the making of a culture that had not previously existed, that of the Luso-Asian world. While in no sense homogeneous unto itself, it nevertheless exhibits commonalities from one setting to another, and does so across time and space. Whether we characterize this culture as an admixture, an amalgam, a fusion or a hybrid, its complexities continue to challenge our intellectual and analytical skills. As we persist in charting a path for understanding these kinds of mixed cultural models, it is our hope that with our findings will also come greater clarity in interpreting the phenomenon itself. We already know that this meeting served as a catalyst for fostering communication among a group of scholars that might not otherwise have occurred — a kind of hybridity in its own right. For our readers, we hope that these studies — and the perspectives they may engender and inform — will leave a bit of a legacy of their own.

Notes

1 Robert D. Kaplan, "CNAS – RSIS [Center for a New American Security – S. Rajaratnam School of International Studies] Panel Discussion on 'The United States and Asia: Prospects and Challenges in 2010'" (remarks, Four Seasons Hotel, Singapore, 20 January 2010).

2 Robert D. Kaplan, "Obama Takes Asia by Sea", *New York Times*, 11 November 2010 <http://www.nytimes.com/2010/11/12/opinion/12kaplan.html?pagewanted=all> (accessed 23 March 2011).

3 Victor Liberman, "Local Integration and Eurasian Analogies: Structuring Southeast Asian History, c. 1350–c. 1830", *Modern Asian Studies* 27, no. 3 (1993): 547.

4 For an exposé about the debate sparked in Western Europe by the early Portuguese and Spanish presence in Asian waters, which ultimately provided a rationale for the Dutch to venture into the same territory by virtue of a philosophical argument for "freedom of the seas", see Peter Borschberg, *Hugo Grotius, the Portuguese and Free Trade in the East Indies* (Singapore: NUS Press, 2011).

5 See, for example, Francisco Bethencourt and Diogo Ramada Curto, eds., *Portuguese Oceanic Expansion, 1400–1800* (Cambridge: Cambridge University Press, 2007).

6 See, for example, Ricardo Roque, *Headhunting and Colonialism: Anthropology and the Circulation of Human Skulls in the Portuguese Empire, 1870–1930* (Basingstoke: Palgrave Macmillan, 2010); Sten Pultz Moslund, *Migration Literature and Hybridity: The Different Speeds of Transcultural Change* (Basingstoke: Palgrave Macmillan, 2010); Robert Young, *Colonial Desire: Hybridity in Theory, Culture and Race*, 2nd ed. (London: Routledge, 2010); and Avtar Brah and Annie E. Coombes, *Hybridity and Its Discontents: Politics, Science, Culture* (London: Routledge, 2000).

7 The Estado da Índia should be understood in a formal sense as having comprised the aggregate of Portugal's colonial holdings along the rim of East Africa and the Indian Ocean, that is, a set of forts and ports plus some minor territorial dependencies, all governed by the viceroy and his council in Goa. The status of each of these dependencies ranged from a contractually secured possession to an outright colony over which Portugal claimed sovereign rights, although the latter were few in number. Informally, the Estado was also about interconnected networks — personal, kinship and business. Over time, with the diminution or removal of formal structures of the Estado, these informal networks were often able to continue.

PART ONE

Adaptations and Transitions in the South and Southeast Asian Theatres, Sixteenth through Eighteenth Centuries

1

SUPPLYING SIMPLES FOR THE ROYAL HOSPITAL: AN INDO-PORTUGUESE MEDICINAL GARDEN IN GOA (1520–1830)[1]

Timothy D. Walker

By the mid-seventeenth century, medical practice in the Portuguese-held enclaves of southern India had become thoroughly hybridized, with applied remedies in colonial health institutions relying heavily on indigenous medicinal plants.[2] To ensure a ready supply of common local and imported healing herbs in the administrative hub of the Portuguese Asian empire, the Hospital Real Militar in Goa maintained on its premises a medicinal herb garden, supervised directly by the chief physician of the Estado da Índia.

This chapter will explore the form, function and role of this Portuguese medical garden as a multicultural space within a larger "hybridized" colonial medical sphere, wherein European and South Asian (and, indeed, even African, South American and Chinese) concepts about healing blended. The chapter will describe the physical space of the garden, its Indo-Portuguese caretakers and their unique medical cosmology, and the hospital's intellectual environment, which placed so much value on the indigenous remedies supplied through this garden's bounty. Further, the chapter will describe various medicinal plants cultivated in Indo-Portuguese hospital gardens, their applications and effects, as well as the social context in which the medical practitioners who employed these plants operated.

In view of the horticultural nature of this work, modern usage of the term "hybrid" demands comment. As employed above, the word today has come to mean simply a "mixed" or "blended" product derived from dissimilar components — in this case, to describe a process of shared acculturation unavoidable in a colonial context. In the early seventeenth century, however, the word, newly minted in English and with origins in farming and animal husbandry, had a much more specific connotation, referring to the offspring of two animals of different breeds, species or varieties. Usually the word implied deliberate cross-breeding to obtain beneficial genetic characteristics. "Hybrid" was soon applied in gardening as well as to refer to the cross-fertilization of different plants. The word did not achieve wide circulation outside of scientific or agrarian circles until after 1850, when it began to take on its broader current meaning.[3] "Hybrid" will crop up frequently in this chapter, not employed as originally intended but instead in the modern sense, to refer to the unique blended culture found in the Portuguese Indian colonies. Thus, this essay suggests that medicinal garden culture in Goa can itself be seen as a hybrid entity, drawing useful components from disparate healing and gardening traditions to shape the form, concept and purpose of a specialized horticultural space.

THE HOSPITAL REAL MILITAR AND ITS GARDENS: AN OVERVIEW

The Hospital Real Militar (royal military hospital) in Goa, capably administered for most of the early modern period by the Society of Jesus, was a major medical facility — the first, largest and most important Portuguese colonial health installation in Asia. Its origins date from the very earliest days of the colony. Crown directives created a framework for its administration in 1520, a decade after the Portuguese took Goa and established this key port, roughly halfway between Bombay and Cochin, as their capital for operations in all of Asia.[4] In the early seventeenth century, some European travellers considered the Hospital Real Militar one of the finest and best equipped healing facilities anywhere in the world.[5] Not only did it treat some 3,000 patients per year on average during the eighteenth century,[6] but, to provide ample quantities of medicines for so many invalids, it boasted a grand pharmacy staffed by more than twenty-five apothecaries and their assistants.[7]

Why the need for such a large apothecary team? Clearly, many of the hospital servants assigned to the pharmacy were employed in the institution's medicinal herb gardens and in processing newly harvested medical plants into prepared remedies for the soldiers and colonial authorities interned in the hospital. Of necessity, many of the medicinal plants used were of local origin. Substantial quantities of these indigenous South Asian simples, in fact, were home-grown, having been raised for practical reasons in the spacious gardens just outside the hospital walls, near the Mandovi River in Old Goa.[8] According to the hospital's official regulations, it was the head pharmacist's duty to oversee the cultivation, harvest, drying and conservation of the medicinal plants "that grew in *conturnos* [in contours of land, or along the perimeter] around the Hospital grounds".[9] Moreover, the chief apothecary was to make sure that his staff, composed entirely of indigenous Goan Christians, learnt the skills necessary for performing this essential work.

Of course, given the hospital's frequently precarious financial straits (securing adequate operating funds from the royal purse was a chronic administrative challenge), surplus medicinal plants from the gardens could be sold in the hospital pharmacy for institutional profit or exported under colonial government contract to regions of need within the empire. For this reason alone, the garden's medicinal production must have been closely regimented, reliably producing large quantities of fungible natural drugs. In 1682, for example, after the Portuguese Conselho Ultramarino (or Overseas Council, the Lisbon-based ruling body for the maritime colonies) decided to reorganize the degenerate Royal Hospital at Mozambique, the Hospital Militar in Goa collected, prepared and forwarded a very large consignment of diverse medicines, valued at over 3,100 *xerafins* (an enormous government expenditure at the time), to stock the African facility's pharmacy. Imperial medical officials in Goa included in this initial shipment a broad range of South Asian remedies, with many medicinal preparations made from traditional Malabar Coast ingredients harvested in the Hospital Real Militar's own gardens.[10]

Similarly, in 1785, the apothecary of the Goa hospital gathered a massive shipment of drugs and medical equipment destined for the Portuguese fortress of Diu in northwest India. The lengthy bill of goods included some eighty-five items totalling hundreds of pounds of medicines.[11] In addition, fiscal documents in Portuguese India reveal that the colonial government typically expended large sums annually to outfit state-owned vessels with appropriate medicines against tropical disease. A chart of colonial revenues and expenditures for 1762, for example, records that the apothecary of the Hospital Militar in Goa distributed drugs that year worth 5,287 *xerafins* to the medicine chests of various vessels of the Portuguese fleet bound for other destinations in the maritime empire.[12] (To give a sense of the value of these drug transactions, the chief physician of the Hospital Real Militar in Goa, the highest medical authority of the Portuguese Asian empire, earned an official salary of only 300 *xerafins* per annum in the seventeenth and eighteenth centuries.)[13] Most of these medicines, of course, originated in India, and a substantial proportion of them would have been grown in standard institutional operating procedure by the hospital pharmacy's indigenous resident gardeners.

Such healing herbs as could not be grown in the hospital gardens the head pharmacist was authorized to source and requisition from merchants or indigenous "herbalists", but only after having approved the purchase with the *físico-môr*, or chief physician of the Estado da Índia, who was ultimately responsible for all hospital healing operations.[14] Consignments of some rarer drugs were often supplied directly by Hindu merchants — wholesalers of medicinal plants — who procured bulk quantities of indigenous remedies from distant South Asian regions for Portuguese medical facilities in Goa. For example, during the suppression and expulsion of the Jesuit religious brotherhood from all Portuguese territories in 1759–60, the colonial authorities awarded part of the value of their confiscated goods to the prominent Goan Hindu merchant Suba Camotim Mamay; this payment mainly covered consignments of medicinal plants destined for the royal hospital and pharmacy that the Jesuits had faithfully administered for generations.[15]

Aside from the bare fact of its existence, which is noted in several contemporary sixteenth- to nineteenth-century sources, direct documentation about the appearance and composition of the Portuguese colonial medicinal gardens at Goa is virtually non-existent. Therefore, information about these gardens must be constructed indirectly, teased out through documentary inferences, or with context provided by the extant sources that describe general medical structures and conditions in the capital of the Portuguese Estado da Índia.

THE FOUNDING OF THE GARDENS AND THE ROLE OF THE JESUITS IN THEIR DEVELOPMENT

The origins of these particular gardens may date from the efforts of the famous Portuguese physician Garcia da Orta (whose surname means, in fact, "of the garden"), who served as chief physician of the Estado da Índia in the mid-sixteenth century. Da Orta arrived in Goa in 1534; his official title was *físico d'el Rei*, or "physician named by the king".[16] He spent thirty years in India, studying, cataloguing and experimenting with regional medicinal plants. In 1563, da Orta published his seminal book, *Colóquios dos simples e drogas e cousas medicianais da Índia* (*Colloquies on the Simples and Drugs and Medicinal Things of India*), the first systematic description of Asian *materia medica* written by a European. This work, quickly translated into Latin and

French, circulated widely in Europe; it introduced Western science and medical practitioners to many Indian healing plants and methods.[17] Da Orta was renowned for his garden of medicinal plants, grown for his own observations and trials, but also to supply drugs for his patients in the hospitals of Goa. It is reasonable to assume that, while he was the chief resident physician in Goa, da Orta's house and gardens were in close proximity to the medical facility he was charged with overseeing. It may well be that he initiated the practice of keeping a garden of healing herbs and simples on the hospital grounds, or perhaps his successors merely followed his practical example and grew their own local components for remedies.

In either case, the Portuguese motives for producing medical drugs independently when possible are easy to understand. Fresh plant medicines were of course considered to be more efficacious, and an on-site garden would have allowed for the hospital apothecary staff to create curative compounds with newly picked ingredients near to hand. Medicines that were stale or had travelled a great distance might have lost some of their healing potency.[18] Second, hospital officials worried about the poor quality or possible adulteration of medicines purchased from outside sources.[19] Moreover, maintaining a reliable facility for growing frequently used local herbs and other healing plants (or medicinal species introduced from other parts of the empire) would have been an attractive option, since the garden's bounty would have increased the hospital's self-sufficiency, reduced some uncertainty about procuring a supply of healing plants, lowered operating costs and increased revenues through sales of surplus medicines.

One factor accounting for the lack of documentary information about this garden, of course, is that the need for a medicinal herb garden in Goa was simply too prosaic to bear much comment. After all, acquiring a mastery of local healing knowledge was a basic strategic goal of the early Portuguese colonial and missionary enterprise; imperial success depended on keeping very limited human resources (soldiers, sailors, settlers, priests) alive and on winning Christian conversions to further expand a culturally sympathetic population base.[20] For the majority of its history, highly trained Jesuit missionaries, whose interest in indigenous healing plants was well established, administered the Goa royal hospital. The Society of Jesus assumed responsibility in 1579 at the request of the Portuguese viceroy in India;[21] they maintained oversight of the hospice until news of the royal decree suppressing their brotherhood reached Goa in 1760.[22] Every hospital of any size needed its own discrete supply of medicinal plants. Thus, to contemporaries, the existence of a special hospital garden set aside for cultivating healing plants was about as noteworthy as the presence of a freshwater well or latrines.

In a *regimento* (governing by-laws) promulgated for the royal hospital in Goa in 1583, shortly after the Jesuits took on the administration of the facility, the existence of a medicinals garden is referenced obliquely and only by inference. The *regimento* section outlining the apothecary's duties says that he is obliged to "always have at the hospital, or *next to his apothecary shop* [italics added], perfectly preserved and in good supply, those medicinal ingredients that are good, clean, and fresh, when possible".[23] The *regimento* goes on to say that, should the apothecary find his stock lacking in some medicine called for by the hospital nurses or physicians, he may buy such ingredients from a neighbouring apothecary.

A revision of this *regimento* written the following year says that the apothecary should "diligently and immediately" make up fresh medicines when the hospital staff order them, in strict accordance with the recipes stipulated by the *médicos* (physicians), and to send the medicines to be administered to the patients without delay. This *regimento* further enjoins the apothecary not to administer syrups and other medicinal compositions more than a day after they have been made up.[24] By implication, these passages indicate that the Jesuit apothecary was expected to have fresh ingredients always near to hand, including herbs, roots and simples plucked as needed from the apothecary's garden on the hospital grounds.

In Portuguese colonies from Brazil to Macao, Jesuit missionaries were acknowledged by their contemporaries as masters of medicinal herb-lore. Jesuit padres and lay clergy in South Asia, as elsewhere in the Iberian colonial world, excelled in discovering and experimenting with indigenous medicinal substances, knowledge that they carefully recorded in manuscript texts circulated among their brethren. Even their secular contemporaries in the medical field acknowledged the intrepid, learned Jesuits as the leaders in indigenous medical prospecting.[25] Most permanent Jesuit colonial missions around the world operated medical facilities — typically an infirmary and a pharmacy — from which they dispensed medical compositions for a profit. Jesuit mission apothecary shops were common throughout colonial settlements in early modern southern India, particularly in Goa and Maduri Province (modern Tamil Nadu).[26] Moreover, from earlier experience in Africa and South America, missionaries recognized that indigenous cultures often harboured a great store of folk knowledge about highly efficacious local medicinal plants. The same intellectual proclivities that led missionaries to study indigenous languages and customs (strategic knowledge for winning conversions) also led them to gather detailed information about native healing arts — traditional remedies and their natural ingredients. Within a generation of the initial Portuguese occupation of colonized regions, Jesuit missionaries began to write and circulate protracted descriptions of indigenous healing plants, including advice about how to identify, prepare, and apply native drugs.[27] So, it should come as no surprise that, once in charge of the royal hospital in Goa, the Jesuits would cultivate their own medicines, even importing and experimenting with plants brought from other colonial regions.

GOA MEDICINAL GARDENS CONSTRUCTION AND LAYOUT

The Goan royal hospital gardens went through periods of expansion, contraction, deterioration and rehabilitation over time. Their exact location, layout, size and contents probably changed many times over the centuries. We know, for example, that the entire hospital was rebuilt and greatly expanded in the late sixteenth century, when the Jesuits assumed administration and the Portuguese crown provided additional revenue to augment and maintain the facilities.[28] In the late eighteenth century, the hospital was moved from its location of over two centuries to a new area that was thought to be healthier, built on higher ground ten kilometres to the west, downstream and nearer to the sea, at the new capital of Panjim by the mouth of the Mandovi River, where it was thought that the new health facility would be "washed" with fresh ocean breezes.[29]

At the beginning of the nineteenth century, the governor-general of the Estado da Índia, Dom Rodrigo de Sousa Coutinho, wrote to the Prince Regent Dom João and his overseas governing council to complain that the botanical garden, "the conservation of which your Royal Highness has mandated to me", was totally ruined and "had already been so for a long time" before the governor's term of office began.[30] He went on to say that "it is not considered practical" to rebuild the garden on its present location, so he "ordered the chief physician of the colony to choose another plot of land that he judged more appropriate for the execution of its given royally determined" purpose.[31]

It seems reasonable to assume, however, given contemporary conventional thinking about garden design and layouts, that, for most of its history, the royal hospital's medicinal herb garden was planted in an enclosed quadrilateral yard. An enclosure was necessary to keep out pigs, cattle and other animals that in India roamed free for grazing. Perhaps a simple curtain wall built between two wings of the hospital had originally defined one of the garden's parameters. At other times, the garden may have been planted in a separate and free-standing rectangle, removed from the main hospital building but lying adjacent on the institution's grounds.

The garden layout for much of its history was likely designed in a simplified seventeenth- or eighteenth-century European style, a lozenge-shaped central hub, perhaps with a fountain or water tank, and radiating garden walks to divide and define the plots. Large corner plots might have been rectangular, to make the most efficient use of space for medicinal herb cultivation. The garden was almost certainly laid out on a symmetrical plan, consistent with contemporary garden culture in early modern Europe (or, for that matter, neighbouring Mughal India).[32] However, because the garden filled a critical institutional purpose and was not merely decorative, practical need likely kept aesthetic embellishments in the organic cultivation space to a minimum.

Whatever the case, the garden walls were undoubtedly formed of locally quarried laterite stone. Laterite was a porous, soft stone easily cut and shaped with simple iron tools. Malabar Coast stonemasons had been building all manner of structures — temples, mosques, fortresses, palaces — from this material since time immemorial. Heavy lime whitewash and thick plaster, manufactured from crushed seashells harvested along Goan beaches, covered the walls to form a smooth surface that reflected brilliantly in the tropical sun. Portuguese authorities mandated that, to maintain the noble appearance of public buildings, the whitewash be renewed every year after monsoon rains had washed much of it away.[33]

Roman Catholic religious devices and symbols (simple shapes formed by moulded plaster) likely adorned the walls, though it is possible that traditional Portuguese decorative tile panels (*azulejos*) depicting Catholic religious themes had also been set into the plaster. Stone statues of saints or Jesuit priests, carved with a distinctive style by local Indo-Portuguese artisans and set either on stone bases in the garden or recessed into niches in the walls, could also have been included in the decoration of the garden yard. These embellishments would again have been consistent with contemporary garden design and decoration in contemporary Portugal.[34]

It is highly likely that, for at least part of its history, the garden's main exterior entryway was a modest gate surmounted by an overhead arch, rounded in the seventeenth- and eighteenth-century Indo-Portuguese colonial style. Atop the arch may have stood a cross, or the distinctive crest of the Jesuit order.[35] Such decoration defined the space and identified the hospital proprietors. It served as a reminder for the Europeans of their colonial and spiritual mission as much as it was aimed at indigenous peoples, to affirm or reinforce the ascendant position of European Christianity (and "superior" Western medical practice) over traditional local cultures or belief systems.[36]

A contemporary illustration of the Hospital Real Militar buildings, painted in the 1780s, shows a large, whitewashed building with a red tiled roof situated along the waterfront of the Mandovi River in Old Goa. A verdant and thickly forested hillside rises behind the hospital, but to the east are depicted what seem to be enclosed garden spaces.[37] Another contemporary image, executed as an engraving in the nineteenth century, shows the old royal hospital built along a stone quayside with what appears to be an attached walled garden space on the eastern side.[38]

Still another primary source is a simple outline map created in the middle 1800s of the ruins of Goa City; it includes the old palace (the Casa da Pólvora[39]) that had constituted the hospital building and grounds. The terrain clearly shows space where gardens would have been, behind the main buildings, away from the river, in enclosed yards that climbed the hillside above the hospital.[40] Such garden planning is perfectly in keeping with the way palace and convent or monastery gardens in Lisbon were laid out during the sixteenth to eighteenth centuries.[41]

The best extant documentary source for apothecary gardens in Goa is an architect's structural diagram, executed in the mid-eighteenth century, of the converted palace that housed the royal hospital. Depicted behind and adjacent to the east wing of the building is a garden space labelled "quintal" (plant nursery). The garden layout is shown in an irregular rectangle following the parameters of the palace's rear outer walls. The garden's western edge is defined by a small wing of the former palace, built behind and perpendicular to the main structure. The architect's plan identified the chambers in this wing as those of the apothecary workshop and offices. The diagram shows another large pharmacy chamber, also adjacent to the garden, in the main body of the hospital building.[42] Clearly, the proximity of the apothecary workshops to the hospital garden served a professional purpose, facilitating medical operations.

The *quintal* extended behind the main hospital building for roughly one-third of the palace's length. A scale provided with the architect's plan allows for a calculation of the garden's size. The original scale is in *palmos* ("palms", or a hand span), an archaic Portuguese measurement, but an equivalent can be calculated to show that the garden's length was approximately 44 metres, or about 150 feet. For most of its length, the width was about 15.5 metres, or 50 feet. However, for about one-quarter of its length (11 metres), the garden plan broadened to a width of 22 metres.[43] These dimensions provided a substantial ground area for the pharmacy staff to cultivate the hospital's necessary medicinal plants. Unfortunately, the architect's diagram provides no details about the *quintal's* design, layout or walking spaces within the enclosure.

According to the architectural plan, the hospital director's chambers and administrative offices looked out over the garden; the *quintal* would have been visible from some of the patients' wards, as well. A broad, shaded veranda at the rear of the palace was perched above the garden, with stone steps descending into the enclosed garden yard. This must have been a pleasant refuge perfumed with aromatic herbs for those recovering from wounds or disease.

This impression is borne out by travellers' accounts. French voyager François Pyrard de Laval, interned at the Goa hospital in 1608, described the facility as having numerous "gardens with pretty walks".[44] He reported that the hospital building "and its appurtenances" were renowned for being able to "supply all comforts that can be wished for, whether in regard to doctors, drugs, and appliances for restoring the health", or high-quality food and spiritual consolation.[45] Later in his account, he noted that the hospital building was "very large and ample", with "many galleries, porticoes [and] ponds … where the patients that are beginning to recover go to take the air and a bath".[46] Pyrard also mentioned the appointed chief apothecary, who "lives in the hospital, and has his own shop well stocked at the hospital's expense".[47]

Three decades later, the itinerant merchant Albert de Mandelslo appraised the Portuguese hospital when he accompanied the English East India Company president of Surat to Goa in 1639. He described its galleries and wards in glowing terms, writing that "the noblest apartments of the hospital were the kitchen and apothecaries' shop, both well-furnished with all things necessary for the accommodation of the sick".[48] If Mandelslo recognized the underlying link between the hospital's attractive gardens and the ample stocks of drugs filling shelves in the apothecaries' workrooms, he made no direct comment to that effect.

In one way, the Goa royal hospital garden represents the imposition of European ideas of garden architecture and design of the physical space, as well as utilitarian concepts about botanical gardening, on South Asian indigenous culture. And yet, within its walls, it was South Asian medical culture that triumphed, dominating with traditional local flora the intellectual healing cosmology that defined the use of the garden. Europeans may have determined the expressed function of the space, but Malabar Coast peoples, employing mainly medical herbs from southern India according to their own indigenous traditions, accomplished the execution of that plan. Further, though the Europeans who directed hospital operations may initially have co-opted indigenous plants for their own imperial ends, over time, long-established dependence on local healing knowledge, and on Indian personnel to cultivate those medicinal plants on which European health relied, meant that, effectively, inside the garden and indeed within the hybridized healing environment of the royal hospital, South Asian medical culture flourished, became resurgent and eventually dominated.

Not that the Portuguese did not play an active role in facilitating cultural syncretism. The Europeans' herb garden blended medicinal knowledge from different parts of the Portuguese empire. Deccan and Malabar healing plants may have been predominate in the garden, but it was not an exclusively South Asian botanical space. The genius and singularity of Portuguese botanical activity within their colonial domains is that it was redistributive along practical and commercial lines — the Iberians transplanted useful flora around the world if it suited their imperial needs. Plants from Brazil, Africa and China came to India courtesy of Portuguese imperial designs.[49] Non-Indian roots, fruits, barks and vines deemed efficacious in preserving health would certainly have been found cultivated in the Goa hospital gardens. Cashew and cinchona trees from the Amazon, *pereira* or *pareira brava*[50] vines and the root of the João Lopes pine tree from East Africa — Portuguese médicos at the Goa Royal Hospital knew, used and wrote about these plants as part of their daily tropical healing repertoire.[51]

THE GARDEN AS A MULTICULTURAL HUMAN SPACE: SOUTH ASIAN CHRISTIAN FUNCTIONARIES

Portuguese India had a lengthy tradition of supporting medical facilities that blended Western and Eastern influences. However, if the Hospital Real Militar garden layout was European, its organic contents — both the plants and the workers — were predominantly South Asian. The garden should therefore be understood as a space that was the product of unique multicultural blending, where South Asian Christian functionaries treated European soldiers, sailors and colonial officials with healing plants from India, the Persian Gulf, East Africa, Brazil, China and Ceylon. The Portuguese colonies in India achieved a level of hybridization unlike that in any other European colonial experience. Nowhere was this more evident than in the institutional medical sphere of the Estado da Índia.

The high tide of Portuguese power in Goa was brief. After about 1625, the luster of Goa Dourada ("Gilded Goa") faded because of commercial competition in Asian ports from Dutch and English merchants. With the discovery of gold in Brazil in the late seventeenth century, the economic focus of the Portuguese empire shifted to the Atlantic Ocean, and Goa slid into a long, irreversible decline. With no fortunes to be made, few continental Portuguese wished to relocate to India. But the infrastructure of empire remained, and the Christianized indigenous population assumed social roles previously filled by European colonizers.

By the mid-eighteenth century, following the stark decline of Goa, the European-born population of Portuguese in India had been reduced to just a few hundred souls, most of whom were illiterate convict soldiers.[52] The day-to-day activities of maintaining the Indian colonies — carrying on the commerce, administration, health care, missionary work and defence measures that made the enclaves viable — were executed mainly by mixed-race descendants of earlier Portuguese settlers, along with Luso-acculturated indigenous peoples whose ancestors had long ago converted to Christianity.

Reluctance to serve in the Indian colonies naturally extended to licensed Portuguese physicians and surgeons. The reduced social and economic circumstances in the Estado da Índia after the mid-seventeenth century had significant implications for Indo-Portuguese medical services, and led to the increased hybridization, or cultural sharing, of healing knowledge. As the number of European-born residents in the eastern colonial enclaves diminished, practical need dictated that medical attention for the indigenous population and for colonial troops sent from Portugal had to be met by indigenous practitioners and apothecaries. Because of the tiny number of European physicians and surgeons in the Estado da Índia at this time (perhaps two or three, never reaching even half a dozen), colonial officials increasingly acquiesced to the pragmatic expedience of filling vacant medical posts with locally trained indigenous physicians and surgeons (though they had to be of Christian families).[53] For lack of European-trained medical practitioners, hospital installations in the Estado da Índia were gradually forced to rely on locally born and cultured healers, who typically used a blend of Indian and imported medical plants to treat illness.

As European medical influence waned in the Asian colonies during the seventeenth and eighteenth centuries, the remedies prescribed in Indo-Portuguese hospitals and infirmaries were increasingly of indigenous origin and applied by indigenous practitioners.[54] Eventually, as many local Goan healers found their way into Portuguese service, the widespread introduction and use of indigenous medicine in Goa's medical institutions became inevitable, and the hybridization of Indo-Portuguese medical culture was complete.

For example, as early as 1608, when the French voyager François Pyrard de Laval recorded his impressions of his stay at the royal hospital of Goa, he observed with some surprise the number of indigenous staff engaged in healing work:

> Be it noted that the superiors and officers of this hospital are Portuguese; the servants are *Bramenis*, or Christian *Canarins* of Goa, who have to feed and attend upon the sick with great care, and to be always at hand ... as for the servants ... they are all Christian Indians.[55]

A century afterwards, many of the hospital posts for "superiors and officers" would also be filled by indigenous Indian Christians.

Later still, during the closing decades of the eighteenth century, even the chief physician of the Estado da Índia was a native Goan: Inácio Caetano Afonso, born into an elite Portuguese-speaking Indo-European family. Though he had access to little formal medical training in the European sense, he gained a very favourable reputation as a healer. In March 1798, in a letter to the Portuguese secretary of state in Lisbon, the governor of the Estado da Índia, Dom Rodrigo de Sousa Coutinho, described Afonso as "a Brahmin ... favoured with natural talents" for healing. The governor continued, saying that "notable cures" had been attributed to him, even though he "had not opened any [medical] book for many years".[56] The following year, after Afonso's death, Governor Sousa Coutinho would write that Afonso had "the sense of a *Médico*, and practised for many years, which compensated for the defects of his [medical] education".[57]

Afonso appears to have studied informally in Goa at the Hospital Militar under his predecessor, the Portuguese-born, Coimbra University-trained physician Luís da Costa Portugal (who, it is worth noting, had made a practice of taking in promising Goan healers and training them in Western medical techniques[58]). Afonso's medical knowledge consisted primarily of native Indian plants and their medicinal applications. In the main, Afonso treated Portuguese soldiers, officials and colonists with local remedies derived from indigenous Indian drugs — medicines that Afonso learnt from older Goan healers, who had employed them since time out of memory. Inácio Caetano Afonso was a product of this rich, hybridized healing culture.

Thus, at a time when other European powers (notably the British in India) often sought to impose Western medicine on their colonial subjects, the chief state physician and his staff in Portuguese India used an innovative, unorthodox blend of contemporary European and traditional indigenous South Asian medical practices. "Doctor" Afonso is just one example of a common phenomenon in the Goan medical institutions of the late seventeenth to the early nineteenth centuries: hospitals, pharmacies and infirmaries depended almost exclusively on native-born practitioners whose training and outlook towards healing reflected a blend of Indian and European cultural influences.

In the Portuguese enclaves on the Malabar Coast of India, then, state hospitals and pharmacies came to rely on native-born staff to fill even the highest medical posts. Although colonial government policies advocated the nomination of European physicians, surgeons and pharmacists whenever possible, in practice a chronic lack of medical staff with Western qualifications meant that treatment of government and military personnel was often of necessity entrusted to native-born, locally trained healers.[59] This situation continued until the founding of the Goan School of Medicine and Surgery in 1842.[60]

In a surviving hospital staff list of the 1770s, the pattern is clear: hospital administrators, ward overseers, male nurses, pharmacy assistants, pharmacists, barber-surgeons and *sangradores* (phlebotomists) were all native Goans.[61] While required to be practising Christians, of course, they were from birth steeped in local healing culture. The pharmacists' "boys" listed on this staff roster were young indigenous men who, among their other duties, tended the medical herb garden.[62] They were among the lowest paid staff, but they ultimately had a very large influence on the types of medicines being cultivated, distributed and applied throughout the Portuguese enclaves in India. This is a crystalline example of the pattern that prevailed within later Portuguese colonialism in Asia: ostensible European rule shaped indelibly by a resilient subaltern sensibility.

Moreover, under Portuguese rule, indigenous medical influence was exported from India and disseminated broadly to other points within the Lusophone world. In 1801, the Prince Regent Dom João charged his colonial governor in India with collecting, cataloguing and remitting a "collection" of seeds for "all of the plants, that vegetate on the Islands and Provinces" of the Portuguese South Asian enclaves.[63] Seed specimens of the medicinal plants and other flora of interest were to be carefully boxed and sent back to the metropole to be cultivated at the Royal Botanical Gardens of the Ajuda Palace in Lisbon. The seeds were, according to the regal order, to be assembled by a local "Herbalist or Gardener" who could provide instructions for their proper cultivation, as well as commentary about the plants' useful application.[64] In the event, the colonial governor entrusted this duty to the chief physician of the Estado da Índia, Dr. António José de Miranda e Almeida, whose responsibilities of course included oversight of the medicinal herb gardens of the royal hospital in Goa. The physician duly submitted his (surely incomplete) specimens and report, mentioning a mere thirty useful and efficacious plants; he noted that many were cultivated in gardens and greenhouses in Goa.[65]

PLANTS GROWN IN THE GOA ROYAL HOSPITAL GARDEN

What types of medicinal plants might have been harvested regularly in the gardens of the Hospital Real Militar in Goa, and how were these indigenous remedies understood by the colonial authorities who employed them? This is a matter of some speculation, but enough documentary evidence exists to identify many of the most likely botanical candidates. We also have sufficient descriptions of the native medicinal plants most widely used in the hospitals and infirmaries of Goa to create a picture of how they were perceived and applied within the hybridized, Indo-Portuguese colonial medical establishment of the seventeenth and eighteenth centuries.

We will begin by looking briefly at some practices of the indigenous Goan physician Inácio Caetano Afonso. During the 1780s and 1790s, when Afonso undertook the treatment of Portuguese soldiers and mariners afflicted with the seasonal fevers associated with the onset of the monsoon, he resorted to familiar Indian medical techniques and medicines at his disposal. While some medicines for combatting fevers had been sent from Brazil via Portugal and were available in the hospital *botica*, or pharmacy, the ethnically diverse colonial staff commonly made use of two indigenous plant-based remedies. One was sandalwood, usually imported from Kerala but widely available in Goa. Ground into dust and mixed with water or other plant juices to make a cooling paste, this Malabar Coast aromatic wood had been spread on the body of patients to reduce fever for generations. In classical Ayurvedic medicine as in traditional Goan folk healing (called *ganvti vokot*, or "medicine of the land"[66]), sandalwood was a long-accepted treatment for fever.[67] Another treatment utilized the root of a thorny tree found in abundance in Goa, which the Portuguese called the João Lopes *pinheiro*, or pine tree. Known in the Konkani language of Goa as *tefoláns*, this plant also was precious to Goan practitioners of traditional medicine as a fever-reducer.[68] Because of its esteemed qualities as a febrifuge, the João Lopes *pinheiro* was almost certainly cultivated in the gardens of the military hospital in Goa.

In 1794, the Conselho Ultramarino called upon Inácio Caetano Afonso to report on the efficacious medicinal plants available in Goa. One example of the several medicinal roots to which Afonso referred in his subsequent descriptions was the celebrated *pau cobra*, or "cobra wood", a name applied to several varieties of plant root known across south India and thought to be effective against snakebite and other venomous animal stings. According to Afonso's manuscript report, *pau cobra* was known in Ceylon, the plant's native home, as "*Hampaddu Tanah*", as Afonso rendered the name phonetically in his Portuguese-language text. In Goa, Afonso wrote, the plant was well known among indigenous "herbalists", but that it was generally referred to by its Portuguese name.[69]

Pau cobra had long held a place in Indo-Portuguese medicine. A discussion of this root appears in Garcia da Orta's text of 1563; three varieties are named, plants with origins in Ceylon and south India. Da Orta asserts that at least one of these varieties, called *mordexi*, grew on the "island of Goa", and that south Indian healers also used the root to treat rheumatism, smallpox, measles and cholera.[70] Similarly, colonial Portuguese linguist Sebastião Dalgado's *Glossário Luso-Asiático* includes an extensive entry on *pau de cobra*, and cites references to this medicine in half a dozen Indo-Portuguese publications of the sixteenth and seventeenth centuries.[71] Dalgado identified the root with *Aristolochia indica*, *Rauwolfia serpentaria* and *Strichnos colubrina* (named under Linnaeus's system), all of which have accepted analogous applications according to classical Indian healing texts.[72] Again, the Goa hospital apothecary staff likely cultivated quantities of this local healing plant root in their institutional gardens.

Because of problems with the health of soldiers and colonial officials in the tropics that persisted into the nineteenth century, imperial authorities in Lisbon maintained their interest in discovering new indigenous remedies from India that could be of use in crown endeavours. In a royal directive dated 2 April 1798, the *cirurgião-môr* (chief surgeon) and other *médicos* of the Hospital Real Militar in Goa were tasked with reporting on their application of indigenous Indian remedies in Portuguese colonial medical institutions. Queen Maria I and the Conselho Ultramarino, seeking medicines for tropical diseases throughout the Portuguese maritime network, commissioned the Hospital Militar staff physicians and surgeons to write a description of all the useful medicinal plants found along the Malabar Coast and in the other remaining Portuguese enclaves at Diu and Daman.

The following year, *cirurgião-môr* Dr. José Abriz and his colleagues produced a report, dated 29 April 1799 and extending to nearly forty manuscript pages, in which they provided thorough descriptions of important indigenous roots and plants then in use in the medical facilities of Portuguese India.[73] As a result, we have a record of several healing plants that were likely grown on the premises of the Goa royal military hospital at the end of the eighteenth century. The following four excerpts from the Abriz report give a sense of these plants as they were understood by contemporary Indo-Portuguese medical practitioners.

Bangue (known in Indian languages as *bhang*, or *Cannabis*) was described in the following terms:

> It is a shrub similar to hemp of Europe and is the height, more or less, of a man. It is ... found in Goa in diverse places as well as in Africa ... and other parts. The vegetation is narcotic, very acrid and pungent, and sulphuric; it has deleterious or venomous qualities, from the leaves, of

> which the Moors and Blacks make the same use, as tobacco to smoke … and which they introduce into sweets and spirituous drinks. It is not known in what dose, but it causes the action of the spirit to be enlivened and sharpened, like wine. Some practitioners advise that one should put it as a lotion in the hair of women who are old or nervous, to guard against hysterical accidents and apoplectic fits.[74]

The pine tree known as the João Lopes *pinheiro* received the following description: "This root comes from Africa, and in Goa there is an abundance of it … Its virtue is as an anti-fever medicine, carminative, as applied in dentistry, dissolver of cold tumours, much valued for neurotic pains and ailments, and against the venom of cobras."[75]

The African connection surfaces again in the plant *butua* (also known as *pereira brava* or *pareira brava*):

> There are three species of it, one of which is called *Butua*, the other two *Parreiras*. The *Butua* is a vine … It is found in diverse places in this country [Goa], one of which is certain to have come from Africa. Its virtue is as a solvent or anticoagulant, aperitif and diuretic, administered internally in contusions, puncture wounds, lymphatic tumors, and externally as a topical in liniment form or fomentation. *Pereira Brava* exists in two qualities, one white and one red … Its virtue is as an expectorant, solvent, and in incidents of wounds or injuries. Administered to inflammations, cataracts, rabies, physical problems from excess drinking and asthma attacks.[76]

The description of the *raíz de cobra* (snake root) was also African in origin and stated that it was

> a plant that grows in the manner of a vine; it grows in mountains, and is found in abundance in Goa … . It comes from Africa, where they make general use of it … . The blacks use it for animal and insect bites … there it is called "*Gangar*" … . Its pharmaceutical virtues help respiration, and is an admirable and a most efficacious remedy, specifically against the venom of cobras, all qualities of insects & venomous animals, being administered internally … and on the exterior, applied to [the area] around the bitten part in the form of a liniment, introducing more into the wound, by means of an incision, the work done of course in this case to purge the virulent serum from that wound.[77]

In addition to locally grown medicinal plants listed in the 1799 Abriz report, the following South Asian simples were also prime candidates for institutional cultivation at the Goa hospital gardens during the seventeenth and eighteenth centuries. How can this assertion be made with confidence? The selected plants are easily cultivated along the Malabar Coast: documentation exists showing the plants were indigenous to Goa, and that Portuguese health practitioners in the Indian colonies had long been aware of their medical applications, sometimes for centuries. Recorded evidence (hospital ward day books detailing patients' treatment[78] and Goan pharmacy records[79]) shows that these plants were commonly applied medicinally in the colonial hospitals and missionary infirmaries of Goa from the seventeenth to nineteenth centuries. Indeed, consignments of drugs gathered for export from the Goan royal hospital often included remedies made from these very same plants.[80]

Further, these plants are known to have been favoured by local Goan *vaidyas* (indigenous healers), so the plants formed part of a pre-colonial medical culture that shaped the awareness of the indigenous Christians who made up the corps of assistants and clerks on the pharmacy staff. It is easy to imagine a scenario whereby Konkani hospital staffers in the pharmacy division advocated for the cultivation of the very plants that had been best known to them as remedies since childhood.

What follows, therefore, is an admittedly speculative list of indigenous healing plants that nevertheless were, in all probability, grown by the apothecary staff of the royal military hospital in Goa at various times during their medicinal herb garden's long existence:

Aloe (in Portuguese, *aloes*; also known as *azebre*). The general name for the sap of diverse species of the genus *Aloe* found in the environs of India. In European medical tradition, it was used in concert with other drugs for the mixture of medicinal plasters or poultices, or as a topical external ointment. The substance was also attributed with powers as a purgative to clear the bowels or as an emetic to induce vomiting; it was further employed topically in Goa as a cooling agent to treat fevers. This latter use was taken directly from Indian practice: indigenous healers on the Malabar Coast employed the fresh pulp of aloe leaves as a cooling compress.[81]

Althea (in Portuguese, *altea*). A plant of the genus *Malva*, also known as *Sida* or "marsh mallow". A small shrub, several types of althea grew all over India as a common weed. The plant's seeds saw popular use in Goa as an aphrodisiac and for increasing sexual potency; in combination with ginger (as a decoction), it was applied in Goan colonial infirmaries for certain fevers (an analogous use is documented in Ayurvedic texts); the powdered root bark of althea was given with milk to women for nervous disorders; the root juice was used topically to help heal wounds.[82] A dose of althea was a common daily treatment for patients in some Indo-Portuguese healing facilities in the middle of the eighteenth century.[83]

Cardamom (in Portuguese, *cardamomo*). A common medicinal plant that grows wild in south India and was long known to Ayurveda and other indigenous healing systems. The drug consists of the dried fruits and seeds of the plant. Often used in combination with cloves, ginger or caraway seeds, Indian *vaidyas* saw it as effective for indigestion, or administered it with a purgative to relieve digestive problems.[84] Indo-Portuguese colonial pharmacies commonly stocked this *droga* from the mid-sixteenth century onwards.

Cashew fruit. Cashew wine, or *feni* (in Portuguese, *vinho de caju*) was employed as a healing agent in the Estado da Índia. The fruit of the cashew tree became the basis of a fermented or distilled alcoholic beverage. Administered at home as an infusion and decoction, *feni* was also served in colonial hospitals as a heated medicinal beverage. The Portuguese, of course, introduced cashew trees into India from Brazil, but indigenous medicine along the Malabar Coast soon embraced "cashew wine" and spirits as a pain killer and decongestant, and for relief of respiratory ailments. This is a clear instance, then, of Portuguese distilling practices and introduced species of flora adding to the medical lexicon of Konkani-speaking peoples in Goa.[85]

Ginger (in Portuguese, *gingebre*). A "universal remedy", according to classical Ayurveda.[86] This plant is widely cultivated throughout south India and had been central to Ayurvedic principles long before the arrival of the Europeans. As an acrid, heat-inducing food, it was valued as an anti-rhuematic, carminative, diuretic and aphrodisiac. Ginger root, dried and powdered, was thought to cure cardiac disorders, stop vomiting and coughing, and help liver inflammation. It addresses such conditions as constipation, fever, swelling, flatulence and colic. Ginger is also applied to treat diarrhoea, cholera, dyspepsia and eye diseases.[87] Portuguese colonial medical facilities dispensed large quantities and made broad use of ginger during the early modern colonial era.

Sarsaparilla (in Portuguese, *sarsaparilha*). A perennial climbing vine that is found throughout India, this plant drug has long been employed by Ayurvedic healers. The woody root, powdered and mixed with water or other plant juice, constitutes the drug. Sarsaparilla is useful as a fever-reducer and anti-rhuematic; it can also be used to treat skin diseases, syphilis and urinary disorders. Ingested, its diuretic effect was used to purify the blood.[88] Indo-Portuguese surgeons and physicians prescribed sarsaparilla for the same maladies and made sure that colonial pharmacies were well stocked with the substance.[89]

Tamarind (in Portuguese, *tamarindo*). A pulp made of the body and seed pod of the tamarind plant, a leafy, vegetable-like tree common to the Indian tropics. Alternatively, this preparation could consist of the stems, roots and bark of the plant, reduced to a consistent paste. As a medicine, it was used for its qualities as a digestive, as a laxative, and to reduce fever. Indo-Portuguese practitioners often mixed tamarind paste with other plants. It is rich in organic acids (citric and tartaric), as well as sugars and pectins.[90] This preparation was also a common ingredient in medicinal *águas*, preserves and syrups consumed in other Portuguese dominions.[91]

Zedoaria (in Portuguese, *zedoária*). The root of *Curcuma zedoaria*, originating in southern India and the Molucca islands. Associated with the root of *Angelica* and diluted in vinegar, this plant was used by Europeans and South Asians to perfume the mouth during times of plague or epidemic, or to ward off disease. This bitter substance was used in a balm, together with licorice and gentian, to soothe and protect burns; the drug was also considered a stimulant and an anti-spasmodic.[92]

CONCLUSION

No matter what their appearance at any given time, the medical gardens of the Portuguese Hospital Real Militar at Goa represented an exceptional multicultural space in South Asia, wherein European, Malabar and non-Indian concepts of healing were blended. The social context in which the Indo-Portuguese medical practitioners operated was hybridized like no other, owing to the global scope of the Portuguese colonial dominions, combined with a willingness to experiment with indigenous medicines and a tropical disease environment that caused the European colonizers to turn pragmatically to local medical expertise when their own knowledge and resources were insufficient. The garden's Indo-Portuguese caretakers thus developed and held a unique medical cosmology that inculcated indigenous and European conceits regarding health and medicine, and that employed indigenous plants according to a fusion of cultural exigencies that was neither fully Indian nor European. The Goa royal hospital garden thus emerges as a vivid symbol of the profound cultural hybridization common across Indo-Portuguese colonial regions.

Notes

1 The author wishes to express his gratitude to the American Institute of Indian Studies and the National Endowment for the Humanities of the United States; this paper was produced with research made possible by a generous grant provided through these organizations. In addition, for logistical support in Goa, India, I am grateful to the Portuguese Fundação Oriente and the Xavier Centre for Historical Research. For support of research in the United Kingdom, I wish to thank the Wellcome Trust Centre for the History of Medicine at University College London.

2 Please see the arguments presented in Michael N. Pearson, "The Thin End of the Wedge: Medical Relativities as a Paradigm of Early Modern Indian-European Relations", in *Modern Asian Studies* 29, no. 1 (1995): 141–70; and Timothy Walker, "Evidence of the Use of Ayurvedic Medicine in the Medical Institutions of Portuguese India, 1680–1830", in *Ayurveda at the Crossroads of Care and Cure*, edited by A. Salema (Lisbon: Centro de História de Além-Mar, Universidade Nova de Lisboa, 2002).

3 John Simpson and Edmund Weiner, eds., *Oxford English Dictionary*, 2nd ed. (Oxford: Oxford University Press, 1989).

4 José Nicolau da Fonseca, *An Historical and Archaeological Sketch of the City of Goa* (Bombay: Thacker & Co., 1878; 2nd repr., New Delhi: Asia Educational Services, 1994), p. 228.

5 François Pyrard, Pierre de Bergeron and Jérôme Bignon, *The Voyage of François Pyrard of Laval to the East Indies, the Maldives, the Moluccas and Brazil* (London: Printed for the Hakluyt Society, 1887; repr., New Delhi: Asia Educational Services, 2000), 2:1:5. See also the testimony of Albert de Mandelslo in Adam Olearius and Johann Albrecht von Mandelslo, *The Voyages and Travels of J. Albert de Mandelslo* (London: Starkey, 1669), 2:1:81, cited in Fonseca, *An Historical and Archaeological Sketch*, p. 232.

6 For figures of the annual number of patients treated at the Hospital Militar at the end of the eighteenth century, see Livros das Monções do Reino (hereafter cited as MR) 173, fol. 168, 1791 (3,476 patients); MR 176B, fol. 436, 1793 (3,858 patients); MR 176B, fol. 448, 1794 (3,076 patients); and MR 177A, fol. 218, 1797 (1,932 patients), Historical Archives of Goa (hereafter cited as HAG), Panaji, Goa. N.b.: Many collections in the HAG have no title and thus are referenced by a number only. Dates appearing in the HAG citations herein pertain only to the specific folios cited.

7 MR 115, fols. 88–89, 1742.

8 M.J. Gabriel de Saldanha, *História de Goa (Política e Arqueológica)* (Bastorá, Goa, 1925–26; repr., New Delhi: Asia Educational Services, 2002), 2:183; and Fonseca, *An Historical and Archaeological Sketch*, p. 228.

9 HAG 646, fol. 39, n.d.

10 MR 46A, fols. 96r–97v, 1681–82.

11 HAG 7926, fol. 56–56v, 1785.

12 MR 135B, fol. 489v, 1762.

13 Pessoal do Real Hospital Militar, HAG 4508, fol. 5, 1777–79.

14 Ibid., fols. 40–41.

15 The merchant's name in the Goan Konkani language would be Subbha Kamat Mhami; HAG 1736, fols. 9v–12, n.d.

16 J.B. Amancio Gracias, *Médicos Europeus em Goa e nas Cortes Indianas nos Séculos XVI a XVIII* (Bastorá, Goa: Tipografia Rangel, 1939), p. 31.

17 Garcia da Orta, *Colóquios dos Simples e Drogas e Cousas Medicianais da Índia* (Rachol Seminary, Goa, 1563; facsimile ed., Lisbon: Academia das Ciências de Lisboa, 1963).

18 Gregório Pereira Ribeiro, substitute *médico* of the royal hospital of Goa, to the governor-general of the Estado da Índia, MR 99, fol. 286, 25 January 1732.

19 Statement of Dr António José de Miranda e Almeida, *físico-môr* of the Estado da Índia, Panjim, MR 185, fols. 17v–18, 1 May 1806.

20 For further discussion on this point, see Timothy Walker, "Acquisition and Circulation of Medical Knowledge within the Portuguese Colonial Empire during the Early Modern Period", in *Science, Power and the Order of Nature in the Spanish and Portuguese Empires*, edited by Daniela Bleichmar, Kristin Huffine and Paula De Vos (Stanford: Stanford University Press, 2008), pp. 247–56.

21 Dauril Alden, *The Making of an Enterprise: The Society of Jesus in Portugal, Its Empire, and Beyond, 1540–1750* (Stanford: Stanford University Press, 1996), p. 338.

22 Fátima da Silva Gracias, *Health and Hygiene in Colonial Goa, 1510–1961* (New Delhi: Concept Publishing, 1994), p. 126.

23 "Regimento do Hospital Real da Cidade de Goa", 23 August 1583, doc. 838, in *Archivo Portuguez-Oriental: Fasc. 5*, vol. 3, edited by J.H. da Cunha Rivara (Nova Goa: Imprensa Nacional, 1865; repr., New Delhi: Asia Educational Services, 1992), pp. 1006–67.

24 "Regimento do Hospital Real da Cidade de Goa", 28 May 1584, in *Documenta Indica*, vol. 13, *1583–1585*, edited by Joseph Wicki (Rome: Institutum Historicum Societus Jesu, 1975), pp. 867–73.

25 Lycurgo de Castro Santos Filho, *História de Medicina no Brasil, do Século XVI ao Século XIX* (São Paulo: Editora Brasiliense, 1947), 2:26–30.

26 See Annual Jesuit Missionary Letters of the Maduri Province, shelf 211, bk. 34 (1606–43), pp. 30–44, 47–50, 52–53 and 78; see also shelf 211, bk. 102 (1655–66), pp. 87–91 and 221–27, Shembaganur Province Archives, Sacred Heart College, Kodaikanal, Tamil Nadu, India.

27 See, for example, *Breve Compendio de Varias Receitas de Medicina*, 1598, fols. 2–79v, Fonds Portugais No. 59, Département des Manuscrits, Biblioteque National de France, Paris; see also *Curiosidad: Un Libro de Medicina Escrito por los Jesuitas en las Misiones del Paraguay en el Año 1580*, nos. 1–15, 02, 026, fols. 1–280, Setor de Manuscritos, Biblioteca Nacional, Rio de Janeiro; and *Colecção de Varias Receitas e Segredos Particulares das Principais Boticas da Nossa*

Companhia de Portugal, da India, de Macao e do Brazil, 1766, Opp. NN. 17, fols. 1–688, Archivum Romanum Societatis Iesu, Rome.

28 Fonseca, *An Historical and Archaeological Sketch*, pp. 229–30.

29 Statement of Dr. António José de Miranda e Almeida, fols. 17v–18, 1 May 1806; and Fonseca, *An Historical and Archaeological Sketch*, p. 236.

30 Letter, Goa, MR 181A, fol. 121, 18 April 1802.

31 Ibid.

32 Heta Pandit, *Hidden Hands: Master Builders of Goa* (Porvorim, Goa: Heritage Network, 2003), pp. 183–94. See also Helena Attlee, *The Gardens of Portugal* (London: Francis Lincoln, 2008), pp. 9–17, 67–70, 115–19 and 131–37.

33 See Heldar Carita, *Palácios de Goa*, 2nd ed. (Lisbon: Quetzal Editores, 1996), pp. 52–53; and Pandit, *Hidden Hands*, pp. 7–12, 35–39 and 85–94.

34 See Carita, *Palácios de Goa*, pp. 15–38; and Attlee, *The Gardens of Portugal*, pp. 67–70, 115–19 and 131–37.

35 See comments in Fonseca, *An Historical and Archaeological Sketch*, p. 232, and Pandit, *Hidden Hands*, pp. 175–94.

36 For a discussion on this point, see Robert M. Hayden, "Antagonistic Tolerance: Competitive Sharing of Religious Sites in South Asia and the Balkans", *Current Anthropology* 42, no. 2 (April 2002).

37 Detail from a painting (ca. 1780) held in the private collection of Alpoim Galvão in Cascais, Portugal. Image published in Carita, *Palácios de Goa*, p. 28.

38 Engraving by António Lopes Mendes, published in António Lopes Mendes, *A India Portuguesa: Breve Descripção das Possessões Portuguezas na Asia* (Lisbon: Imprensa Nacional, 1886).

39 The name means "Gunpowder House", since the site had originally been used as a munitions magazine. See Carita, *Palácios de Goa*, p. 28.

40 Foldout engraved map in Fonseca, *An Historical and Archaeological Sketch*, n.p.

41 Attlee, *The Gardens of Portugal*, pp. 130–59.

42 Plan of the Palácio da Casa da Pólvora, Goa (n.d.; mid-eighteenth century), held by the Biblioteca da Ajuda, Lisbon; image reproduced in Carita, *Palácios de Goa*, p. 29.

43 Ibid. A *palmo* measured 22 centimetres, or 8.8 inches.

44 Pyrard, Bergeron and Bignon, *The Voyage of François Pyrard*, 2:1:14.

45 Ibid., 2:1:5.

46 Ibid., 2:1:14–15.

47 Ibid., 2:1:6–7.

48 See the testimony of Albert de Mandelslo in Olearius and Mandelslo, *The Voyages and Travels of J. Albert de Mandelslo*, 2:1:81, cited in Fonseca, *An Historical and Archaeological Sketch*, p. 232.

49 José E. Mendes Ferrão, *A Aventura das Plantas e os Descubrimentos Portugueses*, 3rd ed. (Lisbon: Instituto de Investigação Científica Tropical and Chaves Ferreira Publicações, 2005), pp. 14–23.

50 Although this plant is commonly known today as *pareira brava* (or *pareyra*

brava), original manuscript sources consulted by this author normally spelled it *pereira brava*. *Pereira* is a common Portuguese surname that also means "pear tree", whereas *pareira* has no meaning in Portuguese.

51 See MR 178B, fols. 644–64, 1798–99; and MR 831, fol. 72, 27 July 1735.

52 In 1791, for example, the population of all territories in Portuguese India was reported as 201,919 souls; barely over 1,000 (under 0.5 per cent) were Portuguese natives. See MR 173, fol. 227, 1791. For detailed 1788 population statistics, see MR 169A, fols. 305–7, 1788. See also Timothy J. Coates, *Convicts and Orphans: Forced and State-Sponsored Colonization in the Portuguese Empire, 1550–1755* (Stanford: Stanford University Press, 2002), pp. 35 and 69–71.

53 See Maria de Jesus dos Mártires Lopes, *Goa Setecentista: Tradição e Modernidade (1750–1800)*, 2nd ed. (Lisbon: Universidade Católica Portuguesa, 1999), pp. 90–94 and 115–23.

54 For further discussion on this point, see Walker, "Acquisition and Circulation of Medical Knowledge", pp. 257–60.

55 Pyrard, Bergeron and Bignon, *The Voyage of François Pyrard*, 2:1:14–16.

56 Letter, MR 177A, fol. 212, 14 March 1798.

57 Letter, MR 178A, fol. 272, 28 April 1799.

58 Letter, MR 177A, fol. 212, 14 March 1798.

59 For early seventeenth-century royal restrictions on local healers practising their craft in Goa, see Livro das Posturas, HAG 7795, fols. 25–27, 3 November 1618. For a 1695 royal directive advocating a shift towards training and employing locally born healers in the Estado da Índia, see MR 59, fol. 305v, 24 March 1695.

60 However, even though the school was created to teach "scientific Western" medicine, the demographics of the student body remained thoroughly Indian.

61 Pessoal do Real Hospital Militar, HAG 4508, 1777–79.

62 Statement of Dr António José de Miranda e Almeida, fol. 18v, 1 May 1806.

63 See the letters of the Portuguese Secretary of State, Mafra, Portugal, 12 November 1801, and the response of the Portuguese Governor General of India, Goa, MR 182, fols. 322–24, 18 February 1803.

64 Ibid.

65 Report by Dr António José de Miranda e Almeida, Goa, MR 182, fols. 325–25v, n.d.

66 Maria Bernadette Gomes, "Ethnomedicine and Healing Practices in Goa" (Ph. D. dissertation, University of Goa, India, 1993), introduction.

67 Ibid., chap. 2; and S.K. Jain, *Medicinal Plants* (New Delhi: National Book Trust, India, 1999), pp. 154–55. For evidence of use in Portuguese medical facilities, see Despezas do Convento do São João de Deus, HAG 7887, fol. 197, n.d.; and MR 46A, fol. 96, 1681–82.

68 MR 178B, fol. 646, 1798–99; and MR 175, fols. 222v–23v, n.d. See also V.V. Sivarajan and Indira Balachandran, *Ayurvedic Drugs and Their Plant Sources* (New Delhi: Oxford & IBH Publishing Co., 1994), pp. 111–12.

69 MR 175, fols. 220–21v, 1794.
70 Da Orta, *Colóquios dos Simples e Drogas*, Colloquy 42.
71 Sebastião Rodolfo Dalgado, *Glossário Luso-Asiático* (Coimbra: Imprensa da Universidade, 1919–21; repr., New Delhi: Asian Educational Services, 1988), 2: 196–97.
72 Sivarajan and Balachandran, *Ayurvedic Drugs*, pp. 185–86 and 218.
73 MR 178B, fols. 644–64, 1798–99.
74 Ibid., fol. 647.
75 Ibid., fol. 646.
76 Ibid., fols. 645v–46.
77 MR 178B, fol. 645, 1798–99.
78 For examples, see Doentes do Hospital Real do Baçaim, HAG 865, n.d.
79 Representative examples include Livro da Receita e Despeza de Medicamentos do Hospital do Convento de São João de Deus, HAG 831, n.d.; and Botica do Convento do Santo Agostinho, HAG 8032, n.d.
80 See, for example, MR 46A, fols. 96–97v, 1681–82; and Relação de Medicamentos que Vão da Botica do Hospital Real [de Goa] para a Fortaleza de Diu, HAG 7926, fols. 56–56v, n.d.
81 Da Orta, *Colóquios dos simples e drogas*, pp. 4–9, 38, 40 and 42; Maria Benedita Araújo, "A Medicina Popular e a Magia no Sul de Portugal" (Ph.D. dissertation, Universidade de Lisboa, 1988), 3: 144.
82 Jain, *Medicinal Plants*, pp. 160–61; and Sivarajan and Balachandran, *Ayurvedic Drugs*, pp. 71–79.
83 Livro da Receita e Despeza de Medicamentos do Hospital do Convento de São João de Deus, HAG 831, fol. 3, 18 May 1733 (and many subsequent days).
84 Jain, *Medicinal Plants*, pp. 72–74; and Sivarajan and Balachandran, *Ayurvedic Drugs*, 398–99. See also da Orta, *Colóquios dos Simples e Drogas*, Colloquy 13.
85 HAG 831, fol. 72, 27 July 1735.
86 Robert E. Svoboda, *Ayurveda: Life, Health and Longevity* (New Delhi: Penguin Books, 1993), pp. 130–31.
87 Sivarajan and Balachandran, *Ayurvedic Drugs*, pp. 50–51. See also da Orta, *Colóquios dos Simples e Drogas*, Colloquy 26.
88 Jain, *Medicinal Plants*, pp. 96–97. Sivarajan and Balachandran, pp. 434–38.
89 See, for example, HAG 8030, fol. 37, n.d.
90 Ibid., fol. 214, n.d.
91 Manuel Azevedo, *Correcçam de Abusos* (Lisbon: Officina de Joam da Costa, a custa Martim Vaz Tagarro, 1680), 3: 292; Brás Luís de Abreu, *Portugal Médico: Ou Monarchia Médico-Lusitana* (Coimbra: Joam Antunes, 1726), pp. 192–93 and 386; da Orta, *Colóquios dos Simples e Drogas*, p. 203; George Bate and Caetano de Santo António, *Pharmacopea Bateana na quel Se Contem Quasi Oytocentos Medicamentos Tirados de Pratica de Jorge Bateo* (Lisbon: Officina Real Deslandesiana, 1713), p. 105.
92 Araújo, "A medicina popular", 3: 217–18.

2

MALACCA IN THE ERA OF VICEROY LINHARES (1629–35)

Anthony Disney

On 14 January 1641, after a protracted siege lasting five and a half months, Portuguese Malacca surrendered to the Dutch. The loss of Malacca, which had been in Portuguese hands since its capture by Albuquerque from Sultan Mahmud 140 years earlier, was a crushing blow to the Portuguese. At the time the greatest loss the Estado da Índia had ever suffered in the East, it proved a setback from which there would never be a full recovery. Effectively, it marked the end of Portugal's status as a first-rate power in maritime Asia, especially east of Cape Comorin.

The story of the final siege of Malacca by the Dutch in 1640–41 is well known and need not detain us here.[1] But the build-up towards that climax, particularly in the decade or so preceding it, is less clear. What follows is an investigation into a crucial part of this build-up — the rapidly moving situation at Malacca during the administration of Dom Miguel de Noronha, fourth Conde de Linhares. This viceroy, who held office at Goa from 21 October 1629 to 9 December 1635, was an intelligent and hard-working proconsul, tireless in his efforts to sustain the Estado da Índia. Nevertheless, only five years after his departure, Malacca fell. The questions addressed here are to what extent did Portuguese Malacca cease to be militarily and commercially viable during the course of Linhares's term — and, insofar as this did happen, how and why did it happen?

SEVENTEENTH-CENTURY PORTUGUESE MALACCA

Seventeenth-century Portuguese Malacca consisted of an inner city surrounded by defensive walls, within which were the citadel and the Augustinian, Dominican and Jesuit churches and establishments clustered on and around St Paul's hill. Most of the townspeople lived outside the walls in Malay-style thatched houses, particularly to the north of the river. Here were also orchards, gardens and the *dusun,* or small rural properties on the fringes of the forest. But there was insufficient arable land in Portuguese-controlled territory for the city to feed itself — it was therefore obliged to import rice and other foodstuffs from Java, Siam and elsewhere in peninsular Malaya.[2] Malacca's population under Linhares remained quite cosmopolitan, but the mixture was rather different from what it had been for much of the sixteenth century. Naturally the indigenous Malays formed a substantial majority, but their political influence was limited and they seldom feature in the Portuguese sources. Most remained Muslims, but their religious practice was apparently quite lax. Many were fishermen or seamen, but there were also numerous Malay small traders and craftsmen. There were also the Minangs or Minangkabau, many of whom lived in the area adjoining Malacca to the east. Several thousand of these Minangs had come under Portuguese administration but retained their own *tumenggung* (an official responsible for law and order), who was usually a Malacca *casado* (a married man in the reserve army). These people were primarily farmers, especially of betel, but they also brought supplies of tin to Malacca from the interior.[3]

The various non-Malay, non-Portuguese trading groups that had earlier dominated Malacca's maritime commerce — the Gujaratis, Klings, Javanese and Chinese — are hardly mentioned in the Portuguese written sources for the Linhares period. In fact, the Gujaratis appear to have left soon after the Portuguese conquest in 1511, and while many Klings and Chinese stayed on and cooperated with the Portuguese, remaining important in Malaccan trade through the first half of the sixteenth century, their numbers gradually dwindled. In Linhares's time, those who still remained had mostly merged into the dominant Portuguese culture, many becoming Catholic Christians. There were reportedly over 7,000 Asian Christians in Malacca by the early seventeenth century, most being of Chinese or South Indian extraction.[4]

The politically dominant element in Portuguese Malacca's population was, of course, the Portuguese themselves. Broadly speaking, there were three major

Portuguese interest groups in the city in this period: the colonial Portuguese, the Portuguese from Portugal and the religious. The colonial Portuguese consisted of Portuguese and Eurasians born in Malacca or elsewhere in maritime Asia, Portuguese immigrants who had effectively become permanent settlers and Lusitanized Asians. These people were sometimes referred to collectively as *castiços*. The second major group — the Portuguese from Portugal — comprised primarily young metropolitan Portuguese men shipped out from Europe as *soldados* (soldiers); it also included a handful of senior officials, who were mostly *fidalgos* (noblemen), and represented, at least in theory, the interests of the crown. These metropolitan Portuguese were referred to locally in Asia as *reinóis*, a term that roughly corresponds to the various derogatory terms for Britons such as *limeys* in British North America, *poms* in Australia and *rooineks* in colonial South Africa. The interests of the colonial Portuguese and the Portuguese from Portugal sometimes coincided, but were at other times in conflict. The third element — the Catholic religious — had a foot in both camps, but was in important respects a separate force with its own interests. Moreover, there were important internal divisions among the various religious, especially between members of the different regular orders. Power and influence in seventeenth-century Portuguese Malacca was shared among these three groups.

THE FINAL PHASE OF PORTUGUESE OFFENSIVE ACTION (1629–30)

The principal military role of Portuguese Malacca was, of course, defensive. Like all the Portuguese possessions in maritime Asia, it had to guard against the possibility of attack from external enemies, whether local or European, with constant vigilance. However, Malacca also engaged from time to time in offensive operations. These varied from mere corsair ventures and the mounting of predatory raids to actual campaigns of conquest. For most of Linhares's viceroyalty, the city was involved in defensive operations only, but in the first year or two there was some vigorous offensive action.

When Linhares arrived in Goa on 21 October 1629, Malacca was under siege from a massive expeditionary force sent against it by the formidable Iskandar Muda, sultan of Aceh (1607–36). However, on the very day the viceroy reached his capital, a Portuguese relief fleet, comprising twenty-nine warships carrying approximately 900 officers and soldiers, also arrived at Malacca, under the command of Captain-General (and Acting Governor) Nuno Álvares Botelho.[5] Malacca was soon further strengthened by the appearance of a large force from Johor led by its sultan in person, who at the time was a Portuguese ally. Under Botelho's energetic leadership, the Portuguese had the Acehnese rapidly cornered, bottled up in the River Pangor some five kilometres from Malacca, from where there was no escape. There, on 6 and 7 December 1629, Iskandar Muda's great expedition, said by the Portuguese to have comprised 236 ships and 19,000 men, was utterly annihilated by Botelho and his allies.[6]

After this outstanding victory, Botelho was welcomed back to Malacca in euphoric triumph by António Pinto da Fonseca, the city's long-serving but ageing captain-general, and by the populace. Presented with the city's keys, Botelho was cheered through streets festooned with triumphal arches and richly decorated with Chinese silk hangings, as he made his way to the cathedral for the obligatory thanksgiving mass and sermon.[7] The defeated Acehnese commander, called Laksamana by the Portuguese, was sent as a trophy, along with his captured galley, to be displayed in Goa and ultimately in Lisbon — but died en route while the vessel was wintering in Colombo.[8] The Malacca Jesuits, who had particularly warm relations with Nuno Álvares, staged their own ceremonial thanksgiving at Malacca's St Paul's church, complete with triumphal car, richly dressed symbolic figures, sonorous music and numerous orations.[9] News of Botelho's great victory reached Goa itself in late February 1630, where it again inspired great rejoicing. An elated Viceroy Linhares commented, "I can affirm that all the victories that we read about in the chronicles of India cannot compare with this one."[10] Thus, at the start of the Linhares era, the situation at Malacca, from a Portuguese viewpoint, appeared to have taken a distinctly positive turn.

Following his victory, Nuno Álvares moved swiftly to seize the initiative. First, only five days after his triumph, he sailed to rendezvous with Portuguese commercial shipping expected from Macao, to protect it from the Dutch. Then, early in 1630, with the backing of the Malacca council, he launched an expedition to attack Dutch shipping and trading facilities, pay a visit to Batavia, then proceed to Siam.[11] Precisely what Botelho intended to do at Batavia is unclear. Perhaps he wanted to carry out a reconnaissance of the Dutch fortifications — or he may have been planning something more ambitious. In any event, Portuguese optimism about taking the fight to the Dutch was apparently greater at this time than it had been for many years. Linhares himself wrote in his diary, "from all these journeys I conceive great hopes".[12] Taking the offensive against Aceh was also in Botelho's mind in early 1630, for that March he wrote to the viceroy urging him to come in person at the head of an expedition to seize the sultanate — or, alternatively, to send him an additional 1,000 troops. With these, Botelho affirmed, he would gladly undertake the task himself. In July 1630 Linhares put this proposal to his council, but it unanimously advised that the viceroyalty could not afford to divert its limited resources to the purpose.[13]

Meanwhile, Botelho had left Malacca for his cruise to the south on 22 March 1630. He proceeded first to the River Jambi in southeastern Sumatra, where there was reported to be enemy shipping.[14] At the mouth of the river he found three Dutch ships, which he duly burned or captured. Proceeding upstream he next encountered a large Dutch carrack, which he immediately attacked. This vessel blew up when a cannon-ball ignited its magazine. Then, further up the river, he located two more Dutch carracks that had been loading pepper. These he successfully fired. Meanwhile, yet another Dutch carrack — identified as the forty-four-gun *Walcheren* — arrived off the mouth of the Jambi on 5 May 1630. Botelho promptly attacked this vessel too, assaulting it from all sides with his fleet of small ships. Portuguese boarders quickly secured its forecastle and the Dutch crew fled below decks. The Portuguese thereupon fired the ship and withdrew — but one of their craft became entangled with the *Walcheren*'s prow. Fearing this ship would also catch fire, Botelho brought up his own *jália* (a small galley-type ship) to its assistance — but at this critical moment the Dutchman's magazine exploded, destroying the *jália* with it. Botelho, who could not swim, was thrown into the water. Though — according to Manuel Xavier, who wrote the principal contemporary account of these events — his heart was still beating when he was retrieved by rescuers, he died shortly afterwards in the arms of his chaplain.[15] Stunned by his loss, his captains immediately aborted the expedition and returned to Malacca, where they arrived flying black flags of mourning.[16]

The first rumours of Botelho's death did not reach Linhares at Goa until six months later on 8 November 1630, when he dismissed them as being probably Dutch lies. When the unwelcome report was confirmed in early February 1631, he was only too well aware of the implications, describing it as "the worst news possible". A few days later he informed the crown, "I write this letter … with tears in my eyes because I'm giving in it news to Your Majesty of the death in India … of the man who with the cleanest heart and hands was serving Your Majesty there."[17] The loss of Botelho was indeed a heavy blow to Portuguese hopes, effectively ending any chance of their conducting further offensive operations in the Malacca region. Thereafter there was occasionally talk of conducting some initiative or other, but never again did it lead to positive action. For example, in 1632 the viceroy's council considered a proposal from the sultan of Mataram to mount joint operations against Batavia — but did nothing. At about the same time Linhares was urged by the crown to cooperate with the Spanish governor in Manila to expel the Dutch from Taiwan — but, again, was unable to contribute.[18] Later in 1635, on hearing of renewed threats from Aceh against Malacca, Linhares declared himself ready to sail to its relief in person. However, his council was adamantly opposed to the suggestion — and it is doubtful whether he ever seriously expected to go.[19] In fact, all the evidence suggests that Goa's commitment to conducting offensive military operations in the Malacca region had died with Botelho.

Offensive operations like those of Botelho were clearly official undertakings of the Estado da Índia; but there was also a well-established tradition in Southeast Asia of unofficial elements — that is, Portuguese adventurers, mercenaries and settlers — proposing, urging and sometimes actually conducting Portuguese military raids and schemes of conquest. Such enterprises were at their peak in approximately the years 1570–1610 — and in hindsight often look astonishingly ambitious. A prominent proponent then had been Dom João Ribeiro Gaio, bishop of Malacca from 1570 to 1601. Gaio proposed that the Portuguese and Spaniards conquer Aceh and Johor, then move on to subjugate Siam, Cambodia, Vietnam and southern China.[20] Such schemes were less common by Linhares's time, but were nevertheless from time to time still submitted to the Goa government. In 1634 Linhares was presented with one such proposal, composed by a certain Gaspar Soares, who was probably a Malacca *casado.* Soares, who had been a prisoner in Siam, wanted the viceroy to send an expedition to plunder the Thai capital, Ayutthaya, which he claimed could be seized and sacked "without danger and at very little expense".[21] He claimed the loot would be immense, yielding gold, silver, rubies and bronze pagodas to fill many galleons. A mere twenty ships (*navios*), six *jálias*, and 400 musketeers would suffice for the raid. There would be spoils enough to sustain many future fleets — and make a substantial contribution to "restoring" the Estado da Índia. Soares's proposal appears to have had some significant backing, including that of Malacca's long-serving captain-general, António Pinto da Fonseca. But Linhares himself merely appended the letter to his official diary entry for 26 April 1634. He made no comment on it, and certainly never attempted to implement it.

THE FINAL DEFENSIVE PHASE (1631–36)

The reality, of course, was that under Linhares, especially after Botelho's death, the main Portuguese military focus in Malacca — as in Southeast Asia more generally — was not offensive, but defensive, as it had been since the Dutch achieved maritime predominance in the first decade of the seventeenth century. Moreover, successful Portuguese defence of Malacca depended on four principal components. These were the maintenance of an effective fortifications system; provision of an adequate garrison; the presence of naval forces capable of keeping maritime communications open; and a sufficient supply of arms, ammunition and military materials generally. How and how successfully were these needs met in the Linhares years?

Malacca's fortifications are described in some detail by António Bocarro, who served as state archivist in Goa during Linhares's viceregal term.[22] According to Bocarro, the city was surrounded by a stone wall twenty feet high, with six major bastions. These bastions boasted forty-one cannon, nine of which were iron and the rest bronze, and possessed an adequate supply of powder and munitions.[23] Within the walls, near the mouth of the river, stood A Famosa, the celebrated fortress built by Afonso de Albuquerque. This was a five-storey citadel of medieval design, surrounded by its own wall equipped with a parapet of the same height and width as that on the city walls.[24] During the Linhares period, some attempt was made to improve these fortifications under the supervision of Captain-General Pinto da Fonseca, himself a military engineer. The nature of the work undertaken is not specified in detail, but it included the removal of palm trees without owner compensation, to clear a field of fire in case there was a siege.[25] The construction of a new fortress on the offshore island of Pulau Malacca (known in the Portuguese sources as Ilha das Naus) was also approved, and commenced upon. This island was strategically important because it provided an anchorage for vessels that were too big to enter the river. According to Bocarro, the foundations of a fortress on Pulau Malacca had already been laid and construction materials assembled, at the time of his writing. But the fort had not been completed by the time Linhares's term came to an end — and it was still unfinished at the final Dutch siege of 1640–41.[26] Another project that had been officially approved was the construction of a fort on an "elevated site" occupied by a Jesuit *casa* (house) in Malacca. To make room for this fort, the *casa* was to be moved to another location within the old walls. It is not clear what eventually happened concerning this project, though work on it was obstructed, at least for a while, by a church-imposed embargo.[27]

Of course, any fortification system also requires an effective garrison. The Malacca garrison consisted in theory of four companies of sixty soldiers each, plus their captains, *alferes* (ensigns; in this case, second in command), and sergeants — that is, a total of just over 240 men. But in practice numbers were usually much less, Bocarro even stating that there were at most one hundred garrison soldiers actually serving. This was nothing new — indeed, a few years earlier, in 1626, there had allegedly been only seventy-five.[28] One explanation is the alarmingly high rate of desertion, for the troops lived in desperately poor conditions and received low pay at unreliable intervals, while the cost of living in Malacca was high.[29] On the other hand there were also the Malacca *casados* and their dependants, who provided an important second line of defence. Bocarro states there were some 250 *casados* in Malacca — roughly the same as there had been in the late sixteenth century.[30] These Malacca citizens were able to deploy between them about 2,000 slave soldiers, armed with arquebuses and flint muskets. The men had various origins, but many apparently came from East Africa. The available military manpower could also be boosted, if necessary, by arming local Malay and other converts and, on occasion, by employing Japanese mercenaries.[31]

Nevertheless, a lack of soldiers was a chronic problem for Malacca in the Linhares years. The viceroy did what he could to remedy the situation, sending reinforcements from Goa whenever possible. But Goa's limited resources had to be eked out to meet many needs, including some serious emergencies elsewhere. In 1631 Linhares had decided to include 250 men from his recently formed *terço* (the equivalent of an infantry regiment) at Goa, to serve with naval reinforcements he was sending to Malacca; in the event, these forces were diverted to Ceylon, where a dire situation had arisen following a major Portuguese defeat by the king of Kandy.[32] In 1634 a desperate Linhares wrote to the crown that Malacca needed a garrison of 300 soldiers and that its naval forces required another 300. He also bluntly informed Lisbon and Madrid that, to meet the military needs of the Estado da Índia as a whole, Portugal must immediately send to Goa 4,000 additional men — and then reinforce them at the rate of 1,000 a year. Of course, this requirement never came close to being met.[33]

Quality of military leadership was becoming another significant issue by Linhares's time, there being an alarming lack of able and experienced fighting *fidalgos*.[34] Of course, Nuno Álvares Botelho had been a notable exception — as, to a lesser extent, was António Pinto da Fonseca. The latter had been *visitador* (an outside official appointed to conduct a review) and inspector-general of fortresses in the Estado da Índia before going on to serve as captain-general of Malacca for the exceptionally long term of roughly twenty years, encompassing the period from 1615 to his death, in office, in 1635. Despite his metropolitan origins, Pinto da Fonseca, over the many years he spent in Southeast Asia, came to identify increasingly with Portuguese settler interests — indeed, he has been aptly described by Manuel Lobato as the Malacca *casados*' "chefe natural", who did much to integrate the *casados* into the city's defence system.[35] Linhares had great respect for Pinto da Fonseca, going so far as to declare in 1630 that this captain-general was so worthy, and such a good servant of the crown, that "after his death his relics should be preserved for the defence of Malacca" and his views should continue to be consulted even from the grave.[36] It was Pinto da Fonseca who oversaw the repairs and extensions to Malacca's fortifications.[37] It was also Pinto da Fonseca who, after the death of Nuno Álvares, took command of most of that remarkable leader's ships and sailed them to the Singapore Straits to meet and escort the merchantmen due from Macao.[38] Linhares was fortunate to have had leaders of the calibre of Botelho and Pinto da Fonseca in command in the Malacca region, but both these men passed from the scene before the viceroy's term ended.

The third major ingredient of Malacca's defences — its naval forces — had always been central to Portugal's presence in Asia. In the case of Malacca these naval forces were especially important, for they kept open the city's maritime communications, which were its lifeblood. Every year, during the southwest monsoon, fleets of *jálias* and other small warships were dispatched to the Singapore Straits to meet merchantmen heading for Malacca from Goa, Nagapattinam and other centres to the west. Then, during the northeast monsoon between October and February, the *jálias* met shipping coming from Macao, Manila and other ports to the east.[39] These fleets of small, nimble warships (large warships were seldom used by the Portuguese in Southeast Asian waters in this period) were based in Malacca itself — and their deployment was vital for deflecting Dutch attacks, most of which occurred in or near the Singapore Straits.

The largest, most powerful naval force to operate out of Malacca during Linhares's viceroyalty was, of course, that of Nuno Álvares Botelho. As we have seen, Botelho was strong enough to take the offensive. Moreover, after his victory over the Acehnese he even sent captured ships back to Goa — most notably the enemy's flagship galley — along with six impressive artillery pieces.[40] This was quite exceptional, for normally Goa had to send ships to reinforce Malacca. Linhares accepted that such reinforcements needed to be sent more or less on a yearly basis, though in practice he was not always able to achieve this.[41] Particularly significant setbacks occurred in 1632 and 1634. In May 1632 it was decided to assemble a fleet of at least eight ships to send to Malacca that September. Eventually ten *galeotas* (small sailing vessels propelled by oars and sails) were fitted out, at much expense and with considerable difficulty; but just as this fleet was about to sail, with a full load of supplies and 250 desperately needed soldiers on board, it was ordered instead to Ceylon.[42] In 1634 Linhares determined to send to Malacca two galleys, newly built in Goa, plus a number of *jálias*. But, unfortunately, when this force sailed in October, it ran into a Dutch fleet off the southwest coast of India and suffered disastrous losses, including that of its flagship galley.[43] In April 1635 six *jálias* were sent from Cochin to Malacca with eighty-two soldiers aboard — and in September of the same year, after receiving reports that another hostile Acehnese fleet was assembling, Linhares sent Malacca three more ships with fifty *soldados.*[44] Thus, as time passed, the reinforcements received from Goa became more modest — if they got to Malacca at all. The overall pattern of naval movements during the Linhares period suggests a gradual weakening of the Portuguese presence in Southeast Asian waters generally. By the time Linhares left for Europe, Malacca's interests were significantly less well defended at sea than they had been in 1629.

One of the reasons Linhares's Malacca required constant naval reinforcements was that it had no shipyards of its own.[45] Nor, for that matter, did it produce internally most of its other military and naval supplies — and it was desperately short of money to buy what was needed. Nevertheless, the crown impressed on Linhares that he *must* see that Malacca was adequately provided for — and he was ordered to report each year what he had done to fulfil this obligation.[46]

Particularly regarding supplies, the beleaguered viceroy did indeed make serious efforts to comply. For instance, in September 1631 he sent to Malacca 200 barrels of gunpowder, matches and other items. In April 1633 he sent rice, wheat, pharmaceuticals, gunpowder and munitions. In April 1634 he sent money, cannon-balls and other supplies — and in April 1635 gunpowder, cannon balls, muskets and more cash. This last consignment he was able to freight aboard the *London*, an English East India Company carrack — a move that followed the Anglo-Portuguese truce signed in Goa in January of that year.[47] But, while this signalled a useful new means of getting supplies through, it was also yet another sign of growing Portuguese weakness.

COMMERCIAL DECLINE

Malacca's increased dependence in this period on support from Goa was linked to a drastic decline in its own revenues. Bocarro wrote that by Linhares's time the Malacca government's total expenditure was exceeding its revenue by more than 10,000 *ashrafi* per year.[48] This revenue came overwhelmingly from customs returns, but with the VOC's stranglehold over Southeast Asian trade, and its constant harassment of communications between Malacca and Macao, customs returns had fallen drastically since early in the century. Sanjay Subrahmanyam, who has written cogently about the situation in the 1620s, concluded that the customs revenue at Malacca declined by approximately 33 per cent between 1606 and 1620 and then another 33 per cent between 1620 and 1635.[49] Consequently, the Malacca government could not meet even such basic obligations as the salaries of the clergy — and, by Linhares's time, the Portuguese were regularly subsidizing Malacca from Goa.[50] Thus Linhares told the crown in October 1632 that he had sent "great quantities" of money to Malacca because its customs provided "almost no revenue". He expressed his desire to pay the Malacca clergy — but, frankly, did not know where the money for this could come from.[51] Linhares sent 10,000 *cruzados* (a Portuguese monetary unit) to Malacca in 1632 specifically for work on the new Pulau Malacca fortress, almost 10,000 Malacca *tangas* (a local monetary unit) in April 1634, about 12,500 *ashrafi* in September 1634, nearly 20,000 Malacca *tangas* (shipped aboard the *London*) in April 1635, and 14,000 Malacca *tangas* in September 1635.[52] Some of this money seems to have come from cash subsidies shipped out from Lisbon to Goa. There therefore seems little doubt that a massive collapse of the crown revenue base occurred in Malacca during the first third of the seventeenth century — and that this, in turn, was a reflection of the decline in the city's maritime trade. Further, it is not unreasonable to suppose that, if these trends could not be arrested, the point would soon be reached when the city became functionally unviable as a commercial centre.

Although the volume of trade through Malacca had already shrunk appreciably when Linhares reached Goa in 1629 — Subrahmanyam puts it at about 50 per cent less than it had been half a century before — the city's situation as a commercial entrepôt was not yet hopeless.[53] Indeed, there are occasional glimpses in the sources of quite vigorous trade activity continuing. For instance, in February 1631 the Goa board of the short-lived Portuguese India Company reported the arrival in Goa of a consignment of cloves from Malacca. A couple of months later Linhares himself noted with satisfaction that seven merchant ships had reached Malacca from Macao.[54]

But perhaps the most striking evidence that at least some significant commercial interests still thought business through Malacca remained viable was a request made by the Lisbon board of the Portuguese India Company that it be allowed to participate in the China-Malacca-Goa trade. Essentially, what the board asked was that the company be allowed to send several well-gunned ships of about 300 *toneladas* (tonnes) — that is, effectively of galleon class — on trading voyages directly from Lisbon to Malacca, then on to Macao and Japan. Private traders would be permitted to freight their goods aboard these galleons — which could also, it was pointed out, be used to transport military reinforcements to Malacca. Such sailings, the board argued, would benefit Malacca greatly, both through the trade they generated and also through the duties that would have to be paid at the *alfândega* (custom house). To the objection that such ships would be at serious risk of capture by the Dutch, the board blandly replied with an optimistic proverb: *debaixo do risquo estava o ganho* (profits come from taking risks). It added that trade and navigation between Goa, Chaul, Cochin, São Tomé and various Indian ports, on the one hand, and Malacca and Macao, on the other, had never ceased — and that while some ships had been taken by the enemy, many others had got through safely.[55] Nevertheless, this proposal was rejected by a majority on the Conselho da Fazenda on the grounds that it was too risky, given the Dutch and English corsairs lurking in such places as the Nicobar Islands and the Singapore Straits.

Who then was right? Was the Lisbon board of the Portuguese India Company correct in concluding in the early 1630s that, despite some problems, trade with and through Malacca was still sufficiently attractive to justify a significant investment, or were the sceptics of the Conselho da Fazenda better advised? Is it possible to evaluate the risk more precisely? Of some help in attempting this is a document entitled "Résumé of the losses which the Estado da Índia Oriental incurred during the time in which its viceroy was D. Miguel de Noronha, Conde de Linhares, who governed it for more than six years, beginning on 21 October 1629 and concluding on 8 December 1635". This document was apparently drawn up by Augustinian friar Diogo de Santa Anna, who came to India in 1595 and eventually died there in Goa in 1644, after serving many years as the administrator of the convent of Santa Monica.[56] As its title suggests, the document purports to list all significant maritime losses incurred by the Portuguese during Linhares's term. Extrapolating from the list those losses which appear to have occurred on voyages involving, or likely to have involved, Malacca, and adding them up, we get a total of 2,633,000 *ashrafi*.[57] This is a huge sum — especially when compared with the annual revenue at this time of the Malacca customs, which Bocarro stated was the equivalent of 42,000 *ashrafi*.[58] In other words, if these statistics are to be believed, the losses during the five and a half years of Linhares's term amounted to over sixty times the annual revenues accruing to the crown at Malacca. When the hard-nosed Lisbon directors of the Portuguese India Company put their proposal to the Conselho da Fazenda in February 1631, they would not have had this information. Nor could they have yet known of the death of Nuno Álvares Botelho and the subsequent abandonment of Portugal's last offensive initiative in Southeast Asia. Finally, they would possess no inkling of the series of major setbacks the Estado da Índia was to suffer as Linhares's term progressed: the defeat and death of Constantino de Sá in Ceylon (1630), the rebellion of Sultan Yusuf of Mombasa and massacre of the unsuspecting Portuguese garrison of Fort Jesus (1631), and the fall of Hugli (1632). Nor would they have been privy to the extent of losses now being incurred, according to Friar Diogo de Santa Anna, in Malaccan waters.

CONCLUSION

Although not obvious at the time, during the Linhares years the Estado da Índia was in fact just beginning what would eventually prove a fundamental shift — namely, its transformation from a widespread "maritime" entity focused primarily on the control and management of commercial networks to a small, more coherent landed empire. In the new model, there was less room for possessions like Malacca, which had only a limited territorial hinterland and little prospect of acquiring more.[59] For Malacca itself, perhaps the key turning point was reached on 27 September 1631, when the viceroy's council decided to divert the relief fleet Linhares had so painstakingly assembled at Goa over the previous months from the Malayan city to Ceylon. This amounted to formally acknowledging that the Estado da Índia simply could not plug all the holes in its extended maritime network — in particular, it no longer had the capacity to protect even its most important Southeast Asian possession. Tough choices had had to be made — in the final analysis, it was Ceylon that took priority. Not only was Ceylon much closer to Goa, and therefore to the heart of the Estado da Índia, it also offered more plausible prospects of contributing to a Portuguese land empire than Malacca ever did.[60]

The consequences for private traders operating from or through Malacca were fundamental. Sanjay Subrahmanyam has remarked that, in the 1620s, Malacca's traders did not see that city's situation as hopeless.[61] But, by the mid-1630s, there were signs that attitudes were changing, and a steady drift away from Malacca to other trade centres was gathering pace. In 1633 the Dutch began their systematic blockade of Malacca and intensified their efforts to impose a stranglehold on the Straits of Singapore. While only partially successful, there is little doubt these measures seriously disrupted the business activities of Malacca-based private Portuguese traders.[62] As the mid-1630s approached, Malacca encountered more and more economic problems. The importation of essential food supplies became problematic, the price of rice rose and there were sometimes near-famine conditions.[63] In October 1635 Linhares's enemies in Goa hanged him in effigy — one of the accusations they attached to his image was that he had assembled a fleet to bring succour to Malacca but then, at the last moment, sent it to Ceylon. As a consequence, his detractors claimed, the Dutch had been able to seize five merchantmen en route from China, allegedly worth a total of "six millions in gold".[64] With a viceroyalty apparently unable to provide protection — or unwilling to give Malacca priority — what did that beleaguered city now have to offer its private traders?

Circumstantial evidence suggests that, by the mid-1630s, many had decided that the answer to this question was "not much". Accordingly, the drift away from Malacca accelerated, more and more individuals deciding to conduct their business through other Southeast Asian ports. Indeed, there is evidence that as early as the mid-1620s Portuguese private-trader business through Makassar in particular was becoming brisk. It was reported that Makassar had already acquired as many as 500 Portuguese — and that it had begun to be seen as "a second and better Malacca".[65] Objectively, the traders who abandoned Malacca were simply being realistic. When the final Dutch siege of Malacca began in 1640, Goa did not, and probably could not, provide relief — and so the city, after months of desperate resistance, finally fell. By then Malacca had to all intents and purposes ceased to be a major commercial entrepôt.[66] Ironically, it was precisely in the Linhares years, which had begun with such optimism, that Portuguese Malacca seems to have lost much of its viability as a significant concentration of private trade and private traders.

Notes

1 For the fall of Malacca in 1640–41, see Manuel Teixeira, *The Portuguese Missions in Malacca and Singapore (1511–1958)* (Lisbon: Agência Geral do Ultramar, 1961), 1: 285–97; Anthony Disney, "A queda de Ormuz, Malaca e Mombaça", in *Portugal no Mundo*, edited by Luís de Albuquerque (Lisbon: Publicações Alfa, 1989), 5: 42–46.

2 António Bocarro, "Livro das plantas de todas as fortalezas, cidades e povoações do Estado da India Oriental", in *Arquivo Português Oriental*, new ed., bk. 4, *História Administrativa*, vol. 2, *1600–1699*, pt. 1, edited by A.B. de Bragança Pereira (Bastorá, Goa: Tipografia Rangel, 1937), p. 15. For a much fuller description of Portuguese Malacca, albeit in an earlier period, see Luís Filipe F. Reis Thomaz, *Early Portuguese Malacca* (Macao: CTMCDP, 2000), pp. 35–60.

3 Bocarro, "Livro das plantas", p. 22; and Thomaz, *Early Portuguese Malacca*, pp. 55 and 62–70.

4 Thomaz, *Early Portuguese Malacca*, pp. 71–72, 107–12 and 119–23.

5 Nuno Álvares Botelho's fleet consisted of twenty-eight *galeotas* and a pinnace, and was reported to have carried 769 soldiers, 113 officers and 29 "pages". There were no galleons with Nuno Álvares, but he was counting on the presence of a squadron of five vessels under Miguel Pereira Borralho, which had been sent to Malacca earlier from Coromandel, and also on a host of small craft — *jálias* and *bantins* (banteens) — based in Malacca itself. See A. Botelho de Sousa, ed.,

Nuno Álvares Botelho: Capitão Geral das Armadas de Alto Bordo e Governador da Índia (Lisbon: Agência Geral das Colónias, 1940), pp. 66–67.

6 A detailed narrative of these events is provided by Botelho de Sousa in his introduction to *Nuno Álvares Botelho*, pp. 11–92. Easily the most detailed contemporary account of what happened is Manuel Xavier's "Vitórias do Governador da Índia, Nuno Álvares Botelho", which is reproduced on pp. 113–212 of Botelho de Sousa's work (hereafter cited as Xavier in *Nuno Álvares Botelho*). Several shorter contemporary accounts (but not Xavier's) are translated into English in Charles Boxer, "The Achinese Attack on Malacca in 1629, as Described in Contemporary Portuguese Sources", in *Malayan and Indonesian Studies: Essays Presented to Sir Richard Winstedt on His Eighty-fifth Birthday*, edited by John Bastin and R. Roolvink (Oxford: Clarendon Press, 1964), pp. 105–21.

7 Botelho de Sousa, *Nuno Álvares Botelho*, pp. 79–80; and Xavier in *Nuno Álvares Botelho*, pp. 177–81.

8 Botelho de Sousa, *Nuno Álvares Botelho*, pp. 82–83; Xavier in *Nuno Álvares Botelho*, pp. 187–89; and Boxer, "The Achinese Attack on Malacca", pp. 120–21.

9 Xavier in *Nuno Álvares Botelho*, pp. 177–78 and 193–94.

10 Botelho de Sousa, *Nuno Álvares Botelho,* pp. 85 and 243. See also Xavier in *Nuno Álvares Botelho*, pp. 195–98.

11 Diary, Miguel de Noronha, fourth Conde de Linhares (hereafter cited as D-CL), 19 April 1630, codex 51-7-12, fols. 24v–25, Biblioteca da Ajuda (hereafter cited as BA), Lisbon; Xavier in *Nuno Álvares Botelho*, pp. 187 and 197–98; minutes of Council of State, Goa, 18 April 1630, in *Assentos do Conselho de Estado*, edited by Panduronga S.S. Pissurlencar and Vithal Trimbak Gune, vol. 1, *1618–1633* (hereafter cited as *ACE* 1) (Bastorá, Goa: Tipografia Rangel, 1953), pp. 272–73.

12 D-CL, 3 February 1631, codex 51-7-12, fol. 64.

13 Minutes of Council of State, Goa, 15 July 1630, *ACE* 1: 279.

14 Botelho de Sousa, *Nuno Álvares Botelho*, p. 86; Xavier in *Nuno Álvares Botelho*, pp. 203–4; minutes of Council of State, Goa, 18 April 1630, *ACE* 1: 272–73; D-CL, 6 July 1630, codex 51-7-12, fol. 64.

15 Botelho de Sousa, *Nuno Álvares Botelho*, pp. 86–90; and Xavier in *Nuno Álvares Botelho,* pp. 203–8. See also account in D-CL, 3 February 1631, codex 51-7-12, fols. 138v–39.

16 An offensive strategy in some respects remarkably similar to that adopted by Nuno Álvares Botelho in 1629–30 had been proposed in 1626 by Dom Gonçalo da Silva, bishop of Malacca from 1613 to 1636. Dom Gonçalo's suggestion was, in part, that a Portuguese fleet be sent from the west coast of India to Malacca, where it would take on supplies before proceeding to Jambi. There it would destroy the Dutch factory before moving on to Batavia, which it would attack, hopefully with backing from the sultans of Mataram and Banten. Sanjay Subrahmanyam regards this proposal as "unrealistic and fanciful"; but

Botelho's proceedings in 1630 suggest that perhaps it should not be dismissed so lightly. See Sanjay Subrahmanyam, *Improvising Empire: Portuguese Trade and Settlement in the Bay of Bengal, 1500–1700* (Delhi: Oxford University Press, 1990), pp. 179–80.

17 D-CL, 8 November 1630 and 3 February 1631, codex 51-7-12, fols. 108v and 138v–39; and Linhares to crown, 8 February 1631, *ACE* 1: 535–36.

18 Minutes of Council of State, Goa, 18 April 1632, in *ACE* 1: 419; crown to Linhares, 1632, *Boletim da Filmoteca Ultramarina Portuguesa* (hereafter cited as *BF*) 9 (1958): 233; and crown to Linhares, 20 December 1632, *BF* 9 (1958): 325–26.

19 Minutes of Council of State, Goa, 4 June 1635, in *Assentos do Conselho de Estado*, edited by Panduronga S.S. Pissurlencar and Vithal Trimbak Gune, vol. 2, *1634–1643* (hereafter cited as *ACE* 2) (Bastorá, Goa: Tipografia Rangel, 1953), pp. 14–16.

20 See especially Jorge M. Santos Alves and Pierre-Yves Manguin, *O Roteiro das Cousas do Achem de D. João Ribeiro Gaio: Um Olhar Português sobre o Norte de Samatra em Finais do Século XVI* (Lisbon: CNCDP, 1997); C.R. Boxer, "Portuguese and Spanish Projects for the Conquest of Southeast Asia, 1580–1600", *Journal of Asian Studies* 3 (1969): 118–36; Subrahmanyam, *Improvising Empire*, pp. 137–60; Paulo Jorge de Sousa Pinto, *Portugueses e Malaios: Malaca e os Sultanatos de Johor e Achém, 1575–1619* (Lisbon: Sociedade Histórica da Independência de Portugal, 1997), pp. 62–63, 80 and 88–90.

21 Soares's proposal, dated 20 December 1633, is appended by Viceroy Linhares to his diary entry for 26 April 1634. See *Diário do Terceiro Conde de Linhares* (Lisbon: Biblioteca Nacional, 1937), pp. 82–85.

22 Bocarro's *Livro do Estado da Índia Oriental*, which was completed in 1635, was described by Charles Boxer as "a veritable mine of information". C.R. Boxer, "Three Historians of Portuguese Asia (Barros, Couto and Bocarro)", *Boletim* (Instituto Português de Hongkong) 1 (1948): 37.

23 Bocarro, "Livro das plantas", p. 14. In 1626 there had allegedly been only thirty-two or thirty-three cannons. See Subrahmanyam, *Improvising Empire*, p. 177.

24 Bocarro, "Livro das plantas", p. 15. See also Thomaz, *Early Portuguese Malacca*, pp. 37–40, for these fortifications in an earlier era.

25 See minutes of Council of State, Goa, 1 April 1632, *ACE* 1: 421; see also crown to Linhares, 13 February 1629, Documentos Remetidos da Índia (hereafter cited as Doc. Rem.) 26, fol. 302, Arquivo Nacional da Torre do Tombo (hereafter cited as ANTT), Lisbon.

26 The work seems to have been delayed partly because of lack of funds, partly because the Malacca *câmara* (local governing council) wished to complete alterations to the city walls first and partly because it was felt that, once started, construction would have to be completed and artillery put in place very swiftly. It was feared that, if the Dutch got wind of what was happening, they would try to interfere before the new cannon were available. See Bocarro, "Livro das

plantas", pp. 14 and 23; crown to Linhares, 6 March 1630, Doc. Rem. 27, fol. 24; Linhares to crown, 18 November 1632, *BF* 8 (1958): 24–25; Linhares to António Pinto da Fonseca, 26 September 1634, *BF* 12 (1959): 436–38; minutes of Council of State, Goa, 18 April 1632, *ACE* 1: 420–21.

27 Crown to Linhares, 28 February 1632, and Linhares to crown, 8 January 1633, Doc. Rem. 30, fol. 15.

28 Bocarro, "Livro das plantas", p. 21; and Subrahmanyam, *Improvising Empire,* p. 177.

29 Bocarro, "Livro das plantas", p. 25; and Sousa Pinto, *Portugueses e Malaios,* p. 63.

30 Bocarro, "Livro das plantas", p. 14; and Thomaz, *Early Portuguese Malacca,* p. 88. Subrahmanyam, *Improvising Empire,* p. 178, however, cites a figure of only 125 *casados* in 1626. Lobato gives 300 *casados* for 1613, 100 for 1620, 126 for 1626 and 250 for 1634. See Manuel Lobato, "Malaca", in *História dos Portugueses no Extremo Oriente,* vol. 1, bk. 2, *De Macau à Perifeira,* edited by A.H. de Oliveira Marques (Lisbon: Fundação Oriente, 2000), p. 54.

31 Subrahmanyam, *Improvising Empire,* p. 178; Lobato, "Malaca", pp. 53–54.

32 Diary, Miguel de Noronha, fourth Conde de Linhares (1631) (hereafter cited as D-CL/2), 1 September 1631, codex 939, pt. 2, fols. 71 and 77v, Biblioteca Nacional de Portugal, Lisbon.

33 Linhares to crown, 29 November 1634, Coimbra, Codex 459, fols. 390–91v.

34 Paulo Jorge da Sousa Pinto notes that most *fidalgos* in maritime Asia by this time were interested more in trade and administration than in military activity. See Sousa Pinto, *Portugueses e Malaios,* pp. 65–66.

35 Lobato, "Malaca", p. 61.

36 Linhares to crown, 12 December 1630, *ACE* 1: 421–22. Bocarro likewise referred to António Pinto da Fonseca as "a person of great talent and experience". Bocarro, "Livro das plantas", p. 15. But Linhares did eventually acknowledge that by 1635, shortly before Pinto da Fonseca died, the captain-general had become enfeebled and much less able to maintain effective control. Linhares to crown, 2 June 1635, Doc. Rem. 34, fols. 7–7v.

37 Crown to Linhares, 13 February 1629, Doc. Rem. 26, fol. 302.

38 D-CL, 3 February 1631, codex 51-7-12, fols. 138v–39.

39 Bocarro, "Livro das plantas", p. 25. See also Sousa Pinto, *Portugueses e Malaios,* pp. 68–69; Lobato, " Malaca", p. 57; Peter Borschberg, *The Singapore and Melaka Straits: Violence, Security and Diplomacy in the Seventeenth Century* (Singapore: NUS Press, 2010), pp. 11–12, 63 and 288n18.

40 See minutes of Council of State, 3 December 1630, *ACE* 1: 520. For a description of Acehnese galleys at this time, see Anthony Reid, *Southeast Asia in the Age of Commerce,* vol. 2 (New Haven: Yale University Press, 1993), pp. 232–33.

41 Linhares to crown, 18 May 1631, Doc. Rem. 28, fol. 41.

42 D-CL/2, 14 May and 26 September 1631, codex 939, pt. 2, fols. 27 and 77v; and minutes of Council of State, Goa, 14 May and 26 September 1631, *ACE* 1: 350 and 377–78.

43 *Diário do Terceiro Conde de Linhares,* pp. 107, 151, 156, 158 and 206–7.

44 Linhares to crown, 2 June 1635, Doc. Rem. 34, fols. 7–7v, and Linhares to crown, 30 September 1635, Doc. Rem. 34, fols. 17–17v.

45 Lobato, "Malaca", p. 50.

46 Crown to Linhares, 21 February 1629, Doc. Rem. 26, fol. 225, and crown to Linhares, 28 March 1629, Doc. Rem. 26, fol. 109.

47 See Assentos do Conselho da Fazenda, 1631–37, fols. 66v, 122, 161v, 170v and 174v, Historical Archives of Goa, Panaji, Goa; Linhares to crown, 2 June 1635, Doc. Rem. 34, fols. 7–7v; minutes of Council of State, 4 June 1635, *ACE* 2: 15.

48 Bocarro, "Livro das plantas", p. 21. An *ashrafi* was a gold or silver coin minted in Goa and other western parts of maritime Asia worth 300 *réis* (the main Portuguese monetary unit), or standard money of account to the same value, as used in this context; also known as *xerafim* (pl. *xerafins*).

49 Subrahmanyam cites customs returns of 27 million *réis* in 1606, 18 million *réis* in 1620, and 11 million to 13 million *réis* in 1635. See Subrahmanyam, *Improvising Empire*, pp. 176–77. See also Lobato, "Malaca", p. 43.

50 Bocarro, "Livro das plantas", p. 21.

51 Linhares to crown, 13 October 1632, *BF* 8 (1958): 86–87.

52 Assentos do Conselho da Fazenda, 1631–37, fols. 122, 133v, 161v and 170v; and *BF* 8 (1958): 137.

53 Subrahmanyam, *Improvising Empire*, pp. 175 and 183.

54 Goa board of Portuguese India Company to crown, 14 February 1631, codex 46-13-30, fols. 37–37v, BA; D-CL/2, 19 April 1631, codex 939, pt. 2, fol. 21v; and D-CL, 19 April 1630, codex 51-7-12, fols. 24v–25.

55 Proposal of Lisbon board of Portuguese India Company to crown, 28 February 1630, Doc. Rem. 27, fols. 521–24v.

56 A manuscript of this document exists in the Torre do Tombo. See Manuscritos da Livraria, 816, fols. 257–63v, ANTT (I am grateful to Mr Pedro Pinto for pointing out to me the existence of this manuscript). The same list, with very minor variations, was published in Agostinho de Santa Maria, *História da Fundação do Real Convento de Santa Mónica* (Lisbon: Antonio Pedrozo Galram, 1699), pp. 334–43, which is the source used here.

57 Santa Maria, *História da Fundação*. Most of this total came from relatively small multiple losses — such as 12,000 *ashrafi* for the cargo of a pinnace belonging to Pedro Soares de Brito, en route from Macao to Goa. But there was also a single, very large loss of 900,000 *ashrafi* for five *galeotas* and a pinnace under Capitão-Môr Dom Jerónimo da Silveira, taken by the Dutch while en route from China; see p. 336.

58 Bocarro, "Livro das plantas", p. 21.

59 This situation appears to have been the case despite early seventeenth-century attempts to control more nearby territory, such as the mouth of the Muar River. See Borschberg, *The Singapore and Melaka Straits*, p. 57.

60 See note 40 above.

61 Subrahmanyam, *Improvising Empire*, p. 175.

62 Borschberg, *The Singapore and Melaka Straits*, pp. 13, 171 and 177.

63 Peter Borschberg, "VOC Blockade of the Singapore and Malacca Straits: Diplomacy, Trade and Survival, 1633–1641", in *O Estado da Índia e os Desafios Europeus: Actas do XII Seminário Internacional de História Indo-Portuguesa* (Lisbon: CHAM/CEPCEP, 2010), pp. 163–86, esp. pp. 173–75 and 180–82.

64 Cited in *ACE* 2: 21.

65 The report, made at Batavia, came from an Englishman, Henry Short. See C.R. Boxer, *Francisco Vieira de Figueiredo: A Portuguese Merchant-Adventurer in South East Asia, 1624–1667* (The Hague: Martinus Nijhoff, 1967), p. 3. See also James C. Boyajian, *Portuguese Trade in Asia under the Habsburgs, 1580–1640* (Baltimore: The Johns Hopkins University Press, 1993), pp. 231–32.

66 Cf. M.A.P. Meilink-Roelofsz, *Asian Trade and European Influence in the Indonesian Archipelago between 1500 and about 1630* (The Hague: Martinus Nijhoff, 1962), p. 172.

3

FROM MELIAPOR TO MYLAPORE, 1662–1749: THE PORTUGUESE PRESENCE IN SÃO TOMÉ BETWEEN THE QUṬB SHĀHĪ CONQUEST AND ITS INCORPORATION INTO BRITISH MADRAS

Paolo Aranha

Along the seashore of Chennai, the capital of Tamil Nadu state, known previously as Madras, runs the Santhome Highway. It links Marina Beach in the north, a highly popular sightseeing attraction and a place of socialization in the Tamil metropole, with the Adyar area in the south, where the headquarters of the Theosophical Society and its renowned library are. Between these two landmarks is placed Santhome Cathedral, the centre of Catholic life in Chennai.

The toponym "Santhome" is probably the most visible legacy of the ancient Portuguese settlement of São Tomé (originally "Thomé", and hence today's toponym "Santhome") de Meliapor. What used to be a fortress that preceded and then competed with the English Fort St George is now only a borough in the Tamil capital. However, it is remarkable that the Portuguese settlement had a compound denomination: São Tomé de Meliapor. Before the advent of the Lusitans there had already been an Indian town today called Mylapore (originally "Mailapur"), or the "city of the peacocks". Archaeological excavations in Mylapore demonstrate that the city was already an important trading post in the second century and that around the seventh century it counted at least a *śaivite*, a *vaiṣṇavite,* and a *jaina* temple.[1]

The purpose of this chapter is to propose some preliminary lines of research that may allow us to understand the strategies of resilience of the Portuguese in São Tomé de Meliapor between its conquest in 1662 by the Quṭb Shāhī dynasty of Golconda and its incorporation into British Madras in 1749. By examining archival documents kept in Goa and Lisbon, it will be possible to see better how an autonomous Portuguese community, perfectly exemplifying what has been defined the "shadow empire",[2] persisted in a corner of the Coromandel Coast, blessed by the memory of the Apostle Thomas and still considered economically viable.

RELIQUARY CITY OR A PORTUGUESE RELIC?

Ines Županov has explored how the "discovery" in 1517 of the sepulchre of Saint Thomas in Mylapore made possible the creation of a "factory settlement of independent merchants". Thanks also to "the elaboration of the legends around the life of Saint Thomas, the rearrangement of the sacred geography around the burial site, and the 'invention' or superposition of subsidiary sacred places and objects — all the work of Jesuits and other religious specialists", the *casados* (married men of the reserve army) of São Tomé de Meliapor were able to resist "the centralizing efforts emanating from Goa and could legitimate the mercantile, indigenized, and consequently independent status of the town".[3]

São Tomé was born as a "reliquary town", a settlement whose location was primarily determined by the special grace emanating from the sacred places related to the life and death of the Apostle of India: the Great Mount (Periya Malai), the Small Mountain (Cinna Malai) and the so-called Samta Casa,[4] where the apostle was buried. São Tomé grew steadily in the course of the sixteenth century. In a letter that the *moradores* (residents) addressed in 1535 to Dom João III, it was specified that sixty Portuguese families already lived around the apostle's tomb.[5] The presence of religious and secular priests made it possible to undertake evangelical activities even among the local population, so that by 1559 there were already about 2,000 Indian converts.[6]

In that same year, a military event clarified the specific nature of the Portuguese presence in São Tomé, insofar as that was necessary. The town was laid siege to by Rāma Rāja, a powerful *mahāmaṇḍaleśvara* (provincial governor) of the Vijayanāgara Empire, in order to assert his tributary rights. The *casados* accepted the demand that they pay the tribute, against pressures received from Goa to offer military resistance.[7] A few decades later, it was stated in the Jesuit Annual Letter between 1604 and 1606 that the Portuguese governed themselves, having their own captain and judge (*ouvidor*), while a governor of the "King of Bisnaga" resided in a town near São Tomé, leasing out the collection of port dues and governing the Hindu population.[8]

São Tomé became a major centre of religious life. The Franciscans had a friary outside the walls dedicated to Saint Anthony of Lisbon (or Padua) and the Igreja da Nossa Senhora da Luz, where they took care of the Indian Christians.[9] The Jesuits provided educational services through their college, where it was possible to learn "cases of conscience, Latin, reading, writing, and counting".[10] According to a description that Pedro Barreto de Rezende, secretary to the Conde de Linhares, wrote, probably around 1635, within the walls of São Tomé there was the cathedral and also three churches belonging to the Dominicans, the Augustinians and the Jesuits. Outside the wall there were, in addition to the Igreja da Nossa Senhora da Luz, two other churches: the Jesuit one known as the Madre de Deus and the São Lázaro.[11]

In 1606 São Tomé was elevated to a bishopric, after having been part of the Goa diocese that then belonged to the jurisdiction of the bishop of Cochin since 1558. André de Santa Maria, the Franciscan prelate in charge of Cochin, who was particularly hostile to the Jesuits, persistently requested the Holy See to create the new bishopric, most probably as a way to check the pretensions to jurisdictional autonomy claimed by the Jesuit missionaries on the Costa da Piscaria.[12] This anti-Jesuitic stance is somewhat ironical, inasmuch as the episcopal see of Meliapor, under the Jesuit bishops Gaspar Afonso Álvares (1691–1708), Francisco Laynes (1708–14) and José Pinheiro (1724–44), became a stronghold in the defence of the Malabar Rites allowed by the missionaries of the Society of Jesus in the regions of Madurai, Mysore and the Karnatik during the first half of the eighteenth century.[13]

Around 1635 there were 120 Portuguese families and 200 Indian Christian families living within the walls of São Tomé, whereas 6,000 Indian Christians lived outside them.[14] The settlement beyond the walls — that is, Meliapor in the strictest sense — had settlements of weavers producing for the export market, so that São Tomé could be considered an extended port with an inland market and manufacturing facilities.[15]

A major town along the Coromandel Coast, São Tomé suffered from Dutch competition and then entered into a totally new phase once the English East India Company obtained permission in 1639 to establish Fort St George just three miles north.[16] The English took positive steps to attract the Portuguese and Indian Christian population to their new town.[17] São Tomé found itself deprived also of the institutional support provided by its bishops: no appointments were made by the Holy See between 1640 and 1691, due to both the delay in the Roman recognition of the Braganza dynasty and as a consequence of the tensions between the Portuguese Padroado and the Congregation of Propaganda Fide.[18] The demographical decay of São Tomé can be measured by a discussion that took place in 1652–53 between Dom João IV and the viceroy, Vasco Mascarenhas. The decrease in the population of São Tomé made it necessary to reduce the extent of the fortification so as to better defend the town.[19] Already weakened by European competition, São Tomé fell under the forces of the Quṭb Shāhī dynasty of Golconda in 1662 and was placed under the control of the minister Nekhnām Khān.[20] The town was expanded and fortified massively by the conquerors. Most Portuguese fled to Madras. However, the militarization of São Tomé did not affect the freedom to practise the Catholic religion, and the churches were fully respected by the new Muslim rulers.[21] Several attempts were made by the viceroys António de Melo e Castro (1662–66) and João Nunes da Cunha to get back the town of the Apostle Thomas. Negotiations with the Quṭb Shāhī kings Abdullah and Abu'l Hasan swung between respectful requests and hostile actions of retaliation, such as seizing a very rich ship near the Straits of Hormuz. Both strategies failed.[22]

Despite all the efforts spent by the Portuguese, the French fleet of Admiral de le Haye was able to seize São Tomé in 1672 with a fortunate blitz. As France and the United Provinces were at war in Europe, the Dutch reached an agreement with the Sultan of Golconda for a joint attack to dislodge the newcomers from the town. In 1674 the French occupation came to an end, and the forces of Golconda destroyed all the fortifications. The Dutch received substantial trade advantages within the territory of the Quṭb Shāhī sultanate in exchange.[23] From being a "reliquary town", São Tomé was now reduced to a Portuguese relic; deprived of military defence, population and trade, it could be imagined at the time that 150 years of Lusitan presence around the sepulchre of the Apostle Thomas had been cancelled forever. Such a simplistic prediction was not fulfilled, and this is precisely what makes the case of São Tomé so interesting.

A RENASCENT TOWN

The idea that the Estado da Índia can be adequately described just in terms of stagnation and decline during the second half of the seventeenth century is today less obvious than in the past. As Glenn Ames argued a decade ago, the House of Braganza was able to stabilize its possessions in Asia after its restoration to the Portuguese throne so that the Estado da Índia could be considered a "renascent empire". If it is true that "the Portuguese were never able to reestablish themselves in any significant fashion on the Coromandel coast",[24] nonetheless they achieved the goal of going back to São Tomé. As the first foundation of the town in the sixteenth century was the effect of the autonomous agency of the *casados*, in the same way the reconstruction of São Tomé became possible thanks to an initiative undertaken directly by the Portuguese inhabitants themselves, although in coordination with the authorities in Goa.

They accomplished their reinstitution in São Tomé by way of a delegation led by the Augustinian, Friar Luís da Piedade, plus ten other Portuguese, including the governor of the São Tomé bishopric, Friar Constantino Sardinha Rangel. The sultan of Golconda, Abu'l Hasan, had issued a *farmān* (a royal decree or charter)[25] on 18 October 1686 with which he allowed the Portuguese to settle again in São Tomé, build houses, plant orchards and trade freely, paying the royal dues every year to the same extent that the English and the Dutch did in the port of Masulipatnam (known as Massulipatão in Portuguese). Moreover, the Portuguese would be free to come and go from Golconda.[26]

From a memorandum drafted on 15 April of that year by four of the members of the Portuguese delegation, it can be understood that the mission had been solicited by the viceroy Francisco da Távora (1681–86), Conde de Alvor. The latter had suggested in particular offering gifts (*segoate*) to both the sultan (*rey*) of Golconda and the *nawāb* (*nababo*, governor) who had jurisdiction over São Tomé. The success in obtaining the *farmān* had been particularly relevant because, at the same time, both the French and the Dutch were exerting pressures to acquire São Tomé. After the *farmān*, negotiations shifted to the local level in order to establish a monopoly on the collection of custom dues by all the traders who called at São Tomé, whether Europeans ("estrangeiroz", literally, "strangers"), Muslims or Hindus. At the moment at which the memorandum was composed, there were good prospects for success. The final section of the document is badly damaged, but it can be understood to express a concern for establishing regular officers for the government of São Tomé and to suggest that the Portuguese who refused to come back to the town (most likely those from Madras) should be punished by being deprived of their nationality.[27] The negotiation eventually led to a favourable solution. In a letter sent to the viceroy on 8 October 1687, it was reported that, on that very day, the Portuguese flag was raised on São Tomé, notwithstanding the attempt made by the English to impede the re-establishment of the Lusitan presence. Moreover, the *nawāb* had agreed to grant the Portuguese half of the rights due on sea trade ("a metade dos direitoz do mar").[28] The English had entrusted the Company's merchant, Chinna Venkatadri,[29] to prosecute the business so as to disappoint the Portuguese,

> though we pay something more for it [the lease of São Tomé port] than they offer, which we doubt not in time to recover from them. Besides it is of such absolute necessity to rent that town, as well for preventing the diminishing of our trade and customs, as also our force; five parts of our soldiers being Portuguese topasses, who if they should settle at Saint Tomé would certainly run thither from us in our necessity.[30]

The choice to use a middleman such as Chinna Venkatadri instead of to undertake direct talks with local administrators was explained in the general letter sent from the board of directors on 14 January 1685. It was feared that direct involvement by the "Right Honorable Company" could cause "many scruples and difficulties" to the *divan* (council), and in particular induce it to "enhance the rent".[31] On 4 August, Chinna Venkatadri informed the council of Fort St George that he had been able to obtain from Mādanānta Pantulu, the Brahmin governor of Kanchipuram, the offer of a triennial lease of the São Tomé "Town, Customs, and Adjacent Towns and Paddy grounds".[32] However, this was not yet a concession but only a conditioned proposal, always keeping open the possibility of striking a deal with the Portuguese instead.[33] It seems therefore that between August and October the Portuguese were able to counter the English manoeuvre and win the lease of São Tomé.[34]

The Lusitan recovery of São Tomé took place during a major political change in the Deccan region. In the course of 1687, the Quṭb Shāhī sultanate was conquered by the Mughal Empire, with the fortress of Golconda finally surrendering on 2 October after eight months of a laborious siege and just a week before the return of the Portuguese to São Tomé.[35] The concrete enforcement of the decisions in favour of the Portuguese granted by the sultan of Golconda was therefore the fruit of further negotiations with the Mughal emperor, undertaken once again by Friar Luís da Piedade, defined by the Portuguese governor, Rodrigo da Costa, as a "friar of very good proceeding" (*frade de muito bom procedimento*).[36]

Only four years after the re-establishment of a Lusitan presence in São Tomé, the situation seemed again critical. In a letter sent by the viceroy Miguel de Almeida to Dom Pedro II on 22 January 1690, it was reported that the inhabitants of São Tomé had suffered as a consequence of the war against the Mughal emperor Rāma Rāja (also known as Rama Raza in the Portuguese text), brother of the Maratha ruler Shambaji. Rāma Rāja had requested the Portuguese to pay dues in arrears on the port of São Tomé.

Since the Portuguese had not been able to fulfil their obligations, they had lost the customs contract. In fact, as can be gleaned from an English record of 23 August 1688, by that time Chinna Venkatadri had been able to obtain a *cowle* (a written lease or grant) for renting São Tomé town, its customs, "and the adjacent countries as far as Saint Thomas Mount".[37] The choice of obtaining the *cowle* in the name of Chinna Venkatadri had been made on account of tensions between the English and the Mughal Empire, but also so as "not too much [to] exasperate the Portuguese in their loss and disappointment of a place they retain a most superstitious veneration for, which possibly might provoke them to mutiny or rebellion, or at least some disturbance or mischief; they being at present two-thirds of our soldiers, and at least six for one to the English inhabitants".[38]

In his letter sent to Dom Pedro II, the viceroy Miguel de Almeida observed that, in addition to their precarious economic foundation, the Portuguese of São Tomé had no fortifications and needed artillery for the defence of the town. Moreover, a stable civic government had not yet been established. While an *ouvidor* and a *juíz dos órfãos* (judge for orphans) were in place, at the death of the *capitão-môr* (local commander), Manuel Teixeira Pinto, the office was replaced with three deputies, elected by the inhabitants. This collegial arrangement did not seem expedient to the viceroy.[39]

From the Portuguese and English records it is possible to understand how the appointment in 1695 of Luís Francisco Coutinho, relative of the viceroy Pedro António de Meneses Noronha de Albuquerque (1692–98), as "General of the Coast of Coromandel" was probably devised as a way to strengthen ties with Goa and enhance the Portuguese presence in São Tomé. In the town, Coutinho, provided with secret patent letters, established an office of the Inquisition and summoned back all the Portuguese who had moved to Fort St George in previous decades, but he did not achieve much success. He was not able to obtain from the English company the guns necessary to arm the fifty soldiers that he commanded, and his attempts to rebuild the walls of São Tomé were frustrated in particular by the intervention of the local Mughal governor (*avaldar*), Hājī Muhāmmad Ali, with the demolition of three bastions in January 1697. Coutinho also failed in an attempt to pacify the inhabitants of São Tomé, who were divided into two opposite groups (*ranchos*). Soon, Thomas de Maya, *capitão môr* of the town, sided against the general.[40]

In order to address the problems of São Tomé, as well as to improve overall relations with the Mughal Empire, the Augustinian friar Luís da Piedade was sent on a second diplomatic mission in 1700, this time by the viceroy António Luís Gonçalves da Câmara Coutinho (1698–1701). As far as São Tomé specifically was concerned, the task of the Augustinian was to obtain a *parvāna* (a decree or written warrant)[41] addressed to General Yaqub Khān (*Yacubcan*) so that he would return to the Portuguese all the landed properties that had once belonged to them ("todas as quintas, e ortas dos Portuguezes q[ue] tinhão sido suas antigam[en]te" [all the farms/orchards and vegetable gardens of the Portuguese that had been theirs previously]). The mission was accomplished: the original of the *parvāna* was handed over to the bishop of São Tomé.[42] However, it seems that the problem of the *quintas* (farms/orchards) and *hortas* (vegetable gardens) was not solved in a lasting way with that *parvāna*, since on 8 January 1708 the viceroy Rodrigo da Costa (1701–12) informed Dom João V that he had sent two Jesuit envoys, Josef de Magalhães and Manuel Dessá, to the Mughal court, once again to negotiate the same question.[43]

Meanwhile, the inhabitants of São Tomé had written on 6 October 1706 to inform the king about the pitiful condition of their "Lusitan Troy" (Troja Lucitana). They denounced the ill treatment that they suffered at the hands of the Moors, who did not respect the *farmāns* issued by the Mughal emperor. They deprived the Portuguese of the contract on the port custom and even disturbed religious worship. The solution to all of these problems was to find someone who would ensure the observance of the statutory exemptions (*icençoens decretais*) obtained from the Mughal emperor. The conservation of São Tomé, labelled by the inhabitants as a shrine, resided more in zeal than in military cunningness ("a concervação deste Santuario depende mais de hum zello, q. de huma astuçia militar"); therefore, they suggested the appointment of the Dominican visitor, Friar Tomás de Santo António, who was then residing in Goa. He had gained merits already in Siam, where he was able to pacify the Portuguese of that land and was even invited twice by the king to give advice on political matters.[44] The initiative of the inhabitants of São Tomé clearly displeased the viceroy, Rodrigo da Costa. In a letter sent to Dom João V on 21 November 1709, he complained that the Portuguese had not informed him of the problems they were experiencing. He then defined them as "naturalm[en]te revoltozos" (naturally rebellious), so that it was no surprise to him if the *shāhbandar* (or *xabandar*, harbourmaster) of that land compelled them to pay heavy tributes.[45] The viceroy's attack also included criticism of Friar Tomás de Santo António, who was not so good as the inhabitants of São Tomé represented him to be. Finally, since those *moradores* had no landed properties, it was obvious that the salary for any office entrusted to the Dominican would have to be paid by the royal treasury.[46]

The obvious hostility of the viceroy towards the inhabitants of São Tomé should be related to a conflict that had placed them in opposition to the *capitão-môr* of the town, (João?) Matheus Carneiro da Silva. At the onset of the clash, there was the alleged deception that Carneiro da Silva had committed by presenting himself as a person who was positively requested by the inhabitants. Moreover, once the inhabitants had complained against him, attempts were to replace him with his son-in-law. On 6 August 1706 the Conselho Ultramarino (overseas council) endorsed the request of the *moradores* and ordered the removal of Carneiro da Silva as well as cancelling the appointment of his relative, taking into account his violent behaviour, which included arson of his adversaries' houses.[47]

It could be argued that anarchy had been a feature of São Tomé since its beginning. At the opening of the seventeenth century, the internal dissensions that characterized the Portuguese town had displeased Venkata II, the emperor of Vijāyanagar.[48] François Martin spoke of internal fights within São Tomé during the few years before it fell to Golconda, which may in part explain its defeat; in turn, Portuguese Governor Rodrigo da Costa complained about the spirit of rivalry ("emulação") prevalent among the inhabitants of São Tomé.[49] From this point of view it appears that the Portuguese recovery of São Tomé implied first an internal reorganization, the resolution of internal factional strife (attempted unsuccessfully by Luís Francisco Coutinho) and only subsequently the achievement of better relations with the rulers of the land.

The extent to which internal stabilization was eventually achieved is not clear. Definitely, the diplomatic strategies on behalf of the city did not succeed in renewing its pristine glory. Attempts were made in 1712 to involve Juliana Dias da Costa,[50] a major figure in the relations between Goa and the Mughal Empire.[51] On the other hand, the diplomatic steps undertaken by the viceroy Vasco Fernandes César de Menezes (1712–17) were frustrated by the actions of individuals such as the Dominican friar Sebastião de Miranda. He had supported the patriarch Carlo Tomaso Maillard de Tournon in Macao in his claims on the superiority of the jurisdiction of Propaganda Fide over that of the Portuguese Padroado Real. Because of this attitude, he had been sent to India. However, he was able to escape from Goa and sided with the English, informing them about the steps that the Portuguese undertook to improve the condition of São Tomé.

The viceroy was then trying to use the mediation of the French medical doctor Jean de Saint-Hilaire. A courtier (*válido*) of the *nawāb* of Karnatik, he appeared almost more Portuguese in affectation and inclination than French as by birth ("mais parece Portuguez no affeito e inclinação que Francez em *[sic]* o nascimento").[52] Another foreign doctor, the Castilian Francisco Pereira, was employed in the years 1720 to 1722 in order to bring presents to the Mughal emperor and obtain concessions from him concerning the restitution of all the landed properties that had once belonged to the Portuguese. This envoy, defined regularly in official documents as the "Castilian doctor", ran away to Cochin with the gifts designated for the emperor.[53] The choice of a foreigner obviously triggered polemics once it appeared clear that he had deceived the trust placed in him by the Estado da Índia at its highest levels. In a letter of 22 December 1722, Dom João V asked why a Portuguese had not been chosen for such an important task. Archbishop Dom Inácio de Santa Theresa, together with two other officers, replied simply on 10 January 1724 that the Castilian had been selected because he was an expert in the affairs of the Mughal Empire and because he had come of his own from Madras to Goa so as to propose himself as a mediator.[54] An answer of this kind could suggest to Dom João V that the political agency of the Estado da Índia was seriously constrained. However, Santa Theresa and the other officers were not misled in considering Francisco Pereira as a possible diplomatic mediator with the Mughal Empire. In the following years he became the personal physician of Chanda Sahib, son-in-law of Dost Ali Khān, Nawāb of the Karnatic. It was thanks to his mediation that the French East India Company took possession of the Tamil port town of Karaikal (Kāraikkāl).[55]

CONCLUSION

In this chapter I have presented the first results of an ongoing research project on life in São Tomé after its conquest by the Golconda sultanate. The vast documentation available in Goa, Lisbon, Rome and elsewhere might cast a clearer light on the ways in which a Portuguese presence continued in the "reliquary town" until its annexation to the British settlement of Madras in 1749 — made in order to prevent its acquisition by Joseph François Dupleix, the French governor-general in India, and supported by the Franciscan friar and adventurer António da Purificação (António José de Noronha).[56]

On 14 May 1750, the Council of Fort St George replied to the vibrant protest made on 5 February by the Marquês de Alorna (Pedro Miguel Almeida Portugal, viceroy of Portuguese India, 1744–50) against the occupation of São Tomé, defined as a dominion of the king of Portugal. The English officers simply observed that "no Revenue has Accrued to His Majesty of Portugall from that Place for these fifty Years Past".[57] It was a brutal but realistic way to describe the relation of the Estado da Índia with a territory that had continued to be Portuguese more in terms of desire and imagination than in concrete ways.

However, the case of São Tomé shows the inadequacy of a simple dichotomy between absolute hegemony and a fate of stagnation and decline. Even if São Tomé was no longer a source of wealth for the Estado da Índia, nonetheless a Portuguese presence on the sacred site of the Apostle Thomas amounted indeed to a political asset. Scholars have already examined how the uncorrupted body of Saint Francis Xavier, the "Lord of Goa" (Goemcho Sahib) played a central role in the ritual representation of the Portuguese enterprise in India until its very end in 1961.[58] In a similar way, contact with the memory of the first Apostle of India — origin of the *cristãos* (Christians) for whom, together with *especiarias* (spices), the Portuguese were looking at the end of the fifteenth century[59] — was a reassurance and a source of meaning for a Luso-Indian community scattered throughout the Coromandel Coast. Only from the point of view of power politics could it then be feared that in the future even the memory of the Portuguese in São Tomé would be lost, as the highest officers of the Estado da Índia argued in a letter sent from Goa on 23 December 1723 to Dom João V.[60] If the political influence achieved during the sixteenth century could not be replicated, nonetheless the Portuguese left lasting traces in São Tomé de Meliapor, as well as in vast regions throughout Asia.

Notes

1 Benedict A. Figredo, *Voices from the Dust: Archeological Finds in San Thome and Mylapore* (Madras: Archdiocese of Madras-Mylapore, 1953), pp. 9–10, quoted in Antony Mathias Mundadan, "History of Christianity in Madras and Mylapore from the Beginning Up until the End of the Seventeenth Century", *Indian Church History Review* 39, no. 1 (2005): 21–46. Mundadan's article is an expansion of sections on São Tomé presented in his *History of Christianity in India,* vol. 1, *From the Beginning Up to the Middle of the Sixteenth Century (Up to 1542),* (Bangalore: published for the Church History Association of India by Theological Publications in India, 1943; repr. Bangalore: Bangalore Church History Association of India, 1989), as well as in his "The Portuguese Settlement in Mylapore", *Indian Church History Review* 3, no. 2 (1969): 103–14.

2 George D. Winius, "Embassies from Malacca and the 'Shadow Empire' ", *Proceedings of the International Colloquium on the Portuguese and the Pacific,* edited by Francis A. Dutra and João Camilo dos Santos (Santa Barbara: Center for Portuguese Studies, 1995), pp. 170–78; "Early Portuguese Travel and Influence at the Corner of Asia", in George D. Winius, *Studies on Portuguese Asia, 1495–1689* (Aldershot: Ashgate, 2001), pp. 213–28.

3 Ines G. Županov, "A Reliquary Town: São Tomé de Meliapor: The Political and the Sacred in Portuguese India", in *Missionary Tropics: The Catholic Frontier in India (Sixteenth-Seventeenth Centuries)* (Ann Arbor: University of Michigan Press, 2005), pp. 87–110.

4 "Samta" is the correct spelling in this case, not "Santa".

5 Letter, 27 December 1535, Arquivo Nacional da Torre do Tombo, Lisbon,

published in António da Silva Rego, ed., *As Gavetas da Torre do Tombo*, vol. 2, *Gavetas III–XII* (Lisbon: Centro de Estudos Históricos Ultramarinos, 1962), pp. 712–15.

6 Joseph Wicki, ed., *Documenta Indica*, vol. 5, *1561–1563* (Rome: Monumenta Historica Soc. Iesu, 1958), p. 181.

7 Županov, *Missionary Tropics*, pp. 104–5.

8 Achilles Meersman, *The Franciscans in Tamilnad* (Schöneck, Germany: Nouvelle Revue de Science Missionnaire, 1962), pp. 7–8.

9 Ibid., pp. 7–47.

10 "Breve relação das Christand[ad]es da Prov[inci]a do Malavar na India oriental (1609)", unsigned, fol. 162, Goa 48, Archivum Romanum Societatis Iesu, Rome.

11 Henry Davison Love, *Vestiges of Old Madras, 1640–1800: Traced from the East India Company's Records Preserved at Fort St. George and the India Office, and from Other Sources* (London: John Murray, 1913), 1: 298.

12 Meersman, *Franciscans in Tamilnad*, p. 48; Anthony Mathias Mundadan, Joseph Thekkedath and Hugald Grafe, *History of Christianity in India*, vol. 2, *From the Middle of the Sixteenth to the End of the Seventeenth Century (1542–1700)* (Bangalore: Church History Association of India, 1988), p. 130.

13 Ángel Santos Hernández, *Jesuitas y Obispados*, vol. 2, *Los Jesuitas Obispos Misioneros y los Obispos Jesuitas de la Extinción* (Madrid: Universidad Pontificia de Comillas, 2000), pp. 126–35. The Malabar Rites controversy has been mentioned often by historians but has never been studied in depth on the basis of original documents. An attempt to fill this lacuna is my doctoral thesis, "Malabar Rites: An Eighteenth-Century Conflict on the Catholic Missions in South India" (European University Institute, Florence). I have anticipated some of my findings in two articles, "Sacramenti o *saṃskārāḥ*? L'illusione dell'*accommodatio* nella controversia dei riti malabarici", in *Politiche sacramentali tra Vecchio e Nuovi Mondi*, edited by Maria Teresa Fattori, monographic issue of *Cristianesimo nella storia* 2, no. 31 (2010): 621–46; and " 'Glocal' Conflicts: Missionary Controversies on the Coromandel Coast between the Seventeenth and the Eighteenth Centuries", in *Evangelizzazione e Globalizzazione: Le missioni gesuitiche nell'età moderna tra storia e storiografia*, edited by Michela Catto, Guido Mongini and Silvia Mostaccio (Rome: Società editrice Dante Alighieri, 2010), pp. 79–104.

14 António Bocarro, "Livro das plantas de todas as fortalezas, cidades e povoações do Estado da India Oriental", in *Arquivo Português Oriental*, new ed., bk. 4, *História administrativa*, vol. 2, *1600–1699*, pt. 1, edited by A.B. de Bragança Pereira (Bastorá, Goa: Typografia Rangel, 1937), p. 8.

15 Sinnapah Arasaratnam, *Merchants, Companies and Commerce on the Coromandel Coast, 1650–1740* (Delhi: Oxford University Press, 1986), p. 22.

16 Love, *Vestiges of Old Madras*, 1: 15–24.

17 Ibid., 1: 304. Important to understanding the relation between São Tomé and Madras is George D. Winius, "A Tale of Two Coromandel Towns: Madraspatam

(Fort St. George) and São Thomé de Meliapur", *Itinerario* 18, no. 1 (1994): 51–64. Winius's most important contention is that the Indo-Portuguese traders of São Tomé were able to overcome the naval blockades organized by the Dutch Vereenigde Oostindische Compagnie, thanks to the partnership established with the English Honorable Company's settlement of Fort St George. In fact they "had taken to flying English colours on their vessels and sometimes even had an Englishman on board to warn the Dutch in no uncertain terms to keep their hands off" (p. 59). Winius also observes very appropriately how Love's *Vestiges of Old Madras* — notwithstanding its lack of documentary references — is still the main source on the early history of Fort St George, given the catastrophic conditions in which the Tamil Nadu State Archives are currently kept. This situation is particularly deplorable considering that "next to the former Portuguese archive in Goa, Egmore [a borough of Madras where the archives are located] is the richest depository in Asia for the history of European expansion" (p. 51).

18 Santos Hernández, *Jesuitas y Obispados*, 2: 126. The appointment of new Portuguese bishops in the East was a specific trait of the new course followed by Alexander VIII in relation to the Padroado. António Vasconcelos Saldanha, *De Kangxi para o Papa, pela Via de Portugal: Memória e Documentos Relativos à Intervenção de Portugal e da Companhia de Jesus na Questão dos Ritos Chineses e nas Relações entre o Imperador Kangxi e a Santa Sé* (Macao: Instituto Português do Oriente, 2002), 1: 26.

19 King of Portugal to viceroy, and viceroy to king of Portugal, Livros dos Monções do Reino (hereafter cited as MR) 22A, fols. 242 and 243, 4 March 1652 and 13 January 1653, respectively, Historical Archives of Goa (hereafter cited as HAG), Panaji, Goa. N.b.: Many collections in the HAG have no title and thus are referenced by a number only. Dates appearing in the HAG citations herein pertain only to the specific folios cited.

20 François Martin, "Mémoire sur l'établissement des Colonies françoises aux Indes orientales", manuscript, Archives Nationales, Paris, quoted in Love, *Vestiges of Old Madras*, p. 305.

21 François L'Estra, *Relation ou Journal d'un voyage fait aux Indes Orientales:contenant l'Etat des affaires du Païs, & les établissemens de plusieuss Nations, qui s'y sont faits dépuis quelques années. Avec la description des principales Villes, les mœurs, coûtumes & Religions des Indiens* (Paris: E. Michallet, 1677), p. 174.

22 Glenn Joseph Ames, *Renascent Empire? The House of Braganza and the Quest for Stability in Portuguese Monsoon Asia, c. 1640–1683* (Amsterdam: Amsterdam University Press, 2000), pp. 160–63.

23 Arasaratnam, *Merchants, Companies and Commerce,* p. 62.

24 Ames, *Renascent Empire*, p. 163.

25 *Farmān* is a Persian word meaning royal decree or charter; in Portuguese, *formão*, and in English, *firman*. See Sebastião Rodolfo Dalgado, *Glossário Luso-Asiático*, vol. 1 (Coimbra: Imprensa da Universidade, 1919), pp. 402–3.

26 [Treslado do] fermão q. El Rey da Golcondâ pa[ssou aos Portu]guezes p[ara]

povoarem Meliapor, vertido bem e fielm.e do [Persi]anio [sic] em P[ortu]guez, MR 52, fol. 408, 18 October 1686. Among the Portuguese delegation, the *farmān* specified not only the Augustinian leader and friar Rangel, but also Álvaro Cancella (or "Castella") do Valle, Lucas Luis de Oliv[eir]a, and Ant[oni]o F[er]r[eir]a. This document has been published (without specifying its archival location) by Julio Firmino Judice Biker, *Collecção de Tratados e Concertos de Pazes que o Estado da India Portugueza Fez com os Reis e Senhores com Quem Teve Relações nas Partes da Asia e Africa Oriental desde o Principio da Conquista até o Fim do Seculo XVIII* (Lisbon: Imprensa Nacional, 1884), 4: 227–28, and then by Panduronga S.S. Pissurlencar, *Assentos do Conselho do Estodo*, vol. 5, *1696–1750* (Bastorá, Goa: Typografia Rangel, 1957), 573–74.

27 MR 52, fol. 410, 15 April 1686.

28 MR 52, fol. 412, 8 October 1687.

29 On the Venkatadri family, see Kanakalatha Mukund, *The Trading World of the Tamil Merchant: Evolution of Merchant Capitalism in the Coromandel* (Chennai: Orient Longman Limited, 1999), pp. 110–15.

30 James Talboys Wheeler, *Madras in the Olden Time: Being a History of the Presidency from the First Foundation to the Governorship of Thomas Pitt, Grandfather of the Earl of Chatham, 1639–1702. Compiled from Official Records* (Madras: printed for J. Higginbotham, by Graves and Co., Scottish Press, 1861), p. 175.

31 Wheeler, *Madras in the Olden Time,* p. 174.

32 Ibid.

33 Wheeler, *Madras in the Olden Time,* pp. 175–76.

34 It cannot be concluded, therefore, that Chinna Venkatadri "just before the fall of Golkonda Kingdom … rented San Thome", as it is affirmed in Mukund, *The Trading World of the Tamil Merchant,* p. 115.

35 Wolseley Haig and Richard Burn, eds., *The Cambridge History of India,* vol. 4, *The Mughal Period* (Cambridge: Cambridge University Press, 1937), pp. 286–90.

36 Letter of Dom Rodrigo da Costa to Dom Pedro II, fol. 369, MR 53, published in Panduronga S.S. Pissurlencar, *Assentos do Conselho do Estado*, vol. 4, *1659–1695* (Bastorá, Goa: Typografia Rangel, 1956), 576–77. See also a memorandum of the very Friar Luis da Piedade, composed in Goa on 9 January 1708 and referring to a mission to the Mughal in 1700 and to another one that led to a *farmān* addressed to the viceroy Rodrigo da Costa "restituindo a Coroa de Portugal a Cid[ad]e de S. Thomé" (restoring to the Crown of Portugal the City of S. Tomé). MR 71, fols. 82–83v, specifically fol. 82, 9 January 1708.

37 For a definition of the *cowlee*, see Henry Yule, Arthur Coke Burnell and William Crooke, eds., *Hobson-Jobson: A Glossary of Colloquial Anglo-Indian Words and Phrases, and of Kindred Terms, Etymological, Historical, Geographical and Discursive,* new ed. (London: John Murray, 1903; 4th repr., New Delhi: Rupa & Co., 2002), pp. 268–69.

38 Wheeler, *Madras in the Olden Time,* pp. 176–77.

39 MR 55B fol. 430, 1691[?]. The document seems to be dated 1691; however, the correct date should be 1690 because there is a response from Dom Pedro II

clearly referring to the topics discussed in the letter examined above, dated Lisbon, 22 October 1690.

40 Letter of Pedro António de Meneses Noronha de Albuquerque, Conde de Vila Verde, to Dom Pedro II, Goa, 10 December 1695, fol. 124, MR 59, published in Pissurlencar, *Assentos*, 4: 579–80; and Love, *Vestiges of Old Madras*, 1: 574–77. Whilst the *Public Consultations* and the *Public Letters to England* quoted by Love say that Luís Francisco Coutinho was a relative of the viceroy in charge in 1695, that is, Pedro António de Noronha de Albuquerque, he would appear more obviously a relation of the following viceroy, António Luís Gonçalves da Câmara Coutinho (1698–1701).

41 Dalgado, *Glossário Luso-Asiático*, vol. 2 (1921), pp. 183–84.

42 Letter, MR 71, fols. 82–83v, specifically fol. 83, 9 January 1708.

43 The king wrote on 20 December 1706 to the viceroy Caetano de Mello de Castro, mentioning what the latter had written in this respect on 15 January 1704. Dom Pedro II decided to resort to the Jesuits. MR 71, fol. 81, 20 December 1706. The name of the Jesuits is mentioned in a letter addressed to Dom João V, Goa, 8 January 1708, fol. 84, MR 71.

44 MR 74A, fol. 25, 6 October 1706.

45 In the Indian Ocean, *shāhbandars* were much more than simple "harbourmasters". For instance, "in Malacca at the time of the Portuguese conquest in 1511, four merchant communities were dominant, each of them living autonomous lives with their own headmen, called *shahbandars,* and governing themselves with little or no reference to the ruler, the sultan, who provided facilities, law and order, and fair dealing in return for customs duties"; see Michael N. Pearson, "Markets and Merchant Communities in the Indian Ocean: Locating the Portuguese", in *Portuguese Oceanic Expansion, 1400–1800,* edited by Francisco Bethencourt and Diogo Ramada Curto (New York: Cambridge University Press, 2007), p. 95.

46 MR 74A, fol. 26, 24 November 1708. The viceroy replied to a letter from Dom João V, sent from Lisbon on 24 November 1708, which included the petition made by the inhabitants of São Tomé on 6 October 1706.

47 Índia, 6 August 1706, codex 88, doc. 25, Arquivo Histórico Ultramarino (hereafter cited as AHU), Lisbon.

48 Henry Heras, *South India under the Vijayanagara Empire: The Aravidu Dynasty* (New Delhi: Cosmo Publications, 1980), 2: 437–38.

49 Martin, "Mémoire", quoted in Love, *Vestiges of Old Madras*, p. 305; and letter of Dom Rodrigo da Costa to Dom Pedro II, Goa, 24 January 1866, published in Pissurlencar, *Assentos*, 4: 574–75.

50 Vasco Fernandes César de Menezes to Dom João V. Goa, HAG 85, fol. 88, 23 December 1712.

51 José António Ismael Gracias, *Uma Dona Portugueza na Côrte do Grão-Mogol: Documentos de 1710 a 1719 Precedidos d'um Esboço Historico das Relações Politicas e Diplomaticas entre o Estado da India e o Grão-Mogol nos Seculos XVI, XVII* (Nova Goa: Imprensa Nacional, 1907).

52 Índia, 10 January 1715, codex 107, doc. 6, AHU.

53 In a letter of 16 January 1721, the viceroy Francisco José de Sampaio e Castro informed Dom João V that the Castilian had gone to Cochin and that there were doubts about his conduct. See MR 86B, fol. 504, 16 January 1721. The doctor's name is established from a 15 January 1720 letter from Sampaio e Castro to the Mughal emperor Muhammad Shah (designed with the honorific titles of Padxa Alamagir Gagir), stating that he was sending to him a person of his full confidence, the doctor Francisco Pereira, in order to discuss the restitution of "as hortas, e a mayor parte das vargeas [*sic*? *várzea*?] de Mailapour[,] a Aldea Mamboleo, e a Aldea Alemdur, e Anadamba, e outras" (the gardens, and the greater part of the rice fields [?] of Meliapor[,] the village Mamboleo, and the village Alemdur, and Anadamba, and others). See MR 86B, fol. 668, 15 January 1720.

54 Índia, 9 March 1723 [erroneous], codex 120, doc. s.n., AHU. The motivation was stated as follows: "O motivo que teve o V. Rey Conde da Ericeyra para encarregar a hum estrangeiro, e que morava fora das terras deste Estado o negocio de que trata a Real carta de V. Magestade foi o ser elle pratico, e intelligente das couzas dos Mogoles, e o vir de Madrasta a esta Cidade somente a offerecerselhe para a negociação delle" (The motive that the viceroy Conde de Ericeyra had to employ a foreigner, and one who lived outside the territory of this State[,] [was that] the business that Your Majesty's royal letter dealt with was such that he was practical, and intelligent in the ways of the Mughals, and he came from Madrasta to this City only to offer himself to negotiate this deal).

55 Aniruddha Ray, *The Merchant and the State: The French in India, 1666–1739* (New Delhi: Munshiram Manoharlal, 2004), 2: 780–83.

56 Love, *Vestiges of Old Madras*, 2: 398–401. On the life of the Franciscan adventurer, see Ismael Gracias, *Dom Antonio José de Noronha Évêque d'Halicarnasse: Les aventures d'un pseudo neveu de Madame Dupleix (1720–1776)* (Pondicherry: Imprimerie moderne, 1933).

57 Love, *Vestiges of Old Madras*, 2: 400–401.

58 Pamila Gupta, "The Relic State: St. Francis Xavier and the Politics of Ritual in Portuguese India" (Ph.D. dissertation, Columbia University, 2004).

59 "Searching for 'christãos e especiarias' [Christians and spices]" was the answer that a member of the expedition of Vasco da Gama gave to two Muslims from Tunis whom they met in Calicut on 21 May 1498 and who were curious to know why the Portuguese had sailed to India. Álvaro Velho, *Roteiro da Primeira Viagem de Vasco da Gama*, (Lisboa: Agência Geral do Ultramar, 1960), p. 40.

60 MR 89A, fol. 41, 23 December 1723.

4

EIGHTEENTH-CENTURY DIPLOMATIC RELATIONS BETWEEN PORTUGUESE MACAO AND AYUTTHAYA: THE 1721 DEBT REPAYMENT EMBASSY FROM MACAO

Stefan Halikowski Smith

One of the pre-eminent, current historiographical debates in Thai history concerns the nature of the "National Revolution" of 1688 and whether it genuinely ushered in a period of xenophobia and retreat from international engagement, with Siam becoming a "hermit kingdom" in the language of the academic literature. Traditionally, historians like Hutchinson have insisted that the country became moved by "a spirit of blind and arrogant self-sufficiency".[1] Revisionist historians like Anthony Reid would like to suggest that this was not necessarily the case, since relations between Siam and China were strengthened in this period, and that Phetracha (ruled 1688–1703) was not personally motivated by xenophobia but used it to motivate political support.[2]

The European population remaining in Ayutthaya nevertheless suffered considerable hardships when we compare their situation to earlier times. Fernão Mendes Pinto created an enduring myth of the "good king" (*bom rei*) of Siam, which we can accommodate to the long reign of Naraï (ruled 1656–88).[3] Under Phetracha, on the other hand, some of the leading European families were enslaved, and — to quote from a Portuguese document produced shortly after the climactic events — "the college of the Bishop has been turned into a pagoda and the Christians among the local population under the bishop were seized, the King forcing them to apostize."[4] Of the European trading companies, only the Dutch factory managed to limp on, the French colonial entrepreneur Pierre Poivre reporting in 1745 that "today, the Dutch are the only Europeans who go to trade in Siam", sending three regular ships from Batavia per annum, plus one East Indiaman that stopped in Siam on its way to Japan.[5] In 1715, the once burgeoning company trade in deerskins came to an abrupt end, as it was decided that the two East Indiamen allowed annually to Deshima would be more profitably laden with other goods taken on board in Batavia.[6] Final closure of the *logie* (the Dutch trading factory), however, came only in 1765.[7]

Thai historiography traditionally does not really accept, or even engage, with the debate about xenophobia and long-term retreat and presents circumstances in Siam at the time as peaceable and stable in this period.[8] King Taisra (1709–33) is seen to have enjoyed a peaceful, twenty-four-year reign, punctuated only by an "intervention in the internal affairs of Cambodia in 1717 in order to maintain overlordship".[9] According to primary sources like Hamilton, however, the campaign was a resounding failure, with trenchant consequences for the Siamese military both on land and at sea, with the army subject to an epidemic and the fleet trapped in small creeks where the "great vessels" were set ablaze.[10] Taisra is otherwise seen to have spent his time improving the internal water communications and foreign trade. His reign is considered noteworthy for the renewal of Spanish Philippine trade with Siam, severed for at least sixty years. On this point, Taisra's initiative seems to make sense, other historians like Arasaratnam suggesting that the Philippines mark "the only bright spot in [an] overall gloomy picture" of Indian Ocean trade between 1700 and 1740.[11] Besides, the political pragmatism of the Thai monarchy, siding with more successful and useful foreign parties in the kingdom, is well known, and frequently commented upon by external sources.[12]

I have argued recently that the Portuguese mixed-blood community fared somewhat better in Ayutthaya than other European nations in this period, primarily because their political allegiances were no longer to Europe: the Portuguese were a rootless "tribe" of individuals, many of whom had come in repeated displacements from Southeast Asia, racked by Dutch military seizures and eviction orders.[13] In the climactic circumstances surrounding the court revolution of 1688, Phetracha even extended an arm of friendship to the Portuguese community. As the *Novas do Reyno* reports:

> The King asked the captains of foreign ships who were in the port to defend the river [the Chao Phraya]. The captains of the two ships from our [city of] Macao offered him their ships, their crew, and their assistance. The King accepted this offer and as a gesture of thanks he gave and dressed with his own hands some coats (*casacos*), which he gave to Andre Gomez, Gaspar Franco, Francisco Ferreira and other Portuguese, promising remuneration on completion of the job. And so our boats stayed, with their galleys protecting the river.[14]

HISTORICAL BACKGROUND TO SIAM-MACAO RELATIONS IN THE SEVENTEENTH CENTURY

Macao, to which China missionaries regularly hoped to sail from Siam during "high summer" (the month of July) by the southwestern monsoon, was, prior to 1688, in close contact with the Kingdom.[15] The international commerce of the Portuguese "tribe" in Ayutthaya was almost all in the hands of successfully established shipowners from Macao, who sailed — as Friar Valentim Carvalho, the rector of Macao, reported in a letter of 4 November 1606 — "every two years" under captains that Dutch sources refer to pejoratively as "crusaders" (*kruisvaarders*).[16] The Siamese authorities — who increasingly employed foreign captains, such as the two Englishmen whose two Siamese vessels had met with contrary winds and been blown off course — chose to put into Macao to effect repairs.[17] Thus, Macao was not slow to profess friendship with the new regime in Ayutthaya, in an embassy sent from the "City of the Name of God" in 1688. The Macanese wanted to see for themselves what the turn of events entailed, because "this [*sic*] city needs friendship and trade with the aforementioned kingdom" as well as on account of the "obligations of the Portuguese nation, principally this city".[18] Unfortunately, we know very little other than the Senate's deliberations that led to this earlier embassy's dispatch.[19]

There was also the matter of a long-standing loan to be repaid. This had been incurred in 1667, when the king of Siam was generous enough to grant the Macanese a considerable loan of 120,000 taels to defray the costs of an expensive Portuguese embassy to China under Ambassador Manuel Saldanha following an embassy of two prominent Macanese shipowners active in the Senado da Câmara who had visited the river-state.[20] The Goan Council, while voting unanimously for the embassy, had supplied neither cash nor presents for the Macanese embassy to Siam and instead sent a letter to the king of Siam asking him to continue advancing funds to Macao (suggesting this was not the first time the Siamese had played this role), promising that the Goan authorities would reimburse him.[21] Repayment was never forthcoming from Goa, but initially the debt was lessened by the payment of customs duties incurred by Siamese Crown vessels at Canton by the Portuguese in Macao. Secondly, payment was sent in the form of silk aboard the same returning vessels that had brought the silver to Macao in 1667. While the spirit of later negotiations regarding this loan was decidedly stickling for pennies from the Siamese side, it is perhaps most importantly a tribute to the generosity of King Naraï that this loan was initially made.

After a letter from the Siamese authorities in 1716, a Portuguese embassy was sent from Macao in 1721 to pay off the last instalment of this debt.[22] Seventy-two catties of silver were promptly transported in "twenty-one bags of white silk" alongside presents (*sagoate*).[23] The progress of this embassy is quite well documented from the Portuguese side in papers held in the Arquivo Histórico de Macau; four primary documents relating to it are reproduced at the end of this article in translation, for the first time.

THE 1721 DEBT REPAYMENT EMBASSY FROM MACAO TO SIAM

Having sketched the historical background to relations between Macao and Siam, and the question of the long-standing debt, I will now elucidate the specific circumstances surrounding this embassy. On the one hand, we have a letter from the viceroy in Goa to the Senate in Macao from the second decade of the eighteenth century. It explains that, beyond any possible profit, it was important that the Portuguese community in Thailand see "the people and flags of its nation" for it to be invigorated (*animado*).[24] It was probably an expression of triumph over the fact that the "one-armed fidalgo of Brazilian origin" and governor of Macao, António de Albuquerque Coelho, had been able to restore prosperity to the city "with prudence and skill" after many decades of political and economic uncertainty — what António de Aguiar refers to in his letter as the "calamities of those times".[25] The quarrels surrounding the papal legate Charles Maillard de Tournon's death in Macanese captivity in June 1710 had subsided, and the Chinese rites controversy laid to temporary rest with the next papal legate Carlos Melchior Mezzabarba's declaration of 4 November 1721, which afforded a loophole for the evasion of the papal brief *Ex illa die*.[26] Similarly, the war with Timor, an "unsuccessful Project of Domination", in which the Scottish sea captain Alexander Hamilton claimed to have "ruined … that rich and flourishing city", had arrived at a temporary calm.[27] A third boon was the promulgation of an imperial edict that prohibited the sailing of Chinese junks to all foreign countries save Japan. This edict of Kangxi (Kang-hsi) gave the death blow to the flourishing trade of Cantonese junks to Batavia, and the burgeoning supply of tea to the Dutch at Batavia now became a Macanese monopoly, with the number of ships registered in Macao rising from nine to twenty-three in a single year.[28] A further edict from the Chinese emperor, following a very successful exchange of embassies between Macao and Canton in 1717, exempted Macao from "whatever tribute payments" (*quaisquer tributações*). The historian António da Silva Rego thinks that, because of this, Macao could now afford to pay the Siamese debt.[29]

Then, we also need to situate the Siamese embassy within a general resurgence of commercial relations with other neighbouring states such as Cochinchina in 1712. This move was initiated by the "King of Cochinchina" via the intercession of the Jesuit missionary João António Arnedo, together with other foreign policy initiatives like negotiations with the prefectural authorities of Huangshan-hsien (黃山); it may also have been sent after news of a Spanish embassy to Siam accompanied by a Polish Reformed Franciscan Placidus (Placido Albrecht de Valcio) reached Macao in 1718.[30]

The Senate requested that Siam grant the Portuguese the same commercial privileges as had at one time been established, following the Frei de Annunciação embassy of 1616 and confirmed under King Ekathotsarot, and whose terms António Soares was able to refer to as some sort of lapidary benchmark of the Portuguese presence in Ayutthaya in his letter of 1721 (see Letter 1).[31] As António Soares's letter makes clear, however, what transpired is that the king "revoked his decision with regard to the duties owing the mandarins, foregoing us only those duties owed his estate".[32] Furthermore, unlike the contemporary commercial embassy from the Philippines, no binding treaty was forthcoming from the 1721 embassy from Macao.

Had the days when Europeans were regaled with privileges and incentives to come and do trade in Siam clearly passed? As contemporary European traders like Alexander Hamilton discovered, it was now a real challenge to trade with Siam for profit when "measurage dues" of 8 per cent were expected, and when commodity purchase was sanctioned only through Siamese customs officials. Even in better days, Macanese trade had found in Siam only "an outlet for certain Chinese goods on a modest scale".[33] Part of the problem now was that ancient agreements such as that signed in London between the king and Thai emissaries in 1684, or that the Portuguese had signed in 1616 and thereafter carved on the gates of entry into the Portuguese *campo* (grounds or compound) were no longer accepted, neither by the Thai authorities nor by European groups operating in the area, now jealously guarding their personal privileges to trade and using those as leverage to secure better conditions than their rivals.[34] Thus Collet, governor of Fort St George, wanted only "his" men to be able to do business in Siam.

Hamilton's experience in Siam in 1718 was a thoroughly negative one. He held unsuccessful talks with the chief minister or *phraklang* (the Persian Oi-ya Sennerat) and was warned off approaching the court, via a proclamation prohibiting approaching the king's palace on pain of very severe penalties. A court case followed, in which Hamilton was indicted by his enemies of "imposing upon the king", but acquitted himself by proving that the chief witness on the prosecuting bench, Collison (Ambassador Powny's man in Siam), had not been in a position to understand the key conversation Hamilton had held with the *phrakhlang* in Hindustani. Hamilton left Siam with relief in December 1718.[35]

In comparison, the Portuguese embassy of 1721 went fairly well, and the documents offer detailed description of the protocol followed, the processions that began at the focal point of Portuguese religious life, the Jesuit Church of São Paulo, the richly decorated ceremonial barges (*balões*), the individuals involved and their station, and the pride of place given to the "letters [of credence]".[36] As Simon de la Loubère had explained thirty years earlier, "an Ambassador throughout the East is no other than a King's messenger: he represents not his Master. They honour him little in comparison of the respects which are render'd to the Letters of Credence whereof he is Bearer."[37] The "friendship of kings", which in Europe was held to reside in the ambassadors was, in Southeast Asia, distinctly not the case; Captain Manuel de Vidigal Gião hardly emerges as an individual from the documents.[38]

The ceremony was in many ways identical to that held for considerably more important embassies, such as that of the Chevalier de Chaumont, who travelled from Paris in 1685. Chaumont's letter, too, was transported in a *balon* which had "four umbrellas, one at each corner of the Seat".[39] Indeed, while Chaumont was attended with "four other Balons of the Body, adorn'd with their Umbrellas, but empty", in 1721 Captain Manuel de Vidigal Gião's party required six *balons*.[40] Soares's claim that the mandarins came for the party "with more pomp than that which is meted out to the letters from the Governor General of Batavia and the Governor of Madras" does not appear to be an exaggeration.[41]

Unlike Lopes de Siqueira's embassy in 1684, in 1721 the Portuguese ambassador met with the king. In another divergence from ritual precedent, the "Chaqueri" — the First Minister, or "foremost person in this realm beneath the Prince" — took a very active role in the audience, asking all the leading questions on behalf of the king. Van Vliet otherwise relates how in 1639 he "remained immobile throughout the ceremony, with folded hands and body bowed, sitting so far away from the king they were out of his sight".[42] According to Van Vliet, the *opperhoofd* (head of the Dutch logie) thought this indicated their subjection or fear of the king.[43]

One Siamese mandarin complained that the presents were not enough. These are most explicitly enumerated in the letter of the *phrakhlang* (see Letter 4), as if he wanted the authorities in Macao to be in a position to check that what had originally been sent had indeed arrived, perhaps suspecting things to have been purloined along the way:

> six pieces of mother-of-pearl damask, five pieces of yellow damask, another three pieces of mother-of-pearl damask, and two of yellow damask, four *Loôs* with golden threads,[44] twelve *Tochas* (large candles, or firebrands), twelve catties of lozenges, and thirty jars of sweets. Besides this, he [Vidigal Gião] consigned a further seven mother-of-pearl damasks, eight yellow ones, three pieces of *Tabi*,[45] twelve *Pivetes* (a kind of aromatic substance), and 22 jars of sweets for the Most Serene Prince.

The Jesuit Superior Francisco Teles (see Letter 2) does much the same as the *phrakhlang* in his letter (see Letter 3), going to great lengths to explain why the original gift offered by the Siamese king was reduced to fifteen pieces of silk. It is interesting how the *phrakhlang*'s list of Portuguese gifts appears much more extensive than that declared by António de Aguiar in his letter from the Noble Senate; when it comes to "jars of sweets", for example, the *phrakhlang* has twenty-two jars on his books, whereas Aguiar declares only seven. We must put this down to Padre Soares's wise and generous intercession. At any rate, if gifts constituted an important display of both largesse and recognition of a fellow monarch, then the Noble Senate of Macao stood rather poorly next to the governor general of the Netherlands Indies in Batavia in the Thai monarch's estimation. In 1650, for example, the Thai king sent to Batavia an impressive array of gifts, including a gold crown and twelve large elephants.[46] As we will see in a minute, the Siamese were also far more magnanimous in their gifts to a simultaneous embassy from the Philippines, rendering the *phrakhlang*'s excuse that "the circumstances do not currently permit it" something of a lie. The quantity of identical silks proferred the Macanese appears a purely perfunctory gesture when we recall the highly personalized presents Naraï sent to Louis XIV, "novelties admired by the monarch himself".[47] In the case of the Philippine embassy, gifts were not only offered the Spanish king (a one-year-old elephant, although it never finally left Bangkok), but to the governor of the Philippines and the ambassador himself, including elephant tusks, exotic birds, a ceramic slab from Japan, pieces of European velvet and gold and silver fabric, Persian carpets, taffetas and cotton and silk materials, as well as a gold-plated, bronze-cast bathtub.[48]

The meanness of the Macanese gifts became apparent even after Portuguese intermediaries in Ayutthaya used their better judgement to open and change the official letters, and add supplementary presents for the Crown Prince and for the *phrakhlang*. The presentation was also judged somewhat wanting, so that two "dignified packing-boxes" were requisitioned from Padre Manuel de Queirós for suitable effect. This was of the utmost political importance, Soares arguing that "because these gentiles are so untrusting, they immediately think they are being cheated, and from one small ambiguity that they notice, they will heap upon the embassy a thousand disgraces [*precepissios*]".[49]

At the solemn presentation of the repayment, where the Portuguese were represented by the Jesuit Superior, Padre Francisco Teles, on the instruction of the viceroy in Goa, the Siamese wanted to know why Macanese ships had not called at Bangkok as previously, adding that if Macao needed more silver, the king was ready to help. In effect, the conclusive solemnity of the occasion was a bit misplaced, in that Siamese debt assessors judged that the goods accompanying the silver so as to make up the missing amount were not yet sufficient. Soares explained that the arrival of lots of Chinese goods in Siam at this time only diminished the value of the Portuguese imports.

Besides the exchange of gifts and auguries for the future, and making the debt repayment, the Portuguese ambassador clearly did not have much further business, unlike with Lopes Vaz de Siqueira's visit to Siam twenty-seven years earlier. On that occasion, the ambassador was asked to adjudicate on matters of civil justice, assess the reigning headman of the Bandel, and reprehend clergy judged to be footloose and no longer creditworthy of the Catholic church.[50] Nor does it appear that the Macanese brought with them missionaries from their much-respected seminaries to foster Christianity,[51] so blatant a motivation behind the simultaneous Philippine embassy. Although the explicit link between commercial activity and the spread of the Christian faith was mentioned in a letter of 1712 from the provincial of the Company of Jesus in Cochinchina, Padre Miguel de Amaral,[52] Rego suggests that the Portuguese from Macao had learnt the hard way that doing diplomacy with its neighbours required generosity and genuine professions of friendship, not pretexts for exploitation and expansion. At any rate, in many ways the prospects of the Jesuit church in Ayutthaya under Taisra had definitely improved from the miserable situation in which it found itself at the beginning of the eighteenth century, when, following the death of Gaspard da Costa in 1709, the Jesuit residence was without personnel for some time.[53] The *Catalogue of the Japan-Chinese Province* explains how the Jesuit order now tried to appoint a team of priests for the Ayutthayan mission. There were at least two individuals: Friar Joseph Anselmus as Superior and António Soares as member of the Collegium Siamense.[54]

At this point I would like to open comparative vistas to the aforementioned simultaneous Philippine embassy to Ayutthaya, which had been occasioned by soaring rice prices in Manila as a result of a local locust infestation. Historian Ferdinand Llanes, however, sees it as indicative of a bold new Bourbon policy initiative.[55] Other sources point to Bustamante's profiteering, exporting rice even at a time of dire national shortages.[56] The mission was entrusted to Governor General Fernando Manuel Bustamante's nephew, Alexandro Bustamante, who kept an account of the mission. Spanish officials sought a more permanent trading agreement not just for rice, but also teak and iron. Just as with the Portuguese mission, there were difficult protocol issues. Like Alexander Hamilton, the Spaniards were obliged to leave their artillery and weaponry in Bangkok before proceeding up the river. Another issue was the degree to which the Thai monarch should reveal his face to the visitors in audience: previously, as in famous illustrations of the Chaumont embassy, the king was seated elevated and behind a wooden screen, and took the ambassadorial letters that were offered him on a wooden tray painted with gold, to which was attached a long handle.[57] Unlike the Portuguese mission, the Philippine visit culminated in a comprehensive commercial treaty being signed. The king promptly sent out two junks (*somas*) of rice to the port of Cavite ahead of the embassy's return. In recompense, the Siamese shipmen were provided with letters of recommendation that would ensure they were treated well in Manila and enable them to buy horses in the provinces (traditionally a product Persians had supplied Siam, but the Persian trading community was one of the noticeable retractions, both from the trading scene in Ayutthaya in the 1670s and from Masulipatam in this period).

Llanes's verdict is that the treaty was more favourable to Manila than to Ayutthaya. It allowed Spain to open a factory there, and even to build ships. Learning from experience, the Siamese stipulated that everything had to be declared so as to prevent fraudulence, and monetary exchange was to be fixed. The Manila traders were allowed all forms of purchase except of saltpetre, ivory, cattle and deer hides, which were the preserve of the Siamese authorities and the Dutch company. A related article went further than the offer made the Portuguese, exempting Manila and Siamese ships from paying port duties.

CONCLUSION

By way of conclusion, it is clear that these two embassies represented an active engagement on the part of Siam with the wider world, rather than retreat, albeit on a new playing field where old conventions no longer held sway. In terms of trade, these were hard times in the region as a whole, though we need to remember that the trading crisis of the 1730s, so marked in Coromandel, had other principal factors, including a crisis in the irrigation system of the central Coromandel plain, endemic internecine wars, and short-term revenue-raising arrangements.[58] Commentators like Bishop Pallegoix, however, do not fail to mention the "dearness of everyday goods" in Siam at this time.[59] Although no determining commercial treaty was signed following the 1721 embassy, for Macao these were times when feelers were slowly extended into the wider world. The French traveller Bennetat in 1753 could record that the Macanese shipping presence in the Cochinchinese kingdom of Đàng Trong was on a par with that of the French, and twice that of the Dutch.[60] A little later, Howard Tyrell Fry could describe how "70 or 80 junks resort to the single port of Turon in Cochinchina in one season, and that the trade is the chief support of the town of Macao".[61] Reconnecting with Siam in 1721 was all about re-establishing old links.

Meanwhile, a far more ground-breaking agreement with Manila, for all the hyperbole surrounding it, did not live up to expectations. It was an agreement based on hope and the fine commercial prospects of the time, but it could not predict the political turn of events. Bustamante was assassinated in an uprising aimed at his personal rapacity in appropriating the goods of those he imprisoned, and more generally at the obligations levied on those living in great poverty and those who had recently died, while his nephew was imprisoned in Mexico on unclear charges.[62] A Siamese mission did arrive in Manila to reciprocate but was ignored and had to return to Siam. Thus, in all likelihood, Macao remained considerably more important to Siam than the Philippines over the course of the eighteenth century.

DOCUMENTARY APPENDICES

Letter 1. Padre António Soares, Company of Jesus, written from Siam to the Noble Senate of Macao, 20 June 1721.[63]

To the Noble Senate,

With the arrival of the boats which departed from this [your] city for that kingdom, I received a letter from Your Graces, which was given to me by Captain Manuel de Vidigal Giaõ; in it, I was ordered to defer to the Captain in every respect which, from the experience I have of this land, I judged to be judicious and convenient, in order for the prompt dispatch of the boats and conclusion to the business undertaken on his account. I did what my minor contribution allowed to ensure that business was concluded to the credit of the Portuguese nation, as well as to that of the Noble Senate; in which I had great difficulties, for not having the necessary notification ["notícia"] for such a political undertaking given the customs of this Kingdom, one of which was the fact that the Noble Senate did not write to the Prince of this kingdom, nor send him gifts ["saguate"].

As soon as I read your letter, I immediately gave notice of everything to Guilherme Dam, who is the only and the most capable man that there is in this kingdom for seeing to such business; for his knowledge of reading and writing in Siamese, as for his contacts with all, or almost all the mandarins of this kingdom, both important and less important; and I asked him if he could handle this business. He replied to me that it would please him to have the occasion to serve the Noble Senate, and that he would do everything he could for his part.

But when he came to know that neither letter nor gifts would arrive for the Prince, and of the type of gift that would arrive for the King, which he judged mean, not because in reality it was, but because it appeared so in comparison with the great [gifts] which are given by the [Governor] General of Batavia or Governor of Madras, for reasons I will explain below, he became so confused that he rescinded [his offer], and told me that I had to forgive him; for he could not get mixed up in this business because it was not only probable, but almost certain that the three boats would be ruined, or at the very least would receive interference ["trabalhos"] and damages, and he would also run the same risk for not having letters or gifts for the Prince, as many [boats] had been for the same reason, of which he gave me a good number of examples, of which I already knew some, because the conditions were the same as those I had proposed to him. And he gave me such reasons (which I confess are true) that I also wished to get out [of this business]: but for the desire which I hold to serve the Noble Senate, and the other Gentlemen of Macao which was very great, [and so] I resolved to continue, because if I didn't no lesser damages and troubles might follow. Which is what I did.

After considering things, and possible solutions: he agreed with me that there was no other way than to increase the gifts to the King, and to make a gift in the name of the Noble Senate to the Prince, as well as a letter; and as this could not be done in a way to concur with the letter and gifts to the King and the Phrakhlang, he also agreed to open everything to make everything fully coherent; because as these gentiles are so untrusting, they immediately think they are being deceived, and from small incoherence they perceive "a musketeer from a piece of straw", as one can say proverbially, and they will attribute to the ships one thousand calamities, all of which can be avoided; conducting things [in this way], he [Guilherme Dam] agreed to conduct this business.

Having concluded on these points, we agreed to give account of all this to Captains Manuel de Vidigal Gião, Luís Roiz dos Santos, and also to the Father

Superior of this House, who, having listened and considered our reasons for doing things [this way], all uniformly agreed with us, having no other solution than to open the letters and draft new ones to the King, the Prince, the Phrakhlang, increasing the gift for the King, and to make up another one in the name of the Noble Senate for the Prince, as indeed we did, as the Noble Senate will be able to see from the certificates that Captains Manuel de Vidigal and Luís Roiz will bring with them, [being able to] judge us, and that in such a delicate matter the prudence of the Noble Senate [will sanction] the opening of its letters. And in this way the letters [were handled], as well as it being necessary to change some of the words for a greater clarity in affairs.

Having managed the letters, another difficulty appeared, which was the bags in which they were to be carried. Because, despite a lot of care and attention, the necessary was still not accomplished; to make them appear suitable for appearing before the King, and Prince. But there was no other remedy than to put [things] in two dignified packing-boxes belonging to Padre Manuel de Queirós, and which Captain Manuel de Vidigal was to present, with the agreement of everybody.

Having prepared the letters, the mandarins came for them in our house where we were, for it being the most repectable ["authorisada"] which there is in the Bandel, with more pomp than that which is meted out to the letters from the Governor General of Batavia and the Governor of Madras, in three great state *Balõens* [Siamese ceremonial barges] with another of the same sort to carry the letters, with two more for Manuel de Vidigal Gião and Luís Roiz, the Squire of Pedro Roiz, and a number of other *balõens* belonging to residents here, making a pompous accompaniment, which was completed by two small boats of Blekboi,[64] and the large boat which, for being adorned with branches and draped in flags, made a strong impression.

From the gates of S. Paulo to the banks of the river the two packing-boxes with the Portuguese letters were transported under four umbrellas, by two Portuguese Manuel Gomes and Manuel Roiz, who went in the same *balão* with the letters; arriving in the place where we were to disembark, a bier immediately drew up, although a little old, on which the two boxes were placed. A short distance from this place horses were brought on which the mandarins, the Captains, and other Portuguese were mounted, and who accompanied the letters, and in this way they proceeded to the royal [audience] chamber, in which were a good number of mandarins, of greater and lesser importance, among whom the Chaqueri, who beneath the Prince is the foremost person in this realm, and President. With everyone seated in their respective places, two wooden boxes were immediately set in front of the Captains Manuel de Vidigal and Luís Roiz, as well as golden batons ["sancos"], with betel and Areca. The Chaqueri immediately began to ask in the name of the King about the health of the Noble Senate and the other Gentlemen of Macao; if, in the City of Macao there were many boats, and a lot of trade; and why no boats had come to Siam for so many years; if they had had a good voyage, or encountered contrary winds; what business did they wish to conduct? And finally, he asked if the Noble Senate needed more silver, the King would lend them [some] willingly, and if any of the boats needed anything whatsoever, or if anybody treated them badly, the Captains were to say so; because all favour was to be accorded them.

To all of this Manuel de Vidigal replied with great satisfaction and prudence.

Having completed these compliments, the Chaqueri ordered the gifts to be opened, both for the King as for the Prince, and having seen them, one of the mandarins immediately said they were small for who desired the restoration of ancient privileges.

From this Your Graces will be able to judge our resolution and what would have happened if we did not do what was done; he [the Chaqueri] immediately ordered the letters to be opened, and their contents were translated by Guilherme Dam, who was the interpreter and who was present. He [the Chaqueri] said that they would be translated and presented to the King, from whose greatness ["grandeza", here meaning "magnanimity"] it was hoped the Portuguese would emerge safely.

After all this we departed generally very satisfied with the honour with which the letters were received, and the courtesy with which we were treated.

Four or five days after this event more or less, I received news from a sure source that the King, after learning of the contents of the letters, would forgo all duties upon us that were due his estate, as well as those due the mandarins, two of whom did not like at all this decision, pleading with the King to revoke them, who indeed revoked his decision with regard to the duties owing the mandarins, forgoing us only those duties owed his estate. On this point, I spoke with Manuel de Vidigal and I told him that it was a necessary thing to make a petition to the King that the rights owing the mandarins also be forgone: he replied that it was not convenient to do such a thing, which ended up thus wise. The reasons for this [decision] he would send to our Noble Senate, as well as a report of what had transpired, and that this was already too generous. My reasons for why we were to be conceded the same privileges as before, and to not pay any duties whatsoever were what was agreed by the Siamese kings in 1616, on the occasion of a solemn embassy sent from Goa to this kingdom, as can be read in *Asia Portugueza,* tome 3, parte 39, cap. 19, nos. 6 and 7, which Your Graces should, indeed must see, to be attached to the letters that you are to send this year, as is convenient to you.

It was said that the gifts for the King were very small when compared to those given by the [Governor] General of Batavia and the Governor of Madras.

The reason is this: Because the King of Siam is used to profiting [from these encounters], they are given not by those who [traditionally] proffer presents, but by those who seal business contracts; it is for this reason that in Madras it is not the Governor who makes up the gift, but the outfitters of the visiting vessel, those who make a profit on the return voyage, that it is always up to them, they always give very generously. Nor was it possible to make such grandiose gifts every year. Our Noble Senate could do the same, not at its cost, but at the cost of the outfitters of the visiting ships, who, as well as having to invest, will receive returns from the return

voyage. I do not want to tire Your Graces any more, I only ask you earnestly that you recommence giving gifts to the Prince via those who will be returning, namely Manuel de Vidigal, Luís Roiz and Manuel Ribeiro: I ask for this because just as I did, they will also solicit remuneration. And in this you will do me a great service. Thus I await your generosity and Your Graces' decency ["primôr"], whose persons God Our Lord may protect for many happy years.
20 June 1721
Your Graces' very humble servant
António Soares.

Letter 2. Siam Resident Padre Francisco Teles to the Noble Senate of Macao, 28 June 1721.[65]

Lords of the Noble Senate. As there is presently no Captain General of the Bandel here in Siam and as the Lord Viceroy wrote in a letter commanding that the Superior of this House act in as much as his religious status allows, I received [notice] from Your Lordships via the Captain General that he was to serve the very illustrious and noble Senate to their best interests. In [those instructions] Your Lordships instructed me to ensure the prompt dispatch of the boats in order that the city could continue the commerce that it has historically undertaken with this kingdom. In this way I, together with Padre Antonio Soares, did as much as we could and we were only left with the feeling that we did not conclude business as we would have liked, as the same Padre Antonio Soares will notify you in greater detail. As far as the debt is concerned, it is still not completely paid off, as the Chinese estimate the goods that our Senate sent to be of lesser worth; such that a debt remains amounting to 21 catties and so-and-so taels. This is no doubt a result of the fact that this year there was great abundance of Chinese goods which this year arrived in Siam. As far as the *saguate* that the King of Siam is to send to the Noble Senate, according to the letter from the Phrakhlang which serves as reply to all those concerned according to the traditions of this land, it is to consist of twenty pieces of silk and fourteen of linen; however, I also heard after the letter was handed over that there will only be fifteen [pieces of silk], which Your Lordships must attribute to nothing other than negligence ["inadvertencia"] on the part of the person who translated the letter for me, as well as the great speed with which it was done; in such a way that there was no time to discover the mistake or negligence of my translator.

This letter finally is to serve in giving notice of how Cap.tam Manuel Vidigal Giam gave me a piece of black satin for the Captain General and how up till now I was unable to accept it on behalf of the Church, discounting that Your Lordships would take it away for good.

The only thing that remains is to express my hopes to serve the Most Noble and Illustrious Senate once again, which God may protect.
Siam, 28 June 1721.
From Your Lordships' Least Servant, Francisco Telles.

Letter 3. The City of Macao to Siam, 20 March 1720.[66]

Most Excellent Lord,

This our city of Macao and its residents find themselves owing many favours to His Most Serene Highness, which is the reason for which we are striving to show the continuity [*vinco*] of our thanks for the perpetual memory of, not least when in times of our greatest extremities it was His Highness, illuminated by God who, with the generosity of his spirit, lent us 650 catties of silver which went towards alleviating our troubles; such a generous act that only one like His Highness as such a great monarch could carry out. The repayment ["satisfação"] of this sum took place continually, this our Senate meeting every year as suited the calamities of those times, and on this occasion God allowed us to remit the rest which we were still owing, which amounts to almost 72 catties of silver, which are to travel in this boat given to the command of Captain Francisco Correia de Liger in [the shape of] 21 rolls of white silk of the first worm [an expression of quality] amounting to 179 taels, as well as 10 pieces of yellow damask costing 66 taels a bundle and 9 *condrins,* [hoping] it will be of use to His Excellency to whom we pray and declare that this repayment of His Highness's capital be presented to him. We are presenting our wishes to his Excellency as much to Himself as for a means ensuring His Majesty treat the ship, which is presently leaving this city to continue its commerce, with the same ancient benevolence that you used to treat our ships of Macao in the past. And we hope not to exceed the measure of the accustomed favour which in past times His Highness has shown us. We would also like to alert His Excellency that the same Captain is bringing a small tribute ["mimozinho"] constituted of eleven pieces, four in gold, and some coats-of-arms ["armerias"], which we ask Your Excellency to bring into the presence of His Highness, and deign to accept as a symbol of our affection and thanks. The same Captain Francisco Correa will pass on to His Excellency a demonstration of our affection, which we ask His Excellency to deign to accept, which would amount to five large pieces ["pessas"] [of silk], five jars of sweet pears, two jars of *broas* [a sweet, made with eggs, rice, and bread of maize] and two cakes. Nothing more is to be proferred than to wish His Excellency all the best with his trade and a pleasant journey for those who are about to make the journey there and will do so in the future and [to wish] all fortune and good favour.

May God grant His Excellency many years [of life]. Written at the aldermen's table, by me Manuel Pires de Moura Alferes and Scribe to the Chamber of this City.
20 March, 1720. António de Aguiar.

Letter 4. The Phrakhlang of Siam to the Noble Senate of Macao, June 1721.[67]

[To the] Very Illustrious and Noble Senate of Macao.

The present [letter] is to serve as notice of how much the Noble Senate continues to owe his Most High, and Powerful King of Siam, our Lord and Patron. This is to serve here to signify how Captain Manuel de Vidigal Gião consigned the gifts to His Majesty, which consisted of six pieces of mother-of-pearl damask, five pieces of yellow damask, another three pieces of mother-of-pearl damask, and two of yellow damask, four *Loôs* with golden threads, twelve *Tochas* [large candles, or firebrands], twelve catties of lozenges, and thirty jars of sweets. Besides this, he consigned a further seven mother-of-pearl damasks, eight yellow ones, three pieces of *Tabi,* twelve *Pivetes* [a kind of aromatic substance], and 22 jars of sweets for the Most Serene Prince.

His Royal Highness as indeed the Most Serene Prince greatly give praise to the Noble Senate for successfully remitting the said gifts. The Most High and Powerful King our Lord also deigned to send further things to the Noble Senate via the same carrier. The gifts of His Highness consist of six pieces of silk including *Melleques* and *Atalazes,* and fourteen including *Chitas Paquiãns* [a type of block-printed chintz], and cloths of Pafsatã, which amount to twenty pieces.[68] The Most Serene Prince also sends seven pieces of silk including Melleques and Atalazes, and 16 including chintzes ["chitas"], and other textiles of different types, which altogether amount to 23 pieces. These are the gifts of the most high and powerful King, and our Most Serene Prince to the Noble Senate of Macao, which altogether amount to 43 pieces, which Captain Manuel de Vidigal Giam will deliver.

We also give notice to the Most Illustrious and Noble Senate how the Most High and Powerful King our Spirit and Lord used his royal benevolence to pardon the duties owing the royal estate to each of the three boats which in this year of 1721 arrived at the Court of Siam, just as the Noble Senate requested in its letter, to which His Majesty responded by deducting that which is owing his royal ministers, as in fact occurred, which the bearer [of this letter] will be able to provide more information about; whom we have instructed that he is to inform every member of the Noble Senate that henceforth it is to continue its commerce, which in past times it conducted with this kingdom, and from our side will continue to be conducted. We will treat all those who make this journey with favour, as we have done this year, even if we did not grant everything that the Ten [Senate] requested, but the circumstances do not currently permit it.

This is to thank you for the present that the Very Illustrious and Noble Senate sent us, namely the five pieces of mother-of-pearl damask, the ten jars of sweets, and as a symbol of our thanks we will reciprocate by sending four *chitas* de Masulipatão and one white cloth of Pafsatã [*Bofetá*][69] to the Most Illustrious Senate, the offering of which we make also for the good friendship and correspondence of His Most High and Powerful King of Siam with the Most High and Powerful King of Portugal; and with this may God bless the most Illustrious and Noble Senate.

Made in this the court of the Kingdom of Siam on a Sunday the 14th of the New Moon, in the month *Du'anchôt hera* 1083 of the year *Pây Chulu' Trinisôc*. This the month of June 1721. From the Illustrious and Noble Senate's great friend Chau' Payâ, Sitamarât, Chau'Paya Praclâ, the Minister that governs foreigners, who is the same as his Excellency, the Lord Phrakhlang.

Notes

1 Edward Hutchinson, *Adventurers in Siam in the Seventeenth Century* (London: Royal Asiatic Society, 1940), pp. 192–93.

2 Anthony Reid, "Changing Perceptions of the 'Hermit Kingdoms' of Asia", in *Charting the Shape of Early Modern Southeast Asia* (Chiang Mai: Silkworm Books, 1999), pp. 235–45. See also Dhiravat na Pombejra, "Ayutthaya at the End of the Seventeenth Century: Was There a Shift to Isolation?", in *Southeast Asia in the Early Modern Era: Trade, Power and Belief*, edited by Anthony Reid (Ithaca, NY: Cornell University Press, 1993), pp. 250–72.

3 Fernão de Mendes Pinto, *Peregrinacam de Fernam Mendez Pinto, em que Da Conta de Muytas et Muyto Estranhas Cousas que Vio et Ouvio no Reyno da China, no da Tartaria, no do Sornau* (Lisbon: P. Crasbeeck, 1614), chap. 183, p. 234v ff.

4 "As Novas do Reyno de Sião", fol. 186, n.d., Biblioteca Nacional, Lisbon.

5 Kennon Breazeale, ed. and trans., "Memoirs of Pierre Poivre: The Thai Port of Mergui in 1745", *Journal of the Siam Society* 97 (2009): 193; E.M. Jacobs, *Merchant in Asia: The Trade of the Dutch East India Company during the Eighteenth Century* (Leiden: CNWS Publications, 2006), p. 211.

6 Jacobs, *Merchant in Asia*, p. 213.

7 Bhawan Ruangsilp, *Dutch East India Company Merchants at the Court of Ayutthaya: Dutch Perceptions of the Thai Kingdom, c. 1604–1765* (Leiden: Brill, 2007), p. 18.

8 See, for example, the preamble to Surachai Chumsriphan, "The Great Role of Jean-Louis Vey, Vicar of Siam (1875–1909), in the Church History of Thailand during the Reformation Period of King Rama V, the Great (1868–1910)" (Ph. D. dissertation, Pontificiae Universitatis Gregorianae, 1990), p. 37.

9 Ibid. Recent authorities such as David Wyatt, *Thailand: A Short History* (New Haven: Yale University Press, 1984), p. 126, prefer to refer to this king as Thai Sa. Cf. Dhiravat na Pombejra, "Princes, Pretenders and the Chinese Phrakhlang", in *On the Eighteenth Century as a Category of Asian History: Van Leur in Retrospect*, edited by Leonard Blussé and Femme Gaastra (Aldershot: Ashgate, 1998), pp. 114–20, where Thai politics are seen to take a Chinese turn.

10 Alexander Hamilton, *A New Account of the East Indies, Being the Observations and Remarks of Capt. Alexander Hamilton, Who Spent His Time There from the Year 1688 to 1723* (Edinburgh: J. Mosman, 1727), 2:196.

11 Sinnappah Arasaratnam, "Coromandel Trade, 1700–1740: Stagnation or Decline?" in *Merchants, Companies and Commerce on the Coromandel Coast, 1650–1740* (Delhi: Oxford University Press, 1986).

12 Bhawan Ruangsilp, who has just written a book about relations with the Dutch, explicitly pursues the pragmatist line of argument, using the concept of "conditional partnership" to remind us that the coexistence was not born of

authentic, original mutual respect, in *Dutch East India Company Merchants at the Court of Ayutthaya.* Despite assurances of "the firm and unchanging nature of his friendship", backed up by appeals to treat the Siamese "as [the French King's] enemies if they neglect to carry out his wishes", Europeans often railed at what they perceived as the fickle and treacherous nature of the Siamese and their king; see for example "Reply to M. de Chaumont", in E.W. Hutchinson, ed., "Four French State Manuscripts", *Journal of the Siam Society*, 27, no. 2 (1935): 220.

13 Stefan Halikowski Smith, *Creolization and Diaspora in the Portuguese Indies, 1640–1720: The Social World of Ayutthaya* (Leiden: Brill, 2011), pp. 32–35.

14 "As Novas do Reyno de Siam", fol. 186. I have transcribed this document in Appendix 12 of *Creolization and Diaspora in the Portuguese Indies.*

15 Henri Cordier, *Mélanges d'histoire et de géographie orientales*, vol. 4 (Paris: Jean Maisonneuve, 1923), pp. 11–13; Jean de Fontaney, *Lettres édifiantes et curieuses*, tome 17, new ed. (Paris: J.G. Merigot le Jeune, 1781), pp. 222–23.

16 Lettere dalla Cina, lap. Sin. 14, 2, fols. 263–64v, Archivum Romanum Societatis Iesu, Rome.

17 "Termo do Conselho Geral do Leal Senado sobre uma carta que o capitão-geral de Macau escreveu à Mesa da Câmara acerca do requerimento que lhe foi feito pelos capitães das naus do rei de Sião para se recolherem nesta cidade", *Arquivos de Macau,* 2nd ser., 1 no. 3 (April–May 1941): 157–58.

18 Ibid.

19 Ibid., pp. 275–76.

20 For Saldanha's embassy, see John Wills Jr., *Embassies and Illusions: Dutch and Portuguese Envoys to K'ang-hsi 1666–1687* (Cambridge, MA: Harvard University Press, 1984); 100,000 taels was the value ascribed the cargo of two Macanese cargo ships with up to 300 nautical tonnes carrying capacity each; see Tana Li, *Nguyên Cochinchina: Southern Vietnam in the Seventeenth and Eighteenth Centuries*, (Ithaca, NY: Southeast Asia Program Publications, 1998).

21 Embaixada de China, Historical Archives of Goa (hereafter cited as HAG) 1210, fols. 28–33, HAG, Panaji, Goa; see also João Feliciano Marques Pereira, ed., "Uma resurreição histórica (paginas ineditas d'um visitador dos jesuitas, 1665–1671)", *Ta-Ssi-Yang-Kuo: Archivos e Annaes do Extremo-Oriente Portuguez,* 1st–2nd ser. (Lisbon: Antiga Livraria Bertrand – José Bastos, 1899–1903), 2: 755–56; Cartas Patentes e Alvarás, 44, fols. 36v–37, 29 April 1667, HAG; and Assentos do Conselho da Fazenda, 11, fols. 108v–109, 27 April 1667, HAG. The loan became a very controversial issue in Macanese politics, the local populace enraged that the captains-general asked for loans but left office before paying them off, leading to a situation in which the city itself suffered a "notavel detrimento em seu credito" (notable detriment to its credit). The Proceedings of the State Council of Goa henceforth decided that the city itself was to give its *concentimento* (consent) before loans were contracted, and Governor Simão Gomes da Silva was instructed to "dar inteira satisfação" (give complete satisfaction)

before leaving Macao; see Assentos do Conselho da Fazenda, 27 April 1667. The loan, however, had still not been paid off by 30 January 1687, at which point the Senado da Câmara in Macao decided henceforth to reserve one per cent of its revenue for that purpose; see "Termo do Conselho Geral do Leal Senado", pp. 147–48.

22 Correspondência recebida e expedida, 319, Leal Senado, 1 July 1716, fols. 115–15v, Arquivos de Macau, Macao. "Carta das autoridades de Sião para Manuel Favacho acerca da dívida do Leal Senado para com o dito reino", *Arquivos de Macau*, 3rd ser., 6, no. 1 (July 1966): 15–16.

23 See João Vicente Melo, "The Sagoate: Diplomacy and Gift Exchange in the Eighteenth-Century Estado da Índia", paper presented at the 13th International Seminar on Indo-Portuguese History, Aix-en-Provence, France, 24 March 2010.

24 Paulo Miguel Martins, *Percorrendo o Oriente: A Vida de António de Albuquerque Coelho (1682–1745)*, (Lisbon: Livros Horizonte, 1998), p. 59.

25 Charles R. Boxer, "The One-Armed Governor", in *Fidalgos in the Far East, 1550–1770*, 2nd rev. ed., reprinted with corrections (Hong Kong: Oxford University Press, 1968); and C.R. Boxer, "A Fidalgo in the Far East: Antonio de Albuquerque Coelho in Macao", *Far Eastern Quarterly* 5, no. 4 (1946): 387–410. For Aguiar, see Letter 3 in the Documentary Appendices of this chapter.

26 Boxer, *Fidalgos in the Far East*, pp. 166–68.

27 Hamilton, *A New Account of the East Indies*, 2: 218.

28 Ibid., 2: 211; see also António da Silva Rego, *O Ultramar Português no Século XVIII (1700–1833)*, (Lisbon: Agência Geral do Ultramar, 1967).

29 Rego, *O Ultramar Português*, p. 107.

30 For the Cochinchinese negotiations and follow-through, see Anders [Andrew] Ljungstedt, *An Historical Sketch of the Portuguese Settlements in China and of the Roman Catholic Church and Mission in China* (Boston: John Munroe, 1836), p. 127. For Placidus, see Pietro Antonio da Venezia, *Giardino Serafico Istorico fecondo di Fiori e Frutti di Virtù di Zelo e di Santità nelli trè Ordini Instituiti da S. Francesco*, (Venice: Lovisa, 1710), 1: 100; see also Stanisław Kleczewski, *Kalendarz seraficzny zamykaiący w sobie zywoty wielebnych Sług Boskich Zakonu S.O. Franciszka Reformatów Polskich Osobliwą Swiątobliwoscią znamienitych. Przez X. Stanisława Kleczewskiego, tegoż Zakonu Kapłana zebrany, Dla pożytku Wiernych, y nasladowania cnoty Do Druku podany* (Lwow: I.K.M. y Bractwa Swętej Troycy, 1760), p. 12.

31 "[T]he same privileges as before, and to not pay any duties whatsoever were what was agreed by the Siamese kings in 1616, on the occasion of a solemn embassy sent from Goa to this kingdom, as can be read in *Asia Portugueza*, tome 3, parte 39, cap. 19, nos. 6 and 7, which Your Graces should, indeed must see." This reference is to António Bocarro, *Década 13 da História da India* (Lisbon: Typographia da Academia Real das Sciencias, 1876 [written before 1642]), chap. 118, p. 524.

32 Padre António Soares, Company of Jesus, to the Noble Senate [of Macao], 20 June 1721, published in *Arquivos de Macau*, 1st ser., 1, no. 3 (August 1929): 157–61. See Documentary Appendices, Letter 1, in this chapter.

33 Boxer, *Fidalgos in the Far East*, p. 10. It should be said that Macao typically levied 7 per cent duties on incoming merchandise during the eighteenth century (5 per cent went to royal coffers, 2 per cent went towards supporting the Misericórdia and the Convent of Santa Clara); see António Martins do Vale, "Macau: Uma 'república de mercadores' ", in *Espaços de um Império: Estudos*, ed. Mafalda Soares da Cunha (Lisbon: Commissão Nacional dos Descobrimentos, 1999), p. 210.

34 For the 1684 embassy to the Court of St James, see M.L. Manich Jumsai, *A History of Anglo-Thai Relations* (Bangkok: Chalermnit, 1970), pp. 2–3. Bèze reports that at the entrance to the camp the Portuguese erected a cross upon which "is engraved the terms of the concession, as a permanent memorial of the rights acquired by the King of Portugal"; see Claude de Bèze, *Mémoire du Père de Bèze sur la vie de Constance Phaulkon, premier ministre du Roi de Siam, Phra Narai, et sa triste fin: Suivi de lettres et de documents* (Tokyo: Presses Salésiennes, 1947), p. 40.

35 Michael Smithies, ed., *Alexander Hamilton: A Scottish Sea Captain in South-East Asia, 1689–1723* (Chiang Mai: Silkworm Books, 1997), pp. 174–81; see also William Foster, *The English Factories in India, 1618–1669: A Calendar of Documents in the India Office, British Museum and Public Record Office*, vol. 1 (Oxford: Clarendon Press, 1906), p. xxxi.

36 For a description of the religious activities of the Jesuits in Siam in this period, see Phillip Sibin, *Brieff Defz Ehrw. Paters Philippus Sibin Aufs der Gesellschafft JESU, An Ihro Churfürstl. Durchl. zu Cöllen &c. &c.* (Cölln, 1737). Sibin was a Jesuit from the Province of the Lower Rhine visiting in 1724. See also Pietro Cerutti, "The Jesuits in Thailand: Part I, 1607–1767", Society of Jesus Thailand <http://www.sjthailand.org/english/historythai1.htm> (accessed 29 November 2009).

37 Simon de la Loubère, *A New Historical Relation of the Kingdom of Siam* (London: Printed by F.L. for Tho. Horne ... Francis Saunders ... and Tho. Bennet, 1693), 3: 108.

38 This statement refers to a declaration by Braym Beça and forms the point of departure for an article I have written, "'The Friendship of Kings Was in the Ambassadors': Portuguese Diplomatic Embassies in Asia and Africa during the Sixteenth and Seventeenth Centuries", in *Portuguese Studies* 22, no. 1 (2006): 101–34.

39 La Loubère, *A New Historical Relation*, 3: 108.

40 There is a picture of this *balon* in *Descriptions of Old Siam*, edited by Michael Smithies (Kuala Lumpur: Oxford University Press, 1995), p. 45.

41 Soares to the Noble Senate, 20 June 1721 (see Appendices, Letter 1).

42 *Dagregister Van Vliet*, 16 April 1639, fols. 868–69, VOC 1131, Nationaal Archief, The Hague, Netherlands.

43 Ibid. In neighbouring Cambodia, the *chakri* is considered the "minister of war"; see David P. Chandler, *A History of Cambodia* (Boulder, CO: Westview Press, 2008), p. 114.

44 The "lo" (羅) as defined in Robert Henry Mathews, *Chinese-English Dictionary*, rev. ed. (Cambridge, MA: Harvard University Press, 1943) is a "gauze, a thin kind of silk"; see also Lillian M. Li, *China's Silk Trade: Traditional Industry in the Modern World, 1842–1937* (Cambridge, MA: Council on East Asian Studies, Harvard University, 1981), p. 278.

45 Tabi, or Tabbee was a medium-quality fabric, of pure silk or mixed with a weft of waste silk and flax; see Luca Molà, *The Silk Industry of Renaissance Venice* (Baltimore: The Johns Hopkins University Press, 2000), p. 408.

46 Alfons van der Kraan, "On Company Business: The Rijckloff van Goens Mission to Siam, 1650", *Itinerario,* 22, pt. 2 (1998): 42.

47 Luigi Bressan and Michael Smithies, *Siam and the Vatican in the Seventeenth Century* (Bangkok: River Books, 2001). The list from Chaumont specifies: "Two Chinese ladies, each of them on a peacock, carrying in their hands a small silver cup, enamelled, the peacocks by turning a spring walk on a table, according to the way they are placed, the cups staying upright in their hands. Two Chinese horsemen carrying in their hands two small cups, who walk by a motion of springs, all of silver in the Chinese fashion", and "Two silver covers, Japan work, which had a motion by a spring, and carry each of them a small cup". Michael Smithies, ed., *Aspects of the Embassy to Siam, 1685: The Chevalier de Chaumont and the Abbé de Choisy* (Chiang Mai: Silkworm Books, 1997), pp. 137–49.

48 Cf. the gifts in Alfons van der Kraan, "On Company Business", pp. 42–84.

49 Soares to the Noble Senate, 20 June 1721 (see Appendices, Letter 1).

50 Leonor de Seabra, *The Embassy of Pero Vaz de Siqueira (1684–1686)*, (Macao: Instituto Português do Oriente and Fundação Oriente, 2005).

51 Macao's seminaries were among the best in the Catholic world, attracting not just Portuguese but Italians, Frenchmen and Germans in equal measure. The four-tiered stone Madre de Deus college founded by the Jesuits in Macao in 1593 became one of the city's most splendid keystones; today only the façade remains. For a seventeenth-century description of the college, see Peter Mundy, *The Travels of Peter Mundy in Europe and Asia, 1608–1687,* edited by Richard Carnac Temple and Lavinia Mary Antsey (London: Hakluyt Society, 1919), pp. 162–63.

52 "O comercio desta cidade de Macao com a Cochinchina foy o meyo pello qual a providencia e bondade Divina quiz que se dilatace a nossa Santa Fé", *Arquivos de Macau,* 1st ser. (December 1929): 355.

53 Jean Burnay, "Notes chronologiques sur les missions Jésuites du Siam au XVIIe siècle", *Archivum Historicum Societatis Iesu* 43, no. 22 (1953): 191.

54 "Actus Sociorum Prouinciae Japoniae per loca, et official confectus", Jap./Sin. 25, fol. 249, Japonica-Sinica collection, Archivum Romanum Societatis Iesu, Rome.

55 Ferdinand Llanes, "Food Crisis of 1718: Siam Rice, Diplomacy and Reforms", *Philippine Daily Inquirer,* 10 May 2008; and Ferdinand Llanes, "New Knowledge in an Old Account: The Bustamante Diplomatic Mission to Ayudhya, 1718", (Ph.D. dissertation, University of the Philippines, 2005). The primary sources for this mission are principally Fray Juan Francisco de San Antonio, *Cronicas de la Provincia de San Gregorio Magno* (1738–44). Sections of this have been translated into English as *The Philippine Chronicles of Fray San Antonio: A Translation from the Spanish,* edited by Pedro Picornell (Manila: Casalinda, 1977), and as "A Royal Reception of Spaniards from the Philippines", in Smithies, *Descriptions of Old Siam,* pp. 102–5.

56 Joaquin Martínez de Zúñiga, *História de las Islas Philipinas* (Manila: Impreso en Sampoloc, 1803), pp. 443 and 469. See also Rosario Mendoza Cortes, *Pangasinan, 1572–1800,* (Quezon City: University of the Philippines Press, 1974), p. 170.

57 See Jean-Baptiste Nolin's painting of Chaumont's audience with King Naraï, 18 October 1685, commissioned by Chaumont.

58 Bhaskar Jyoti Bask, "The Trading World of Coromandel and the Crisis of the 1730s", in *Proceedings of the Indian History Congress, Forty-Second Session, Magadh University, Bodhgaya, 1981* (New Delhi: Indian History Congress, 1982), pp. 333–39; and Sanjay Subrahmanyam, "Asian Trade and European Affluence? Coromandel, 1650–1740", *Modern Asian Studies* 22, no. 1 (1988): 179–88.

59 Jean Baptiste Pallegoix, *Description du Royaume Thai ou Siam: comprenant la topographie, histoire naturelle, moeurs et coutumes, legislation, commerce, industrie, langue, littérature, religion, annales des Thai et précis historique de la mission: avec cartes et gravures* (Paris, 1854; repr., Farnborough: Gregg International Publishers, 1969), 2: 208.

60 Cited in Adrien Launay, *Histoire de la mission de Cochinchine, 1658–1823: Documents historiques,* vol. 2, *1728–1771* (Paris: Charles Douniol et Réteaux, Tequi successeurs, 1924), p. 354.

61 Howard Tyrrell Fry, *Alexander Dalrymple (1737–1808) and the Expansion of British Trade* (London: Routledge, 1970).

62 For more on the popular uprisings in the period, see John Leddy Phelan, *Hispanization of the Philippines* (Madison: University of Wisconsin Press, 1967), pp. 136–52; Cortes, *Pangasinan,* pp. 145–222; and Juan de la Concepción, *Historia General de Philipinas,* vol. 9 (Manila: Imprenta del Seminar de San Carlos, 1790), 205 ff.

63 Soares to the Noble Senate, 20 June 1721 (see Appendices, Letter 1).

64 This term is mysterious, and means "the black boy". Probably it refers to the offspring of one of the many passing Dutch officials through the *logie,* one of the many *mestiços* (individuals of mixed race) in the Ayutthayan world. Dhiravat na Pombejra, "VOC Employees and Their Relationships with Mon and Siamese Women", in *Other Pasts: Women, Gender and History in Early Modern Southeast Asia,* edited by Barbara Watson Andaya (Honolulu: Center for Southeast Asian Studies, 2000), pp. 195–215.

[65] Francisco Telles to the Noble Senate of Macao, 28 June 1721, published in *Arquivos de Macau,* 1st ser., 1, no. 3 (Aug. 1929): 165.

[66] The City of Macao to Siam, 20 March 1720, published in *Arquivos de Macau,* 1st ser., 1, no. 3 (August 1929): 151–52.

[67] The Phrakhlang of Siam to the Noble Senate of Macao, June 1721, published in *Arquivos de Macau,* 1st ser., 1, no. 3 (August 1929): 163–64.

[68] None of these textiles appears in "The Grouped List and the Glossary of Indian Textile Types", in K.N. Chaudhuri, *The Trading World of Asia and the English East India Company, 1660–1760* (Cambridge: Cambridge University Press, 1978), app. 4, pp. 500–505, or in Tapan Raychaudhuri, *Jan Company in Coromandel, 1605–1690* (The Hague: Martinus Nijhoff, 1962), app. C, "A Note on Some Varieties of Coromandel Cloth".

[69] A cotton cloth defined by Dalgado's *Glossário Luso-Asiático* as "muito fino e tapado" (very fine and dense), produced principally in Baroche; see Diogo do Couto and others, *Décadas na Asia*, vol. 1, *Décadas IV e V* (Lisboa Occidental: Officina de Domingos Gonsalves, 1736), p. 7.

5

CONTINUITIES IN BENGAL'S CONTACT WITH THE PORTUGUESE AND ITS LEGACY: A COMMUNITY'S FUTURE ENTANGLED WITH THE PAST

Ujjayan Bhattacharya

Cross-cultural interactions were a significant feature of the sixteenth-century phase of Portuguese expansion. Sanjay Subrahmanyam, who has extensively examined this theme, suggests viewing this phenomenon as "a part of the history of the Portuguese presence in maritime Asia at a time when Portugal was itself under Habsburg rule", that is, the late sixteenth and early seventeenth centuries.[1] One may recall the individual prototypes who exemplified such cross-cultural interactions, namely, Felipe de Brito e Nicote, governor of Syriam in the early seventeenth century, and Gabriel Quiroga de San Antonio in Cambodia at the end of the sixteenth century. This chapter will argue that, if cross-cultural interactions in Portuguese settlements were characteristic of this expansive phase, the inversion of it, implying inward-looking tendencies, was its trait in the phase of imperial decline and contraction.

I contend that cross-cultural interactions were vibrant and vigorous so long as the Portuguese remained a dynamic power in colonization, maritime commerce, and political and diplomatic affairs. Once maritime links weakened or snapped, and the Portuguese developed an inclination to become more territorially based, interactions *within* cultures, rather than ones *across* cultures, found more intensity. Cross-cultural interactions abated or waned, and a process of narrowing down the ambit of the foreign culture set in, as the Portuguese identity absorbed local or native traits unto itself. Territorial or maritime extensions of Portuguese Asia were dependent on strategic and political factors, and the diversities that it could include were variables set by the degree of hegemony it could assert. Once that hegemony fell apart, the same niches of Portuguese existence could no longer be described as parts of "Portuguese Asia", but rather as "Portuguese-speaking spaces".

Subrahmanyam's argument, intended for a completely different purpose, has been taken here in its broadest implication to demonstrate processes within the shrinking spaces of Portuguese Asia. Subrahmanyam argues that there was a process in operation as of the sixteenth century that produced a "trans-cultural" synthesis.[2] However, such a synthesis could only be possible while "Portuguese Asia" was expanding, not while it was struggling to survive and conceding physical space to its rivals. By the eighteenth century, the empire was militarily weakened and the white Eurasian population had failed to "reproduce itself in adequate numbers" all over Portuguese Asia.[3] Thus a weakening of linkages and the collapse of the imperial structure produced Indo-Portuguese culture(s) within local settings. I would like to call this phenomenon the *parochialization of an erstwhile imperial culture* that produced identity tensions in a later period.

THE HISTORIOGRAPHY OF THE PORTUGUESE IN DECINE

The historiography of the Portuguese maritime empire raises critical questions regarding its political and economic strength in the post-expansion period, such as whether the Estado da Índia could, in this period, affect or alter the position or status of its distant settlements; whether the "frontier milieu" character of distant settlements was equally applicable as an idea for all outposts; and how vivacious and continuous Portuguese maritime commerce was. To these, one may add questions: how strong was the contact of these settlements with Lisbon?; did the ecclesiastical domain became the focal point of these settlements instead of the politico-juridical one?; and what was the relation between the two? The last point has some significance in light of the statement by António Bocarro in the mid-seventeenth century that "now that trade is almost extinct, the only sense it [Portuguese Asia] has through this [is] Christianity", implying that religion and congregations would be the central focus of the communities' attention.[4]

A number of factors contributed to narrowing down the Portuguese presence into small hubs of minuscule communities and to the formation of an Indo-Portuguese society with varied features. One would do well to remember that Portuguese India from the second half of the seventeenth century bore a frontier character and had a low demographic trend that had important consequences for the composition of the population. Bengal was almost literally a frontier for the Portuguese, and the dictum of C.R. Boxer is applicable here. According to Boxer, "this frontier milieu of continuous warfare, which lasted with few intermissions until the end of the eighteenth century, helps to explain why so few Portuguese women went out to India in comparison with men; and why peasants emigrating voluntarily from Portugal ... preferred to take their chances in Brazil."[5]

In the seventeenth century, the Portuguese maritime position had been severely undermined by the Dutch and the Omani on sea and by the Marathas on land.[6] The impact of this changing situation was felt in myriad ways. First, maritime careers were offering fewer prospects for profit and advancement while greater importance accrued to settled, land-based professions and economic activities like small trade and skilled workmanship.[7] An indirect and perhaps normal result of this was migration, but the Portuguese encountered the phenomenon of migration in graver forms as well, such as desertion from the ranks of the army. Thus the second impact, namely demographic imbalance, was acutely felt when there was a shortfall in the number of male Europeans ready to take up arms against hostile attacks by the enemies. The reason for such dwindling numbers was desertion, as pointed out by Boxer, and according to him it reached a crescendo from 1650 to 1750.[8] The third impact of the changing conditions in Portuguese Asia was a landward reorientation in the policy of the Estado.[9] Goa became the territorial *cum* cultural nucleus of the "Portuguese" populace of South Asia, rather than a satellite location of an extensive thalassocracy based in Portugal. This fact had great significance for the native ethnic *mestiços* (individuals of mixed race), as they were identified with the region, language and customs of the place of their birth, rather than distant centres of imperial power.

Holden Furber once stated that "nationality stopped east of Cape", and Kenneth McPherson, following this line of argument, demonstrated that an aspect of the development of the Indo-Portuguese society in the subcontinent, particularly in coastal regions to the east of Cape Comorin, was its connection with the British.[10] McPherson argued on very strong grounds that Portuguese private commercial enterprise continued in the zone east of Cape Comorin, particularly with the cooperation of the British, from Madras and Calcutta.[11] To him the question of defining the "Portuguese", in terms of their origin, was quite irrelevant, because the term was not defined by the English themselves in any strict manner. Discrimination on grounds of colour did not come into play if a concerned "Portuguese" had acquired status. Far from being relegated to the "bounds of decayed mestiço communities", the "post-Estado Portuguese life" was continuous and active in the commercial domain of eighteenth-century Asia. This study seeks to confirm this point through the presentation of further data regarding their presence in Bengal.

M.N. Pearson gave a rough sketch of the development of *mestiço* society through its linkages with trade and professions. Pearson argued that the usual participants and beneficiaries of trade in the eighteenth century were not the Portuguese state or the Portuguese-born people, but "a few local Portuguese, quite a number of mestiços, and especially Indians resident in Portuguese India, and usually citizens of Portugal".[12] Pearson noted that "Portuguese India's traders filled in some gaps, operating within and without the British-dominated Indian Ocean trade of the nineteenth century".[13] Pearson's general point is that though Portuguese India — which includes all the settlements that had existed under Portugal's control — did not contribute at all to the trade of the Portuguese empire in the eighteenth and nineteenth centuries, "its inhabitants participated in a quite flourishing Indian Ocean trade", and he makes a special mention of the "Portuguese" of Bengal — 20,000 by a late seventeenth-century estimate — who played "some role in the trade of the Bay of Bengal and also worked as artisans, soldiers, and petty traders."[14]

An important question that can be raised is whether the Portuguese imperial dream, especially in the eastern Indian Ocean region, was revived or was being given a fresh lease on life at that time. Jorge Manuel Flores in his article "Relic or Springboard? A Note on the 'Rebirth' of Portuguese Hughli, ca. 1632–1820",[15] considers the history of the Portuguese in eighteenth-century Bengal as that of an active field or a "springboard" from which actions could be launched, rather than as static history of a surviving "relic" that waited passively for the changes of history to occur. Along with this, a lingering imperial dream of the Portuguese also survived for some time.

An important component of British commercial domination in the region was collaboration with the Portuguese, which was true, as McPherson has shown, not only for Coromandel but also for Bengal. But this collaboration was weighted very heavily in favour of the British. The Anglo-Portuguese Methuen Treaty of 1703 is cited as the cause behind the success of trade collaboration between the two nations in Asia, but Boxer states that it was primarily intended to keep the way open for accrual of English advantages in the re-export trade in the Atlantic.[16] The asymmetry in economic relations was also reflected in political relations when later it was repeatedly suggested that the Indo-Portuguese territories be amalgamated with the British Indian empire.[17]

Between the sixteenth century and the eighteenth there had been a shift in the balance of power in favour of Europeans who could demonstrate their superiority, not only on the seas but also on land and in the dominance of politics territorially on the Indian subcontinent. These Europeans had greater access to capital, a point that McPherson has emphasized. Thus the combination of economic and political power together gave the newly arrived Europeans a sense of superiority, mastery and power that allowed them to create distances between rulers and subjects, which included Luso-Indians.[18] Thus, the gradual acceptance of the British Raj by the Portuguese as loyal subjects, with all attendant anxieties regarding original identity, involved recognition of the fact that the British were the first Europeans to have defeated an Indian power.

THE PORTUGUESE IN BENGAL DURING THE EIGHTEENTH CENTURY

The Portuguese settlement at Hugli capitulated to the Mughal forces after a three-month siege in 1632. The following year, however, they were rehabilitated at the same site. Between 1633 and the end of the seventeenth century, the relation between the settlement and the Portuguese imperial structure operating from Lisbon was rather uncertain. Sanjay Subrahmanyam has pointed out that, in the third quarter of the seventeenth century, Lisbon seemed to have completely forgotten this region (not only Bengal but Coromandel too), which had been a crucial component of its territorial scheme during the Habsburg period. For Hugli, however, there is some evidence that suggests that even in this period the internal administrative structure of the settlement was being remotely supervised from Goa. Subrahmanyam has also shown that in 1665 "the Christians", numbering 6,000, residing in Bandel of Hugli, made a representation before the viceroy of Goa, António de Castro Melo, to elect several officers in different positions like captain, justices of the peace, administrator of the orphans and so forth, all of which until then were managed by a single person. He also mentions that occasional references to names of officers in position during the period also occur. In 1667 Francisco Cabreira de Seixas held the position of captain at the same time when the legendary merchant of Bandel, João Gomes de Soto, was actively pursuing his trade and philanthropic activities.

The principal landmark of Bandel — the "village" immediately adjoining Hugli — is the Convento da Virgem Nossa Senhora de Rosário, which suffered the onslaught of the Mughal attack in 1633 and later was pulled down by settlers in 1640.[19] It was rebuilt by Gomes de Soto and his wife in 1661, and they buried their kin and relations there. Settlements of the English, the Dutch and the Portuguese — Hugli, Chinsura and Bandel, respectively — together were "distinct names for what may be called one city". Chandernagore, the French settlement established in 1673 and built as an elegant colony, was adorned with many fine buildings.

It was here, at Chandernagore, that we find a replay of the ecclesiastical politics of south India, involving the missionaries of the Capuchin and Augustinian orders, the Congregation of Propaganda Fide, the Padroado of Lisbon and Goa and — the ultimate ecclesiastical authority — the pope. J.H. da Cunha Rivara has referred to this period as that of "notorious" politics when ministers of the Congregation of Propaganda Fide were usurping church prerogatives until the pope put an end to it and entrusted those to the care of bishops and diocesan clergy.[20] Chandernagore's ecclesiastical domain was a contested matter between the powerful Augustinians of Bandel, who were parish priests of the town, until the bishop of Mylapore invested the Jesuits with the power of a special parish in 1696 and confirmed it after 1726.[21] But it was later that the Capuchins, who were charged by the Congregation with the duty of spreading religion in south India, involved the Mylapore diocese in wrangles. Nevertheless, they succeeded in entrenching their mission at Chandernagore against opposition by Augustinians, whose powers by then had been reduced through the intercession of political and ecclesiastical powers. The main opposition to the entry of agents of the Congregation came from the Augustinians, who were represented by Friar Francisco da Purificação.[22]

The Augustinians of Bandel, perhaps as a result of an exaggerated estimation of their own strength, had defied the authority of the diocese of Mylapore and were placed under interdict by Bishop Dom Francisco Laynes (a Portuguese cleric who died at Chandernagore in 1715).[23] With the Augustinians' power eclipsed, the Capuchins, who were under severe restriction of activities in the south due to an interdict by Cardinal Tournon,[24] made an inroad to Chandernagore and sought, between 1714 and 1726, interventions by the pope, the king of Portugal and the viceroy of Goa to open a chapel and oratory at this place. The English, who were favourably disposed towards the Capuchins, later regretted their decision and instead suspected them of being French agents. With this turn of events, one might say that the position of Bandel as a settlement and its ecclesiastical standing had been considerably affected and almost challenged by the rise of Chandernagore as a political, commercial and ecclesiastical centre of Catholic France. The Jesuits — who held spiritual charge at Chandernagore after 1726 — and the Capuchins were Catholics, but by the mid-eighteenth century they were also beyond the control of the Portuguese Padroado.[25]

Thus the Portuguese "traded simply as natives at their ancient settlement of Bandel, to the north of Hugli"; so said S.C. Hill while introducing European settlements in the mid-eighteenth century to the reader.[26] But their trade was on a footing that was different from European companies. In fact, when the *nawab* insisted that the English give up the benefits of the *farmān* (royal decree or charter) conferred by the Mughals, he intended to reduce them to the status of the Portuguese and Armenians.[27] The French distinguished the Bandel Portuguese from Europeans, but kept their identity distinct from natives. Usually referred to as *topasses*, meaning the offspring of Portuguese men and South Asian women,[28] such Portuguese numbered 105 at Chandernagore.[29] The French connection with the Portuguese was revealed when it was found that the *topasses* in Nawab Murshidabad's employ were commanded by a French renegade.[30] The French and the Portuguese served as gunners in the *nawab*'s army, particularly for the Cossimbazar cannons.[31] During the siege of Calcutta by Nawab Siraj-ud-daulah in 1756, these gunners seemed to be the most dreaded threat to the English, and thus the intercession of the Christian priests was sought to neutralize them. It was conveyed to the Cossimbazar Portuguese that it was contrary to their religious tenets to take up "arms in service of the Moors against Christians."[32]

The English had their share of Portuguese connections too, and probably the most important turn of events in the history of the Portuguese *descendentes* (descendants) in Bengal was their migration to Calcutta, which began with the establishment of the town as an English settlement. It is believed that Portuguese and Armenians began to migrate to Calcutta from Bandel around the same time as the families of traditional businessmen like Setts and Basaks came to town.[33] Writing in 1756, William Tooke explained the rising number of Portuguese (and Armenians) to be a result of the policy of the *zamindar* of the English East India Company (EEIC), John Zephaniah Holwell, to bring "every Portugueze, Armenian and others not born of European parents but in the country … under his zamindarry [the office or jurisdiction of a *zamindar*, a superintendent of lands in a district]" for the purpose of enhancing the power of his *cutcherry* (revenue collection office or court of justice) over those "who were deemed Christians, let them be of whatsoever denomination", and who were not excluded from the company's jurisdiction like the "Mogul's subjects", who were "understood by the Company's Charter should be excluded from having recourse to our Courts".[34] In fact it was Tooke's argument that this policy was flawed because it looked for revenue maximization and extension of control rather than promoting the collaborative interests of a trading settlement. Tooke lamented that the merchants of Calcutta "neglected by us ... took all measures of encouraging the Danes ... as well as the Portuguese ... supplying them plentifully with whatever they want".[35]

Thus relations with the English were marked by a deficit of trust and ambivalence right from the beginning. The most glaring instance of this occurred after the siege of 1756, when rumours of war with the French began circulating among the Portuguese of Calcutta, whom the English thought were friends of the former, as they were Catholics.[36] The council decided to prohibit the public exercise of Catholicism and turned the priests out of Calcutta. They were employed in the EEIC's army as militia, but it was felt that they had behaved badly during the siege of 1756[37] by making it a condition that their families should be admitted into the fort if they were required to fight,[38] and by refusing to come out and fight when they were called.[39] The company's army had 3,000 *topasses* from Madras,[40] but Drake's testimony says that they numbered about 180 and were "extremely awkward at their arms". This dispirited Portuguese militia, without food and water, disappeared at the time of the siege when the *nawab* allowed them to go free,[41] and M. Renault reported that about 3,000 half-castes and Portuguese reached Chandernagore as refugees.[42]

Despite the inexactness of the number of people involved, one can say that the Portuguese presence in Calcutta in the mid-eighteenth century was substantial, irrespective of their origin or the nature of their employment. The population was also a circulating one among Calcutta, Bandel and Chandernagore, but not Chinsurah, which was under Dutch control. However, their social condition was precarious and their identity as Europeans generally recognized as marginal. Otherwise they were seen as a floating and mercenary population without much commitment to a cause or a contract that could turn adverse. But their European identity seemed particularly dangerous to new European masters when they were found in the company of the latter's enemies, as in the case of a suspected Portuguese liaison with the *nawab* or the French. In this characterization, the prejudiced representation of the Portuguese by nineteenth-century admirers of the British Indian Raj and its culture definitely had a role to play.[43] In their perception, the Portuguese were no longer foreigners to the British, but a part of the multitude of subjects in British India, who were divided into many groups.[44]

A steady stream of immigration into Calcutta from adjoining areas that the British later called Lower Bengal can be surmised, but there is no serial data to confirm this assumption. The view emerging from Calcutta through the *Complete Monumental Registers,* the *Compendius Eccelsiastical Chronological*

Sketches, and the *Historical and Ecclesiastical Sketches,* between 1815 and 1831, was a reconstructed narrative of the Portuguese arrival in Bengal and Calcutta, which was placed within the general conspectus of the narrative regarding the arrival of the Portuguese in India.[45] It sought to give the impression that a demographic shift in the characteristically itinerant Portuguese population had occurred, from initially being concentrated in Bandel and Hugli to being relocated to Calcutta, due to what might be called the "pull factor" exerted by that up-and-coming city. However, this narrative is devoid of any empirical historical evidence. Instead, this contemporary reconstruction of events began with the arrival of Job Charnock at Calcutta in the early 1690s and thereafter followed a trail of factual detail regarding religious matters in the city, which was avowedly the purpose for which the texts were compiled. But incidentally it also provided information about persons who were important in the world of trade and Calcutta's civic life.

The history of the beginnings of Portuguese religious activity in Calcutta is the same as the history of ecclesiastical establishments there. It began with the erection of a chapel "of mats and straw" by the friars of the Order of Saint Augustine of Bandel, which very quickly developed into a brick chapel that was later enlarged by 1720 under the direction of Friar Francisco da Assumpção at the expense of Mrs Sebastian Shaw. Ecclesiastical administration was directed from Goa and Mylapore, but there seemed to be a conflict of interest between those nominated by them and the inhabitants of Calcutta. The Portuguese community as a whole resisted Goa's control in these matters and, through the intervention of the bishop of Mylapore, retained a hold over the management of funds. But because the wardens were appointed in perpetuity, the interests of the inhabitants were affected, and thus a conflict ensued which was settled through the courts.

Rather than a simple history of Christian ecclesiastical establishments of Calcutta, this dispute is a history of participation in civic life by members of the civil society of Calcutta, which included the Portuguese and their religious establishment. Through this narrative, we come to know some of the energetic personalities involved in civic community action, through their participation in philanthropy, charity and donations to religious institutions. Religion served as an ideological guide for their actions that were in effect directed towards community welfare. Their material basis was collaborative trade, and in this enterprise two siblings among the Portuguese of Bengal stood out prominently. They were the "two opulent brothers Mr. Joseph Barretto and Mr. Luis Barretto, [who] stepped forward and shewed the same zeal as Gomes de Soto", implying that they were as successful in business as in philanthropic activities.

From the English, for whom trade was a more venerable activity than mercenary soldiering, the successful Portuguese traders and collaborators received greater respect. To this were added respectable civic activities as mentioned earlier, which placed individuals like the Barrettos in a higher social stratum than those innocent souls who, through no fault of their own, drew the most unpleasant scorn from English authors of the Raj vintage.[46]

Manuel de Rosário, who authored the dedication to the Barrettos after Luis's death, held that enterprise, philanthropy and illustrious lineage made them comparable to models of virtue like Gomes de Soto.[47] According to Rosário, the Barretto family came very early to Asia. Manuel Teles Barreto arrived in 1505, in the fleet with Admiral "Lopez Suarez".[48] Their distinguished line included, according to Rosário, two governors of the Estado da Índia in the sixteenth century and one patriarch-designate of Ethiopia in the middle of the sixteenth century: "Such were the Asian heads of this high, favoured, and munificent family, that we now see founding and endowing Churches in Bengal."[49] The new church at Calcutta was called The Virgin Mary of the Rosary. Joseph Barretto was the benefactor of a few other pious sites for the welfare of the community. He purchased lands for a cemetery at Boitokh-khana at 8,000 *reis* (the Portuguese monetary unit) in 1785; for the Roman Catholic Church of Madre de Deus at Serampore in 1783 at 14,000 *reis*; and for a domestic chapel at Sukhsagar, built and consecrated in October 1789, and dedicated to the Virgin Mary of Parma, costing 9,000 *reis*.[50]

TRADE AND THE FLAG

Joseph Barretto made use of his Portuguese connections to promote his trade in Bengal. He imported a quantity of chank shells in 1783 on the Portuguese ship *Nossa Senhora de Carmo Santa Evililia e Almas*.[51] He also extended the use of this vessel to his English partner: John Fergusson used a Portuguese ship, the *Monte d'Carmo*, to transport English goods from Bombay to Calcutta, and he dispatched bales of cloth by the ship *Princess of Brazil*.[52] An aspect of their collaboration was the export of rice to Coromandel for which they were engaged by the government.[53] The manufacture and trade of arrack was another area of their collaboration. As the wars of the late eighteenth century obstructed the importation of arrack from Batavia,[54] Barretto, Fergusson and Finny "erected distillerys at very great expence for the particular purpose of supplying the army and squadron with Rum and Arrack". However, they suffered a financial loss on the venture after the war and had to ask for a remission of duties.[55] This partnership stretched across a long span of time and opened trading avenues into Southeast Asia.[56]

Ships bearing Portuguese names like *Santa Rita, Louiza Teresa, São António, Santo António* and *Miguel Roza de Barros* landed at Calcutta port, paid government duties for import and export cargoes, and obtained regular navigational assistance from the customs authorities.[57] The question of payment of duties at Calcutta port assumed significance because goods were very often laden on the ship outside the settlement and the charge of smuggling could be levelled if it was apprehended that a part of the consignment had been landed too.[58] Such allegations could be critical for individuals whose identity could be questioned, as in the case of Luís da Costa, a merchant and an official agent of the Portuguese state in Calcutta.

In Indian Ocean trade and its collaborative ventures, an issue that frequently caused controversy was the use of flags of a nation to which the ship or the owner did not belong. Goods exempted from certain duties or allowed certain privileges at Calcutta were obliged to use the British flag, but quite often in practice certain departures took place that produced strong resentments. The Portuguese, being the erstwhile "rulers" of the eastern seas, persisted with certain powers that had some effect on the maritime world of the East. One was the power to issue maritime passports, or *cartazes*. Two incidents of a slightly later date come to notice. One involved Mahomed Zulfee Bohra, a Bombay merchant, and his Parsee partner, Nusretjee Manchorjee, while the second concerned Luís da Costa and his ship *Enterprise*. In the first case, the ship carrying English government papers and a passport was found with a Portuguese flag on arrival at Calcutta, which as the owner explained was obligatory because it had obtained from Goa a Portuguese *cartaz* to mislead the French at sea. But when it actually encountered a French fleet at sea, it threw the papers into the water and as a result was asked to pay customs according to the rate imposed on foreign goods.[59]

Luís da Costa's ship *Enterprise*, bound for Manila, landed in greater trouble. It was understood by the British that, after obtaining the benefit of a British pass, his ship would change colours midway on its journey and land at Manila to get goods from there under a foreign flag.[60] Because imports from Manila were prohibited by a trade treaty between Spain and Britain, Luís da Costa found the demand for a declaration to abide by these instructions very strange.[61] This attitude raised suspicions.

The complexities of Anglo-Portuguese collaboration and their attendant trading relations were to an extent responsible for Luís da Costa's predicament, but responsibility was also due to ambiguity in the latter's identity as a Portuguese and his status as the EEIC's subject. The mechanics of collaboration had taken a turn in the 1750s, when the English were legislating to favour their own cargoes by "preventing the vessels from flying Portuguese and French flags" because there was an increase in English tonnage.[62] This affected shipping in both sectors of trade from India — towards Manila as well as towards Macao. From the1740s, fewer Portuguese ships were plying from Manila, and it is evident that in the 1760s they were not very welcome at Calcutta. The captain of the *São João Nepomuceno* (*Sao Joao Nepomencino* in the original source) from Macao landed in 1766, faced a demand of duty on the cargo from the "Moors", and was advised to settle the matter with Governor Verelst. But, as the captain perceived, this was a ploy to permit the "Moors" to plague and insult him and to prevent the goods from landing, because Mr Verelst had a view "to discourage the Macao's [*sic*, meaning Macanese] from coming here, as there were these Council ship that made the voyages to China, to whose private trade the coming of the Macaos [*sic*] was thought prejudicial and deemed an intrusion".[63] When he returned to Calcutta again in 1775, he remonstrated before Warren Hastings that 7.5 per cent was too heavy for a nation "always in alliance of friendship with the English", while in Bengal, those who were not so affiliated — such as the French in Chandernagore, the Dutch at Chinsura and the Danes at Sriampur — paid a trifle to the "Moors".[64]

Luís da Costa had imported goods from Macao by the *São João Nepomuceno* in 1775. His advocacy of the captain's case was compounded by his personal interests and the umbrage caused to him by being placed "on the same footing with them [the Macanese] without having any regard to my being [an] inhabitant of Calcutta who pays no other Duty on Foreign imported goods than that of the Hon'ble Company's".[65]

In spite of the avowal of his own status, it is clear that Luís da Costa had a dual political loyalty, one as the subject of a British colony and an inhabitant of Calcutta, and the other as the business agent (*agente de negócios*) for the port of Calcutta of the Estado da Índia. However, the Estado stood by him on occasion by issuing a *carta de crença* (a letter of credence), which mentioned his good conduct and regulated behaviour, and also expressed much satisfaction on account of his promotion of the benefits of the nation by exhibiting his patriotic zeal.[66] Dom Frederico Guilherme de Sousa Holstein (governor of Portuguese India, 1779–86) wrote to Warren Hastings and the Council of Bengal regarding his agent, in order to avoid arrests and predicaments of this sort in future.[67]

One cannot say that such problems had adversely affected Portuguese trade. It appears from the number of ships arriving and departing from Bengal that the imports into and exports from that port by Portuguese carriers were quite regular (see Table 5.1).

TABLE 5.1
Arrival and Departure of Portuguese Ships at Calcutta, 1785 and 1786
(Names of ships appear in the original spellings used in the document)

ARRIVALS Ship	From	DEPARTURES Ship	To
1785		1785	
Ship Santa Antonio	Madeira	Neptune	Madras
Nossa Senhora Derozario	China	Sacramento	Madras and Lisbon
Marquize De Anjengo	Lisbon	Augustinha	Madras and Lisbon
Santa Antonia	China	Monte de Carmo	Lisbon
Flower of Funchal	Macao	Maria Primina	Lisbon
Premize de Asia	Macao	Belzario	Lisbon
Snow Minerva	Madras	Resgate	Macao
Ship Rainha De Monte	Lisbon	Grao Nossa Senhora	Macao
Ship Nossa Senhora Derozario	China	Primeza de Asia	Macao
Nossa Senhora De Luz	Macao	Santa Antonio	Macao
Snow Saint Lewis	Macao	Minerva	Portugal
Nossa Senhora de Risgate	Macao	Flower of Funchal	Lisbon
		Santo Antonio	Lisbon
		Marquiz de Anjego	Corenga
		Ship Rainha de Monte	Madras
1786		1786	
Senhora de Bomfim Santa Maria	Madras	Senhora de Bomfim Santa Mario	Madras
Bilazario	Madras	Bilazario	Madras
Duque de Braganca	Madras	Duque de Braganca	Madras
Bow Kora	Pegu	Boa Kora	Madras
Trindade	Madras	Trindade	Madras

Source: "A List of Foreign Vessels that have exported from the Port of Calcutta between the 1st of January & 31st December 1785 & between 1st January & 31st October 1786 being one years and ten months", with appendix, 6–30 November 1786, Proceedings of the Board of Revenue, vol. 6, West Bengal State Archives.

THE COMMUNITY IN EXISTENCE: LAND AND LIVELIHOOD

The sale of landed assets at one end in Hugli[68] and the propensity to purchase the same at another end in Calcutta[69] in the eighteenth century does indicate a new tendency at that time on the part of the Portuguese *mestiços* to disperse from their erstwhile centre and settle in a newer one permanently. This is indicated by the fact that every property deal had to be confirmed by a *patta* (a government-granted lease to farmers).[70] Records presented at the meetings of the provincial councils of the 1770s show dealings in landed property between Portuguese *mestiços* and native Bengali inhabitants as of the early 1750s.[71] Transactions and deals bring in intermediaries, and one such prominent mediator was Luís da Costa, mentioned earlier.[72] It seems that he was a professional attorney and broker who mediated on behalf of many Bengali gentlemen and Europeans.[73] From the testimony given before officials, it also appears that he was not wary of engaging in disputes with the high and mighty of the town. He accused Gokul Ghoshal, a big-time revenue farmer and *banian* (Hindu merchant or shopkeeper), of obstructing useful activities like the construction of a wall to prevent encroachment by the river.[74]

Disputes are an inevitable consequence of proprietorial acquisition, especially in land matters, which lead to attrition within a community. This was evident at Bandel, the symbolic relic of the Portuguese community that preserved its links with the past. In 1632, conflict at this site ensued, due to alleged encroachments made by the Portuguese in the imperial *mahals* (place or lands yielding revenue) under the Mughals, but they were restituted with some rights to autonomy in governance directly under the government or its *faujdar* (magistrate of the police over a large district) without any interposition of authority by the *zamindars*. In 1773 when João Mercado, a "Black Portuguese", obtained a regular grant from the *zamindar* of Burdwan giving him ownership "of the whole village of Bandel" (except such parts as had been restituted by the *zamindar*),[75] it was a case of *déjà vu*: now it was the *zamindar* who was accused of interfering in the imperial *mahal* and the authority of the *faujdar*, with the Portuguese prior of Bandel complaining that the land granted by the *farmān* of 1633 had been usurped.[76] Mercado, a Portuguese registrar at the Burdwan collectorate, obtained a *mahattaran* (lands given to "respectable", non-Brahmin people; also *motran*) in Balagarh village without the prior's permission, and it was confirmed by the EEIC's *parwana* (a warrant to summon or arrest).

The Augustinian prior of the Bandel convent who challenged Mercado's claim did so on this basis of the *farmān* of 1633 that had given the community control over 777 *bighas* (roughly a third of an acre) of land. But in reality the convent had retained only a fraction of it — including a restitution grant of 72 *bighas* by the *zamindar* of Burdwan in 1768 — and "the rest being lost through many litigations and bad management of the Priors."[77] Thus the EEIC's administration refused to wholly entertain the claim of the prior, that the convent had a right to all the land that had been granted, or admit the plea that the *ryots* (tenants of a house or land) paying rent to Mercado ought to be under their control.[78]

Disputes and narrations of wrongful dispossession by proprietors were particularly evident among Portuguese *jagir*[79] holders. Such *jagir* holders were soldiers in the employ of the government, in this case for the defence of the fort of Hugli (also known as Shawbad). In 1780 Ignácio Correa of Bandel and Hugli petitioned that "a *jakeer* [*jagir*] … was possessed and enjoyed by petitoner's ancestors from time immemorial" by inheritance until his grandfather, Francisco de Melo, was dispossessed by one António Jorge, a surgeon living in Murshidabad at the time of Alivardi Khan (see Table 5.2).[80] Jorge had succeeded due to his influence at the *nawab*'s court.[81] The family of a former *jagirdar* (*jagir* grantee) could maintain themselves by relegating themselves to the position of estate manager. Finally, the Provincial Council of Revenue of Burdwan declared after an enquiry by the *faujdar* that the *jagir* was in a mismanaged state.[82]

The Portuguese living in English settlements gravitated to urban professions and trade early on. Portuguese "lads" were employed as registrars as early as 1701. At government customs in Calcutta in 1783, the majority of the staff were Luso-Indians who worked along with individuals having common Bengali names. Custom offices at Patna and Dacca (Dhaka) also employed Luso-Indians, and on one occasion the Patna office reported that a deficiency in the number of Portuguese registrars held up work.[83] Their familiarity with the commercial milieu and environment, where native merchants' accounts were in the "Bengal language", made them indispensable. They also knew "Malabar, Coromandel, Portuguese and French all of which have often business to do at the office."[84]

A seventeenth-century Portuguese document, "Requests under the Seal and Signature of Nawab Khan Khanan Bahadur",[85] placed before English authorities, stated that they were like any other small trader who brought several things from diverse places and had to put up with exactions by the *sarkar mutsuddie* (an accountant or clerk in a public office) who asked for duty. This included things "for our own provision" or "our own eating", but some of them also shipped grains "for a voyage", which resulted in grain scarcity in the "parganas [small district] of the neighbourhood of Hooghly".

TABLE 5.2
***Sanads* of *Jagir* (Documentary Verification of Land Grants) of Pedro Jorge**

(Names appear in the original spellings used in the document)

Name of Jagirdar as Recorded in Dewani Daftar	*Date*	*Appointing Authorities*	*Reasons for Change of Jagirdar*
Joao de Fermar	1626	Islam Khan, Wazir Khan, Faujdar of chakla Satgong	Incumbent's death
Joao de Silia	1645	Subahdar Shah Shuja	Incumbent old, dismissed
Paglade (?) Silia	1680	Malik Kasim, Faujdar	Incumbent's death
Son of Above	1707	Zainullah Khan, Faujdar of Peloon	Incumbent's death
Salin de Antonio	1717	Assumullah Khan, Faujdar of the chakla	Incumbent's death
Domingo Tabarez	1724	Assumullah Khan, Faujdar of the chakla	Incumbent's death
Antonio Tehrzek Feringhy (Antonio Jorge)	1726	Nawab Shujauddin, Muhammad Khan, Emperor Muhammad Shah	Incumbent dismissed, tender age
Pedro Jorge	1770s	Company	Death
Iago de Mello, Carol Baz, and 15 companions	1766	Company, Sanad — Shah Alam, Yar Beg Khan	Incumbent resigned
Pedro	1767	Sanad — Amir beg, Khan Faujdar of Hooghly	

Source: List of *sanads* delivered by Pedro Jorge, 13 January 1780, Provincial Council of Revenue at Calcutta, West Bengal State Archives.

But their role in foreign trade comes to light when they state that "when the ships of the *sarkar* [head of government] of the *khalsa* [revenue department] therefore are departing[,] many *firinghees* [*feringhees*; foreigners] send goods with their *gomastas* [commissioned factor or agent] upon these ships" as "the ships of the Feringhees have no ingress or egress in the Royal country from fear of the Dutch." They said that the Dutch stopped the entry of their ships from Europe. Such traders were "constantly coming and going from Hooghly to Ingellee" and on the way encountered six *chowkies* (tax or custom collection stations).[86]

The orientation of the Portuguese made them natural traders in Bengal. They traded in *chunam* (lime), salt and grain. Among *chunam* and salt traders we come across the names of Pedro de Vivanco, Elizabeth da Costa and the ubiquitous Luís da Costa.[87] Salt was perhaps the most ancient business for the Portuguese in Bengal, and all three personalities mentioned were involved in it.[88] But in changing times they confronted many checks and impositions by the revenue farmers and the government.[89] In the grain trade, suppliers like Manuel de Almeida regularly brought grain to Calcutta from Bakharganj,[90] while "Francis" (Francisco) de Rosário entered "into various contracts for chunam with the inhabitants of the town in which they reside."[91]

CONCLUSION: FROM "PORTUGUESE" TO "LUSO-INDIANS"?

In the eighteenth century, the presence of the native-born Portuguese resident in India was marked and widespread in Bengal. Their maritime connections were quite fresh in the memory of the local inhabitants and rulers, and the possibility of reinventing a colonial domain was looming chimerically in the minds of the Portuguese rulers in Lisbon.[92] But through extensive involvement at the social level, especially via economic transactions with the native population, they were entering the mosaic of the society that was in existence in Bengal prior to the arrival of the Portuguese in the sixteenth century". But still there was a distance that was maintained through connections with other European groups rather than with their own nationality. How this "foreignness" that had been conserved since the sixteenth century was dissolved and the gap with the society at large eventually bridged, such that the community subjected itself thoroughly to the Raj, will be found in its history of the nineteenth and twentieth centuries. The collaboration with the English continued until the end of the managing agency system (whereby a firm of professional managers was contracted to run a joint stock company), that is, until the 1820s and for as long as the opportunities opened by the "temporary British control of the Dutch colonies" were there.[93] Joseph Barretto was the leading figure in these collaborations, and as a Luso-Indian he earned for himself and his family a place in the society of Bengal that was respected by both the Bengalis and the English.[94] He was probably the last in the line of *descendentes* whose Portuguese identity served him well.

Notes

1 Sanjay Subrahmanyam, "Manila, Melaka, Mylapore: A Dominican Voyage through the Indies ca. 1600", *Archipel* 57 (1999): 224.
2 Ibid., p. 226.
3 C.R. Boxer, *The Portuguese Seaborne Empire, 1415–1825* (New York: Knopf, 1975), p. 134.
4 Subrahmanyam, "Manila, Melaka, Mylapore", p. 231.
5 Boxer, *The Portuguese Seaborne Empire*, p. 135.
6 Ibid., p. 139.
7 M.N. Pearson, *The Indian Ocean* (London: Routledge, 2007), pp. 250–51.
8 Ibid., p. 134.
9 Anthony Disney, "The Portuguese Empire in India c. 1550–1650" in *Indo-Portuguese History: Sources and Problems*, edited by John Correia-Afonso (Bombay: Oxford University Press, 1981), pp. 148–62.
10 Kenneth McPherson, "Anglo-Portuguese Commercial Relations in the Eastern Indian Ocean from the Seventeenth to the Eighteenth Centuries", *South Asia: Journal of South Asian Studies* 19, supp. 1, Special Issue: Asia and Europe: Commerce, Colonialism and Cultures (1996), p. 43.
11 Ibid., pp. 41–57.
12 M.N. Pearson, *The Portuguese in India* (New York: Cambridge University Press, 1987), p. 152.
13 Ibid.
14 Ibid.
15 Jorge Manuel Flores, "Relic or Springboard? A Note on the 'Rebirth' of Portuguese Hughli, ca. 1632–1820", *Indian Economic and Social History Review* 39, no. 4 (2002): 381–95.
16 Boxer, *The Portuguese Seaborne Empire*, p. 170.
17 Pearson, *The Portuguese in India*, pp. 144 and 151.
18 J.H. Stocqueler, *The Hand-book of India: A Guide to the Stranger and the Traveller, and a Companion to the Resident* (London: W.H. Allen, 1844), pp. 34–35.
19 *A Compendius Ecclesiastical, Chronological and Historical Sketches of Bengal: Since the Foundation of Calcutta* (Calcutta, 1818), p. 162.
20 J.H. da Cunha Rivara, *A Jurisdicção Diocesana do Bispado de S. Thome de Meliapor nas Possessões Inglezas e Francezas* (Nova Goa: Imprensa Nacional, 1867), pp. 5–6.
21 Ibid.; and Leopold Delaunoit, "Archdiocese of Calcutta", *The Catholic Encyclopedia*, vol. 3 (New York: Robert Appleton Company, 1908) <http://www.newadvent.org/cathen/03152a.htm> (accessed 16 July 2010).
22 Julio Firmino Judice Biker, *Collecção de Tratados e Concertos de Pazes que o Estado*

da India Portugueza Fez com os Reis e Senhores com Quem Teve Relações nas Partes da Asia e Africa Oriental desde o Principio da Conquista até o Fim do Seculo XVIII, vol. 8 (Lisbon: Imprensa Nacional, 1885), pp. 70–79.

23 Rivara, *A Jurisdicção Diocesana*, pp. 200–65, especially 240.

24 Biker, *Collecção de tratados*, 8: 70–79; and James Doyle, "Saint Thomas of Mylapur", *The Catholic Encyclopedia*, vol. 13 (New York: Robert Appleton Company, 1912) <http://www.newadvent.org/cathen/13382b.htm> (accessed 16 July 2010).

25 Ibid.; and *Jurisdicção Diocesana do Bispado de S. Thome de Meliapor nas Possessões Inglezas e Francezas* (Nova Goa: Imprensa Nacional, 1867), pp. 258–63.

26 S.C. Hill, comp., *Bengal in 1756–1757: A Selection of Public and Private Papers Dealing with the Affairs of the British in Bengal during the Reign of Siraj-ud-daula* (London: John Murray, 1905), 1: xxxiv.

27 Ibid.

28 Henry Yule, Arthur Coke Burnell and William Crooke, *Hobson-Jobson: A Glossary of Colloquial Anglo-Indian Words and Phrases* (London, 1903), p. 933; and Anthony Xavier Soares, *Portuguese Vocables in Asiatic Languages*, edited and translated by S.R. Dalgado (Baroda, India: Oriental Institute, 1936), pp. 346–48. *Topass* in a Tamil derivation could mean "interpreter". *Topasses* were also referred to as "black Christians", and the men often became professional soldiers, leading to the additional meaning of a "hat-wearing mercenary soldier".

29 "Statement of the Factories in Bengal on 23 January 1756, Archives Coloniales, Paris", in Hill, *Bengal*, 1: 418. The same statement shows that at Cossimbazar the Portuguese mercenary soldiers were referred to as *Portuguese-mesti* soldiers and numbered only thirteen, while at Dacca, Patna and Jugdea, they only numbered seven, seven and two, respectively.

30 "Narrative of the Succession of Souraged Dowlet to the Provinces of Bengal, Bihar and Orixa, and of the Siege of Calcutta Taken by Escalade the 20th June, 1756, by Governor Drake, Dated 11th July 1756", in Hill, *Bengal*, 1: 142–43.

31 Hill, *Bengal*, 1: lxxii–lxxiii.

32 Ibid., 1: lxxxix; and "Narrative of the Succession", pp. 135, 140 and 147.

33 Gourdas Basak, "Kalighat and Calcutta", *Calcutta Review* 92 (1891).

34 "Narrative of the Capture of Calcutta from 10 April, 1756 to 10 November 1756, by William Tooke", in Hill, *Bengal*, 1: 248–301.

35 Ibid.

36 Hill, *Bengal*, 1: cxxxvii.

37 Ibid.

38 Ibid., 1: lxxvi. Portuguese women who lived in houses adjacent to the factory had come into the fort. Captain Grant mentions that Holwell gave orders to clear the factory of the crowd of Portuguese women. The Portuguese lived in brick houses in the vicinity of the fort that the council wanted to raze to clear the line of fire. The women had brought in their slaves, and they created a commotion while fleeing the fort by boat. See "Narrative of the Succession" in Hill, *Bengal*, 1: 91, 144, 154 and 157.

39 "Narrative of the Succession" in Hill, *Bengal,* 1: 131, 144, 152 and 155. See also "Letter from Mr. William Lindsay to Mr. Robert Orme, Concerning the Loss of Calcutta, Dated 'Syren' Sloop, off Fulta, July 1756", in Hill, *Bengal,* 1: 166–67.

40 "Narrative of the Capture of Calcutta", in Hill, *Bengal,* 1: 299.

41 Hill, *Bengal,* 1: lxxxix.

42 Ibid., 1: xciv.

43 Stocqueler, *The Hand-book of India,* p. 44.

44 Ibid., pp. 34–35.

45 The authors expressed their intellectual debt to Manuel Faria y Souza.

46 Stocqueler, *The Hand-book of India,* pp. 34–35. See the remarks of Mrs Postan, an English lady living in India in the mid-nineteenth century, remarking on the countenance, gait, garments and behaviour of the Portuguese in most ungratifying terms, saying that they mimicked European manners.

47 M. de Rozario, *The Complete Monumental Registers Containing all the Epitaphs, Inscriptions, etc. etc. in the Different Churches and Burial-Grounds, in and about Calcutta etc.* (Calcutta, 1815).

48 Ibid. "Lopez Suarez" might be a reference to Lopo Soares de Albergaria, although this cannot be confirmed. However, Lopo Soares de Albergaria arrived in Asia in 1515, not 1505.

49 Ibid.

50 Bengal, *Historical and Ecclesiastical Sketches of Bengal from the Earliest Settlement until the Virtual Conquest of That Country by the English in 1757* (Calcutta, 1831).

51 Joseph Barretto to the President of the Board of Customs (hereafter cited as BOC), 22 January 1783, Proceedings of the Board of Customs (hereafter cited as PBOC), West Bengal State Archives (hereafter cited as WBSA), Calcutta.

52 John Fergusson to the Secretary of the BOC, 17 January 1783, PBOC.

53 BOC proceedings, 28 October 1783, PBOC.

54 Secretary of the Board of Revenue (hereafter cited as BOR) to Governor-General in Council (hereafter cited as GGC), 24 July 1787, Proceedings of the Board of Revenue (hereafter cited as PBOR); Fergusson, Barretto and Finny to BOR, 24 July 1787; Mr Johnson, Mr McKenzie and Acting President of the BOR, opinions, 24 July 1787, PBOR, WBSA.

55 Ibid.

56 Anthony Webster, "British Export Interests in Bengal and Imperial Expansion into South-East Asia, 1780–1824: Origins of the Straits Settlement", in *Development Studies and Colonial Policy,* edited by Barbara Ingham and Colin Simmons (London: F. Cass, 1987), pp. 138, 154 and 169.

57 BOC proceedings, 28 March, 5 April, and 22 August 1783, PBOC.

58 GGC to BOR, 17 November 1786, PBOR.

59 BOC proceedings concerning Fort William, 11 October 1783, PBOC; and Catorjee Moncharjee to BOC, 8 October 1783, stating that the Portuguese

passport was granted, along with a suit of colours carried by a Portuguese captain, PBOC.

60 Government Custom Master to Committee of Revenue (hereafter cited as COR), 19 April 1786; Custom Master to COR, 22 April 1786; Luis da Costa to COR, 22 April 1786; COR to GGC, 22 April 1786; and Secretary of the GGC to COR, 21 April 1786, Proceedings of the Committee of Revenue (hereafter cited as PCOR), vol. 67, WBSA.

61 Luís da Costa to GGC, 19 April 1786, PCOR, vol. 68, stating that he enjoyed the protection of English laws and that his ship "goes now with English colours and will return with the same". But in spite of this statement, the ship was forbidden to sail; see Secretary of the Secret Department to Secretary of the Board of Revenue, 28 June 1786, PBOR, vol. 1, 1–28 June 1786. Luís da Costa to Government Custom Master, 18 April 1786, stating that he felt that the grant of a British pass did not enjoin him "to limit the port she is to proceed to or with what Nation to trade", PCOR.

62 McPherson, "Anglo-Portuguese Commercial Relations", p. 56.

63 Petition by João Carlos Dias, commander of the *São João Nepomencino* [*sic*], to GGC, 14 April 1775, PBOR.

64 Ibid.

65 Luís da Costa to GGC, 12 April 1775, PBOR.

66 Livros de Reis Vizinhos 984, vol. 58, fols. 44–44v, 26 Apr. 1783, Historical Archives of Goa, Panaji, Goa. N.b.: Dates appearing in the HAG citations herein pertain only to the specific folios cited.

67 Ibid., vol. 60, fols. 88v–90v, 3 December 1783.

68 *Bengal Gazette,* 12 February, 26 February and 11 March 1780. Five houses and a piece of land measuring three *bighas* (one *bigha* was roughly a third of an acre) and fifteen *cottahs* (one-twentieth of a *bigha*) were sold in Hugli.

69 Francis de Mello to the Provincial Council of Revenue at Calcutta (hereafter cited as PCR/C), 8 May 1775, stating that he had held the important market of Mechuabazar since 1755, Proceedings of the Provincial Council of Revenue at Calcutta (hereafter cited as PPCR/C), WBSA.

70 Sale of land by Philip da Cruz to Jose Sepandro, 16 June 1777; Bibi Mendes to PCR/C, 11 February 1778; Luís da Costa to PCR/C, 11 February 1778; Luisa de Souza to PCR/C, 21 May and 21 September 1778; application by Maria and Catherine de Rozario, 21 July 1778; application for *patta* by Maria Mesquita for land purchased from Gabriel Rodrigues in 1764, 21 July 1778; and sale of land with a *patta* by Francisco Xavier Gomes to Gokul Ghoshal's descendant, 27 August 1779, PPCR/C.

71 Luisa Cardoso to PCR/C, 31 March 1777, submitting a letter from a painter stating she had purchased property from him in 1752; Luís da Costa to PCR/C, 11 August 1779, stating he had been in possession of a house since 1762; statement of a landed property transaction of 1764 between Mario Rozario and Gabriel Rodrigues (two Portuguese *mestiços*), 11 February 1778;

and a Eurasian to PCR/C, 30 July 1779, stating he had purchased property from Andrew Derozio, PPCR/C.

72 PCR/C, 11 and 19 January 1778, recording landed property transactions with Brindaban Datta and Rottu Sarkar, and 18 February 1778, recording landed property transactions with Ramprasad, Nemai Charan Kundu and Gorachand Kundu, PPCR/C.

73 PCR/C on behalf of Brindaban Datta, 29 December 1777; Brindaban Datta to PCR/C, 3 March 1778, stating that he is the attorney of Tilakchand Das, who in turn was the administrator of the landed estate of Ratneswar Sarkar, PPCR/C. Datta appeared as the executor of the will of Mr Thomas Griffiths that involved landed assets; see *Bengal Gazette,* 26 February 1780.

74 PCR/C proceedings, 20 August 1777, and 18, 20 and 23 August 1779.

75 GGC to BOR, 18 July 1786; BOR minutes, 18 July 1786; GGC to BOR, with enclosures, 17 July 1787; and report by the President of the BOR, 11 May 1787, PBOR. The grant of seven and one-half *bighas* was made on an application by Reverend Prior Friar Bento de Saint Sylvester.

76 GGC to BOR, 17 July 1787, first enclosure, stating that "the 'humble' petition and representation from Padre Fr. Joseph de St. Augustin Prior and Regent of Bandel, for, and on the behalf himself and the Christians, Natives as well as the Portuguese inhabitants of the same, to Hon'ble John McPherson, Governor-General of Bengal", PBOR.

77 J.J.A. Campos, *History of the Portuguese in Bengal,* (Patna: Janaki Prakasham, 1979 [1919]), p. 148.

78 Provincial Council of Revenue of Burdwan to PCR/C, 9 July 1779, PPCR/C.

79 A *jagir* or *jakeer* was a grant of territory to an individual for a temporary period of time (from three years to a lifetime), originally in recognition of military service. The *jagirdar*, or holder of the grant, effectively ruled that region and realized income from the taxes it produced. Although such grants reverted to the ruler upon the grantee's death, they could and usually were re-granted to heirs and successors.

80 PCR/C proceedings concerning Pedro Firngi (Jorge)'s claim to villages of Degrah, conducted by John Shore, 13 March 1780; and petition by Ignatio Correa of Bandel at Hooghly concerning his status as the only surviving executor named in the last will and testament of Thereza de Melo, late of Bandel, 13 March 1780, PPCR/C.

81 *Arzees* (petition) from Pedro Jorge to PCR/C, 30 August 1779 and 26 June 1780; and GGC to PCR/C, 6 and 22 May 1790, consenting to allow Pedro Jorge to be in possession of the *jagir*, PPCR/C.

82 The *faujdar* of Hooghly to the PCR/C, 20 Aug. 1779; and PCR/C proceedings, 17 July 1780, informing the PCR/C that none of his officers held the *pooneah* (rent day), PPCR/C.

83 Collector of Government Customs at Calcutta, to BOC, 6 September 1783,

PBOC; Custom Master to BOC, 6 September 1783, PBOC; and Collector of Government Customs at Patna to COR, 17 April 1786, vol. 67, PCOR.

84 Collector of Government Customs at Calcutta to BOC, 22 August and 6 September 1783, PBOC.

85 GGC to BOR, 17 July 1787, second enclosure, a translated copy of Requests under the Seal and Signature of Nawab Khan Khanan Bahadur, according to the under written [*sic*] particulars, PBOR.

86 Ibid.

87 Luís da Costa to PCR/C, 19 and 24 May 1775; and Pedro Vivanco to PCR/C, 1 July 1775, PPCR/C.

88 Provincial Council of Revenue at Dacca to GGC, 22 September 1775, regarding a delivery of salt by Luis da Costa from Bakharganj; and Provincial Council of Revenue at Dacca to GGC, 23 June 1775, complaining about the inferior quality of salt delivered by da Costa, Proceedings of the Provincial Council of Revenue at Dacca, WBSA.

89 PCR/C proceedings, 10 and 28 October 1776, regarding obstructions to Elizabeth da Costa's trade on the part of Benjamin Lacam, revenue farmer; and complaint by Manuel de Almeida, 30 August 1776, regarding Lacam's obstruction of the grain trade from Bakharganj, PPCR/C.

90 PCR/C proceedings, 30 August 1776, PPCR/C.

91 Petition by Francis de Rozario and Bengali traders, 12 June 1786, regarding *chunam* trade, PBOR.

92 Flores, "Relic or Springboard?", pp. 381–95.

93 Anthony Webster, *Gentlemen Capitalists: British Imperialism in South East Asia, 1770–1890* (London: Tauris Academic Studies, 1998), p. 58.

94 Brajendranath Bandyopadhyay, ed., *Sambadpatre Sekaler Katha,* vol. 2 (Calcutta: Bangiya Sahitya Parisad, 1977), p. 240.

PART TWO

Dispersion, Mobility and Demography from the Sixteenth into the Twenty-first Centuries

6

THE LUSO-ASIANS AND OTHER EURASIANS: THEIR DOMESTIC AND DIASPORIC IDENTITIES

John Byrne

The Luso-Asians are the descendants of sixteenth- and seventeenth-century Portuguese colonists who cohabitated and intermarried with the various indigenous women of Asia: from Diu in India to Nagasaki in Japan; from Macao in China to East Timor in the Pacific. They are also the descendants of slaves belonging to the Portuguese settlers who, over the course of several centuries, merged into the Portuguese mixed-blood societies. These slaves originated from the coasts of India and Sri Lanka, the islands of the Indonesian archipelago, and, in lesser numbers, the Portuguese colonies in Africa. The Luso-Asians are part of the small communities of part-European people who played a significant role in the power politics of colonial Asia. Playing the part of cultural brokers in a complicated relationship between the European administrators and the indigenous peoples, their Western education enabled them to hold posts in government and the professions; they were paid more than other locals, but less than the Europeans. These hybrid groups, who generally comprised 1 to 2 per cent of their national populations, had various local names and identities but have come to be known collectively as Eurasians. The Luso-Asians were the first Eurasians. The non-Luso-Eurasian communities developed later and include the Dutch Burghers of Sri Lanka, the Indo-Dutch of Indonesia, the Anglo-Indians of India, the Anglo-Burmans of Myanmar and other Anglo communities in Sri Lanka, Malaysia/Singapore and Hong Kong.

This chapter examines the fifteen Eurasian communities which emerged during the colonial era. It focuses on their formation, their diverse ancestral combinations and their evolution during the three colonizing periods of the Portuguese, Dutch and British. The original Luso-Asian groups are the Luso-Indians of India, the Portuguese Burghers of Sri Lanka, the Kristang of Malacca in Malaysia, the Macanese of Macao in China, the Larantuqueiros of the Nusa Tenggara province in Indonesia and the Mestizos of East Timor. All these communities originated between 1510 and 1558. On this quincentennial anniversary of Portuguese settlement in the East, we also acknowledge the communities which were very much part of these golden years of the Portuguese "empire", communities which have since been absorbed by other larger ethnicities. These lost communities include the Bayingyis of Myanmar; the Luso-Siamese of Thailand; the mestizos of the Spice Islands, Indonesia; and the Batavian Portuguese and Mardijkers of Indonesia.

This enquiry attempts to go beyond the usual description of the non-Portuguese communities which later developed, with the argument that initial and early intermarriages with the original Luso groups had left a significant proportion of their population part-Portuguese. Additionally, during the British period, many Luso-Asians swapped identities to become Anglo-Asians. In other words, many members of the other (non-Portuguese) Eurasian communities are actually Luso-Asians.

This study also explores the two dispersions of the Luso-Asian groups and, using data from select tables of the different national censuses, is the first to provide estimates of the number of Luso-Asians and other Eurasians in the diaspora. Research on how these overseas-based Eurasians identify themselves will also be analysed.

THE MAJOR LUSO-ASIAN GROUPS

Luso-Indians (India)

The first Luso-Asian was most probably born in India. Cochin (Kochi) became the first European settlement in India when the Portuguese set up a fortified trading post there in 1503. All along the Malabar and Coromandel coasts of India, and later in Bengal, Portuguese missionaries, adventurers, traders and settlers set up Luso centres. The invariably male immigration inevitably resulted in miscegenation. The Luso-Indians — also called *mestiços*, mestizos, *Luso-descendentes*, or Luso-descendants — came into existence from these encounters. Albuquerque's 1510 letter to Portugal's king, Dom Manuel I, informing him of the 450 marriages which had taken place in Goa between Portuguese men and Indian women, has been widely quoted in scholarly works,[1] and together with the continuity of the Goan settlement could give the impression that it was predominantly in Goa where racial intermingling had taken place. In fact, the capital of the Estado da Índia had only 1,500 Portuguese and mestizos in 1660, compared to 2,000 "whites" in Bassein in the 1660s, 4,000 "whites" in Cochin in 1663, and some 400 "white" families in both São Tomé de Meliapor and the Praças do Norte in the 1600s.[2] The Luso-Indians include some of the Goans and also the Portuguese descendants all along both coasts and in Bengal. Not all Luso-Indians are Goans; not all Goans are Luso-Indians.

The Portuguese Burghers (Sri Lanka)

The Portuguese settled in Colombo in 1518 and intermarriages with the Sinhalese and Tamil women of the island resulted in a mestizo community. The darker-skinned descendants of the mestizos who married natives were called *topazes* or *topasses*. The mestizos and *topazes* identified themselves as Portuguese, the term Portuguese Burgher only being used in British times, almost 150 years after the Portuguese had left the country. The Kaffirs (Cafres), descendants of African slaves brought to the island by the early Portuguese settlers, also considered themselves part of the Portuguese community. Many of the Kaffirs intermarried with the Portuguese mestizos. This is not surprising, considering their common language (Portuguese Creole) and religion (Roman Catholicism). In the 1600s Colombo had more than 2,500 families of Portuguese descent.[3]

The Kristang (Malacca, Malaysia)

The Portuguese captured the strategic port of Malacca in 1511. Tomé Pires, a Portuguese scholar and diplomat who went to Malacca in 1512 and stayed for two years, found the multi-ethnic population speaking eighty-four languages.[4] The Portuguese settlers were to add another ethnic group to the list, the *gente Kristang* (Christian people), offspring of their intermarriage with the local Malay women and members of the slave population. These slaves were probably of Javanese, Balinese, Makassarese and Bugis stock, just as they had been before the arrival of the Lusitanians.[5] In 1613 there were 300 *casados* (married Portuguese men, excluding the garrison) and some 7,400 Catholics in Malacca.[6]

The Eurasians (Singapore)

Singapore was founded by the British in 1819, some 308 years after the arrival of the Portuguese in Malacca and 178 years after that city had been taken over by the Dutch. Eurasians were among the first immigrants to the city and they came, "already mixed" from two main sources: neighbouring Malacca and the British territories of India, Sri Lanka and Bencoolen (Bengkulu). In 1836 there were 425 Native Christians and 117 Indo-Britons in Singapore.[7] These categories were replaced in 1849 by the term "Eurasian". The "Native Christians" would have been the Luso-Malays from Malacca. This term had been used in both India and the Dutch East Indies to describe Roman Catholics of remote Portuguese descent. The "Indo-Briton" label had previously been used in India to describe the present Anglo-Indian community; the term would have been used once again to describe those mixed-blood descendants of the British from India, Sri Lanka and elsewhere. It is doubtful if the British would have applied their identity as "Britons" to members of other nationalities — for example, to the Portuguese descendants. The proportion of Luso-Asians in 1836 was approximately 80 per cent. Although there was much intermingling between the subgroups, the Portuguese proportion has remained similar to this day.[8]

The Larantuqueiros (Indonesia)

Originally called *topasses* and the "black Portuguese", the Larantuqueiros of Larantuka, Wureh and Konga on Flores Island, Indonesia are the descendants of the original Portuguese who settled there in the early 1500s and intermarried with the local Malay and Papuan women, together with later Portuguese groups who were expelled from Malacca and Makassar in 1641 and 1660 respectively. In the nineteenth century, Portuguese was replaced by Malay as the day-to-day language of the then 10,000-strong community[9] but it has been retained as their religious medium. The Larantuqueiros remain fervent Catholics in this most Catholic of all Indonesian islands, and they are further identified by their Portuguese surnames.

The Mestizos (East Timor)

Many of the Mestizos of East Timor are the descendants of families who had originated in Larantuka. Others are offspring of more recent mixing, including *deportados*, political exiles from the Salazar regime who married Timorese women. In 1950, the Mestizos numbered 2,022, or about 0.5 per cent of the population.[10]

The Macanese (Macao S.A.R., China)

There has been much debate about the historical point at which Chinese blood entered the Macanese gene pool. However, there seems to be universal acceptance that the first mothers of the Macanese were not the indigenous people of China. In contrast, Portuguese settlers married native Indians in India, native Sinhalese and Tamils in Sri Lanka, and native Malays in Malacca. In Macao, it was not the Chinese but a multi-ethnic selection of women who contributed to the first few generations of Macanese. The Chinese were not permitted to stay within Macao's borders after sundown, and as such, intercourse between the Chinese and the Portuguese was kept at a minimum.[11]

The Macanese Creole reflects the ancestry of the Macanese people, with the following heritages and their order of input: Portuguese, Malay, Japanese, Indian and African.[12] When the Portuguese arrived in Macao in 1553, they had already founded colonies in Malacca and India, and the women who accompanied them were Luso-Malay and Luso-Indian. Malacca was the nearest Portuguese possession; it had the strongest relationship with Macao, through the Malay and Luso-Malay wives and servants of the early settlers. The Japanese component consisted of Japanese Christians and Luso-Japanese children who were expelled from Japan in 1596 and 1636 respectively.[13] The Africans were slaves imported during the sixteenth and seventeenth centuries. In 1583 there were 900 Portuguese men in Macao.[14] The 1834 census of the Portuguese population of Macao listed 3,793 "whites" and 1,300 slaves. The slaves were mostly from Timor and Africa.[15]

The Bayingyis (Myanmar)

The earliest miscegenation in Burma occurred in the sixteenth century between Portuguese traders and Burmese women in the maritime districts of Mergui, Tavoy, Martaban, Pegu and Akyab.[16] One such community was the Bayingyis, who numbered 3,000 in the 1830s.[17] Their descendants today are culturally Burmese, separated from other Burmese peoples only by their Roman Catholic religion.[18]

The Luso-Siamese (Thailand)

Thailand was never a European colony and, as a consequence, the European and Eurasian communities were very small when compared to neighbouring countries. The Portuguese first arrived to trade in 1510; there were 130

Portuguese settled in Ayutthaya, the former Thai capital, by the mid-sixteenth century. Their numbers were augmented by arrivals of Portuguese displaced first from Malacca in 1641, and then from Makassar in the 1660s, as well as the growing number of Portuguese-Siamese mestizo children. By the end of that century there were 4,000 Christians in the city, including 1,300 Portuguese descendants.[19] After the fall of Ayutthaya in 1767, the Portuguese followed King Taksin to settle in Thon Buri near Bangkok, where the church of Santa Cruz was built in 1770. In the mid-nineteenth century the community was joined by Macanese (Portuguese Eurasians) from Macao.[20] Due to their relatively small numbers and the absence of a stratified colonial society which kept ethnic groups clearly identified and ranked, the Luso-Siamese have been completely assimilated into Thai society.[21]

The Mestizos of the Spice Islands (Indonesia)

Kota Ambon in Amboina was founded by the Portuguese in 1516; Ternate was settled in 1522. On both these islands, the Portuguese intermarried with the local women, creating mixed communities that were Catholic and Creole-speaking.[22] These mestizos (originally called Mardijkers, a term applied to all the Christian inhabitants of Ambon)[23] were evicted by the Dutch, and many left for Malacca and Batavia. In 1606, approximately 200 Portuguese-speaking Mardijkers sailed to the Philippines and settled on the south shore of Manila Bay. Their town became known as Ternate, in memory of their island of origin, and their Portuguese Creole was eventually relexified into Spanish Creole.[24] The 2000 Philippine census recorded 18,123 speakers of Ternateno-Chavacano and Caviteno-Chavacano.[25] Their numbers are declining, and their Lusitanian origins are no longer recognized.

The Batavian Portuguese and Mardijkers (Indonesia)

Batavia was never a Portuguese colony. However, as of its foundation in 1610, the Dutch discovered that Portuguese was the only language understood by the slaves, seamen and artisans, as well as the women they took as their wives.[26] Portuguese-speaking merchants and clerks from Malacca, Ceylon, Cochin and Calicut were attracted to this largest settlement in the Dutch East Indies. Along with the Mardijker community, the Portuguese community of Batavia helped perpetuate Portuguese Creole as the lingua franca of the Dutch territories until the late eighteenth century.[27] The Mardijkers (meaning "freed person" in Bahasa Indonesia) were the largest group of Portuguese speakers in Batavia. They originated from the Portuguese coastal settlements in India and arrived as slaves during the seventeenth century. Bearing Portuguese surnames and speaking a Portuguese Creole, they traded their Catholic religion for Calvinism upon emancipation. Most became operators of small businesses, and many took spouses from the other Indonesian Christian communities (those descended from Balinese and Moluccan slaves). A few grew wealthy, and there was considerable social mixing between members of the Mardijker and mestizo (Indo-Dutch mixed-blood) elites. Indeed, the distinction between the two groups was fuzzy.[28] Numbering around 7,500 at their peak, the Mardijkers maintained their separate identity until about 1816 and gradually merged with the Indonesian Christian population as well as the Indo-Dutch minority.

THE PORTUGUESE PERIOD

There was much intermigration between the Portuguese communities, hastened by eviction from their colonies by the Dutch. One interesting example is that of the Malaccan Portuguese shift to Penang. Some Malaccan Portuguese families migrated directly to Penang when the British founded the island in 1736. Others took the long route: from Malacca to Makassar in 1641, from Makassar to Siam in 1661, and finally from Siam to Kedah and Penang in 1736.

This movement resulted in the "eclectic racial makeup"[29] of the Portuguese communities. A case in point was that of Maria Guyomar de Pinha, wife of the Greek adventurer Constantine Phaulkon, who was born in Ayutthaya (Thailand) in 1664. Sitsayamkan[30] described her father as a Goan, of mixed Portuguese-Bengali-Japanese ancestry, and her mother as a Japanese Christian.

Even though the above communities had individual identities, many of which were given to them later by the Dutch and British colonial rulers, they saw themselves as one people. As we have observed, they were racially heterogeneous, having combinations from a variety of ancestries: Portuguese, northern and Dravidian Indian, Sinhalese and Tamil Sri Lankan, Malay and Indonesian, Papuan Timorese, Chinese, Japanese and African. However, they were homogeneous in their ethnic identification as Portuguese. Hallmarks of this identity included their Portuguese surnames, their use of Portuguese or Portuguese Creole and, above all, their Roman Catholic faith.

Distinctions were certainly made between "white" and "black" Portuguese. For example, Bocarro estimated 4,800 white *casados* and 7,485 black *casados* throughout the Estado da Índia in 1635.[31] Also, Albuquerque stressed that the 450 early settlers married good-looking Muslim women of "white" colour.

Rankings were often based on colour and birthplace, with *reinóis* (those born in Portugal) ahead of *castiços* (those born in Asia of Portuguese parentage), followed by *mestiços* (those born of mixed Portuguese and Asian parentage), ahead of native Christians (those of pure Asian parentage). However, the Luso-Asians became more numerous than the "pure" Portuguese, and they occupied a privileged niche in the colonial system, with many of them working for the Portuguese government and in trading companies:[32] "The Portuguese settlements all depended on the local mixed-race 'Portuguese' to provide manpower in every sphere of public life from the military to administration, commerce, and the church".[33]

THE DUTCH PERIOD

Dutch traders had been active in Southeast Asia since 1590. They conquered a few Indian settlements in 1605, defeated the Portuguese at Malacca in 1641 and took Ceylon in 1656. Most of the early Dutch arrivals were, like the Portuguese before them, unmarried men, and they also took local wives — in this case, mostly Luso-Asian women. Within a few months after the takeover of Colombo, about 200 Dutchmen had already married Indo-Portuguese women.[34] These marriages took place mostly in the Catholic Church, and the subsequent offspring were brought up as Roman Catholics.

In the late seventeenth century, the European population of the Dutch East Indies was concentrated around a relatively small number of urban centres scattered across the Indian Ocean. The majority lived in Batavia and Colombo, with smaller numbers in Banda, Kota Ambon, Vlaardingen (Makassar), Ternate, Cochin and Malacca. Almost all these settlements, with the exception of Banda, had a Portuguese residuum in the form of a Luso-Asian community and/or a Portuguese-speaking slave population. The Dutch presence was greatest and longest in Batavia; there they succeeded in converting the Portuguese elements to Calvinism and eventually absorbed them.

Until the mid-nineteenth century, the Dutch communities consisted mostly of men. Thereafter, the numbers of settlers going to the remaining Dutch settlements grew, with an increasing proportion of female arrivals. The Indo-Dutch (Indisch) Eurasians in Indonesia had grown to 250,000 before their exodus to the Netherlands in the late 1940s and 1950s. Sri Lanka, a Dutch possession from 1656 to 1796, had the second-largest European population in the VOC (Dutch East India Company). The Dutch Burghers are those who are descended, in the male line, from the 900 Dutch who remained in Ceylon after the British takeover. They tended to be Protestants, and their community once comprised one-quarter of the total Burgher and Eurasian population of

Sri Lanka, or approximately 10,000 persons.[35] Malacca and the settlements on the Malabar coast of India had much smaller Dutch populations, and the Dutch segment was absorbed by the much larger Luso-Asian groups. For example, in 1675 there were 104 Dutch Freeburghers in Malacca compared to 1,463 Portuguese-Eurasians. By 1688 there were only 43 Freeburghers, 129 Dutch mestizos and 1,445 Portuguese-Eurasians.[36] Likewise, in the case of Cochin, "the [Dutch] numbers were so small that, instead of remaining a distinct entity or a community unto itself, the people merged with the larger Malabar milieu."[37] A few Eurasian families in Singapore and Malaysia have recently rediscovered their Dutch heritage.[38]

THE BRITISH PERIOD

This third and final colonial period saw the arrival of the British colonists and the development of the Anglo-Indian and Anglo-Burmese groups as well as other British-Eurasian groups in Sri Lanka, Malaysia/Singapore and Hong Kong. This period had a profound effect on the future of the Luso-Asian communities.

Originally, the majority of unions by British men were with Luso-Asian women. In Madras, where the English had established Fort St George in 1639, some 3,000 Portuguese soldiers and traders joined the 300-odd English inhabitants.[39] Intermarriages between Englishmen and Luso-Indian women resulted in a substantial proportion of Anglo-Indians in Madras (and greater South India) bearing Portuguese surnames.[40] The situation was similar on the other side of India. In Bengal, from the last half of the eighteenth century onwards, the British married freely with the Luso-Indians; the marriage register of Saint John's Church in Calcutta shows many names of Portuguese women who married Englishmen.[41] When the British founded Singapore in 1819, the Luso-Malay families from Malacca were among the first to migrate to the new settlement. Apart from the local Malay, Bugis and Javanese groups, the Luso-Malays had the only balanced gender ratio. The British, Chinese, Indian and other immigrant communities were predominantly male at the time; it was to be expected that the early British men took these Catholic and Portuguese-speaking women as wives, creating offspring with a new British-Eurasian identity.

The opening of the Suez Canal in 1869 saw large numbers of British women join their menfolk in Asia. The reduction in European and Asian intermarriages resulted in heightened stratification along colour lines. A hierarchy also emerged with Protestant Eurasians of British and Dutch origins believing themselves to be above those Catholic Eurasians of Portuguese descent. In Sri Lanka, Burghers of Dutch origin "were considered and considered themselves superior to Burghers of Portuguese origin, with the former recognised as a successful and articulate middle class, while the latter were regarded as the great Burgher residuum: poorer, darker, more numerous, and less European."[42]

In Malacca, those who identified themselves specifically as "Eurasians" tended to have Dutch or British family names, spoke English as their first language, were educated and were employed in white-collar occupations. Those called "Portuguese" had predominantly Portuguese family names, spoke creolized Portuguese, were largely illiterate and mostly worked as fishermen.[43] In Singapore, the socio-economic classes of the Eurasians had a colour bias. The "Upper Tens" were predominantly fairer members of the community, offspring of more recent mixing with the British and the Dutch. The lower class was dominated by the darker-skinned *geragoks* (shrimp eaters), descendants of the Malaccan Portuguese.[44]

THE FIRST DISPERSION

The first dispersion of the Luso-Asian groups occurred between 1800 and 1900, when they came to serve a new empire in an intermediary role as the British opened up new territories in Asia and Africa. Goans, including Luso-Indians, moved to the neighbouring cities in British India, as well as to British colonies in East Africa. Those who left in search of better opportunities in Bombay, Karachi, Calcutta and Pune climbed in number from 29,216 in 1880 to 47,334 in 1910.[45] The numbers of Goans in Kenya, Tanganyika, Uganda and Zanzibar increased from 4,572 in 1921 to 11,294 in 1948.[46] By 1954 there were an estimated 180,000 Goans living outside Goa, including 80,000 in Bombay and 20,000 elsewhere in India.[47]

In 1789 a number of Luso-Malays left Malacca for Penang when the British colonized the island. As already stated, hundreds more left for Singapore after the British founded the island in 1819. A similar pattern occurred in Macao when Hong Kong was established as a British colony in 1842. By 1896, of the 2,371 Macanese who had left Macao, 1,309 went to Hong Kong and 738 to Shanghai.[48]

This Luso-Asian migration led to the Anglicization of their identities, with most becoming British subjects and English speakers. In 1897, 51 per cent of the 2,263 Macanese in Hong Kong had British nationality, and it has been said that in "around 1900 … it was as hard to find a Macanese [in Hong Kong] who could not speak good English as it was to find one who could speak good Portuguese."[49] "The Shanghai and Hong Kong Macanese tended to consider themselves progressive, speaking English and having better paid jobs. In contrast, the Macao Macanese were Portuguese-educated and largely employed in the Macao civil service."[50]

In India, Anglicization of the Eurasian communities meant wholesale swapping of identities. For example, the 1837 Calcutta census recorded 4,746 Eurasians and 3,181 Luso-Indians. By the time of the 1876 census, there were 10,566 Eurasians and just 707 Luso-Indians in the city. This latter, dwindled number is explained by the fact that the Luso-Indians identified themselves gradually with the Eurasians or Anglo-Indians of the present day.[51] Eurasian Indians of Portuguese origin are no longer identifiable in India, except in the territories which remained Portuguese until 1961.

Many communities of the English-speaking Luso-Asians and other Eurasians developed into well-educated and prosperous colonial elites, creating a social world that closely mirrored that of their British masters. They played cricket, hockey and netball, had music lessons and attended concerts (see Table 6.1).[52]

Data on the Eurasian population have always been difficult to obtain due to several factors. First, varying official attitudes towards their identity have resulted in the lack of statistical information. The Malay lands offer a clear illustration of this. Whereas the former Netherlands Indies enumerated all Eurasians as "Europeans", British Malaysia had a separate "Eurasian" ethnic category in its census returns. The Philippine mestizos, however, have never been officially recognized as an ethnic category and have always been lumped together with the "native" (that is, general) population. Second, many individuals of mixed ancestry were raised by their non-European mothers and socialized into native Asian society without close contact with Western culture. These children, and subsequently their own offspring, have disappeared as identifiable racial hybrids. Likewise, many Eurasians have chosen to conceal their ethnic identity by "passing" as pure-blooded whites. Finally, as illustrated below, the large numbers of Eurasians who elected to leave their Asian homelands to settle in Western countries reduced their already small share of the population to become a part of the "other" category.

THE SECOND DISPERSION

After the Second World War, large numbers of Eurasians elected to leave their Asian homelands for Western countries. The Eurasian exodus could be described as a subgroup of postcolonial migrants returning "home". As the white population, both European- and Asian-born, departed for Britain, the Netherlands, France and Portugal when the various Asian countries gained

TABLE 6.1
Eurasian Population (including Luso-Asians) in Selected Countries in Asia

Country	*Luso-Asians: Portuguese- and Creole-speaking*	*Luso-Asians: English- and Malay-speaking*	*Other (Non-Luso) Eurasians*	*Total Eurasians*	*Year of Census*
India	4,940	?	226,449	231,389	2001
Sri Lanka	500	34,843	2,000	38,388	2001
Malaysia	2,150	6,705	3,795	12,650	2000
Singapore	—	10,555	4,524	15,045	2000
Indonesia	—	30,000	6,000	36,000	
East Timor	1,939	—	—	1,939	1970
Macau S.A.R.	6,825	—	—	6,825	2006
Hong Kong S.A.R.	—	1,500	8,500	10,500	2006
Totals	16,354	83,603	251,268	352,736	

Notes:
India. Luso-Asian Creole-speakers: 4,940 Indo-Portuguese speakers. "Languages of India", *Ethnologue*, 16th ed., Web version <http://www.ethnologue.com/web.asp>, citing Cardoso, 2006. Other Eurasians: 226,449 English-speakers; most of these would be Anglo-Indians. The 1951 census was the last to enumerate Anglo-Indians at 111,637.
Sri Lanka. Luso-Asian Creole speakers: 500. Shihan de S. Jayasuriya, *The Portuguese in the East: A Cultural History of a Maritime Trading Empire* (London: Tauris Academic Studies, 2008). Creole speakers: 30. "Indo-Portuguese", *Ethnologue*, 16th ed., Web version <http://www.ethnologue.com/web.asp>, citing Baker, 1992. Other Eurasians: 2,000 members of Reformed Church, mostly Dutch Burghers.
Malaysia. Luso-Asian Creole-speakers: 2,150 Kristang speakers. Christopher Moseley, *Encyclopedia of the World's Endangered Languages* (London: Routledge, 2007). Luso-Asian English-speakers: based on 70 per cent Portuguese origin. Cutter, Selangor Eurasian Association.
Singapore. Luso-Asian English-speakers: based on 70 per cent Portuguese origin.
Indonesia. Luso-Asian Malay-speakers: 30,000 Larantuqueiros. Ronald Daus, *Portuguese Eurasian Communities in Southeast Asia* (Singapore: Institute of Southeast Asian Studies, 1989), p. 61. Other Eurasians: 6,000 Indo-Dutch. Paul W. Van der Veur, "Luctantur et emergunt: Indo-European tussen 1942 en 1962", in *Het einde van Indië*, edited by Wim Willems and Jaap de Moor (The Hague: Sdu, 1995).
Timor-Leste. Luso-Asian Potuguese-speakers: Mestizos. Portuguese Timor 1970 census.
Macau S.A.R. Luso-Asian Portuguese-speakers: total of all Portuguese ethnicity plus mixed-ethnicity, less European-born Portuguese. Macao, Direcção dos Serviços de Estatística e Censos, 2006 by-census.
Hong Kong S.A.R. Luso-Asian English-speakers: author's estimates based on 14,932 mixed-ethnicity, including Chinese and 3,160 mixed-ethnicity, including non-Chinese. Hong Kong, Census and Statistics Department, 2006 by-census.

their independence, Eurasians were also among the evacuees. Allegiance and language played a major part in settlement patterns. Very few of the Dutch Burghers from Sri Lanka left for their "ancestral homeland" of the Netherlands; hardly any Portuguese-Eurasian families from Malaysia migrated "home" to Portugal. Both groups immigrated to Australia, the United Kingdom and other English-speaking countries. In the territories which had remained Portuguese (Goa, Timor and Macao) the Luso-Asians left mostly for Portugal and the Portuguese colonies in Africa, with much smaller numbers settling in Brazil. English-speaking Luso-Asians chose Britain, the United States, Canada, Australia and New Zealand as destinations. The Luso-Asians originating from Macao went two ways: whereas the Portuguese-speaking Macanese from Macao settled in Portuguese-speaking territories, their fellow Macanese — the English-speaking, so-called "Portuguese" communities of Hong Kong, Shanghai and Canton — preferred the United States and Britain as their new homes.

The migration was a singular occurrence in that a large number left their countries of birth within a relatively short time frame, with very few of the others who had stayed behind wanting to leave later. Those who stayed in Asia have since become more integrated with their surrounding societies. The relatively short time frame mentioned above, between the early 1950s and late 1960s, would have been even more concentrated if the racially select policies of the receiving countries had not existed. The White Australia policy practised from the beginning of the twentieth century until the early 1970s meant that mixed-race applicants such as the Eurasians had to establish that they were of 75 per cent European blood before being allowed into Australia. This rule meant that only 10,000 Eurasians were admitted between 1950 and 1965, mostly fair-skinned Dutch Burghers and Anglo-Indians.[53] However, the Portuguese Burghers and the majority of other Eurasians had to wait until 1964, when part-Europeans (only, and not those who were wholly Asian) were formally permitted into the country. The year 1973 saw the final abolition of the White Australia policy by the Whitlam Labour government. Thousands of people from all over Asia began immigrating into Australia, but the small Eurasian migration was already over.

Just as the Eurasians formed the first wave of post-war Asian immigrants to Australia, so did Eurasians comprise the first post-war arrivals in the United Kingdom, when some 25,000[54] to 30,000[55] Anglo-Indians entered the country between Indian independence in 1947 and 1952. Settling mostly in London, the Anglo-Indians arrived just before hundreds of thousands of Asians in the 1950s and 1960s.

Due to the fact that the exodus ended in the early 1970s and some forty to fifty years have since elapsed, the total Eurasian population size in the diaspora has now passed its maximum. For example, Dr Charles Price, one of Australia's most respected demographic experts, estimated the numbers of "ethno-Europeans" resident in Australia born in the same seven countries as listed in Table 6.2 as 163,814 in 1978.[56] By the time of the 2006 census, as seen in Table 6.2, the number had declined to 100,608.

Table 6.2 also reveals for the first time the numbers of Eurasians who reside in the diaspora. As it is defined here, Eurasians are the Asian-born descendants of colonial relationships between Europeans and Asians. The colonial context is strictly applied here and the Konketsuji (mixed-bloods) born during and after the Second World War in Japan and the other Amerasian groups born during and after the Vietnam War in Indochina, Thailand and the Philippines fall outside this definition. The Table 6.2 figures do not include the descendants of Eurasians born in these Western countries (that is, the second generation), nor does it include the growing numbers of children resulting from intermarriages between Caucasians and Asians in the West.

It must be noted that the data in Table 6.2 derive from different criteria utilized by different nations and include both Europeans and Eurasians born in the various countries of origin. The United States and the United Kingdom apply a race-based measure, with those claiming "white only" origin being clearly separated from those claiming mixed racial origin. The Canadian and New Zealand results are based on ethnic origin; people can belong to one or several ethnicities. For example, an individual could be recorded as "Dutch" in our tables if he or she claimed "Dutch only" ethnicity; another could have ticked both the Dutch and Indonesian boxes and still appear on our tables as "Dutch"; still another could have selected Dutch, Portuguese and Indonesian ethnicities and been counted twice on our tables as both "Dutch" and "Portuguese". (Indonesian is ignored here as we are calculating European ethnicities only.) The Australian data differ from that of these two countries in that it derives from answers to an ancestry question, where a person could go back several generations; in recent years only, the Australian methodology also accepts several local Eurasian identity designations such as "Anglo-Indian", "Anglo-Burmese", "Burgher" and "Eurasian, so described" in its census returns. The Portuguese census does not classify its population into racial, ethnic or ancestral groups; therefore, all data for that country have to be based on estimates.

It is necessary to show both the combined European and part-European (Eurasian) totals for two reasons: first for uniformity, as some figures provide singular and multiple responses whereas others are only combined responses;

TABLE 6.2
Eurasian Population (including Luso-Asians) in the Diaspora

Country of Origin	*Portugal 2010*	*United Kingdom 2001*	*United States 2000*	*Canada 2006*	*Australia 2006*	*New Zealand 2006*
India	**11,000–50,000 (a)**	**62,382** 45,452 White British 7,543 White Other 9,387 Mixed	**52,030** 10,640 White 41,390 Two races +	**22,820** 10,890 British 5,095 Portuguese 320 Dutch	**33,807** 21,444 British 6,864 Anglo-Indian 1,514 Portuguese 246 Dutch	**1,896**
Sri Lanka		**7,850** 4,442 White British 557 White Other 2,851 Mixed	**2,730** 415 White 2,315 Two races +	**13,015** 4,250 British 3,020 Portuguese 1,335 Dutch	**11,862** 4,771 British 3,449 Dutch 772 Burgher 733 Portuguese	**264**
Malaysia		**18,000*** 12,000 White* 6,000 Mixed*	**3,175** 1,125 White 2,050 Two races +	**2,000**†	**14,579** 7,366 British 733 Eurasians 520 Portuguese 457 Dutch	**960**
Singapore		**26,000*** 22,000 White* 4,000 Mixed*	**2,420** 1,465 White 955 Two races +	**1,000**†	**11,788** 6,010 British 1,020 Eurasians 525 Portuguese 457 Dutch	**1,527**
Indonesia		**4,000*** 3,000 White* 1,000 Mixed*	**19,090** 10,025 White 9,065 Two races +	**3,000**†	**7,336** 4,179 Dutch 1,237 British 36 Portuguese	**1,023**

continued on next page

TABLE 6.2 — *cont'd*

Country of Origin	*Portugal 2010*	*United Kingdom 2001*	*United States 2000*	*Canada 2006*	*Australia 2006*	*New Zealand 2006*
East Timor	**1,000 (b)**				**1,080** 895 Portuguese	**9**
Hong Kong. S.A.R.		**18,000*** 16,000 White* 2,000 Mixed*		**5,530** 2,405 British 1,035 Portuguese	**8,556** 5,066 British 374 Portuguese	**807**
Macau S.A.R.	**5,000 (c)**	(included in figures for China)	**475**	(included in figures for China)	(included in figures for China)	**9**
China (PRC)		**3,932** 3,129 White British 349 White Other 454 Mixed	**23,880** 11,330 White 12,550 Two races +	**6,400** 2,055 British 355 Portuguese	**7,781** 5,111 Russian 1,161 British 307 Other European	**819**
TOTALS	**17,000–56,000**	**140,164**	**103,800**	**54,765**	**100,608**	**7,458**

Notes:
* Author's estimates based on data for "Other Far East", United Kingdom, Office for National Statistics, *The 2001 Census.*
† Author's estimates based on data for "Other Southeast Asia", includes Europeans and Eurasians, from Statistics Canada, *2006 Census of Canada.*
Portugal (a): Oscar Lobo "About Goa" < http://malgoans.com/aboutgoa.htm> (accessed July 2010); Jorge Malheiros, *Imigrantes na Região de Lisboa: Os Anos da Mudança* (Lisbon: Colibri, 1996), p. 160; and Teotonio R. de Souza, "Is There One Goan Identity, Several or None?", *Lusotopie 2000* (2000): 494.
Portugal (b): Author's estimates
Portugal (c): Author's estimates
United Kingdom: Data compiled from United Kingdom, Office for National Statistics, *The 2001 Census,* Table S102, "Sex and Country of Birth by Ethnic Group".
United States: Category is designated as two or more races. Data compiled from U.S. Census Bureau, *Census 2000,* Special Tabulations, "Profile of Selected Demographic and Social Characteristics: 2000".
Canada: Figures represent Europeans and Eurasians. Data compiled from Statistics Canada, *2006 Census of Canada,* "Topic-Based Tabulations: Ethnic Origin".
Australia: Data compiled from Australian Bureau of Statistics, *2006 Census,* tables on ancestry by country of birth.
New Zealand: Figures represent persons born in Asia of non-Asian ethnicity, including Europeans and Eurasians. Data compiled from Statistics New Zealand, *2006 Census of Population and Dwellings.*

second, many Eurasians classify themselves as Europeans, especially those who have a European parent and a Eurasian parent. Others know only of their Portuguese or other European heritage (due to their family names, history, cultural traits, language and religion) but are unsure of their specific Asian background. The majority of the totals comprise Eurasians, but the European component is very significant and depends much on the ancestry group. There is a large number of "pure" Europeans among those classified as "British", the last colonial power; a much smaller number among the "Dutch" group (except for a sizeable minority of those born in Indonesia); and hardly any in those listed as "Portuguese" (except for some families whose members were born in Macao and East Timor).

About 462,795 Luso-Asians and other Eurasians live outside Asia. Over 140,000 reside in the United Kingdom, another 100,000 each in the United States and Australia, some 50,000 each in Portugal and Canada, and over 7,000 in New Zealand. The statistics exclude Eurasians beyond the scope of this study such as the large Indo-Dutch communities in the Netherlands and the United States, the growing Filipino-Spanish mestizo communities in North America, the long-established Anglo-Burmese communities in Britain and Australia, and the small French-Indochinese Metis community in France.

Charts 6.1 and 6.2 compare the Sri Lankan-born of European ethnicity in Canada with the Sri Lankan-born of European ancestry in Australia. In 2006, both populations were similar in size — 13,015 and 11,862 respectively — but the subgroup compositions varied considerably. Whereas the proportion of Dutch to Portuguese Burghers among Sri Lankan-born Australians is 3:1, the ratio is reversed among Sri Lankan-born Canadians. This is easily understood when one considers that the Dutch Burgher migration to Australia occurred during the White Australia era when most Portuguese Burghers would have been excluded. However, the number of persons describing themselves as British in both countries is a surprising 33 to 40 per cent. Even allowing for the inclusion of a couple of thousand British Europeans in the total, the percentage is much higher than the actual proportion of Anglo-Eurasians in colonial Ceylon (about 5 to 10 per cent). This tendency for many English-speaking Luso-Asians to identify themselves as British is further illustrated by the data from the Malaysia- and Singapore-born living in Australia.

Charts 6.3 and 6.4 demonstrate the similarities between the Malaysia-born and Singapore-born of European ancestry resident in Australia. In 2006, the populations from the two countries numbered 14,579 and 11,788 respectively. As the table illustrates, about half of each group claimed British

CHART 6.1
Canada: Sri Lanka-born of European Ethnicity by Subgroup, 2006

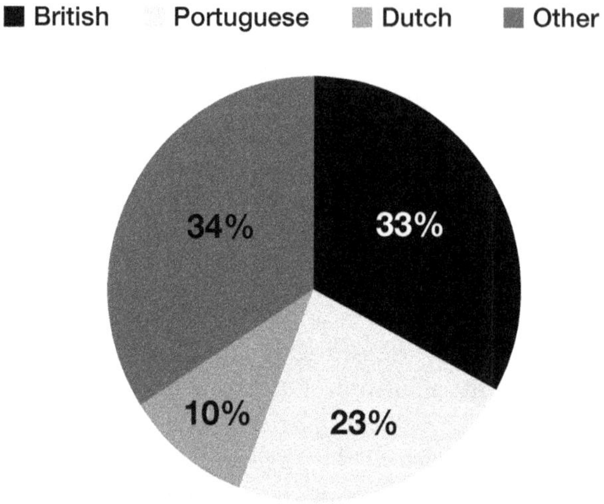

Source: Statistics Canada, *2006 Census of Canada*.

CHART 6.2
Australia: Sri Lanka-born of European Ancestry by Subgroup, 2006

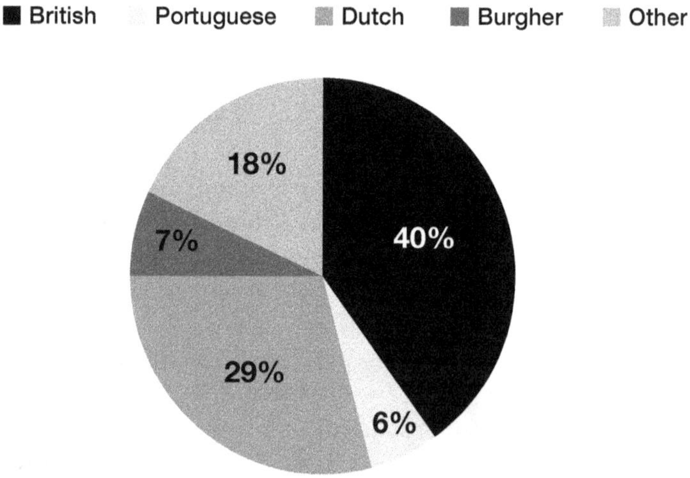

Source: Australian Bureau of Statistics, *2006 Census*.

CHART 6.3
Australia: Malaysia-born of European Ancestry by Subgroup, 2006

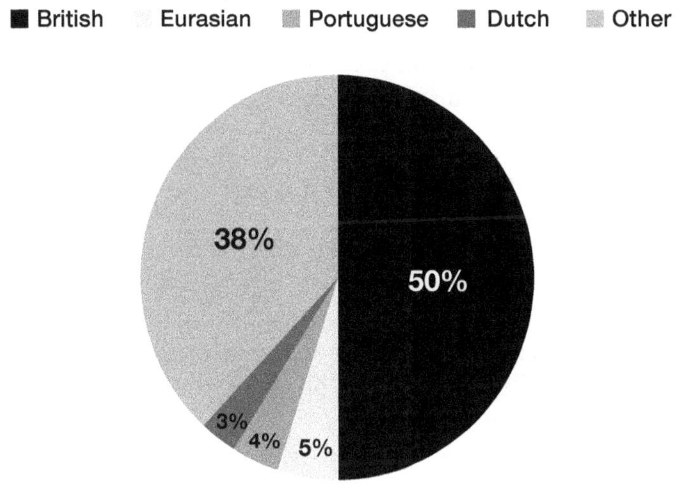

Source: Australian Bureau of Statistics, *2006 Census*.

CHART 6.4
Australia: Singapore-born of European Ancestry by Subgroup, 2006

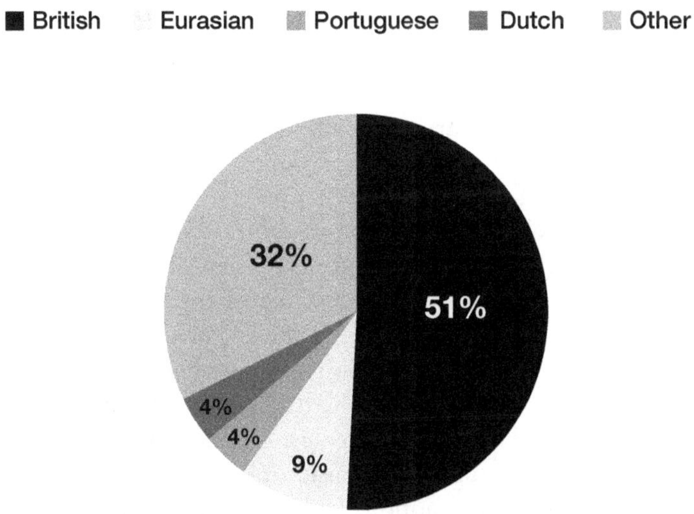

Source: Australian Bureau of Statistics, *2006 Census*.

ancestry, with only 4 per cent recording Portuguese ancestry in both countries. Even allowing for a further 5 to 9 per cent who noted Eurasian ancestry (these could have been Portuguese), the percentage of the Portuguese subgroup (9 to 13 per cent) is much lower than the actual proportion of Luso-Asians in the two countries (about 70 per cent). This could be a reflection of how English-speaking Luso-Asians see themselves.

CONCLUSION

The Luso-Asians, even though they were widely distributed throughout Asia in some dozens of settlements in both the official and unofficial Portuguese empire, were a unified group in their identity. Irrespective of their racial combinations, or their slave origins, they saw themselves as one people, the Portuguese of Asia. The Dutch period "broke up" the Portuguese world, with some territories remaining Portuguese and others becoming Dutch, although in both areas their Portuguese language continued to be spoken. Although new communities with a Dutch identity emerged, the Luso-Asians survived. It was the British period that had the greatest impact on the Luso-Asians. The first dispersion introduced British culture and the English language to the communities. By the time of the second dispersion, parts of their communities were so Anglicized that they chose to emigrate to the English-speaking territories.

As the oldest of the Eurasian groups, the Luso-Asian communities have had to adapt to many changes in their long history and to survive the assimilative processes of both the incoming European colonists as well as their local Asian neighbours. It is truly remarkable that the Luso-Asian communities have survived for 500 years. However, there are very few speakers of Portuguese Creole remaining — less than 7,000 persons — and the number of Luso-Asians in Asia has been greatly reduced by their emigration to the West after the Second World War and the granting of independence for the South and Southeast Asian nations. Their numbers seem to be recovering in recent years, but extensive intermarriage with other ethnicities in Asia is diminishing their "Portugueseness". Similarly, the successful integration of the English-speaking Luso-Asian communities in the Anglo-Saxon world has resulted in the further dilution of their Portuguese identity. The Luso-Asians are a legacy of the sixteenth- and seventeenth-century Portuguese expansion into Asia. The analysis carried out above substantiates the notion that Luso-Asian identity has changed over time and over seas.

Notes

1 António da Silva Rego, *Portuguese Colonization in the Sixteenth Century: A Study of the Royal Ordinances (Regimentos)* (Johannesburg: Witwatersrand University Press, 1959), pp. 35–36.

2 L.A. Rodrigues, "Portuguese-Blood Communities in India", *Boletim do Instituto Menezes Bragança* 108 (1973).

3 Ibid.

4 Armando Cortesão, *The Suma Oriental of Tomé Pires: An Account of the East, from the Red Sea to Japan, Written in Malacca and India in 1512–1515* (London: The Hakluyt Society, 1944), p. 269.

5 Gerard Fernandis, ed., *Save Our Portuguese Heritage Conference 95 Malacca, Malaysia* (Malacca, 1996), p. 45.

6 Manuel Teixeira, *The Portuguese Missions in Malacca and Singapore (1511–1958)* (Lisbon: Agência Geral do Ultramar, 1961). Teixeira's source is Francisco de Souza's two-volume *O Oriente Conquistador a Jesus Christo pelos Padres da Companhia de Jesus* (Lisbon, 1710). See also Geoffrey C. Gunn, *First Globalization: The Eurasian Exchange, 1500–1800* (Lanham, MD: Rowman & Littlefield, 2003), pp. 251–52.

7 T.J. Newbold, *Political and Statistical Account of British Settlements in the Straits of Malacca*, vol. 1 (London: John Murray, 1839).

8 Most writers acknowledge that the Portuguese Eurasians are the majority component of the Singaporean Eurasian community. In the 2000 Singaporean census, 67 per cent of Christians in the "others" group (mostly Eurasians and Europeans) were Catholics. However, it was also stated that "roughly a quarter to a third of Eurasians in Singapore carry Portuguese surnames." See Bee Geok Leow, *Census of Population 2000: Education, Language and Religion, Statistical Release 2* (Singapore: Department of Statistics, Ministry of Trade and Industry, 2001) p. 112, table 39. See also George Yeo, "Foreword", *The Most Comprehensive Eurasian Heritage Dictionary: Kristang-English, English-Kristang* (Singapore: SNP Reference, 2004), p. 7. For discussion on the "Indo-Briton" and other labels in colonial India, see also Adrian Carton, "Beyond 'Cotton Mary': Anglo-Indian Categories and Reclaiming the Diverse Past", 2009 <http://home.alphalink.com.au/~agilbert/ carton.html> (accessed 23 July 2010).

9 Ronald Daus, *Portuguese Eurasian Communities in Southeast Asia* (Singapore: Institute of Southeast Asian Studies, 1989), p. 58.

10 Donald E. Weatherbee, "Portuguese Timor: An Indonesian Dilemma", *Asian Survey* 6, no. 2 (1966): 684. Weatherbee's data are derived from Instituto Nacional de Estatística, *Anuário Estatístico do Império Colonial* (Lisbon: Instituto Nacional de Estatística, 1950).

11 Isabel Tomás, "Makista Creole", *Review of Culture* 5 (1988): 33.

12 Marie Arana-Ward, "A Synchronic and Diachronic Investigation of Macanese:

The Portuguese-Based Creole of Macao" (Ph.D. dissertation, University of Hong Kong, 1977), p. 21; and Gunn, *First Globalization*, pp. 259–60.

13 Madalena Ribeiro, "The Japanese Diaspora in the Seventeenth Century According to Jesuit Sources", *Bulletin of Portuguese/Japanese Studies* 3 (Dec. 2001): 61–62.

14 Anders [Andrew] Ljungstedt, *An Historical Sketch of the Portuguese Settlements in China* (Boston: Adamant Media Corp., 2006), p. 27.

15 Ibid., pp. 205–8.

16 John Clement Koop, *The Eurasian Population in Burma* (New Haven: Yale University Press, 1960), p. 17.

17 Miguel Castelo Branco, "500 Anos Portugal-Tailandia" <http://500anosportugal tailandia.blogspot.com/2009/10/portuguese-minority-in-siam.html> (accessed 23 July 2010).

18 In 2002, Joaquim Magalhães de Castro, sponsored by the Macao International Institute, travelled to Myanmar in search of these Portuguese descendants and published a photographic account of this "lost community". Joaquim Magalhães de Castro, Os *Bayingyis do Vale do Mu: Luso-Descendentes na Birmânia* (Santa Maria da Feira, Portugal: Câmara Municipal, 2002).

19 Stefan Halikowski Smith, "Seventeenth Century Population Displacements in the Portuguese Indies and the Creation of a Portuguese 'Tribe'" in *Christians and Spices: Sri Lanka and the Portuguese Orient*, edited by Gaston Pereira (Sri Lanka: ICESKY, 2010).

20 Barnabas Hon Mun Koo, "The Survival of an Endangered Species: The Macanese in Contemporary Macau." (Ph.D. dissertation, University of Western Sydney, 2004), p. 216.

21 Some individuals, however, proudly acknowledge their remote Portuguese heritage, such as Praphatsorn Seiwikun, Thai diplomat and acclaimed author.

22 Keith Whinnom, *Spanish Contact Vernaculars in the Philippine Islands* (Hong Kong: Hong Kong University Press, 1956).

23 Malyn Newitt, *A History of Portuguese Overseas Expansion, 1400–1668* (New York: Routledge, 2005), p. 256.

24 Whinnom, *Spanish Contact Vernaculars*; and John Holm, *Pidgins and Creoles*, vol. 2, *Reference Survey* (Cambridge: Cambridge University Press, 1989).

25 United Nations Statistics Division, Department of Economic and Social Affairs, *Demographic Yearbook*, Special Census Topics, vol. 2b, "Social Characteristics: Ethnocultural Characteristics", p. 40, table 4 <http://unstats.un.org/unsd/demographic/ products/dyb/DYBcensus/NotesTabSpecial2_4.pdf> (accessed 23 July 2010).

26 Newitt, *A History*, p. 263.

27 Jean Gelman Taylor, *The Social World of Batavia: European and Eurasian in Dutch Asia* (Madison: University of Wisconsin Press, 1983), p. 48.

28 Ulbe Bosma and Remco Raben, *Being "Dutch" in the Indies* (Singapore: National University of Singapore Press, 2008), p. 53.

[29] Smith, *Community Dynamics.*

[30] Luang Sitsayamkan, *The Greek Favourite of the King of Siam* (Singapore: Donald Moore Press, 1967).

[31] Sanjay Subrahmanyam, "Written on Water: Designs and Dynamics in the Portuguese Estado da Índia", in *Empires: Perspectives from Archaeology and History*, edited by Susan E. Alcock (New York: Cambridge University Press, 2001), p. 47.

[32] C.R. Boxer, *The Portuguese Seaborne Empire: 1415–1825* (London: Hutchinson, 1969).

[33] Newitt, *A History*, p. 257.

[34] K.W. Goonewardena, *The Foundation of Dutch Power in Ceylon: 1638–1658* (Amsterdam: Djambatan, 1958), p. 226.

[35] Rodney Ferdinands, *Proud and Prejudiced: The Story of the Burghers of Sri Lanka* (Melbourne: F.R.L. Ferdinands, 1995), p. 93; and Noel P. Gist and Anthony Gary Dworkin, eds., *The Blending of Races: Marginality and Identity in World Perspective* (New York: John Wiley & Sons, 1972), p. 35.

[36] R.J. Barendse, *Arabian Seas, 1700–1763*, vol. 1, *The Western Indian Ocean in the Eighteenth Century* (Leiden: Brill, 2009), pp. 515–16.

[37] Anjana Singh, *Fort Cochin in Kerala, 1750–1830: The Social Condition of a Dutch Community in an Indian Milieu* (Leiden: Brill, 1976), p. 232.

[38] The Malaysian Dutch Descendants Project was founded in 2002. They estimate the number of Dutch descendants in Malaysia at 2,000. See Dennis De Witt, *History of the Dutch in Malaysia* (Petaling Jaya, Malaysia: Nutmeg Publishing, 2009), p. 224.

[39] Lionel Caplan, *Children of Colonialism: Anglo-Indians in a Postcolonial World* (Oxford: Berg, 2001), p. 22.

[40] Caplan, *Children of Colonialism*, p. 23; and Gloria Jean Moore, *The Anglo-Indian Vision* (Melbourne: AE Press, 1986), p. 4.

[41] J.A.A. Campos, *History of the Portuguese in Bengal* (New Delhi: Asian Educational Services, 1998 [1919]), p. 185.

[42] Caplan, *Children of Colonialism*, p. 24.

[43] Margaret Sarkissian, "Being Portuguese in Malacca: The Politics of Folk Culture in Malaysia", *Ethnografica* 9, no. 1 (2005): 152.

[44] Myrna Braga-Blake, *Singapore Eurasians: Memories and Hopes* (Singapore: Times Edition, 1992), p. 119; and Alexius A. Pereira, "No Longer 'Other': The Emergence of the Eurasian Community in Singapore", in *Race, Ethnicity, and the State in Malaysia and Singapore*, edited Lian Kwen Fee (Leiden: Brill, 2006), p. 15.

[45] Fátima da Silva Gracias, "Goans Away from Goa: Migration to the Middle East", *Lusotopie* (2000): 423–32. Gracias's data are derived from the Paco Patriarchal (Patriarchal Archives), Rois de Cristandade: Rois de Ilhas 1870–89 and 1934–41; Rois de Bardez 1870–89; Rois das Novas Conquistas 1870–89 and 1934–41; and Rois de Salcete 1934–41.

[46] Margret Frenz, "Global Goans: Migration Movements and Identity in a Historical Perspective", *Lusotopie* 15, no. 1 (2008): 187. Frenz's data are derived from censuses of Kenya, Tanganyika, Uganda, and Zanzibar for the years 1921 and 1948.

[47] Bento G. D'Souza, *Goan Society in Transition* (Bombay: Popular Prakashan, 1975), p. 203.

[48] Koo, "The Survival", p. 216.

[49] J.E. Reinecke, "Marginal Languages: A Sociological Survey of the Creole Languages and Trade Jargons" (Ph.D. dissertation, Yale University, 1937), p. 206.

[50] Koo, "The Survival", p. 219.

[51] Campos, *History of the Portuguese*, p. 199.

[52] Sarkissian, "Being Portuguese", p. 154.

[53] Gwenda Tavan, *The Long, Slow Death of White Australia* (Melbourne: Scribe Publications, 2005).

[54] Melville de Mellow, "Anglo-Indians", *The Illustrated Weekly of India,* 19 July 1970, p. 12.

[55] Ian McAuley, *Guide to Ethnic London* (London: Immel Publishing, 1999), p. 26.

[56] Charles A. Price, *Immigration and Ethnicity* (Canberra: Commonwealth Department of Immigration and Multicultural Affairs, 1996), pp. 105–8, table 3.3, "Converting Birthplace Origin to Ethnic Origin, 1978".

7

THE POPULATION OF THE PORTUGUESE ESTADO DA ÍNDIA, 1750–1820: SOURCES AND DEMOGRAPHIC TRENDS[1]

Paulo Teodoro de Matos

Beginning in the second half of the eighteenth century, the administration of Portugal's overseas territories came to demand an increasingly detailed and systematic understanding of their inhabitants. This tendency was manifested in the development of the framework known as "political arithmetic", whose effects were felt in Portugal throughout the eighteenth century. Just like other European imperial powers, specifically England and Spain, the Portuguese state came to depend upon specific information about inhabitants and their annual fluxes (births, marriages and deaths) to reinforce its own power.

As a result of the various royal orders sent to overseas governors, there survives an impressive corpus of population *mapas* (statistical tables, referred to throughout this chapter as either "*mapas*" or "statistical charts"), especially after 1776. There are, necessarily, reservations concerning the corpus, especially in regards to the completeness of the coverage of territory and the accuracy of the *mapas* themselves. Nonetheless, by analysing this corpus we are able to delineate with some depth the principal demographic characteristics of certain territories that belonged to the Portuguese Estado da Índia, particularly Goa.

Between 1750 and 1820, the Estado da Índia — comprising the territories of Goa, Daman, Diu, Macao and Timor — underwent some changes in its territorial extension. Beginning in 1752, Mozambique ceased to depend on Goa and received a governor who responded directly to the Conselho Ultramarino (Portugal's overseas administrative council). Goa, a small territory located on the coast of Konkan, included both the so-called Old Conquests (1510) — the provinces of the Islands of Goa (Ilhas de Goa, or simply "Islands"), Bardez and Salcete (745 square kilometres)[2] — and the New Conquests, which were annexed between 1746 and 1782. This annexation nearly quadrupled the Estado da Índia's territorial extension.[3]

During the second half of the eighteenth century, the reforms of the Marquês de Pombal (1755–78) came to hold particular importance. He promoted, on the one hand, both a policy of greater religious tolerance and the clear promotion of local elites; on the other hand, however, he sought to extend the territory of Goa through to its natural limit, the Ghats mountain range, as a means to safeguard the crucial territory from potential attacks by nearby kingdoms. This strategy aimed to reposition Goa in light of the Portuguese loss of various possessions in India (particularly the Praças do Norte, the northern territories), so that the Estado da Índia would have a new kind of viability.[4]

Nonetheless, beginning in the second half of the eighteenth century, if not before, the Goan territory came to suffer a noticeable loss in population, especially in the province of the Ilhas de Goa. A string of epidemics, some of significant impact, appear to have been responsible for an extraordinary loss of life and decrease in the number of inhabitants. Additionally, the reconstruction of the moribund City of Goa, in 1778, contributed to excessive loss of life, the effects of which affected the entire territory.[5]

This chapter consists of two parts. The first presents and discusses several still little-known sources and explains a normative scheme of statistical *mapas*, the grouping of available sources, information typology and notes about the reliability of the documents. The second part presents the demographic structures of diverse territories with an emphasis on the comparative dimension. This analysis rests above all on the number of residents, their rate of growth and their socioreligious makeup. The frequency of production of the *mapas* and their level of information allow for a more detailed view into the territory of the Old Conquests, with the exception of Timor and Macao, for which few sources exist.

The period under consideration extends from 1750 into the 1820s. The first year corresponds to the ascension of Dom José I to king; during his reign the principles of political arithmetic became widely diffused and reforms of significant social and political reach were enacted. The year 1820 marks the inauguration of liberalism in Portugal, which would quickly introduce new directions in the area of demographic statistics. The changes that then took place justify the chronological break for the period under consideration here.

THE SOURCES

The first national census of continental Portugal took place in 1801, giving rise to the period known as "premodern statistics". This fact has at times obscured population counting, which, under the names "enumerations", "computations" or "surveys", took place at various times over the course of the eighteenth century. While the majority of these surveys coincided with the Pombaline period (1750–77), much progress was made towards calculating Portugal's overseas population during the reign of Dom João V (1700–50).[6] We also know of several *mapas* elaborated during this same period for the captaincies in Brazil, a more or less direct consequence of the Treaty of Madrid (1750).

Although such statistics are relatively sparse, corresponding to periodic requests from the Crown, they do reveal two important characteristics. First, the area recorded in the census covers the whole territory; second, the surveys convey exceptionally informative detail. The best examples are those from Cabo Verde (1731)[7] and, above all, those from Goa (1720).[8]

Analysing the statistical charts of the Portuguese possessions shows that regular execution of statistical surveys began, in the majority of the colonies, in 1776. In fact, a few series or isolated *mapas* for the Azores, Madeira, Brazil, Angola, Cape Verde and São Tomé e Príncipe for the period prior to 1776 survive; in several cases, the structure of these *mapas* comes close to that which received such praise in that year.

Among the demographic sources available for the overseas empire, those for Goa (the Old Conquests) stand out. The documentation deposited in the Arquivo Histórico Ultramarino (AHU), the Historical Archives of Goa (HAG) and the Biblioteca Nacional of Rio de Janeiro (BNRJ) cover the years 1749 through 1753 and, later on, 1776 to 1835 in a nearly continuous series.

The situation is different for the other Portuguese holdings in Asia, especially Macao and Timor, for which information is very sparse. The abundance of statistical charts for Goa may be partially explained by four basic reasons: (a) the existence of a highly bureaucratic administration, capable of carrying out the Crown's wishes; (b) the small size of the territory; (c) the dispersion of holdings under the jurisdiction of Goa and the resulting difficulty in the creation of the *mapas*; and (d) a more effective archival system in Portuguese India, especially in the capital, as expressed by the volumes of the Livros das Monções do Reino (the Monsoons collection), into which all documentation received from and sent to Lisbon was copied.

As was the case for some other overseas possessions, statistical charts for the Old Conquests of Goa were produced during the mid-eighteenth century, more specifically between 1749 and 1753.[9] In 1749, the information included the numbers of clerics, whites, "naturals", gentiles, Muslims (called Moors), blacks and Timorese. In the 1753 *mapa*, the designation "slave" replaced "black", while the Timorese became part of another category: "Timores, Chinese, and Bengalis".

The royal order of 21 May 1776, which was expedited to the many overseas governors, regularized and made official the reporting of statistics on basic demographic divisions and the annual flux of births, deaths and marriages.[10] This decree marked a new paradigm in overseas statistics, resulting in consequences on two levels. First, the presentation of information, especially age groups, was standardized, so that comparisons became possible. Second, and perhaps with greater impact, it became obligatory to annually send *mapas* to the Conselho Ultramarino.

In the case of Goa, just as in the other possessions of the Portuguese Atlantic, the royal decree of 21 May 1776 alludes to previous orders sent to the viceroy concerning the elaboration of the *mapas*. In truth, as far back as 1718, some surveys for Goa exist, especially those from 1720, 1749 and 1753. It is quite possible that others were also completed but thus far remain unpublished.[11]

To ensure that the gathering of information would take place with "all possible exactness", the monarch sent an identical notice to the archbishop of the East in 1776 to solicit the collaboration of the parish priests, who, supported by the ministers of justice, would provide the first numbers.[12] As ordered by the decree, the population was to be categorized at the parish level according to the classes found in Table 7.1.

The adopted classification deserves some comment. As is easy to see, these charts are by nature governmental, per the requirement sent from the monarch to the viceroy. Nonetheless, only the ecclesiastical entities were able to gather the information. For this reason, on various occasions the ecclesiastical terminology did not fully coincide with that used by the civil authorities. Furthermore, the small appetite among parish priests for mathematics — and consequently the rigour required to calculate each portion of the survey — creates problems for interpreting the documentation.

To precisely count their residents, the priests relied on rolls of confession (drawn from the lists of worshippers who confessed and took communion at Lent), while population movement was counted via the parochial

TABLE 7.1
Population Classifications for Goa, 1776

Class	*Original Portuguese Classification*	*Equivalent in English*
1	Todas as crianças do sexo masculino até à idade de 7 anos completos	All boys under age 7
2	Todos os rapazes desde a idade de sete anos até a idade de 15	All male youths from ages 7 to 15
3	Todos os homens desde a idade de 15 anos até à idade de 60	All men from ages 15 to 60
4	Todos os velhos desde a idade de 60 anos para cima com especificação particular de todos os que passam de 90 anos	All men from age 60 and up, with special classification for those older than 90
5	Todas as crianças do sexo feminino até à idade de 7 anos completos	All girls under age 7
6	Todas as raparigas desde a idade de 7 anos até à idade de 14	All female youths from ages 7 to 14
7	Todas as mulheres desde a idade de 14 anos até à idade de 40	All women from ages 14 through 40
8	Todas as adultas e velhas desde a idade de 40 anos para cima com especificação particular de todas as que passarem de 90 anos	All adult and elderly women from age 40 and up, with special classification for those older than 90
9	Todos os nascimentos acontecidos no ano em que se tirar cada relação	All births during the calendar year under consideration
10	Todas as mortes acontecidas no mesmo ano	All deaths during the same year

registry books for baptisms, weddings and deaths. By what measure the births in a determined year would be included in classes 0 through 7 is unknown. At the same time, some births may have been omitted when the newborn passed away before baptism.[13] In the same way, there may be an underrepresentation of deaths of young children who passed away before receiving the sacrament of baptism.

Classes 0 through 7 cover all "minors of confession", who were not always counted by the clergy in the confessionary rolls. As a result, the counts for this group may have come from estimates. The class of women aged fourteen through forty was related to the period of fertility and may have therefore contributed to the elaboration of population projections.[14] Finally, the existence of such a wide interval for men — from fifteen to sixty years — corresponded perfectly to the age of conscription according to militia regulations for the so-called "third line" of troops.[15]

The crown did not offer instructions for counting socioreligious groups and minorities (fluctuating population). From 1776 to 1796, the division was based exclusively on religion, dividing the population between Christians and gentiles (Hindus and Muslims). In 1797, however, new demographic classifications were introduced, and they would remain in place through 1825. These charts begin to distinguish between "white Christians", "native Christians" (also known as *canarins*), "blacks", *pardos* (the offspring of individuals who were crosses between Africans and non-Africans) and "gentiles and Muslims". The first category included Portuguese from Portugal (the *reinóis*) and Portuguese born in India (*castiços*). Nevertheless, a Luso-descendant individual could eventually be reclassified as a "white Christian" or a "native Christian", depending on the criteria used by the editor. While "blacks" can be assumed to refer to slaves, the same is not applicable for those of mixed race; the legal status of these persons, the offspring of Africans and non-Africans, was left to the judgement of the specific property owner.[16] As a result, it becomes difficult to quantify in an effective way the size of the slave population.

One may think to ask how Hindus and Muslims were counted, as they were vassals of the king but not subject to the jurisdiction of the Church. It is known that Hindu and Muslim houses of worship kept population registries quite similar to those of the Christians. The information was possibly taken by community leaders, the *gãocares*, to the civil authorities, or was directly collected by the clerics themselves.[17]

In a collective analysis, Goa is the overseas territory with both the greatest number of sources and the greatest homogeneity. This reality contrasts sharply with the other lands of the Estado da Índia. In general, the information is highly irregular and sporadic, so that comparisons across space and time become impossible. Although information on the New Conquests dates back to 1808, it rarely includes social groups or the age breakdown of the persons surveyed. The even fewer statistics for Daman and Diu suffer from the same limitations. For Macao, there are numerous surveys for the eighteenth century, but they provide limited information due to the exclusion of the Chinese population.[18]

In general, the sources consulted here ought to be considered relatively accurate for the period under consideration.[19] The statistical analysis of population flux, percentage of population by age group, and demographic behaviour reveal acceptable oscillations. In spite of the typical undercounting of births and deaths during the period under consideration, the corrected values reveal less fluctuation in birth rates in relation to death rates. This confirms, with a reasonable degree of confidence, the judgement that in pre-industrial societies, mortality underwent significant oscillations due to the appearance of epidemics and food crises.

POPULATION TRENDS

It is difficult, if not altogether impossible, to provide a trustworthy estimate of the population of Portuguese Asia prior to the end of the nineteenth century. This challenge stems principally from the absence of facts for Timor, as the population there was not directly controlled by the Portuguese administration. Furthermore, we must re-emphasize that only fragile information on Macao survives. Robust statistics for Macao go back only as far as the middle of the nineteenth century, due to the frequent difficulties that impeded counting the Chinese population.[20]

Despite the fragility of the statistics available for Portugal's overseas possessions, Vitorino Magalhães Godinho estimates that in 1747 some 243,000 individuals resided in Portuguese Asia, representing approximately 15 per cent of the empire's total global population (see Table 7.2). By 1819, on the eve of liberalism, that sum had grown to 581,000. However, thanks to the continuous and accelerating growth of Portuguese America, the population in Asia had come to represent only 10 per cent of the empire's total.

In 1808, the first statistical charts for the New Conquests (Goa) and for Diu began to circulate. As a result, we can glean information on the population of each of Portuguese India's diverse territories starting from this date (see Table 7.3). In both 1808–10 and 1817–21, the territory of Goa represented close to 90 per cent of all of Portuguese India's population. About 70 per cent was concentrated in the Old Conquests, with 10 per cent in the northern possessions of Diu and Daman. The latter was by far the largest of the northern possessions, as it had 24,000 inhabitants.

It is worth keeping in mind that, while the New Conquests were not incorporated into the territory of Goa until between 1746 and 1782,

TABLE 7.2
Population of Portugal and Its Empire, 1580–1819

	Percentage of Empire Total				Statistics		
Year	*Atlantic Islands*	*Brazil*	*Africa*	*Asia*	*Empire*	*Portugal*	*Asia*
1580	23	15	15	47	381,744	1,300,000	180,000
1695	18	36	17	29	783,195	1,900,000	230,000
1747	14	62	9	15	1,593,572	2,250,000	243,000
1776	11	69	8	12	2,190,051	2,750,000	272,000
1800	5	81	5	9	4,507,247	2,931,930	402,000
1819	4	81	5	10	5,908,160	3,026,000	580,900

Sources: Vitorino Magalhães Godinho, *Estrutura da Antiga Sociedade Portuguesa*, 2nd ed. (Lisbon: Arcádia, 1975), pp. 45–69; Adrien Balbi, *Essai Statistique sur Le Royaume de Portugal et D'Algarve*, vol. 2 (Paris: Rey et Gravier, 1822; repr., Lisbon: Imprensa Nacional Casa da Moeda/Faculdade de Economia da Universidade de Coimbra, 2004), p. 231; and Joel Serrão, *Fontes de Demografia Portuguesa* (Lisbon: Horizonte, 1975), pp. 107–16.

TABLE 7.3
Population of Portuguese India in 1808–10 and 1817–21

Location	*1808–10*	*%*	*1817–21*	*%*	*Variation*
Goa Territory					
Old Conquests					
Islands of Goa	31,643	11.1	33,513	11.0	5.9
Bardez	72,459	25.5	76,484	25.1	5.6
Salcete	70,299	24.7	75,908	25.0	8.0
Subtotal	*174,401*	*61.3*	*185,905*	*61.1*	*6.6*
New Conquests					
Bicholim	7,723	2.7	9,538	3.1	23.5
Canácona and Cabo de Rama	12,773	4.5	12,785	4.2	0.1
Pernén	23,284	8.2	23,358	7.7	0.3
Pondá	32,620	11.5	35,023	11.5	7.4
Tiracol	456	0.2	375	0.1	–17.8
Angediva	779	0.3	744	0.2	–4.5
Sanquelim	—	—	5,755	1.9	
Subtotal	*77,635*	*27.3*	*87,578*	*28.8*	*12.8*
Goa Total	**252,036**	**88.7**	**273,483**	**89.9**	**8.5**
Daman	24,662	8.7	24,396	8.0	–1.1
Diu	7,577	2.7	6,293	2.1	–16.9
Total Portuguese India	**284,275**	**100.0**	**304,172**	**100.0**	**7.0**

Note: These data are drawn from multiple manuscript sources, which are indicated in the appendix.

statistical surveys began only in 1808. This delay was due not only to the large amount of land which these zones covered but also to the slow growth of a bureaucratic apparatus which could carry out censuses in regions with only a tenuous Christian presence.

The Old Conquests, which covered 712 square kilometres, had not only the greatest population in the Estado da Índia but also the highest density: 266 inhabitants per square kilometre. The New Conquests, on the other hand, covered 2,657 square kilometres but had only 32 inhabitants per square kilometre.[21] The recent annexation of the territory and the instability that followed made permanent settlement difficult. Furthermore, the large forested areas and the agrarian structure of the land itself contributed to keeping the population density lower. Further north, the small holdings of Daman (384 square kilometres) and Diu (53 square kilometres) had the intermediate densities of 64 inhabitants per square kilometre and 133 inhabitants per square kilometre, respectively.

The data for counting the population of Macao are scarce and contradictory.[22] In this small possession of only 16 square kilometres, two communities — Chinese and Christian — lived side by side with an additional fluctuating population, almost always absent from the statistics. António Vale considers it reasonable to acknowledge a community of non-Christian Chinese on the order of 20,000 at the end of the eighteenth century. The three surveys completed in the eighteenth century indicate a decline in the Christian population, from 5,212 souls in 1745 to 4,958 in 1774, and then to 4,851 in 1791.[23] This trend continued through at least 1813, when 3,993 Christian residents were counted.[24]

Timor was the largest territory of Portuguese Asia (18,989 square kilometres) and certainly held the greatest demographic weight. However, the statistics reflect the fact that in Timor, just as in Angola and Mozambique, the authorities held only weak control over the local population. For this reason, it is only starting from the decade of the 1880s that there exist some estimates — but even these suffer from a lack of rigour. Examining the military recruitment process for forty-nine Timorese kings, Afonso de Castro calculated the population at 100,000 inhabitants at the end of the nineteenth century.[25] It is certain, however, that the white population was minuscule, with almost everyone linked to the public administration, plus some exiled criminals. Rudy Bauss calculated an 1813 population of only 1,800 white and slave residents.[26]

The existing sources for the Old Conquests allow us to outline the evolution of the number of inhabitants between 1720 and 1820. During this period, the Goan population experienced a decline on the order of 37,000

CHART 7.1
Evolution of the Population of the Old Conquests of Goa

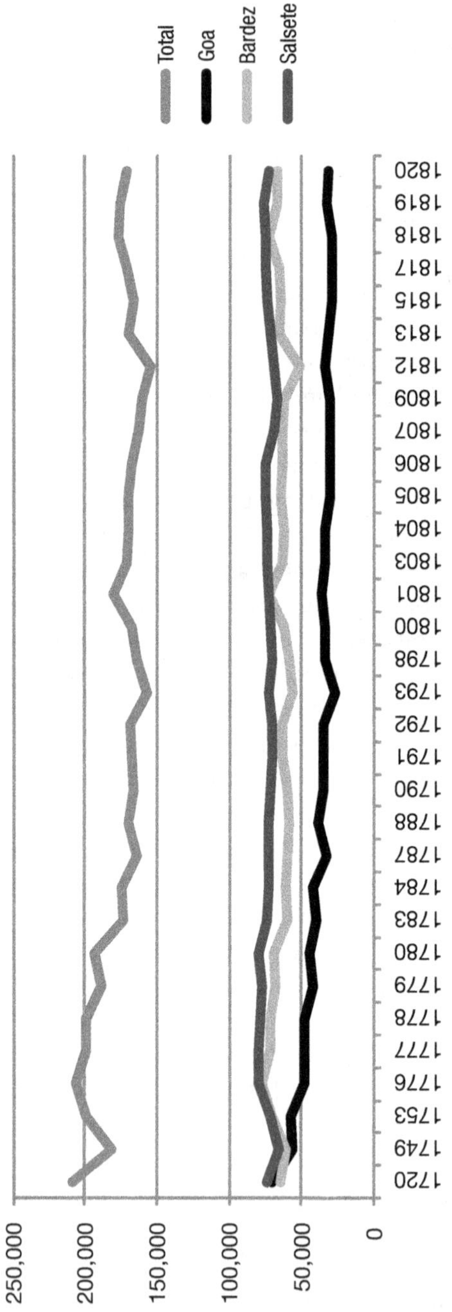

individuals, which translates into a negative average growth of 0.2 per cent per year. This rate, however, subtly obscures different periods of growth. During a first phase, taken to be from 1720 to 1779, a slow decrease took place; but it was in the 1780s and the first years of the following decade that the territory suffered a considerable loss of population: a decline of 19.5 per cent in a mere fourteen years (from 1779 to 1793). This statistic makes sense only in the context of exacerbating conditions of extraordinary mortality, perhaps as a result of serious economic desperation. The recovery from this severe demographic crisis began some time around the end of the eighteenth century.

In comparative terms, the population of the territory of Goa between 1720 and 1820 underwent trends distinct from those that took place in the rest of the Indian subcontinent, where population grew at more than 0.14 per cent per year. Furthermore, the moderate annual population increase of 0.17 per cent in Goa during the nineteenth century was itself significantly lower than the annual 0.35 per cent growth proposed for India during the same time.[27]

When compared to the percentage of population from each province, the Islands of Goa lost much importance during this time, dropping from 34 per cent in 1720 to just 15 per cent in 1820. By a certain measure, the continuous process of ruralization of the population of the Islands, itself partially caused by the high rate of mortality during the period under consideration, may account for this loss.[28] However, the subtle loss of population in the Islands between 1720 and 1753 and during the early years of the nineteenth century and the simultaneous population growth in the province of Bardez appear to reflect strong migratory movements within the heart of the Old Conquests. In truth, while in 1720 Bardez had only 31 per cent of the population surveyed, by 1820 it registered 39 per cent of the inhabitants. Despite the elevated population density, the peopling of the Old Conquests was by nature markedly rural: the inhabitants were dispersed in various villages, some of large size, but with a scarcity of real urban centres. Only the capital (Goa City or "Old City"), stood out as a large city in the Goan context. But in the second half of the eighteenth century, its decline accelerated: the *mapas* state that the population in 1753 numbered only 3,734, a number far lower than 100,000 inhabitants estimated (perhaps exaggeratedly) for the golden age of the mid-seventeenth century.[29]

Again, this scene constrasts with that of the rest of the subcontinent in the eighteenth century, for which estimates put forth an urban population of 13 per cent. This figure is proportionally higher than the contemporary rate for Europe and is due to the existence of the grand urban centres of Agra,

Delhi, Thatta and Surrate.[30] But the specifics of the Goan territory — small in size and long characterized by the lack of cities of the scale seen on the subcontinent — require an analysis focused on medium-sized settlements, which, despite their rural characteristics, could use their size to centralize some services.

Table 7.4 mirrors in a certain way the very demographic evolution attested for the three areas. On the Islands, the strong decline in population was reflected in the shrinkage of the "urban" centres: just four in 1753 and down to only Taleigão in 1819. In Bardez, the demographic crisis of the 1780s triggered the shrinkage of the large centres, but by 1819 it claimed the greatest number — 65 per cent — of inhabitants who resided in large

TABLE 7.4
Principal Urban Centres in the Old Conquests of Goa

1753	*No. of Inhabitants*	*1787*	*No. of Inhabitants*	*1819*	*No. of Inhabitants*
Islands of Goa					
Chimbel	3,899	Chorão	3,060	Taleigão	10,295
Goa Velha	3,734	Taleigão	9,615		
Siridão	7,411				
Taleigão	7,645				
Bardez					
Aldoná	3,918	Aldoná	3,021	Aldoná	3,988
Anjuna	5,657	Anjuna	4,852	Anjuna	4,320
Calangute	4,462	Calangute	5,021	Assagão	3,329
Candolim	3,810	Mapuçá	3,500	Calangute	4,635
Mapuçá	3,194	Sirulá	8,543	Candolim	3,613
Nerul	3,311			Mapuçá	4,864
Pilerne	3,584			Nerul	5,202
Sirulá	11,489			Salgão	5,343
				Siolim	3,684
				Sirulá	9,286
				Tivim	3,120
Salcete					
Cuncolim	5,334	Assolná	6,881	Assolná	7,140
Curtorim	4,895	Benaulim	3,755	Benaulim	4,066
Loutolim	3,159	Cuncolim	4,950	Cuncolim	4,962
Margão	8,882	Curtorim	4,515	Curtorim	4,857
		Margão	7,938	Loutolim	3,571
		Raia	5,242	Margão	9,160

parishes (eleven). During this period of sixty-six years, Sirulá, the largest village from the beginning, stands out, as do Anjuna, Aldoná and (at some distance) Mapuçá, the capital of the province. Salcete, the territory with the greatest stability in growth, experienced demographic development parallel to that which took place in the principal villages: its ranking had increased from four to six by 1787 and, in 1819, 52 per cent of the population was living in seven large centres (see Table 7.4).

Of the remaining Portuguese territories in India, Daman and Diu, only the former showed characteristics of a more or less urban nature. In the thirty-eight districts or *praganas* that existed in 1808, 30 per cent of the inhabitants (9,000) resided in Damão Pequeno (Little Daman), relatively close to the 28 per cent in the district of Nagar Avely. All of the remaining constituencies numbered less than 2,000 surveyed residents.[31] During the period under consideration here, the small territory of Macao was the largest city in the Estado da Índia in demographic terms. Beyond being an important urban centre, it had a periphery concentrated with a large number of inhabitants, many of them undocumented Chinese. For this reason, Macao was the most densely populated Portuguese possession in Asia.

The information available in the majority of the *mapas* allows us to piece together some observations concerning the religious and social makeup of the inhabitants of Portugal's various holdings in Asia. In general terms, the Old Conquests of Goa and Daman were the territories with the greatest Christian character, standing in opposition to the New Conquests, Diu and Macao.

During the period observed, the "gentiles" varied between 9 and 12 per cent in the Old Conquests (see Table 7.5). Once again, though, we find profound differences in the core of the provinces. The greatest number of non-Christians resided in the Islands: about 14 per cent in 1776–79 and

TABLE 7.5
Percentage of Gentiles in the Old Conquests of Goa, 1749–1819

Year(s)	*Islands*	*Bardez*	*Salcete*	*Goa*
1749	15.8	9.4	2.5	8.8
1753	15.4	8.9	4.0	10.3
1776–79	13.9	9.3	2.9	9.6
1780–89	16.8	9.2	2.5	9.4
1790–99	17.8	9.2	2.8	9.1
1801–08	22.9	13.2	4.1	11.2
1814–19	27.5	14.6	3.4	12.3

Note: Here the term "gentile" comes directly from the sources consulted. In context, it meant non-Christians, that is, Hindus or Muslims.

28 per cent in 1814–19. This systematic and significant increase took off beginning with the years 1776–79. In Bardez, the representation of the gentiles was less, with proportions between 9 and 15 per cent, and in Salcete their presence had always been quite low, with an average of only 3 per cent during the period under consideration.

The trend of the non-Christian, and especially Hindu, population growth is partially explained by the policy of promoting local elites and also by greater religious tolerance. While the decree of 2 April 1761 allowed for all natural vassals, being Christians, to enjoy the same prerogatives as those in the kingdom proper, it did not discourage further settlement by the Hindu and Muslim population.[32] The annexation of the New Conquests required a policy of greater social and political tolerance, a policy that was only furthered by the extinction of the Inquisition in Goa, in 1774.[33] As a result of this tolerance, the viceroys increasingly authorized gentile rites in the Goan territory, specifically weddings with the right to dancers.[34]

In the New Conquests, the percentage of non-Christians was, as one would expect, clearly the majority (see Table 7.6). From 1816 to 1820, a period for which there exists information on the four provinces, there were on average only twelve Christians per one hundred inhabitants; at the same time, the scarce Muslim percentage (3.5) stands out for being higher still than the corresponding number in the Old Conquests. Although Hinduism was by far the principal religious creed, there remained some differences between the Provinces. Pondá, the most populous, possessed the greatest diversity, as it had the highest number of Muslims (6 per cent) and of Christians (15 per cent) — versus Perném and Bicholim, where Hindus accounted for over 90 per cent of the population. The different proportion of Christians appears to be related directly to the antiquity of the Portuguese conquest and the subsequent progress made at conversion of the locals. It therefore makes

TABLE 7.6
Percentages of Hindus, Muslims and Christians in the New Conquests, 1816–20

Province	*Hindus*	*Muslims*	*Christians*
Pondá	78.4	6.4	15.1
Pernem	90.3	0.6	9.1
Canácona	84.6	0.4	15.0
Bicholim	92.7	3.3	4.0
Total	**84.8**	**3.5**	**11.7**

sense that Pondá and Canácona, conquered in 1763 and 1764, respectively, had proportionately more Christians than the other two provinces, Perném and Bicholim, which achieved sovereignty in the 1780s.

Goan society was divided fundamentally in two large religious groups — Christians and "gentiles" — accompanied by a division along ethnic and legal lines. The Christians were subdivided into "whites" and those from the "Kingdom" (in other words, those individuals who were born in Portugal and who therefore enjoyed the designation of *reinóis*). The number of *reinóis* was always low. Furthermore, those Portuguese who were distinguished in military service, bureaucracy or financial administration usually stayed in the territory for only brief periods.[35] The *castiços*, or whites born in India, corresponded to those Portuguese who had settled in India and married other Europeans. It is assumed that this community was largely endogamic, though naturally acculturized to Goan customs. Despite their prominence in administrative and military positions, their percentage was likewise quite reduced, above all following the fall of Bassein in 1739. The *mestiços* (people of mixed race), more properly called "Luso-descendants", resulted from the cross between Europeans and locals and as a class came about thanks to the marriage policy implemented by Albuquerque.

The overwhelming majority of the population of the Old Conquests consisted of native Christians, those "from the land", also known as *canarins*. These were further divided into various castes that had lost their ancestral Hindu meaning but which continued to play a fundamental role in social stratification. This stratification affected not only the natives themselves but also their level of acceptance by the Portuguese authorities.[36] The Muslims constituted the remaining practically residual part of the population and were essentially linked to commerce.

No slave society based on agricultural labour developed in Goa, as had occurred in Brazil, but from a legal perspective there was a marked division between the free and the enslaved populations. The slaves were marked by ample ethnic, geographic and even religious heterogeneity, with the greatest number of African origin. Chinese, Bengali, Timorese and Indians from the Malabar region were present as well, albeit on a small scale. It is worth noting that some Chinese natives from Macao were sent to Goa so as to avoid their own infanticide or moral perdition, to be liberated — theoretically — after a determined period of time. Despite the existence of slaves in Timor, the number was lower in Goa and was connected to reselling them to foreigners.[37] Also recorded were some free or emancipated individuals, despite the fact that counting them was very difficult. In the later years of the eighteenth century, the records begin to indicate the number of *pardos*. Their legal condition varied, however, as it fell to the owner to judge their status. As a result, we cannot break down the *pardo* population into the proper percentages of free and enslaved.

The presence of Portuguese in the Old Conquests was quite low, at no point rising above 2,000 individuals (see Table 7.7). Overall, their distribution was most uneven, as more than half resided in the province of the Islands, the home to the principal administrative, military and judicial authorities of the Estado da Índia. The value recorded for 1819 is exaggeratedly high, due perhaps to the inclusion of Luso-descendants in the same group.

A large majority of the slaves was congregated on the Islands of Goa, where their share of the population oscillated between 4.8 per cent in 1753 and 3.5 per cent in 1819. The captives were almost exclusively property of the European population, which occupied them in domestic service and subsequently enjoyed a certain manifestation of status.[38] In the capital's neighbouring parishes, specifically Ribandar, Daugim and Pangim (Panaji), the non-free population reached about 15 per cent, due to the greater concentration of Portuguese and their descendants. An examination into the parishes of Pangim and Morumbim-o-Grande between 1750 and 1819 reveals baptisms of slaves at 6 and 8 per cent, respectively, values which — while low — do demonstrate some presence of this group. The *pardos* also factor in as fluctuating population, although their share was lower than that of the blacks, never exceeding 0.5 per cent of the Old Conquests.

When compared to the remaining territory of the Old Conquests, the high number of Portuguese, blacks and Hindus on the Islands made this province the most complex in terms of socioreligious composition. This complexity explains the strong cosmopolitan nature of some localities, specifically Pangim,

TABLE 7.7
Ethno-religious Groups in the Old Conquests and in the Province of the Islands of Goa, 1753–1819

	1753		*1797*		*1819*	
Classification	*Islands*	*Goa*	*Islands*	*Goa*	*Islands*	*Goa*
Portuguese ("white men")	2.0	0.9	1.4	0.6	4.6	1.1
Natural Christians	77.8	88.1	76.8	90.2	66.3	86.0
Hindus	14.3	8.2	17.6	7.6	23.5	11.5
Muslims	0.1	0.2				
Slaves	4.8	2.3	3.6	1.4	3.5	0.9
Mixed race (*pardos*)	1.0	0.3	0.7	0.3	2.1	0.5

Ribandar and the island of Chorão, not to mention Goa City until the mid-eighteenth century.

The religious and social composition of Goa and of the Old Conquests in particular contrasts sharply with the reality of the fortified holdings of Daman and Diu (see Table 7.8). Although *mapas* with such detailed information exist only from the beginnings of the nineteenth century, the social scheme could have changed only very little between 1750 and 1820.

TABLE 7.8
Ethno-religious Composition of Diu and Daman, 1804–17

Location and Date	*White Christians*	*Natural Christians*	*Pardos*	*Blacks*	*Hindus and Muslims*
Diu, 1804	0.3	4.4	3.7	0.7	91.0
Daman, 1817	0.4	5.1	0.1	1.5	92.6

Practically the entire populations of Diu and Daman were Hindu, with only a small minority of Christians. The Portuguese did not exceed 0.3 per cent of the total, or eighty-six individuals in Daman and just thirteen in Diu. The presence of slaves was also limited, less than that of the Old Conquests of Goa. The number of *pardos* in Diu (3.7 per cent) stands in marked contrast to the weak representation of blacks (just 0.7 per cent).

The statistics for Macao do not allow for a clear measurement of the social-religious makeup, as the Chinese population — certainly the majority — was not counted. Notwithstanding, within the Christian population the Portuguese were rare, whereas slaves were abundant. In 1774, there were 109 Portuguese and 1,060 slaves; and although the number of Portuguese went unrecorded in 1791, the number of slaves had already grown to 1,447, close to 30 per cent of the Christian population.

The data on the ethnicities, religious creeds and socio-economic levels of the populations of the possessions of the Estado da Índia are insufficient for us to compute the society's innumerable social categories. Additionally, we must take into account the presence in Portuguese India of various fluctuating populations — specifically, the Chinese, Timorese, Bengalese and Parsis — as well as the European and Jewish communities, which were a bit disseminated throughout the various possessions. However, as the authorities did not employ systematic records of these groups, we are unable to track their numerical development.

The information provided by the population surveys is invaluable and allows for a strong understanding of the macro-demographic landscape. Nevertheless, in order to capture the extreme social diversity of Portuguese Asia, we require some other kind of primary documentation. The notarial, judicial and administrative information collected by the Catholic Church — and transmitted, in particular, through parochial records — is extremely important for deepening our understanding of the larger demographic panorama.

CONCLUSION

The second half of the eighteenth century marks the beginning of population statistics for Portugal's overseas territories. *Mapas*, required by royal order, were destined to measure the growth, the structure and, later on, the annual fluxes in these populations. A significant number of these *mapas* has survived to the present day, allowing us to make progress towards the quantification of the populations and the description of their composition.

Between 1750 and 1820 the inhabitants of the Estado da Índia did not represent more than 10 per cent of the total overseas population. The vast majority of the inhabitants under the official authorities lived in Goa — especially in the Old Conquests — with only a limited number in the other territories. Even with the integration of the New Conquests, the population of Portuguese Asia grew at only a moderate pace, especially when compared to Brazil.

The population of the Estado da Índia was predominately rural: despite the high population density, true urban centres had been scarce since the decline of Goa City in the first years of the eighteenth century. By this standard, we see that Macao was the largest urban city in the East during the period considered here.

The social and religious composition of the territories contained striking asymmetries, even in the small territory of Goa. Only the Old Conquests had an overwhelming majority of Christians, on the order of 90 per cent. In the New Conquests, the opposite phenomenon obtained. In Daman and Diu, the share held by Christians — around just 5 per cent — was exceedingly small.

One of the most salient characteristics of Portuguese Asia lay in the fact that the white population was almost vanishingly low, not exceeding 5,000 at any time. As a natural result of political, administrative and military necessities, whites were essentially concentrated in Goa. Even so, the records show significant variation between Macao, where whites comprised more than 25 per cent of the Christian population, and Daman and Diu, where the European population stayed lower than 200.

Just like the white population, the slaves were a group in flux and with little representation: they tended to rise in direct proportion to the number of Portuguese who lived in each zone. Quite differently from Brazil — and, in a certain way, from Africa — in Asia the slaves' duties tended to be essentially domestic.

Among the overseas territories, the Estado da Índia stood out as the area with the most complexity and the greatest disparity in social terms. In the case of Portuguese India — especially Goa — not only ethnic criteria but also religious factors, the caste system and judicial statutes concerning liberty affected social composition. Unfortunately, the statistics available today do not allow us to make a detailed comparison among all of these categories.

Despite the relative abundance of statistical charts, there are significant discrepancies in terms of geographic coverage and level of detail. In this way, this study takes on an essentially exploratory character on the level of describing sources and the macro-demographic scene. Future research concerning the demographics of the Estado da Índia will have to rely upon other kinds of documentation, particularly parochial records.

APPENDIX

MANUSCRIPT SOURCES: STATISTICAL CHARTS (MAPAS) OF PORTUGUESE INDIA, 1720–1820

Note: The documents discussed in this study are located in the Arquivo Histórico Ultramarino (AHU) in Lisbon and the Historical Archives of Goa (HAG). They are arranged chronically in this appendix.

1720	HAG, Livros das Monções do Reino (hereafter cited as MR) 86, fols. 10–56v
1722	AHU, Índia, caixa 46, doc. 51
1749	AHU, Códice 449, fol. 115v
1753	HAG, MR 125B, fols. 628–30
1776	AHU, Índia, caixa 346
1777	AHU, Índia, caixa 345
1778	AHU, Índia, caixa 347
1779	AHU, Índia, caixa 362
1780	AHU, Índia, caixa 356, and HAG, MR 161C, fols. 649–50
1781	HAG, MR 162A, fols. 366 a, b and c
1782	HAG, MR 163B, fols. 409–11
1783	AHU, Índia, caixa 366
1784	HAG, MR 164E, fols. 1,326–30
1785	HAG, MR 167A, fols. 94–96
1786	AHU, Índia, caixa 374
1787	AHU, Índia, caixa 379
1789	AHU, Índia, caixa 384
1790	AHU, Índia, caixa 388
1791	AHU, Índia, caixa 390
1792	AHU, Índia, caixa 393
1793	AHU, Índia, caixa 394
1797	AHU, Índia, caixa 398
1799	HAG, MR 179A, fols. 238–41
1803	AHU, Índia, caixa 410
1804	AHU, Índia, caixa 413
1805	AHU, Índia, caixa 415
1808	AHU, Índia, caixa 418
1814	AHU, Índia, caixa 431
1816	AHU, Índia, caixa 434
1817	AHU, Índia, caixa 438
1818	AHU, Índia, caixa 441
1819	HAG, MR 197, fols. 654–59
1820	HAG, MR 198B, fols. 586–89

Notes

1 The author extends his thanks to Adam Roth Singerman for translating this chapter from Portuguese into English.

2 The province of the Islands of Goa was captured in 1510. The other two provinces, Bardez and Salcete, were annexed during the reign of Dom João III (1521–57), king of Portugal.

3 Ernestina Carreira, "O Estado Português do Oriente: Aspectos políticos", in *Nova História da Expansão Portuguesa*, edited by Joel Serrão and A.H. de Oliveira Marques, vol. 5, *O Império Oriental*, edited by Maria de Jesus dos Mártires Lopes, bk. 1 (Lisbon: Estampa, 2006), pp. 91–96.

4 Luís Filipe Thomaz, "Goa: Uma sociedade Luso-Indiana", in *De Ceuta a Timor*, 2nd ed. (Lisbon: Difel, 1998). On this subject, see also Anthony Disney, *A History of Portugal and the Portuguese Empire*, vol. 2, *The Portuguese Empire* (Cambridge: Cambridge University Press, 2010), pp. 319–21.

5 Paulo Teodoro de Matos, "Grupos populacionais e dinâmicas demográficas nas Ilhas de Goa (1720–1830)", in *O Estado da Índia e os Desafios Europeus: Actas do XII Seminário Internacional de História Indo-Portuguesa* (Lisbon: CHAM/ CEPCEP, 2010), pp. 615–32.

6 Paulo Teodoro de Matos, "O Numeramento de Goa de 1720", in *Anais de História de Além-Mar*, vol. 8 (Lisbon: CHAM, 2007), pp. 241–324.

7 António Carreira, "O Primeiro 'censo' de população da Capitania das Ilhas de Cabo Verde (1731)", *Revista de História Económica e Social* 19 (January–April 1987): 33–76.

8 Matos, "O Numeramento", pp. 241–324.

9 Códice 449, fol. 115v, 1749, Arquivo Histórico Ultramarino (hereafter cited as AHU), Lisbon; and Livros das Monções do Reino (hereafter cited as MR) 125B, fol. 167, 1753, Historical Archives of Goa (hereafter cited as HAG), Panaji, Goa. Dates appearing in the HAG citations herein pertain only to the specific folios cited.

10 Dauril Alden, "The Population of Brazil in the Late Eighteenth Century", *Hispanic American Historical Review* 43, no. 2 (1962): 177–80; Ana Paula Wagner, *População no Império Português: Recenseamentos na África Oriental Portuguesa na Segunda Metade do Século XVIII* (Curitiba: Universidade Federal do Paraná, 2009).

11 The figures for 1720 and 1749 were located only very recently. See Paulo Teodoro de Matos, "O Numeramento"; and Miguel Coutinho, *Goa no Tempo do Marquês de Alorna (1744–1750): Uma Sociedade em Transformação* (Lisbon: Universidade Nova de Lisboa, 2008), p. 179.

12 MR 157A, fols. 156–57, AHU (previously housed in HAG).

13 Investigations conducted in the baptism registries of the parishes of Pangim

(Panaji), Santa Bárbara and Taleigão for the eighteenth century (Islands of Goa, currently the province of Tiswadi) revealed that baptisms at home (*sub-conditione*) were frequent, so that there may have been a discrepancy of more than two weeks between the birth and the baptism.

14 Alden, "The Population of Brazil", p. 179.

15 The "third line" of troops performed military training and could be called to serve for defence purposes against invaders.

16 Timothy Walker, "Abolishing the Slave Trade in Portuguese India: Documentary Evidence of Popular and Official Resistance to Crown Policy, 1842–1860", in *Slavery & Abolition* 25, no. 2 (2004): 63–79.

17 In order to carry out the 1720 survey, the priest of Pomburpá (Bardez) affirmed that he gathered information from Hindus "by going directly to their houses". See Matos, "O Numeramento", p. 307.

18 António M.M. do Vale, "A População de Macau na segunda metade do século XVIII", *Povos e Culturas* 5, *Portugal e o Oriente: Passado e Presente* (1996): 241–54.

19 This affirmation rests on comparisons with other, already studied overseas areas, specifically the Azorean archipelago and the Brazilian captaincies of São Paulo, Bahia and Pernambuco. However, we lack specific, statistically grounded studies to measure the quality of these sources or to propose corrective adjustments.

20 Vale, "A População de Macau", pp. 241–54.

21 The basis for these facts comes from *Censo da População do Estado da Índia de 1900* (Panaji: Imprensa Nacional de Goa, 1903), pp. 4–7.

22 Reliable information begins in 1867, when the first surveys were carried out. See José Vicente Serrão, "Macau", in *Nova História da Expansão Portuguesa*, edited by Joel Serrão and A.H. de Oliveira Marques, vol. 10, *O Império Africano, 1825–1890*, edited by Valentim Alexandre (Lisbon, Estampa, 1998), p. 754.

23 Vale, "A População de Macau", p. 246.

24 MR 198B, fol. 608, 1820.

25 Affonso de Castro, *As Possessões Portuguezas na Oceânia* (Lisbon: Imprensa Nacional, 1867), p. 310.

26 Rudy Bauss, "A Demographic Study of Portuguese India and Macau as well as Comments on Mozambique and Timor, 1750–1850", *The Indian Economic and Social History Review* 34, no. 2 (1997): 200.

27 Irfan Habib, "Population", in *The Cambridge Economic History of India*, edited by Dharma Humar and Tapan Raychaudhuri, vol. 1, *c.1200 – c.1750*, 3rd ed. (New Delhi: Orient Longam/Cambridge University Press, 2004), pp. 163–71.

28 Matos, "Grupos populacionais", pp. 619–20.

29 Maria de Jesus dos M. Lopes and Paulo Teodoro de Matos, "Naturais, reinóis e luso-descendentes: A socialização conseguida", in *Nova História da Expansão Portuguesa*, vol. 5, *O Império Oriental (1660–1820)*, edited by Maria de Jesus dos M. Lopes (Lisbon: Presença, 2006), p. 23.

30 Habib, "Population", pp. 167–77.

31 In Daman, the fort of São Jerónimo had only 631 residents in 1808.

32 Maria de Jesus dos Mártires Lopes, *Tradition and Modernity in Eighteenth-Century Goa* (Delhi: Manohar/CHAM, 2006), p. 40.

33 Anthony Disney, *A History of Portugal*, p. 326; and Lopes, *Tradition and Modernity*, p. 49.

34 The dancers, or temple servants, were normally prostitutes who had received instruction in and performed well at the arts, in particular dance.

35 Lopes, *Tradition and Modernity*, pp. 132–39.

36 Ibid., pp. 114–20.

37 Lopes and Matos, "Naturais", pp. 67–68. Concerning the question of Chinese and Timorese enslavement, see Índia, caixa 388, 5 April 1791, AHU, in which their legal status (free versus enslaved) and juridic framework were discussed.

38 In 1720 only 74 of the 4,141 slaves on the Islands were property of Hindus. A full 41 per cent of the total number of slaves were concentrated in the city of Goa. See Matos, "O Numeramento", pp. 241–49.

8

FLYING WITH THE *PAPAGAIO VERDE* (GREEN PARROT): AN INDO-PORTUGUESE FOLKLORIC MOTIF IN SOUTH AND SOUTHEAST ASIA

K. David Jackson

O papagaio do paço
Não falava — assobiava.
Sabia bem que a verdade
Não é coisa de palavra.
Fernando Pessoa[1]

The parrot in the palace never
spoke — whistled instead.
It understood full well the truth's
not something to be said.

The folksong "Papagaio Verde" (Green Parrot) is one of the oldest and most widely known Portuguese *cantigas* — stanzas of verse sung to traditional melodies — that spread from Indo-Portuguese communities to South and Southeast Asia. Sung from Diu to Macao, the *papagaio verde* is a popular and agile motif: it flies in from afar to teach maxims, play the rogue, criticize or insult, sing to a lover, or beat its wings and sing dance tunes. Variants of quatrains on the theme of the green parrot sung in Creole Portuguese have been collected throughout Luso-Asian communities by linguists, folklorists and ethnographers, and remain part of folk traditions performed in Daman, Malacca and Macao.

Parrots — birds of the order *Psittaciformes* found in Portugal and throughout the tropical and semi-tropical lands contacted by the Portuguese voyages — appear as a motif in early Portuguese folk verse and folksong. Popular seven-syllable quatrains or *cantigas,* collected in the field by ethnographer José Leite de Vasconcellos (1858–1941),[2] invoke birds with green feathers, or green parrots, for their intelligence, playful social skills, ability to imitate the human voice and long, direct flight. In the nineteenth century, it was common to give a parrot as a gift. Brazilian statesman Joaquim Nabuco (1849–1910) favoured the English politician Charles Herbert Allen (1824–1904) with two parrots, and the recipient wrote in appreciation on 9 February 1900:

> [Thank you] for so kindly bringing me another beautiful green parrot ... You will be pleased to hear that the beautiful parrot has grown into a very fine bird and ... is so active and lively. He still calls himself "papagaio real" but has already picked up many enough words and phrases. My two daughters are extremely devoted to him and he really comes out of the cage to sit on their hands. The grey African parrot looks on him with contempt ... He is wonderfully imprudent.[3]

The magical presence of a parrot in the home is described by a young narrator in Jorge de Sena's story, "Homenagem ao Papagaio Verde" ("Homage to the Green Parrot"): "Era verde e velho ... Não tinha nome, era o Papagaio, e parecia-me, porque falava, um ser maravilhoso" (It was green and old ... It had no name: it was just the Parrot, and because it could talk it seemed to me a marvellous creature).[4] The naturalist Alexander von Humboldt (1769–1859) recounts hearing at Maypures a parrot that was the last surviving speaker of forty words of the language of the extinct Atures people of the Orinoco:[5]

> A tradition circulates among the Guahiboes, that the warlike Atures, pursued by the Caribbees, escaped to the rocks that rise in the middle of the Great Cataracts; and there that nation, heretofore so numerous, became gradually extinct, as well as its language. The last families of the Atures still existed in 1767, in the time of the missionary Gili. At the period of our voyage an old parrot was shown at Maypures, of which the inhabitants related, and the fact is worthy of observation that "they did not understand what it said, because it spoke the language of the Atures".

The role of parrots in popular Portuguese verse can be considered an extension of their role in the oral folktale and fable dating from ancient times. The *Motif-Index of Folk-Literature* lists more than twenty themes in world folktales centred on the parrot that became part of its lore in different languages and cultures.[6] Aesop's (620–564 BCE) fable "The Parrot and the Cat" features a parrot boasting the advantages of the gift of speech,[7] while "The Tale of the Husband and the Parrot" from the Persian and Arabian oral traditions transcribed in *The Book of the Thousand Nights and a Night* treats the parrot as keen observer of human activities: a truth-telling parrot is killed by mistake for telling of a wife's infidelity.[8] In British and Thai folktales, parrots incapable of deceit tell inconvenient truths that denounce their deceitful owners — a baker whose loaves are too light, a farmer who killed and ate his neighbour's buffalo — for which they receive punishments.[9]

In addition to their roles as truth-tellers, parrots take on magical powers: in a Tibetan folktale, "The Story of the Tree of Life", a parrot king gives a magical seed to a merchant who saves his life, with the promise that after three years its fruit will make the merchant young again.[10] The Brazilian story "O papagaio do limo verde" ("The Parrot of Green Algae") features a royal prince who visits his betrothed in the form of a large and beautiful parrot; on lighting in a basin of water prepared by the lady, the parrot beats its wings until each drop becomes a diamond, while the enchanted parrot turns into a beautiful prince who remains until early morning, when once again he changes into a parrot, beats his wings and flies away.[11] In Sir George Fraser's (1854–1941) study of primitive cultures, *The Golden Bough*, the theme of metempsychosis is illustrated by an invulnerable ruler or giant who removed his soul from his body and hid it in the body of a parrot, kept on a deserted island in a cage under six jugs of water. By capturing the parrot, a hero was able to defeat the ruler. Besides security, the cage was also a symbol of entrapment, whether of bodies, souls, spirits, desires or people incarnated in the parrot.[12] A parrot's fidelity is the theme of "The Steadfast Parrot" (or "The Parrot and the Fig Tree"), a Jataka Buddhist legend in which a parrot who loves a fig tree is tested by the god Shakra, who makes the tree barren, yet the parrot will not abandon the home for which he feels gratitude. As a reward Shakra restores the tree to fruition.[13]

In the Myanmar tale "Shin-Mway-Loon and Min-Nanda", a prince uses his parrot as a matchmaker or messenger to fly to a palace across a wide expanse of water, where the parrot describes his master to a princess, who immediately falls in love with him; and when the parrot describes the princess on its return, the couple become lovers without having seen each other.[14]

The parrot tries unsuccessfully to unite a maid with a rich man's son in the Chinese tale of "The Waiting Maid's Parrot".[15]

Often after telling an inconvenient truth — or explaining a lawsuit, in a village folktale of Ceylon — the parrot flies away, a final touch or coda that emphasizes this authority over the community and the universality of his judgements: "Having said this the Parrot flew away and went to the flock of Parrots".[16] In a survey of the parrot in Western literature, Anthony Gottlieb lists female infidelity, ruse and perjury, unnatural wisdom and foresight, coarse and obscene personae, piety for the Virgin Mary or Trinity, and satire of language itself as main themes.[17] In the bestiary by David Sedaris, *Squirrel Seeks Chipmunk*, the parrot continues to play the role of perching linguist and comedian:

> When asked why she'd chosen to become a journalist, the parrot was known to cock her head a half-inch to the right and pause for a moment before repeating the question. "Why did I choose to become a journalist? Well, the easy answer is fairly obvious, perfect recall is something I was born with, but I guess what really drives me is the money. That, and the free booze." ("The Parrot and the Potbellied Pig")[18]

Images of parrots with green wings were found by Leite de Vasconcellos in *cantigas* in which the parrot — or bird with green plumage — plays the part of an intelligent and often crafty singer who learns by hearing or observation and needs no instruction. The characteristics of intelligence, voice, craftiness and fidelity identify the birds as parrots; in some quatrains the colour green is projected into plants, water or soil. A *cantiga* from Alcoutim, a small town in southeastern Portugal, praises the birds' innate happiness, song and perceptive imitation:

Os alegres passarinhos	(The happy little birds
São cientes no cantar:	Know what they're singing:
Aprenderõ só de ôvir,	They learned by listening,
Sem ninguém nos ensinar.	Didn't need any teaching.)
	(Alcoutim)

In the town of Aguiar da Beira, District of Guarda, the parrot's song celebrates the fruits and spices in a poet's garden:

Papagaio pena verde	(A parrot with green feathers
Foi cantar ao meu jardim;	Came to sing in my garden;

Pôs um pé na laranjeira	He put one foot on the orange tree
E um pé no alecrim.	And another on the rosemary bush.)
	(Aguiar da Beira)

Verses from the northern Minho Dictrict depict the bird's skill in acting and deception, pretending to be thirsty while always keeping its beak in water:

Que passarinho é aquele	(What bird is that
Que anda no lameiro verde,	Walking in the green mud,
Sempre co'o biquinho n'água,	With its beak always in water,
Sempre morrendo á sede?	Always dying of thirst?)
	(Minho)

Que passarinho é aquele,	(What bird is that,
Que canta no galho verde?	Singing on the green branch?
Dorme com o bico na água,	It sleeps with its beak in water,
Está sempre a morrer à sede!	And is always dying of thirst!)
	(Minho)

In the town of Marco de Canaveses, District of Porto, the parrot aggressively demands affection, and in a verse from Salvaterra do Extremo, District of Castelo Branco, is always a faithful companion to the lady in its nest:

Que passarinho é aquele,	(What bird is that,
Que no ar faz ameaços?	Making threats in the air?
Co'o biquinho pede beijos,	Its beak asks for kisses,
Co' as asas seus abraços.	Its wings embraces.)
	(Marco de Canaveses)

O passarinho canta alegre	(The bird sings happily
Por ter a dama no ninho,	With a lady in its nest,
Olha como é constante	Look how constant is
O amor do passarinho!	This bird's love!)
	(Salvaterra do Extremo)

In early Portuguese poetry reflecting oral traditions, the parrot appears in a collection of the Galician-Portuguese lyric in a *pastorela* by Dom Dinis (ruled 1279–1325).[19] In four eight-line strophes, a parrot speaks in reply to reassure a lady of the success of her love complaint: "Ben, per quant' eu sei, senhora" (Good, as far as I know, my Lady). When the lady exhorts the bird to tell the truth, as she is about to die of love, the parrot repeats its hopeful message: "Senhora comprida / de ben, e non vos queixedes, / ca o que vos á servida, / erged' olho e vee-lo edes" (My Lady is overflowing with good, so don't complain, as for what you will receive, just raise your eyes and you shall see it).[20] A parrot also speaks in the baroque fabulary *Aves Ilustradas* (1734) by poet Sóror Maria do Céu (1658–1723),[21] in which fourteen different birds give advice and counsel on religious life in the monasteries, part of spiritualist and moralizing allegory in baroque literature. In "O Papagaio à Rodeira" ("The Parrot and the Wheel"), via rhetorical *impossibilia*, a noisy and exotic Brazilian parrot advises silence and discretion in the use of the cylindrical wheel located at the entrance to convents that allows receipt of objects or even abandoned children: "Aqui ... na roda, senhora, não serve quem fala como papagaio" (Here ... on the wheel, lady, people who talk like parrots are undesirable). The exemplary parrot repeats a story about another of its species that immediately repeated everything it heard, and thus lost its liberty through indiscretion when captured by an old Indian woman.

The parrot's second counsel to observe charity to the poor is exemplified in a second story about a poor old Spaniard in America who alone is rewarded with the discovery of gold because of his simplicity, poverty and goodness. The parrot arrives at its moral through exempla in antonyms: "Papagaio, que grita, papagaio que fala, papagaio que inquieta, não é para aqui, aonde se há de saber que só há pé para servir, e não há voz por conversar" (The parrot that shouts, talks, fusses is not welcome here, where there is only service and no voice for conversation).[22] In the romantic theatre, parrots represent Brazilian indigenism, as in *O Cedro Vermelho* by Francisco Gomes de Amorim (1827–91), first produced in Lisbon in 1856, where the character Lourenço, a Juruna Indian from Pará, appears covered in parrot feathers.[23] In *A Brasileira de Prazins*, a romantic novel by Camilo Castelo Branco (1825–90), the parrot is said to enjoy a long life because of its sordid egotism: "o velho Alexandre Dumas disse que os egoístas e os papagaios viviam cento e cinquenta anos" (old Alexandre Dumas said that egotists and parrots lived to be one hundred and fifty years old).[24] Throughout Portuguese literature, the parrot gives advice or speaks inconvenient truths on the margin of human speech and norms of social relations.

SOUTH ASIA

Verses of "Papagaio Verde" performed in Creole Portuguese communities across South and Southeast Asia attest to the universality of the folksong and the figure of the parrot as a commentator on Indo-Portuguese and Luso-Asian community life. The song is part of a shared legacy of traditional melodies and lyrics that functioned as essential components of social life, festivals, ceremonies and rituals. Lyrics of the *cantigas* described community culture, especially courtship and marriage, and voiced both its social concerns and private desires. Monsenhor Sebastião Rodolfo Dalgado (1855–1922) comments on the spread of folk verses throughout Luso-Asian Creole communities by noting similarities in quatrains of the "Papagaio Verde" from Daman and Malacca: "O passarinho verde (ou *pastorinho verde* dos actuais *cristãos* de Malaca) parece ser uma deturpação de papagaio verde, forma que aparece na seguinte quadra de Damão" (The green parrot, or pastorinho verde of the current Kristangs of Malacca, seems to be a deturpation of the papagaio verde, in a form found in the following quatrain from Daman):

Papagaio verde	(Green parrot
Sentá sobre lêtêr	Sitting on the milk pail
Batê, batê azas, Surumbá	Beats, beats its wings, Surumbá
Chamá rapaz solter ...	Calling the eligible bachelor ...)[25]

Mangalore, Cochin and Sri Lanka

Quatrains from Mangalore (1884) transcribed by Hugo Schuchardt (1842–1927)[26] and from Cochin (Jackson)[27] repeat the general pattern by which the parrot perches on some utilitarian object and beats its wings before performing a service or voicing a comment or message directed at the community as a whole. The green parrot's task in this case is to pick green mangoes, while a variant from Sri Lanka adapts the quatrain to a religious context by adding a verse, "Da per nona Mary" (Gives it to lady Mary).

Mangalore

Ai papagayo verde, Margarida,	(Ah green parrot, Margarita,
Sube riba sebe,	Flies up on the fence,
Ai bate bate aza, Margarida,	Ah beats his wings, Margarita,
Panha manga verde.	Picks a green mango.)[28]

Cochin

Papa gaya vade	(Green parrot
Santhad en tha save	Sitting on the fence
Batha Batha Agu	Beats its wings
Panja manga verde	Picks a green mango)

Sri Lanka

Papugachi vardie	(Green parrot
Riva aka Savie	On top of the fence

Panya manga vardie	Picks a green mango
Da per nona Mary	Gives to lady Mary)[29]

Daman, Diu and Other Northern Enclaves

In verses from Daman and Diu, the parrot returns to the role of messenger, matchmaker and ribald observer of social foibles. In quatrains from Daman, the parrot delivers love letters to ungrateful lovers, throws engagement rings into the sea and joins suitors who drink to drown their lovesick sorrows at local bars:

Daman

Papagai verd	(Green parrot
Sentá sobre lêtêr,	Perched on the milk pail,
Batê, batê azas, Surumbá,	Beats, beats its wings, Surumbá,
Chamá rapaz soltêr.	Calls the eligible bachelor.)
. . . .	. . . .
Papagai verd	(Green parrot
Com bic de prat;	With silver beak;
Levae est cart, Surumbá,	Take this letter, Surumbá,
Entregae com aquel ingrat.	Deliver it to that ingrate.)
Papagai verd	(Green parrot
Com bic de chumb.	With leaden beak.
Levae est anel, Surumbá,	Take this ring, Surumbá,
Mêt no mar fund.	Throw it into the deep sea.)[30]

Northern Enclaves

Dalgado and Jeronynmo Quadros record comparable verses from other Northern enclaves:

Papagaio verde, bai Monquim,	(Green parrot, lady Monquim,
Biquinho de chumbo;	With leaden beak;
Levae esta carta, bai Monquim,	Take this letter, lady Monquim,
E pinchae no mar fundo.	Toss it into the deep sea.)
Papagaio verde, bai Monquim,	(Green parrot, lady Monquim,
Perto de botiça [botija],	Near the bar,
De noite bebo vinho,	Drinks wine at night,
bai Monquim,	lady Monquim,)
Un garafo inteiro.	An entire bottle.)[31]

Papágai verd Com bicc du lacre, Levai est cart Aquell ingrat. Coro:	(Green parrot With a lacquer beak, Deliver this letter To that ingrate.)
Oh! Bahy cur-cú-ry Pentiá cabel pela manh cêd[32]	(Oh! Lady Combing your hair early in the morning)

Additional Sri Lankan Motifs

In variants of the folksong from Sri Lanka, the parrot participates in dancing and singing of the *chikotie*, a fast dance style among the Portuguese Burghers, the term used for mixed-race descendents of the Portuguese. In a collection of *cantigas* from Matara dated 1914, the caged parrot is a metaphor for isolation of young women, as the parrot's beating wings are compared to a lovesick young woman beating her breasts:

Sri Lanka

Papugachi vardie Riva de pikotie Batha Batha asa Vai Kantha chikotie	(Green parrot On top of the well pump Beats its wings Going to sing *chikotie*)
Papegaai ne giola, batté azas quer curre, Menina na janela, batté peto quer morre.	(Parrot in the cage, beats its wings wanting to escape, Young woman in the window, beats her breasts wanting to die.)[33]

Margaret Sarkissian suggests that comparable verses from Malacca may refer to the time of Dutch persecution; the young maiden in the window, however, is a figure of courtship dramas throughout the Portuguese world:

Fina mina nã rentu kama Baté korpu kerê murê	(The virgin girl in her bed Beats her body, wants to die) [34]

The green parrot reaffirms its role of truth-teller through the verses of a Sri Lankan *cantiga*, all of which amount to the collective folk wisdom of a Creole group. *Cantigas* are repeated and reinforced through performance at all important junctures of life, particularly during courtship, marriage and other festive occasions, where they are sung with the force of truth as community lore and lesson:

Maskie tha bunetoee	(But how beautiful is
Papoogagu verdee	The green parrot
Adie iste cantiges	All these *cantigas*
Todoe then verdade	All are true)[35]

MACAO

Verses of the "Papagaio Verde" from Macao appeared in the "Cancioneiro Musical Crioulo" in the turn-of-the-century journal *Ta-Ssi-Yang-Kuo* (1899–1904).[36] The parrot's function is to identify the Macanese by calling out their Portuguese nicknames:

Passarinho verde	(Green parrot
Riva de butan	On top of the buoy
Capi capi aza	Opening and closing wings
Chomá nhum Janjan	Calls the man John)[37]

The attribution of Portuguese names in the folksong was traced by scholar Ana Maria Machado in her book *Filhos da Terra* to twenty-two folk quatrains under the title "Disparates" ("Preposterous Verses"), mailed in 1900 in a letter to João Feliciano Marques Pereira, editor of *Ta-Ssi-Yang-Kuo,* by a Macao Portuguese living in Hong Kong.[38] In her opinion, the verses demonstrate that nicknames used by Macanese come not from Chinese nursemaids but rather from older Portuguese sources:

> Não é nossa intenção fazer, aqui, um estudo comparativo dos hipocorísticos nos vários crioulos portugueses. Apenas se pretende demonstrar que os nominhos de Macau não devem ter sido criados pelas amás chinesas, como alguns autores supõem, apoiados na sua forma dissilábica; outrossim, devem ter uma origem mais antiga.
>
> A rematar este assunto, transcrevemos uma série de quadras cujo primeiro verso corresponde a uma composição cantada, que consta dos papéis de João Feliciano Marques Pereira, como sendo de Macau. Este conjunto de quadras foi-lhe enviado a 20 de Outubro de 1900 por Emílio Honorato de Aquino, português de Macau radicado em Hong Kong, onde o crioulo viveu e se manteve mais puro, durante mais tempo.[39]
>
> (It is not our intention to make a comparative study here of naming in the various Portuguese Creoles. We only want to demonstrate that nicknames in Macao were not coined by Chinese nursemaids, as some authors suppose, based on their multiple syllables; rather they had an older origin.

To deal with this issue, we transcribe a series of quatrains whose first verse is a sung composition, found among the papers of João Feliciano Marques Pereira, as being from Macao. This collection of quatrains was sent to him on 20 October 1900 by Emílio Honorato de Aquino, a Portuguese residing in Hong Kong, where the creole survived and remained pure for a longer time.)

The twenty-two quatrains from 1900 identified by Machado are as follows:

Disparates Passarinho verdi Riba de telhado Capi, capi aza Chomá nhum Ado [Eduardo]	(*Preposterous Verses*) (Green bird Perched on the roof Beats, beats its wings Calls the man Ado)
Passarinho verdi Riba de coco Capi capi aza Choma nhum Toco [Antonio]	(Green bird Perched in the coconut palm Beats, beats its wings Calls the man Toco)
Passarinho verdi Riba de porta Capi, capi, aza Choma nhi Carlotta	(Green bird Perched on the door Beats, beats its wings Calls the maiden Carlotta)
Passarinho vardi Riba de buiam-bico [bule] Capi capí aza Choma nhum Jejico [José]	(Green bird Perched on the teapot Beats, beats its wings Calls the man Jejico [Joe])
Passarinho verdi Riba da janela Capí, capí aza Choma nhi Miquela	(Green bird Perched in the window Beats, beats its wings Calls the maiden Miquela)
Passarinho verdi Riba de bassora [vassoura] Capi capi aza Choma nhi Dora [Theadora]	(Green bird Perched on the broom Beats, beats its wings Calls the maiden Dora)
Passarinho verdi Riba de escada Capi, capi aza Choma nhi Ada [Esmeralda]	(Green bird Perched on the stairs Beats, beats its wings Calls the maiden Ada)

Passarinho verdi Riba de bassora — pena [espanador] Capi capi aza Choma nhi Mena [Philomena]	(Green bird Perched on the sweeper Beats, beats its wings Calls the maiden Mena)
Passarinho verdi Riba de cosinha Capi, capi, aza Choma nhi Anninha	(Green bird Perched over the kitchen Beats, beats its wings Calls the maiden Anninha)
Passarinho verdi Riba de fula [flor] Capi, capi, aza Choma nhum Tula [Boaventura]	(Green bird Perched on the flower Beats, beats its wings Calls the man Tula)
Passarinho verdi Riba de tacho [frigideira] Capi, capi, aza Choma nhum Acho [Ignácio]	(Green bird Perched on the frying pan Beats, beats its wings Calls the man Acho)
Passarinho verdi Rib de caneca Capi, capi, aza Choma nhi Eca [Angélica]	(Green bird Perched on the vessel Beats, beats its wings Calls the maiden Eca)
Passarinho verdi Rib de painel [quadro] Capi, capi, aza Choma nhi Zabel	(Green bird Perched on the painting Beats, beats its wings Calls the maiden Zabel)
Passarinho verdi Riba de lenço Capi, capi, aza Chama nhum Encho [Lourenço]	(Green bird Perched on the handkerchief Beats, beats its wings Calls the man Encho)
Passarinho verdi Riba de fugam Capi, capi, aza Choma nhum Jamjam [João]	(Green bird Perched on the stove Beats, beats its wings Calls the man Jamjam [John])
Passarinho verdi Riba de hospital Capi, capi, aza Choma nhum Vital	(Green bird Perched on the hospital Beats, beats its wings Calls the man Vital)

Passarinho verdi Riba de almario Capi, capi, aza Choma nhum Januario	(Green bird Perched on the almyra Beats, beats its wings Calls the man Januario)
Passarinho verdi Riba de campinha [campainha] Capi, capi, aza Choma chacha-dinha [avó madrinha]	(Green bird Perched on the bell Beats, beats its wings Calls grandma chacha-dinha)
Passarinho verdi Riba de batente Capi, capi, aza Choma nhum Chente [Vicente]	(Green bird Perched on the doorframe Beats, beats its wings Calls the man Chente)
Passarinho verdi Riba de chaminé Capi, capi, aza Choma chacha-néné [parteira]	(Green bird Perched on the chimney Beats, beats its wings Calls the midwife chacha-néné)
Passarinho verdi Riba de maca Capi, capi, aza Choma nhi Caca [Clara]	(Green bird Perched on the stretcher Beats, beats its wings Calls the maiden Caca)
Passarinho verdi Riba de grade (cerca) Capi, capi, aza Choma sium padri [sacerdote]	(Green bird Perched on the grate Beats, beats its wings Calls the man padri [priest)])

MALACCA

The "Papagaio Verde" folk song was transcribed for the first time in Malacca in António da Silva Rêgo's (1905–86) *Dialecto Português de Malaca*.[40] For Silva Rêgo, the *cantigas* function as a mirror of the popular culture of Portuguese descendants in Malacca, across the centuries. In his *Dialecto Português de Malaca*, the author comments on 211 popular quatrains from the Portuguese tradition, which he classifies using two categories borrowed from medieval *cancioneiros*: "Cantigas de Amigo" (female-voice love laments) and "Cantigas de mal-dizer" (satire and personal insult). Silva Rêgo recognizes the importance of music, dance and festivity to the community life of Luso-Asian communities. His first-hand description applies as much to Indian and Sri Lankan groups as it does to Malacca and Singapore:

Os "cristãos" possuem, em geral, um óptimo ouvido musical. Amigos da música e da dança, improvisam de vez em quando um branhô ou festa em que tomam parte homens e mulheres, mancebos e donzelas, que rivalizam uns com os outros nas cantigas ao desafio. Estas festas são vulgares em dias de casamentos, aniversários, etc. Em Singapura encontram-se também festas assim em que se ouve o mesmo.

(The "Kristangs" have in general a sharp musical ear. Friends of music and dance, they throw a *branhô* or party from time to time in which men and women take part, young boys and girls, who compete with each other in singing folk stanzas. These parties are common on wedding days, birthdays, etc. In Singapore one also finds these parties with the same music).[41]

Silva Rêgo provides a rare early description of musical performance by Catholic fishermen in Malacca and, by extension of the role of folksongs, music and dance among speakers of Creole Portuguese throughout Southeast Asia:

Os instrumentos com que acompanham as cantigas variam de número, conforme as circunstâncias. Assim há ocasiões em que se vêem 10 ou mais instrumentos, e outras em que um violino acompanhado por um tambor faz de orquestra sinfônica.

Há em Malaca alguns pescadores que manejam o violino com notável agilidade, para não dizer expressão. As cordas são em geral compradas em lojas chinesas que as fornecem para os instrumentos chineses. São cordas rudimentaríssimas, mas nas mãos dos malaqueiros vibram a valer. E é interessante ver um certo ar de nostalgia brilhar nos olhos dos tocadores, quando eles, descalços e apenas com umas calças muito largas e um casaco mal abotoado, se encostam ao violino, conto a um esteio que os transporta a longínquos paises de mistério e sonho.

Tive ocasião de assistir a vários destes *branhôs* e pude verificar o grande interesse com que todos, velhos e novos, vão seguindo o desenrolar do desafio, aplaudindo as piadas que mais lhes agradam, etc.[42]

(The instruments that accompany the *cantigas* vary in number, according to circumstances. Sometimes one sees 10 or more instruments, and others only a violin and a drum make like a symphony orchestra.

Some fishermen in Malacca play the violin with notable agility, not to say expression. In general the strings come from Chinese stores that provide them for Chinese instruments. They are very rudimentary but in the hands of the Malaccans they vibrate fully. And it's interesting to see a certain air of nostalgia in the shining eyes of the players, barefoot and wearing only long pants and a poorly buttoned jacket, when they take up their violins, as in a story that transports them back to distant countries of mystery and dreams.

I had occasion to attend various of these *branhôs* and could verify the great interest that all, old and young, had in following the unfolding of the challenges, applauding the funniest jokes, etc.)

The eleven quatrains of "Passarinho Berde" were edited by a local speaker of the Creole, David Teixeira, who noted that each song could have numerous different stanzas.[43] Silva Rêgo classifies the category of *cantiga cristão* (Kristang *cantiga*), to which the oldest songs belong, as extremely rare and an inheritance from the past: "As primeiras são raras, muito raras e vêm provàvelmente de seus antepasados. São estas as únicas que nos interessam."[44] (These are rare, [not in original translation] extremely rare, and probably come from their ancestors. These are the only ones that interest us). "Passarinho Berde" is grouped with three other traditional songs "Nina, Boboi, Nina", "Gingli Nona" and "Galinha Caté", each accompanied by a characteristic musical score, which, according to linguist Alan Baxter in his introduction to the second edition, are well-known melodies.[45] "Gingle Nona", or "Singelle Nona", has been traced in variants across South and Southeast Asia.[46]

Folk *cantigas* featuring the green parrot as a metaphor became integrated into popular beliefs and superstitions of the community, featured in three examples noted by Silva Rêgo, who wryly notes[47] that "em Malaca, como em toda a parte, o povo não pode falar durante dez minutos sem se arrimar a metáforas" (in Malacca, as everywhere, people can't talk for ten minutes without resorting to metaphors):

155

Minha pastorinho berde,	(My green little bird
Na qui ramo bôs tá santá?	On which branch are you perched?
Santá na ramo seco,	If you're on a dry branch
Triste bida eu logo passá.	I will soon have a sad life.)[48]

"É uma crendice de Malaca. Se alguém observar um passarinho sentado num ramo seco, é isto sinal de que há-de passar 'triste bida'" (It's a popular belief of Malacca. If someone sees a bird perched on a dry branch, it's a sign that they will certainly have a "sad life").

157

Pastorinho berde,	(Little green bird
Ramo seco já santá;	Lighted on a dry branch;
Santá na ramo seco,	On a dry branch perched,
Qui repairo logo achá?	What remedy will I soon find?)

"Ó meu passarinho verde que estás pousado em ramo seco; se tu assim ficas; que boa fortuna posso eu esperar?" (Oh my green bird perched on a dry branch; if you stay there, what good fortune can I expect?)

158
Pastorinho berde,
Um ramo santá dôs dôs;
Eu nádi more lonzi,
Eu logo more perto bôs.

(Little green bird
Two perched on a single branch
I won't die far away
I will soon die near you).

"Outro crendice de Malaca. Quando algum namorado vê dois pássaros poisados juntos num ramo, acredita que não há-de morrer longe do seu amor." (Another popular belief of Malacca. When someone in love sees two birds perched together on a branch, he believes that he will not die far from his beloved.)[49]

The popularity of folk metaphors is explained by Silva Rêgo by two factors: poetic style and simple vocabulary. The quatrains can be recited on any occasion and at times show surprisingly original content. Improvisation in their performance often results in a lack of logical connection between the first two and last two verses, which may be joined only by rhyme, or as the singer's memory allows.[50]

The "Passarinho Berde" (see Figure 8.1) in Malacca becomes a popular moral tale or fable for the Kristang community, in which the parrot may be an augur of sad or happy destinies, a lover or a faithful friend. The green bird's overseas origin is indicated by the verse "Mas berdi di serindit"

FIGURE 8.1
"Passarinho Berde"

DIALECTO PORTUGUÊS DE MALACA E OUTROS ESCRITOS

PASSARINHO BERDE

3
Pas - sa - ri - nho ber - de, Na gaiola su - bi - á,
Cho - má, Sia - ra, bo - tá per - to, Ou - bí Sia - ra tá can - tá.

(Greener than the green Malay parrot), by its bright green colour ("Greener than the coconut frond"), and by its not being recognized by the local flock. Standard themes reappear, including romance — when the parrot calls a lady, who is later personified as the jasmine rose it smells in the garden — and faithfulness, in the parrot's wish to die near its friends. Superstitions are found in an omnipresence of physical dangers faced by the parrot once outside the protection of its cage, symbolized in the thorny branch, coconut palm or well. Ultimately, the parrot flies away joyfully until it disappears from sight.

PASSARINHO BERDE

1	
Passarinho berde, Na gaiola subiá, Chomá Siara, botá perto, Oubi Siara tá cantá.	(Small green bird, Flying in its cage, It calls a lady to come close, The lady hears it singing.)
2	
Passarinho berde, Más berde di serendê, Já sai di sua gaiola, Que correnti logo corrê.	(Small green bird, Greener than the green Malay parrot, Has just left its cage, Escaped its chains and run away.)
3	
Passarinho berde, Agora ficá largado, Uma vêz já sai di gaiola Mestí aboá com cuidado.	(Small green bird, You now are freed, Once you've left the cage, You'd better fly with caution.)
4	
Passarinho berde Encontrá com sua rancho, Chapá êli perto-perto Por querê fazé cambrado.	(Small green bird, Joining with your flock, He comes very close, Because he wants to make friends.)
5	
Passarinho berde, Rancho nun quê conhecê, Abrí êli sua asa, Aboá até disparecê.	(Small green bird, The flock doesn't recognize him, He opens up his wings, And flies away disappearing from sight.)
6	
Passarinho berde, Más berde di fôla cocu,	(Small green bird, Greener than the coconut frond,

Com alégri tá aboá,	Joyfully flies away,
Já perto cai na fogo.	Here he would fall in the fire.)
7	
Passarinho verde,	(Small green bird,
Aboá dreento di jardim	Flies into the garden,
Já achá unha cheiro,	There he finds an odour,
Sua rosa mungaring.	It is his jasmine rose.)
8	
Passarinho berde,	(Small green bird,
Já bai na mato deserto,	Flies into the deserted woods,
Causo querê morrê,	Wanting to die,
Na cambrado sua perto.	Near his friend.)
9	
Passarinho berde,	(Small green bird,
Santado na ramo espinho,	Perched on the thorny branch,
Olá gente chapá perto,	Sees people coming close,
Bai êle outro caminho.	He goes another direction.)
10	
Passarinho berde,	(Small green bird,
Sua peo ficá fendido,	Gets a wound in its foot,
Num pôdi buscá sua comida,	It can't search for food,
Perdê êli sua sentido.	It passes out.)
11	
Passarinho berde,	(Small green bird,
Santá na rib di poço,	Perched on top of the well,
Tocá um pedaço di pedra,	Touches a piece of stone,
Já quebrá sua osso.	And breaks a bone.)[51]

Silva Rêgo's pioneering transcription was confirmed by similar transcriptions of linguist Ian Hancock, who studied the origin of Malacca Creole Portuguese, as found in his field notes (circa 1960):[52]

Pasarinya bedri	(Green bird
Agora fika lagradu	Now become free
M'bes ja sai di gayola,	At once left the cage
Mesti abua ku kuidadu	And had to fly with care)

It is further reaffirmed in Joan Margaret Marbeck's book (1995) on her family inheritance in the Kristang community:[53]

FIGURE 8.2
"Pasarinya Berdi"

Pasarinya Berdi

Korus 1

Pasarinya berdi,
Na gaiola subih,
Comah siara, botah pertu,
Ubi siara ta kantah.
Cadisa idade Pasarinya berdi (2x)

Pasarinya berdi
Mas berdi di serindit,
Ja sai di sa gaiola, ku kurenti logu kureh.

Korus 2

Pasarinya berdi,
Agora fikah lagado,
Ungua bes ja sai di gaiola,
Misti abuah ku kuidadu.

Pasarinya berdi ngkontrah ku sa rancu,
Pasarinya berdi, rancu ngkereh kuniseh,
Abrih eli sa aza disparseh.

(*The Sly, Wily, Old, Green Bird*
Sly, wily, old, green bird,
Trapped in a cage,
Mounts up to the perch,
A tune to a lover he chirps.

Sly, wily, old, green bird.
Sly, wily, old, green bird.

Sly, wily, old, green bird,
Greener than the green Malay parrot,
Has escaped from captivity,
Despite chains, he's fled into infinity.

Sly, wily, old, green bird,
Is happy to be free,
But must be cautious,
Unseen lie the enemy.

Sly, wily, old, green bird,
Meets his flock,
Keeps close to one,
He desires wedlock.

Sly, wily, old, green bird,
His flock recognizes him not,
Disappointed at her rejection,
He spreads his wings to fly into oblivion.)[54]

CONCLUSION

The folksong "Papagaio Verde", one of a handful of the oldest songs belonging to the musical tradition of the Portuguese maritime voyages, recapitulates many of the themes found in folk literature: the parrot speaks, at times inconveniently, acts out a moral lesson, criticizes and insults, is a lover or matchmaker, delivers messages, keeps a beat with the music, and in the *cantigas* unites the Indo-Portuguese and Luso-Asian communities that have kept traditional performance alive for five centuries. The parrot applies themes of world folklore to local Creole culture; quatrains that invoke the green parrot in the first two lines usually append in the final two an observation on community life, which accounts for their persistence and popularity as local lore.

At the beginning of the twenty-first century, while technological advances and globalization have put the broad Lusophone world into contact through the Internet, forces of war, disaster, immigration and economic necessity have fundamentally changed the old ways of life. Dennis McGilvray documents the disaster to befall the Portuguese Burghers of Sri Lanka's East Coast with the loss of 157 lives at Dutch Bar, Batticaloa in the tsunami of 2004,[55] and Sarkissian describes the politics of folkloric performance for tourism in Malacca's Portuguese town. In all these enclaves, however, the green parrot continues to sing in "Portuguese" and flies away to entertain neighbouring communities. The flying parrot connects them across oceanic distances through shared cultural traditions. Just as the ships of the India fleet connected the communities along the seaborne empire, the *papagaio verde* links them through a common musical folklore.

APPENDIX[56]

D. Dinis – *pastorela ii*

Ua pastora ben talhada
cuidava en seu amigo
e estava, ben vos digo,
per quant' eu vi, mui coitada,
e diss: "Oi mais non é nada
de fiar per namorado
nunca molher namorada,
pois que mh o meu á errado"

Ela tragia na mão
un papagai mui fremoso,
cantando mui saboroso,
ca entrava o verão,
e diss: "Amigo loução,
que faria por amores,
pois m'errastes tan en vão?
E caeu antr uas flores

Ua gran peça do dia
louv'ali, que non falava,
e a vezes acordava,
[e] a vezes esmorecia,
e diss: "Ai santa maria
que será de min agora?"
e o papagai dizia:
"Ben, per quant' eu sei, senhora"

"Se me queres dar guarida"
diss' a pastor, "Di verdade,
papagai, por caridade,
ca morte m'é esta vida";
diss' el<e>: "Senhor comprida
de ben, e non vos queixedes,
ca o que vos á servida,
erged' olho e vee-lo edes"

Sources: Biblioteca Nacional 534, fol. 120v; and Biblioteca Apostolica Vaticana 137, fol. 17.

Notes

1 Fernando Pessoa, *Quadras*, edited by Luísa Freire (Lisbon: Assírio & Alvim, 2002), p. 48. Fernando Pessoa and Philip Krummrich, *A Critical, Dual-Language Edition of Quadras ao Gosta Popular / Quatrains in the Popular Style*, translated by Philip Krummrich (Lewiston, NY: E. Mellen Press, 2003), p. 137.

2 J. Leite de Vasconcellos, comp., *Cancioneiro Popular Português*, vol. 1, edited by Maria Arminda Zaluar Nunes (Coimbra: Universidade de Coimbra, 1975), pp. 32–33.

3 Leslie Bethell and José Murilo de Carvalho, *Joaquim Nabuco, British Abolitionists and the End of Slavery in Brazil* (London: ISA, 2009), pp. 132, 150 and 154.

4 Jorge de Sena, "Homenagem ao Papagaio Verde," in *Os Grão-Capitães: Uma Sequência de Contos* (Lisbon: Edições 70, 1976), pp. 23–52.

5 See David Crystal, *Language Death* (Cambridge: Cambridge University Press, 2000); see also Mark Abley, *Spoken Here: Travels among Threatened Languages* (New York: Houghton Mifflin Co., 2005), pp. 190–200. In 1997 artist Rachel Berweck, based on Humboldt's journals, taught the forty words to Amazonian parrots that were exhibited in 2000 at London's Serpentine Gallery. To read more, see Alexander von Humboldt, Aimé Bonpland and Helen Maria Williams, *Personal Narrative of Travels to the Equinoctial Regions of America during the Years 1799–1804*, vol. 5 (London: Longman, Hurst, Rees, Orme, and Brown, 1821), p. 620.

6 Stith Thompson, *Motif-Index of Folk-Literature: A Classification of Narrative Elements in Folktales, Ballads, Myths, Fables, Mediaeval Romances, Exempla, Fabliaux, Jest-Books, and Local Legends*, rev. enl. ed., 6 vols. (Bloomington: Indiana University Press, 1955–58).

7 Aesop, *Aesopi Fabellas vna cvm argvmentis novis: Vobis admodvm conducibiles accipite adolescentuli, nunc demum ... solertius ...* (Brixiae: Apud hęredes Ludouici Britanici, 1563); and *Fables of Aesop: Selected, Told Anew, and Their History Traced*, selected by Joseph Jacobs (New York: Macmillan, 1946) (see "The Parrot and the Cat").

8 "The Tale of the Husband and the Parrot", *The Book of the Thousand Nights and a Night*, translated by Richard F. Burton (New York: Heritage Press, 1934), 1: 62–64.

9 Katharine Mary Briggs, *A Dictionary of British Folk-Tales in the English Language* (Bloomington: Indiana University Press, 1971), pp. 225–26.

10 Flora Beal Shelton, ed., and A.L. Shelton, trans., *Tibetan Folk Tales* (New York: George H. Doran Co., 1925), pp. 110–12.

11 Sílvio Romero, *Contos Populares do Brasil*, edited by Luís da Câmara Cascudo, illustrated by Santa Rosa (Rio de Janeiro: José Olympio, 1954), pp. 128–36.

12 George Fraser, *The Golden Bough: A Study in Magic and Religion*, 3rd ed. (London: Macmillan, 1906–15; repr., abridged ed., New York: Macmillan, 1922).

13 Rafe Martin, "The Steadfast Parrot" in *The Hungry Tigress: Buddhist Legends and Jataka Tales* (Berkeley: Parallax Press, 1999).

14 Maung Maung Pye, "Shin-Mway-Loon and Min-Nanda", in *Tales of Burma* (New York: Macmillan, 1952), pp. 12–18.

[15] Jane Yolen, ed., "The Waiting Maid's Parrot (China)", in *Favorite Folktales from around the World* (New York: Pantheon, 1986), pp. 90–94.

[16] H. Parker, comp. and trans., *Village Folk-Tales of Ceylon: Collected and Translated by H. Parker*, 2nd ed. (London: Luzac & Co., 1910–14; repr., Dehiwala, Sri Lanka: Tisara Prakasakayo, 1971), 2: 398–401 and 402–3 ("How the Parrot Explained the Law-suit" and "The Parrot and the Crow").

[17] Anthony Gottlieb, "My Parrot, My Self", *New York Times,* 12 October 2008.

[18] David Sedaris, *Squirrel Seeks Chipmunk* (New York: Little Brown, 2010).

[19] Elza Paxeco Machado and José Pedro Machado, *Cancioneiro da Biblioteca Nacional*, vol. 3, *Cantigas 446 a 675* (Lisbon: Edição da *Revista de Portugal*, 1952), Cantiga 534, fol. 120v.

[20] Rip Cohen, *500 Cantigas d'Amigo* (Porto: Campo das Letras, 2003), p. 643.

[21] Maria do Ceo, *Aves Illustradas em Avisos para as Religiosas Servirem os Officios dos Seus Mosteiros* (Lisboa Occidental: Officina de Miguel Rodrigues, 1738).

[22] Sara Augusto, "O papagaio ilustrado: Lição e exemplo na ficção barroca," *Máthesis* 14 (2005): 137–48.

[23] Francisco Gomes de Amorim, *O Cedro Vermelho* (Lisbon: Imprensa Nacional, 1874).

[24] Camilo Castelo Branco, *A Brasileira de Prazins: Scenas do Minho* (Porto: Lello & Irmão, 1882), chap. 20.

[25] Sebastião R. Dalgado, *Dialecto Indo-Português de Damão*, facs. ed. (Lisbon, 1903), 1–36; cited in Ana Maria Amaro, *Filhos da Terra* (Macao: ICM, 1988), p. 65.

[26] Hugo Schuchardt, "Kreolische Studien III: Über das Indoportugiesische von Mangalore", *Sitzungsberichte der kaiserlichen Akademie der Wissenschaften zu Wien (philosophisch-historische Klasse)* 105 (1883b), pp. 881–904.

[27] K. David Jackson, *Sing without Shame* (Amsterdam: John Benjamins; ICM, 1990).

[28] Schuchardt, "Über das Indoportugiesische", p. 888.

[29] Jackson, *Sing without Shame*, p. 26.

[30] Dalgado, *Dialecto Indo-Português de Damão*, p. 693.

[31] Sebastião Rodolfo Dalgado, "Dialecto indo-português do Norte", *Revista Lusitana* 9 (1906): 142–66 and 193–228; and Jeronymo Quadros, *Diu: Apontamentos para sua História e Chorographia* (Nova Goa: Tipographia Fontainhas, 1899), p. 12. See also Hugo Schuchardt, *Kreolisch Studien III: Über das Indoportugiesische von Diu: Sitzungsberichte der kaiserlichen Akademie der Wissenschaften zu Wien (philosophisch-historische Klasse)* 103 (1883a): 3–18.

[32] Dalgado, *Dialecto Indo-Português de Damão*, p. 26; and Schuchardt, *Kreolisch Studien III*, p. 11.

[33] Jackson, *Sing without Shame*, p. 6; and *Cantigas ne o Lingua de Portuguez* (Matre, Ceylon: 23 June 1914). See K. David Jackson, "Indo-Portuguese *Cantigas*: Oral Traditions in Ceylon Portuguese Verse", *Hispania* 74, no. 3 (1991): 618–26.

[34] Margaret Sarkissian, *D'Albuquerque's Children: Performing Tradition in Malaysia's Portuguese Settlement* (Chicago: University of Chicago Press, 2000), p. 195.

[35] Jackson, *Sing without Shame*, p. 47.

[36] João Feliciano Marques Pereira, comp., "Cancioneiro musical crioulo", *Ta-Ssi-Yang-Kuo: Archivos e Annaes do Extremo-Oriente Portuguez,* 1st–2nd ser. (Lisbon: Antiga Livraria Bertrand – José Bastos, 1899–1903), 1: 239–43 and 2: 703–7.

[37] Pereira, "Cancioneiro musical crioulo", p. 705.

[38] Ana Maria Machado, *Filhos da Terra* (Macao: ICM, 1988), pp. 62–65.

[39] Ibid., p. 62.

[40] António da Silva Rêgo, *Dialecto Português de Malaca: Apontamentos para o seu Estudo* (Lisbon: Agência Geral das Colónias, 1942), pp. 228–30; and António da Silva Rêgo and Alan N. Baxter, *Dialecto Português de Malaca e Outros Escritos* (Lisbon: Comissão Nacional para os Descobrimentos Portugueses, Imprensa Nacional, 1998), pp. 266–68.

[41] Silva Rêgo, *Dialecto Português de Malaca* (1942), p. 220.

[42] Ibid., pp. 220–21.

[43] Ibid., p. 221.

[44] Ibid., p. 219.

[45] Alan Baxter, "Introdução", in Rêgo and Baxter, *Dialecto Português de Malaca* (1998), p. 30; and Silva Rêgo and Baxter, *Dialecto Português de Malaca* (1998), pp. 266–68.

[46] K. David Jackson, "Singelle Nona/Jinggli Nona: A Traveling Portuguese Burgher Muse", in *Re-exploring the Links: History and Constructed Histories between Portugal and Sri Lanka*, edited by Jorge Flores (Paris: Calouste Gulbenkian Foundation; and Wiesbaden: Harrassowitz, 2007), pp. 299–323.

[47] Rêgo and Baxter, *Dialecto Português de Malaca* (1998), p. 73.

[48] Rêgo, *Dialecto Português de Malaca* (1942), p. 69; and Silva Rêgo, *Dialecto Português de Malaca* (1998), p. 115.

[49] Rêgo, *Dialecto Português de Malaca* (1942), p. 70; and Silva Rêgo, *Dialecto Português de Malaca* (1998), p. 116.

[50] Rêgo, *Dialecto Português de Malaca* (1942), pp. 25–26.

[51] Ibid., pp. 228–30; and Rêgo and Baxter, *Dialecto Português de Malaca* (1998), pp. 266–68.

[52] Ian Hancock, "Field Notes" (personal copy, ca. 1960).

[53] Joan Margaret Marbeck, *Ungua Adanza: An Inheritance,* trans. Celine J. Ting (Malacca: Loh, 1995), pp. 109–10.

[54] Ibid.

[55] Dennis McGilvray, "The Portuguese Burghers of Eastern Sri Lanka in the Wake of Civil War and Tsunami", in Flores, *Re-exploring the Links*, pp. 325–47; and Dennis B. McGilvray, *Crucible of Conflict: Tamil and Muslim Society on the East Coast of Sri Lanka* (Durham, NC: Duke University Press, 2008), p. 47.

[56] Cohen, *500 Cantigas d'Amigo*, p. 643.

PART THREE

Mixed Legacies: The Portuguese and Luso-Asians in the Twentieth and Twenty-first Centuries

9

PORTUGUESE COMMUNITIES IN EAST AND SOUTHEAST ASIA DURING THE JAPANESE OCCUPATION

Felicia Yap

During the early twentieth century, Portuguese communities formed a prominent element of the social fabric of colonial Hong Kong and Malaya, being one of the largest locally domiciled Eurasian groupings in these territories. Since the late 1940s, however, these communities have gradually declined in number: although a small Portuguese settlement continues to exist in Malacca, the Hong Kong Portuguese community has been almost forgotten today. From the historian's perspective this raises the question, did any specific watershed occur in the twentieth-century evolution of these Portuguese communities? Is it possible to identify a critical moment at which the positions of these communities were irretrievably changed? The twentieth-century development of Portuguese communities in East and Southeast Asia has been explored by only a limited number of studies, and even fewer works have focused on the period of Japanese occupation as a significant epoch in their evolution.[1] In reality, if we hope to unravel the multilayered history of the Portuguese in these regions, their experiences during this tumultuous period merit serious attention. With this aim in mind, this chapter will investigate the compelling wartime experiences of the Portuguese in Japanese-occupied British Asia, with especial focus on colonial Hong Kong and Macao. It will also draw upon the intriguing experiences of Portuguese communities in occupied Malaya and Singapore as supplementary case studies.

The wartime experiences of the Portuguese in British Asia were indeed vastly different from those of any other colonial community during these turbulent years. After these territories were wrenched from British hands by February 1942, most European civilians were herded by the conquering forces into internment camps. Numerous civilians of Portuguese background, however, were not incarcerated by the Japanese. Due to their associations with neutral Portugal, many of them were in fact granted "third national" status and permitted to remain free in the occupied cities. Severe wartime pressures nevertheless compelled hundreds of these civilians to flee to Macao, a tiny colonial outpost of Portugal which was permitted by the Japanese to retain its neutral status. Others were involved in a variety of Allied resistance efforts and clandestine networks during this period. The Japanese conquest of British Asia, for the turmoil and anguish it inflicted, had a critical effect on Portuguese communities despite their neutral position in the region. As this chapter will demonstrate, the Japanese left behind communities that were traumatized, dislocated — and irreversibly altered.

PORTUGUESE COMMUNITIES BEFORE THE WAR

The first portion of this chapter will examine the broader colonial social backgrounds of these communities to provide the necessary framework for this discussion. In twentieth-century Hong Kong, Malacca and the treaty ports of China, most of the people referred to as "Portuguese" had only a tenuous link with Portugal itself. In Hong Kong, they widely described themselves as Macaense, as Filhos de Macau (Sons of Macao) or as the "Portuguese in Hong Kong". Many were descendants of unions between Portuguese and Malaccan, Goan and Timorese migrants. While other European nationalities married into the community over the generations, many Hong Kong Portuguese were also of Chinese descent as a result of intermarriages with Chinese converts to Catholicism.[2] In Malaya and Singapore, many attributed their origins to the Portuguese who conquered Malacca in the sixteenth century and married local women. But generations of intermarriage with local populations had largely blurred these ethnic connections with Portugal, although Catholicism and a creolized version of sixteenth-century Portuguese, known as Kristang, were preserved by the Malaccan community.[3]

From the 1850s, many Portuguese were prompted to migrate to Hong Kong from Macao as a result of declining employment prospects and periods of political turbulence and social unrest. Many were hired by British firms and the great trading houses as interpreters, clerks and bookkeepers. They were deemed suitable for these roles because of their Cantonese-speaking abilities and their ability to speak English, as many of them had attended Catholic mission schools in Macao.[4] As Hong Kong in its early days was characterized by a high incidence of disease, many Portuguese were also able to carve out a thriving niche for themselves as chemists or as workers in medical dispensaries.[5] Like the Eurasians in Hong Kong, the Portuguese eventually came to regard the territory as their home, and their forms of employment tended to follow similar patterns. While a small number became successful businessmen or merchants, the vast majority were employed as clerks or interpreters in the Hong Kong Government or in major European banks, trading companies and other expatriate institutions.[6] The Portuguese were especially well represented in the Hongkong and Shanghai Banking Corporation. Until the late 1950s, most clerical staff members were of Portuguese background.

There was also a considerable number of Portuguese in the colonial military services. Some had enlisted in the locally raised Hong Kong Volunteer Defence Corps (HKVDC) from as early as the First World War. Increasing numbers of recruits from mid-1925 even resulted in the addition of a Portuguese unit to the Corps in April 1927. Another Portuguese company, about 120 in number, was established in the same year as part of the Police Reserve.[7] During the 1930s, two more companies of local Portuguese were created within the HKVDC (No. 5. Coy MMG and No. 6 Coy AALA [Port]). Arthur Gomes joined the Volunteers in 1938 "because it was a popular thing to do. You had a rifle which you could take home and you became a member of the Rifle Club."[8] In Malacca, a Volunteer Defence Force of Eurasians was established in 1902 as an appendage of the Singapore Eurasian Volunteer Company. It was reorganized in 1923 as the "D" Company and consisted of over 200 enlisted men, mostly of Portuguese background.[9]

While the vast majority of Portuguese worked in a humble capacity, as further education was often beyond their means, some individuals nevertheless began to make an impact in commercial and political spheres. As the first Portuguese appointed as an "unofficial member" of the Hong Kong Legislative Council, José Pedro Braga acted as "the community's biggest champion for a long period of years", being "a keen fighter against discrimination".[10] Leonardo Horácio d'Almada e Castro Jr. graduated from Oxford with a degree in jurisprudence in 1926 and was called to the Bar as a member of the Middle Temple in 1927. Upon his return to Hong Kong, he took up private practice as a barrister and was eventually appointed as Braga's successor to the Legislative Council in 1937 and as a Justice of the Peace in 1938. By the turn of the century, several Portuguese trading firms were functioning actively in

Hong Kong (such as the firms of Cruz, Basto, Baretto, Soares, Alvares and Jorge).[11] Some Portuguese merchants even accumulated considerable fortunes on the strength of lucrative interventions in the import-export business or in local property acquisitions.[12]

PORTUGUESE IDENTITY WITHIN THE COLONIAL CONTEXT

During the interwar years, the Portuguese in Hong Kong formed a unique and distinctive community of their own, with clearly defined social, educational, cultural and religious institutions. As a significant proportion of them resided in the enclave of Kowloon on the Chinese mainland, their identity as a community was further strengthened by their residential separateness. The common practice of Roman Catholicism may have also acted as a unifying factor. Indeed, Henry J. Lethbridge has argued that the Hong Kong Portuguese largely maintained their identity as a distinct group and tended to intermarry because of their religion. By the 1920s, these prevailing patterns of intermarriage, after years of continuous residence in the crown colony, had produced a closely knit community.[13] Many acquired British nationality as a result of birth in the territory, although a few families continued to claim Portuguese nationality by descent through the registration of births at Portuguese consulates.[14] By the 1920s, most families spoke English as their primary medium, along with a type of Macao dialect (patois). While all spoke Cantonese with different levels of fluency, most were largely illiterate in that language.[15]

Though the Portuguese were mostly of Eurasian stock, there is evidence to suggest that the British did not discriminate against the Portuguese as heavily as other Eurasian groups in the territory. Jason Wordie has argued that the Hong Kong Portuguese were, for the most part, "the result of religiously solemnized marriages rather than the embarrassing remnants of *ad hoc* 'domestic arrangements', as was the case with many Eurasians, and so did not serve as reminders of moral laxity."[16] Indeed, Eurasians were widely regarded as a threat by the British because of their "anomalous and ambivalent social position", being neither European nor Asian.[17] In contrast to the Eurasians, however, the Portuguese were often regarded by outsiders as a largely homogenous group with a distinct and well-defined identity.[18] There were, however, a few instances of alleged discrimination. While rank-and-file Portuguese employees in British firms may have been trusted marginally more than their Asiatic counterparts, senior Portuguese clerks in the Hongkong and Shanghai Bank were permitted to sign documents only from the mid-1950s.[19]

Frank Correa, a Portuguese employee of the China Light Company, recalled that the firm even instituted separate toilets for its Portuguese and Chinese staff. Though a trained medical doctor, Eduardo (Eddie) Liberato Gosano believed that he was considered "junior" by the British as far as his salary was concerned; he earned just 25 per cent of the salary of his Irish anaesthetist, Dr Esmonde. While Esmonde was granted a five-bedroom flat in the European sector, Gosano was only allocated a four-bedroom flat in the Chinese area. As Wordie has noted, the Gosano family (of part-Goan extraction) were also "viewed askance by some other members of the Portuguese community on account of their racial origins, and more specifically, their skin colour." A number of elderly Portuguese residents remarked that they were "very black", and that this was "a pity".[20] Indeed, there were often tensions between lighter and darker-skinned Eurasians in pre-war Hong Kong, with lighter-coloured Eurasians (a stronger European phenotype) considering themselves "superior" to those of a darker complexion.[21]

THE COMING OF WAR

As war clouds drew ominously closer, several leading Portuguese and Eurasian families in Hong Kong became convinced that a Japanese attack was imminent. Many accordingly wished to flee the territory and believed that their British passports permitted them to do so. In June 1940, alarmed by the possibility of invasion by the Japanese, the British authorities hastily ordered the evacuation of all European women and children from the island. But evacuation was largely confined to those of "pure European descent"; the Australian Government, in particular, had indicated that only "pure" British' evacuees would be accepted in their Dominion.[22] These restrictions infuriated several merchant and professional families of Portuguese background, many of whom were holders of British passports. Their spokesman, the barrister d'Almada e Castro, protested against the "discrimination involved in the said order" and informed the Legislative Council that the government had "placed an appreciable strain on the loyalty of a large section of the [Portuguese] community".[23] Some influential Portuguese even established a Portuguese Evacuation Committee in August 1939 to facilitate the evacuation of the women and children of their community.[24] But other Portuguese residents, for their part, saw little reason to leave. "We didn't believe that war would come to Hong Kong," remarked Margaret Lobo, "It was most farfetched."[25] Thus, as the Japanese began to bombard Hong Kong in December 1941, many of them were caught up in the general mayhem and confusion. "We just threw things into sheets and … walked into town," recalled Lobo, "not knowing where we were going."[26] Her family eventually found shelter in an Indian shop. Amalia Sales and her family sought refuge at the Club Lusitano, where several Portuguese families banded together for mutual protection during the Japanese onslaught.[27]

Prominent among the defenders of Hong Kong who courageously resisted the Japanese were several Portuguese members of the HKVDC. "Although Portugal remained neutral throughout the war and the Portuguese residents of Hong Kong may have carried Portuguese passports," wrote Michael Ferrier, "many regarded Hong Kong as their home which they believed they had a duty to defend. They enlisted in large numbers and were to fight with great bravery."[28] "A lot of my relatives and friends died on the day when they put up a resistance against the Japanese soldiers, especially at Repulse Bay," recalled Reinaldo (Ray) Cordeiro.[29] As Arthur Gomes put it, "the Volunteers fought valiantly and earned their merit. We were roped on as 'Dads Army'; afterwards, they were surprised that dads could fight. Men of sixty were holding up crack Japanese troops. But we had completely underestimated the Japanese, their firepower, the accuracy of their artillery and bombing and their fighting capacity."[30] In Singapore, several Portuguese Volunteers of the "D" Company were part of the advance militia sent to defend the first-line perimeter of Bukit Timah.[31]

UNDER JAPANESE OCCUPATION

During the occupation years, the European populations of Japanese-occupied territories were divided by the conquering forces into two main categories. In the first group were the British, Dutch, Americans and other "enemy aliens" who were technically destined for the civilian internment camps. In the second category were the "third nationals", a loosely defined category which included the Portuguese, the Eurasians and a motley collection of Europeans from the Axis or neutral states (such as Ireland, Switzerland, Norway and Denmark). However, the phrase was often inconsistently used by the Japanese. The Portuguese were categorized as "third nationals" on some occasions, but sometimes they were listed as a distinct group. In February 1943, for example, the *Hong Kong News* reported that there were about 7,000 third nationals in occupied Hong Kong, including 1,203 Portuguese and 614 Eurasians. A month later, however, the Portuguese were denoted as a separate category, and the term "third nationals" was used to refer only to Eurasians and Europeans from neutral or Axis states.[32]

However, the boundaries between "enemy aliens" and "third nationals" in Japanese-occupied Hong Kong were often porous; some resourceful

Europeans were able to evade the internment camps by claiming third national citizenship. While some professed to have Irish connections, a vast majority of tearaways declared that they were of Portuguese background.[33] Indeed, the Portuguese consul himself was said to have remarked on one occasion that he "never at any time realised there were so many Portuguese in Hong Kong".[34] An intelligence report which reached Washington, DC observed that "all they had to do was to sign a paper relinquishing all rights as a British subject to become a Portuguese."[35] There was a widespread belief that the Portuguese would be granted especially favourable treatment by the Japanese, particularly in the allocation of rice supplies. Indeed, it appears that rice rations were initially distributed every morning at the Club Lusitano to the 1,100 Portuguese in Hong Kong.[36] Thus, as the barrister d'Almada e Castro observed:

> Paradoxical as it may sound, it is nevertheless true that never was the name of Portuguese at a greater premium in Hong Kong than immediately after its surrender to the Japanese. People whose only claim to have anything Portuguese in them lay in that they had eaten Portuguese sardines, clamoured for Portuguese Identity Cards. Others of Portuguese descent, and who had previously been at pains to conceal their origin, now openly worn arm-bands bearing the Portuguese colours. All of them sought refuge in Macao, the only place on the China Coast where the Union Jack flew uninterruptedly throughout the Pacific War.[37]

For many Portuguese of moderate income, however, life had to go on in Hong Kong as usual. While some were employed by the Japanese (a job in the new administration often provided the only assurance of a daily "rice bowl"), others were compelled to return to their old positions. A censor's report which reached London in May 1942 noted that "several Portuguese girls and one Portuguese man" were employed in the Japanese Foreign Affairs Department, while the Portuguese foreman of a rope factory was forced "to collect his staff and report back to work".[38] Many were compelled to sell their jewellery or other valuable possessions to make ends meet. Some small-time merchants were eager to reopen their shops as these provided their only means of livelihood. A Portuguese woman named Maria Leigh requested permission from the Japanese to reopen her beauty parlour in the Peninsula Hotel.[39] Emily Hahn remarked that a Portuguese girl named Mercedes found employment at a Japanese store, the Kajima Bazaar, insisting that she had her mother's approval.[40] As John Braga wrote in June 1943, "those early months were terrible times for war prisoners as well as for us outside. With our Portuguese name the Japanese did not intern us, though my wife and

I were in such straights [*sic*] that on many occasions we wished they had."[41] Indeed, as he noted, "we (Louie and I) were so reduced in circumstances that I went out with the fiddle, a street musician to play for Jap soldiers, and when they did not give me money or food, at the risk of my life I often stole food from them."[42]

Having served with the British forces, several Portuguese Volunteers were incarcerated by the Japanese in prisoner-of-war (POW) camps in Hong Kong. Alberto Maria Rodrigues served as a medical officer in the HKVDC Field Ambulance Unit and was interned in the Shamshuipo POW camp between 1942 and 1945. For his medical work in captivity, and in particular for his role in ameliorating a dysentery epidemic within the camp, he was awarded a military MBE in 1948.[43] Eddie Gosano similarly spent six months in a POW camp after the British surrender. He was released in mid-1942 and immediately relocated to Macao.[44] Arthur Gomes was among the Shamshuipo POWs who were forced to work for the Japanese at the Kai Tak aerodrome and Hong Kong harbour. "The work was very hard as our bodies were weakened by malnutrition," he recalled, "Sentries would punch and kick us and we didn't dare to stop working. Hunger was what occupied everyone's minds."[45] What kept him going was the "thought we would be released within three or four months, and so we lived three or four months at a time". Some Portuguese women married to Europeans even voluntarily entered the Stanley camp to be with their spouses.[46]

A few Portuguese and Eurasian individuals, however, were eager to embrace the new possibilities offered by the conquest. Some returned to their traditional intermediary roles by acting as commodity "brokers" for the Japanese, and especially in meeting the conquerors' wartime demand for scrap metals. They paid locals to scour the streets of Hong Kong for iron nails and bits of aluminium or copper, which they then resold to the Japanese.[47] There may have even been a few open shifts of allegiances during this period. An intelligence report received by the Americans in Chungking (Chongqing) suggested that a few "vicious" individuals may have even functioned as spies for the Japanese. One Gus de Rosa (whom a British report pronounced to be "the bad hat of Macao") was said to have

> acted as the intermediary when the Japanese wanted to purchase a Dutch ship in Macao; first buying it himself and then selling it to the Japanese. He also spoke against the British in Macao … it was said that he gave information to the Japanese Consul when the British Consul was sending a party out of Macao. As a result the expedition had to be cancelled.[48]

Life in Japanese-occupied Malaya and Singapore was similarly one of harsh uncertainty; the welfare of local communities often varied according to the whim of Japanese officials on the ground. Several Portuguese families attempted to escape urban hotbeds of fear and suspicion by seeking refuge in villages or smaller towns until the war ended. Many were deprived of their usual means of income and were compelled to depend on the sea as a source of livelihood. The Portuguese settlement in Malacca witnessed an influx of men, women and children from the neighbouring Malay states, especially during the first year of the war. From 1943, large numbers of Eurasians were compelled by the Japanese to open up an agricultural settlement in Bahau (in the centre of the Malayan peninsula), where many eventually perished from diseases like malaria. To escape this fate, many Portuguese sought refuge in Malacca, where they knew large numbers of Eurasians of Portuguese background resided.[49] As Ronald Daus has noted, some Portuguese individuals were believed by the Japanese to be pro-British; community leaders were killed and priests were sent to Singapore, where they perished in captivity. Indeed, a roll of the war dead at the town hall in Malacca suggests that a tenth of the dead were Portuguese.[50]

Indeed, as a result of various wartime pressures, several hundreds of Hong Kong Portuguese quickly boarded ferries to neutral Macao during the first months of 1942. Many of these refugees were left without secure financial means as a result of the collapse of British Hong Kong. As a Hong Kong Portuguese named Lopes described his experiences after the British surrender:

> Our young men including my sons were at Shamshuipo along with other prisoners-of-war. The Allied civilians were at Stanley, but I having lost my home and business had nowhere to go. My only possession was a gold watch. My wife had her jewellery. After roaming the streets, I took my wife and two daughters along to our church. The priest allowed us and other destitute members of our community to sleep upon the floor of the church hall.[51]

Others were driven to Macao by fear or coercion.[52] As Alberto Rodrigues noted,

> many had long and close ties with the British administration and found it prudent to leave. Others, with sons, brothers or fathers interned found life easier in Macao, where food was not as scarce as in Hong Kong, and the risk of harassment by Japanese troops did not exist. In spite of their neutral status, many had been physically or verbally abused on the streets of Hong Kong.[53]

Ray Cordeiro was among the hundreds who sought sanctuary in Macao, as his father (a staff member of the Hongkong and Shanghai Bank) was certain that the Japanese "would come for him".[54] The conquerors were "really abusive and very rough", recalled Cordeiro, "It was a life of fear .... So, I went to Macao and true enough, the next day they came for my dad, but he left just before, so he was lucky to get away."[55]

In Macao, modest subsidies were granted to many of the refugees by the local government, and funds were also remitted from London via the British consulate in Macao for the maintenance and upkeep of specific groups (such as ex-bank clerks of the Hongkong and Shanghai Bank). An English-language curriculum was organized for Hong Kong boys at the Saint Luiz Gonzaga School.[56] Many of the new arrivals resided with relatives or as refugees in the reception centres set up to house them, such as the Bela Vista and the Club Macao. As Arnaldo de Oliveira Sales recalled:

> Life wasn't altogether unpleasant. We had friends and relatives in Macao. I had plenty of volunteer work and studying to do. We had to make our own entertainment, and made do as best we could. There was a bridge club, which the British Consul and the Macao government had set up, so I played bridge in my spare time, and took part in some amateur dramatics, putting on stage plays for the local and refugee community.[57]

Roger Lobo remembered his war years in Macao as being

> pretty good — a lot of girlfriends, a lot of friends from Hong Kong. We played tennis, we went dancing, learnt the jitterbug. Macao really opened up with so many refugees. It was great. People didn't have money in their pockets but the spirit was there and the fun was there too. People were starving but we were not at war; we were just suffering the consequences of war.[58]

Some individuals also found ways to assist their fellow refugees: both de Sales and Cordeiro took up work in refugee centres, while d'Almada e Castro was appointed as a liaison officer in connection with refugee work.[59]

Neutral Macao also sheltered a functioning British consulate headed by a dynamic personage named John Reeves, who came to be actively involved in caring for the numerous Portuguese and Eurasian refugees who streamed in from Hong Kong. Besides offering them succour, Reeves was engaged in facilitating the clandestine passages of several Portuguese and Eurasian individuals into Free China.[60] A number of skilled Portuguese also joined up with the British consulate in Macao and took on jobs in various critical sections of the consulate's staff. The medical doctor António Paulo Guterres was posted to various civilian hospitals during the battle for Hong Kong.

He subsequently sought refuge in Macao, where he worked as a medical officer in the British consulate. Other Portuguese medical recruits at the consulate included Joseph Barnes, Eddie Gosano and G.A.V. Ribeiro.[61] A few Portuguese individuals were also involved in drawing up plans for the eventual British reoccupation of Hong Kong. At the end of the war, the barrister d'Almada e Castro and his wife attempted a difficult journey to the United Kingdom, where he was appointed as a member of the Hong Kong Planning Unit. Consisting largely of veteran civil servants who had held positions in the colony before the war, the unit was involved in drafting the first British policies for post-war Hong Kong and in planning for a "nucleus administration" to restore civil government to the colony immediately after the anticipated defeat of the Japanese.[62]

RESISTANCE TO THE JAPANESE

As the war progressed, a number of Portuguese individuals began to play an increasingly important role in organized Allied resistance movements. Chief of these organizations was the British Army Aid Group (BAAG), an intelligence unit involved in gathering information on Japanese forces in Hong Kong and on general conditions in the colony, as well as in assisting Allied servicemen to escape from the Hong Kong camps. Eddie Gosano served as a BAAG agent in Macao during the war, while the medical doctor Horácio Osório (Ozo) was appointed as a captain in the BAAG.[63] By the summer of 1942, several young Portuguese, Chinese and Eurasians had linked up with the BAAG or other key Allied outfits in Free China. Many of these men and women were Westernized, English-speaking individuals; several were students or staff of Hong Kong University or ex-members of the HKVDC.[64] "My family went to Free China in batches," recalled Margaret Lobo, "because there you could find jobs with the American army and the British army [or] in consulates … I was a stenographer working for the [American] Fourteenth Air Force in Kunming."[65] Many young Portuguese individuals were attracted by the promise of wartime employment, especially as the astronomical cost of living in Macao had put several in difficult straits. As Lobo noted, "most of the young, able people from Macao would go into the interior of China to get jobs … we received a subsidy from the British Consul [in Macao] but that was very meagre; nobody could really live on it."[66] Bernard Xavier, a young signalman of the Royal Navy, was among those who sought employment in Kweilin (Guilin). He was eventually hired as a secret agent by the U.S. Office of Strategic Services (OSS) and dispatched on an intelligence mission to Macao.[67]

Some Portuguese individuals were also involved in facilitating the escape conduits through which Allied workers, refugees and recruits were secretly dispatched from Macao to Free China (and which also served as key channels for BAAG intelligence work). One effective route was by sea from Macao, via boats or motor junks engaged in smuggling goods into China.[68] The BAAG operative Frederic Lobo was involved in rescuing Allied pilots who had been shot down in the Macao region and in transporting them back to Free China via elaborate decoy schemes. As he detailed his experiences:

> I was also involved with British intelligence, through my father ... We were part of the British Army Aid Group, sending back into China pilots who were shot down around this area, or who found themselves in Macao. We'd push them into Kunming to rejoin the airforce. I got quite involved in that. The intelligence group would pass information on to us so we could go along and meet the pilots at an arranged time, make sure the coast was clear, and see them board the junk. We had to send two junks, one with gasoline and other goodies and a noisy engine, designed to be caught by the Japanese, and the other one that the people were hidden on to go right through to Free China. It was risky for us, risky for them, risky for everybody, and we learned not to talk about it.[69]

Some individuals who remained behind in Hong Kong were also involved in Allied resistance efforts. V.N. Atienza, who worked at the Kowloon Hospital during the occupation period, maintained a short-wave radio receiver and secretly distributed news of Allied successes to BAAG agents on the island. In June 1944, Atienza's underground activities were betrayed by an informer; he was subsequently arrested and interrogated by the Japanese who accused him of being a ringleader of pro-British activities in Hong Kong. He was then incarcerated in the prison at Stanley where he was brutally tortured (he confessed that he even attempted to take his own life to end his ordeal). He was eventually released and placed under house arrest until the end of the war.[70] A Portuguese mother with the surname Xavier and her three daughters became actively involved in organizing relief supplies for the beleaguered POWs in the prison camps.[71]

Most strikingly, some Portuguese bank clerks in Hong Kong were also involved in clandestine wartime operations. During the early months of the occupation, a group of sixty British and European bankers — mostly senior personnel of the Hongkong and Shanghai Bank and other financial institutions — were retained at their positions by the Japanese to liquidate their banks' holdings and to sign banknotes for issue. Under the cover of these enforced duties, these British bankers quietly concealed a stash of some HK$2 million, which they eventually smuggled out to the POW and internment camps.[72] The bankers also compiled secret records of all wartime financial transactions that passed through their banks and ensured that information about accounts and notes in circulation were kept up to date, which subsequently assisted the British takeover of the banks in 1945. Some of the clandestine records were smuggled to Macao (where they were stored in the Banco Nacional Ultramarino) and thence to Chungking in Free China.[73] Various Portuguese clerks played a critical role in facilitating "the continuation and storage of the secret records."[74] One of them was the clerk Luis Carlos Rozario Souza; in November 1942, he was asked by a British banker to assist in the devising of short-wave radio reception methods. According to a British intelligence report, Souza "agreed to do this, knowing full well it was strictly forbidden by the Japanese Army . . . from December 1942 to April 1943 he secretly listened to short wave broadcasts from London and other places" and reported them to the British.[75]

As it turned out, these clandestine activities were to rebound heavily on most of the parties involved. When the Japanese decided to intern the British bankers at Stanley, some of the secret records were smuggled out of the banks by Portuguese, Chinese and Indian staff and hidden in various private homes. The Portuguese supervisors of the banks nevertheless facilitated various clandestine operations in the absence of their British bosses. In autumn 1943, the Japanese raided the Club Lusitano in Hong Kong, suspecting that a spy ring was centred there. They found a set of the secret records (it remains unclear as to why the records were taken there) and arrested three Portuguese bank staff. One was eventually executed on charges of espionage while the others were sentenced to long terms of imprisonment.[76] In occupied Malaya, many Portuguese men and youngsters similarly joined resistance efforts and began assisting or supplying information to Allied underground movements. Charles McCormack of the Royal Air Force was aided in his escape from the Pasir Panjang POW camp by some Portuguese Eurasians, and was later asked to contact a guerrilla known as Rodrigues at a secret destination near Kuala Lipis.[77] It appears that plans were even made by some Portuguese Volunteers to raid a Japanese armoury and to escape with the seized weapons to the Asahan jungle in Johor, where it was believed that resistance movements were operating. However, the schemers were betrayed by an informant and arrested in a raid in October 1942. They were interrogated and tortured by the Kempeitai; several later died in prison.[78]

THE EFFECTS OF THE WAR

Upon the recapture of Hong Kong, several Portuguese individuals played prominent roles in the work of post-war reconstruction. There were Portuguese serving in the Legal and Medical departments of the post-war British Military Administration, as well as in Supplies Transport and Industry. As d'Almada e Castro noted, the president of the General Military Court was Portuguese, as well as the custodian of property.[79] Various individuals also returned to Hong Kong and attempted to "rebuild their lives from scratch."[80] Anecdotal evidence suggests that the post-war Hongkong and Shanghai Bank may have adopted an especially favourable policy in the hiring of Portuguese staff. According to George Elliott, the Portuguese were treated "one step higher than the Chinese" out of British "gratitude" for loyal services rendered during the war, and were even paid salaries "slightly higher than the Chinese" immediately after the war.[81]

Like many Eurasians and Baghdadi Jews in Hong Kong, however, many Portuguese left the territory permanently after the war and began new lives elsewhere.[82] During the 1950s and 1960s, entire Portuguese families emigrated from Hong Kong, principally to the United States, Australia, Brazil, Canada and New Zealand. Jason Wordie has suggested that contacts developed during the wartime years (such as with POWs from Britain, Canada and elsewhere) may have encouraged some Portuguese to leave Hong Kong permanently. During the war, fellow POWs had highlighted the favourable employment and educational opportunities that the local Portuguese could obtain if they emigrated from Hong Kong after the hostilities.[83] Many Portuguese ex-POWs who were sent to Britain or Australia for a period of recuperation also never returned.[84]

However, the evidence also suggests that various post-war disturbances and uncertainties were equally critical in encouraging these departures. In January 1946, Admiral Cecil Harcourt of the British reoccupying naval fleet remarked in a letter to the Secretary of State that "we have had a couple of disturbances here that, if they had not been handled well, might have become riots".[85] "These disturbances," he added, "have been primarily racial and chiefly directed against the Portuguese of whom ... there are quite a number in the Colony."[86] While the reasons for these post-war racial agitations against the Portuguese remain unclear, it is indeed possible that they contributed to the decline in Portuguese numbers in the immediate aftermath of the war. Other Portuguese residents were impelled to leave the territory after the Communist takeover of neighbouring China, and especially after the troubles of 1967 when a series of Communist-instigated demonstrations, marches and noisy street protests erupted in the city. "A lot of Portuguese … emigrated when we had the '67 riots," recalled Cordeiro, "People just left Hong Kong, unhappy with their lives here and the future for their kids."[87] Frank Correa similarly felt that various uncertainties prevailing in the post-war territory, especially in the wake of domestic disturbances, prompted the departures of several members of his community.[88]

A few Portuguese individuals who remained behind in post-war Hong Kong nevertheless went on to various positions of prominence in the territory. Eduardo Gosano became increasingly involved in local affairs and was appointed as a member of the Urban Council in 1952. The barrister d'Almada e Castro resumed his distinguished career as a lawyer in Hong Kong as well as his wider role in community affairs during the post-war period. He was appointed to the Executive Council and eventually retired as senior member in 1958. For his services to the public, he was awarded a CBE in 1953. His wife Clothilde was appointed to the bench of Justices of the Peace, thus becoming one of the first female justices in Hong Kong. The physician Alberto Rodrigues was appointed medical superintendent of Saint Paul's Hospital after the war. He served in the Legislative Council (1953–60) and Executive Council (1960–74), and was eventually knighted for his services to Hong Kong in 1960.[89] Roger Lobo similarly rose in post-war Hong Kong to become an influential political adviser and public servant. He was appointed as the head of the Hong Kong Government's media department and served for several years in the Legislative and Executive councils; like Rodrigues, he was eventually knighted for his contributions to Hong Kong.[90] But despite these individual successes, the decline of Portuguese numbers became an increasingly inexorable phenomenon in the post-war period.

CONCLUSION

This chapter argues that the Second World War was a critical turning point in the evolution of Portuguese communities in British Asia. Left without reliable sources of financial support in occupied Hong Kong, many Portuguese families fled to the neighbouring haven of Macao, which was surrounded but not conquered by the Japanese. Most strikingly, "Portugueseness" became a highly prized badge of identification during this period, as many individuals were compelled to identify themselves publicly as such to avoid internment under the Japanese. Indeed, Portuguese connections were even actively sought by British civilians and other "enemy aliens" who attempted to pass themselves off as third nationals during this period. The war was also instrumental in crystallizing the loyalties of numerous Portuguese individuals who became increasingly determined to assist the Allied cause. Several Portuguese who fought with the locally raised HKVDC were incarcerated by the Japanese in POW camps in Hong Kong. Many individuals offered their services to the BAAG and other Allied resistance movements in Free China, while others linked up with the British consulate in Macao.

However, the turbulence of this period also triggered the enduring departures of many members of this community. Some residents who left during the war (such as for Macao) never returned. From the late 1940s, entire Portuguese families emigrated to countries like the United States and Australia. Many Portuguese were persuaded that their opportunities for advancement were higher elsewhere, especially in the light of political disturbances in post-war Hong Kong. Although a few Portuguese who remained behind in the territory went on to positions of considerable political and social influence after the war, the dynamics of this community had been irretrievably altered in just a few years. Indeed, despite colonial roots lasting more than a hundred years, the upheaval and turmoil of the Second World War left more than a just a fleeting impression on the Portuguese. While the period may have consolidated their identity and loyalties, it paradoxically marked the beginning of their community's eventual decline.

Notes

1 For a discussion of the colonial social background of the Hong Kong Portuguese community, see Jason Wordie, "The Hong Kong Portuguese Community and Its Connections with Hong Kong University, 1914–1941", in *An Impossible Dream: Hong Kong University from Foundation to Re-establishment, 1910–1950*, edited by Chan Lau Kit-ching and Peter Cunich (New York: Oxford University Press, 2002), pp. 163–73. An exploration of some of the key themes relating to the Hong Kong Portuguese community during the wartime years is found in Luís Andrade Sá, *The Boys from Macau: Portugueses em Hong Kong* (Macao: Instituto Cultural de Macau, 1999).

2 Wordie, "The Hong Kong Portuguese Community", pp. 163–65.

3 Ronald Daus has argued that "the so-called Portuguese in Malacca were, in most cases not ethnic descendants of the Portuguese, but they used the Portuguese language as an important tool to achieve a dominant position in society". See Ronald Daus, *Portuguese Eurasian Communities in Southeast Asia* (Singapore: Institute of Southeast Asian Studies, 1989), p. 41.

4 Leo d'Almada e Castro, "Some Notes on the Portuguese in Hong Kong", *Boletim* (Instituto Português de Hong Kong), 2 (September 1949): 265–76. Background to the Portuguese in Macao is provided in C.R. Boxer, *Fidalgos in the Far East, 1550–1770* (Hong Kong: Oxford University Press, 1968). Detailed genealogical

information on the Hong Kong Portuguese community is supplied in Jorge Forjaz, *Familias Macaneses*, 3 vols. (Macao: Instituto Cultural de Macau, 1996). For a discussion of the nineteenth-century development of the community, see José Pedro Braga, *The Portuguese in Hong Kong and China* (Macao: Fundação Macau, 1998).

5 One of the first Portuguese to establish a commercial enterprise in Hong Kong was Delfino Noronha, who left Macao for Hong Kong in the early 1840s to set up a small printing plant. He gradually built up a considerable business with a large staff of skilled workmen (mostly Portuguese), and was appointed printer to the Government of Hong Kong "in perpetuum". The families of these early migrants formed the embryo of the Hong Kong Portuguese community. With growing numbers, the need for a social centre for the Portuguese community became obvious. In 1865, the foundation stone of the original Club Lusitano was laid on Elgin Street. The club was constructed largely out of funds contributed by two early pioneers (Delfino Noronha and J.A. Barreto), and contained a dance hall and theatre. See d'Almada e Castro, "Some Notes", pp. 268–69 and 272.

6 During the Communist-inspired strikes of 1922 and 1925–26 that almost paralysed the economic life of Hong Kong, the Portuguese were said to have "played their part loyally by assisting the maintenance of the essential service of the Colony". See d'Almada e Castro, "Some Notes", p. 274; and Philip Snow, *The Fall of Hong Kong: Britain, China and the Japanese Occupation* (New Haven: Yale University Press, 2003), p. 13.

7 Philip Bruce, *Second to None: The Story of the Hong Kong Volunteers* (Hong Kong: Oxford University Press, 1991), pp. 136–38; d'Almada e Castro, "Some Notes", p. 274; and Snow, *The Fall of Hong Kong*, pp. 13 and 355.

8 Arthur Ernesto Gomes, interview by Imperial War Museum, 23 March 2001, interview 21131, reel 2, transcript, Imperial War Museum (hereafter cited as IWM), London.

9 Bernard Sta Maria, *My People, My Country: The Story of the Malacca Portuguese Community* (Malacca: Malacca Portuguese Development Centre, 1982), pp. 170–71.

10 d'Almada e Castro, "Some Notes", p. 272.

11 Arnold Wright and H.A. Cartwright, eds., *Twentieth Century Impressions of Hong Kong: History, People, Commerce, Industry and Resources* (Singapore: Graham Brash, 1990), pp. 218–23.

12 Braga, *The Portuguese in Hong Kong*, p. 223. As Jason Wordie has noted, some of these successful merchants did much to expand educational opportunities for their compatriots in Hong Kong, especially in terms of assisting poorer members of the community in receiving a higher education. Given the generally humble situation of many Portuguese residents in the interwar period, it was tremendously difficult for those without substantial means to further their studies. A scholarship fund known as the Inês Soares Scholarship (established in the

early 1920s by Adão Maria de Lourdes Soares, a wealthy local bullion broker) enabled promising local Portuguese students to pursue medical studies at Hong Kong University. Additional support was offered by the Associação Portuguesa Socorros Mútuos (Portuguese Association for Mutual Assistance). See Wordie, "The Hong Kong Portuguese Community", pp. 165 and 167.

13 Braga, *The Portuguese in Hong Kong*, p. 228; Chris d'Almarda, interview by Charles Allen, BBC Radio 4, 1983, interview 8410, recording, IWM; Barras Botelho, interview by Charles Allen, BBC Radio 4, 1983, interview 8409, recording, IWM; and Frank Correa, interview by Amelia Allsop, 17 October 2008, transcript, p. 4, Archive, Hong Kong Heritage Project <https://www.hongkongheritage.org/Archive/internet/eng/ArchiveBasicSearchForm. aspx (accessed August 2010) (hereafter cited as HKHP)· Henry J. Lethbridge, "Caste, Class and Race in Hong Kong before the Japanese Occupation", in *Hong Kong: Stability and Change: A Collection of Essays* (Hong Kong: Oxford University Press, 1978), p. 179.

14 Wordie, "The Hong Kong Portuguese Community", pp. 163–65.

15 As Jason Wordie has noted, with the exception of some long-established Macanese families who spoke metropolitan Portuguese, few spoke their "mother tongue". There was little commercial advantage in Hong Kong to knowing Portuguese, and most Portuguese students accordingly "concentrated on improving their English" with a view to improving their career prospects. By the 1920s, even the use of patois was somewhat uncommon among the younger generation, being perceived as "socially pretentious" within the community. See Wordie, "The Hong Kong Portuguese Community", p. 166.

16 Wordie, "The Hong Kong Portuguese Community", p. 165. Some notable memoirs and novels by Eurasian authors include Jean Gittins, *Eastern Windows, Western Skies* (Hong Kong: South China Morning Post, 1969); C.H. Crabbe, *Malaya's Eurasians: An Opinion* (Singapore: D. Moore, 1960); and Han Suyin, *A Many-Splendoured Thing* (London: Jonathan Cape, 1952). For studies of Hong Kong Eurasians, see Lethbridge, "Caste, Class and Race", pp. 175–77, and Vicky Lee, *Being Eurasian: Memories across Racial Divides* (Hong Kong; Hong Kong University Press, 2004).

17 Lethbridge, "Caste, Class and Race", p. 176.

18 According to Jason Wordie, the Chinese nevertheless used a variety of terms to describe the Portuguese; these ranged from the derogatory *ham ha chaan* (stupid salty prawns), a reference to a popular Macanese condiment made from salted shrimps, or as *sai yeung jai* (Western Ocean boys), as Portugal was known to the Cantonese as the "Western Ocean Country". The Portuguese in Malaya were occasionally described as *grago* (a reference to the traditional fishermen and a popular condiment made from shrimp). See Wordie, "The Hong Kong Portuguese Community", p. 165; Gerald Fernandis, "Papia, Relijang e Tradisang: The Portuguese Eurasians in Malaysia: *Bumiquest*, A Search for Self Identity", *Lusotopie* (2000): 262.

19 See Correa interview, p. 31; and Frank H.H. King, *History of the Hongkong*

and Shanghai Banking Corporation, vol. 4, *The Hong Kong Bank in the Period of Development and Nationalism, 1941–84: From Regional Bank to Multinational Group* (Cambridge: Cambridge University Press, 1991), pp. 307–8.

20 Eddie Gosano, *Hong Kong Farewell* (privately printed, n.d.), pp. 11–12; and Wordie, "The Hong Kong Portuguese Community", p. 311.

21 Jean Ho Tung's romance with Billy Gittins, a fellow Hong Kong Eurasian, was frowned on by her parents, with her father dismissing her suitor as being "too dark to be considered handsome". See Gittins, *Eastern Windows,* pp. 11 and 64.

22 Snow, *The Fall of Hong Kong,* pp. 42–43.

23 Quoted in Henry J. Lethbridge, "Hong Kong under Japanese Occupation: Changes in Social Structure", in *Hong Kong: A Society in Transition,* edited by I.C. Jarvie and Joseph Agassi (London: Routledge, 1969), p. 92; and Snow, *The Fall of Hong Kong,* pp. 43–44.

24 Lethbridge, "Hong Kong under Japanese Occupation", pp. 91–92; Snow, *The Fall of Hong Kong,* p. 363; G.B. Endacott and Alan Birch, *Hong Kong Eclipse* (Hong Kong: Oxford University Press, 1978), p. 15; and Kent Fedorowich, "The Evacuation of Civilians from Hong Kong and Malaya/Singapore, 1939–1942", in *Sixty Years On: The Fall of Singapore Revisited,* edited by Brian Farrell and Sandy Hunter (Singapore: Eastern Universities Press, 2002), p. 128.

25 Margaret Lobo, interview by Amelia Allsop, 25 August 2009, transcript, p. 4, HKHP.

26 Ibid., p. 5.

27 Ibid., pp. 4–5; and Amalia Sales, interview by Amelia Allsop, 19 May 2008, transcript, pp. 18–19, HKHP.

28 According to Ferrier, "in the days prior to the invasion, the Portuguese distinguished themselves by winning the rifle competition from all and sundry, including the professional soldiers of the regular army. Similarly the Eurasian Company won the machine-gun competition". See Michael Ferrier, "China Boy", pp. 65–66, Special Collections, Hong Kong University Library, Hong Kong.

29 Ray Cordeiro, interview by Amelia Allsop, 4 September 2008, transcript, p. 3, HKHP.

30 Gomes interview, reels 2 and 6.

31 Sta Maria, *My People, My Country,* pp. 172–73.

32 Emily Hahn, *China to Me* (Philadelphia: Blakiston, 1944), pp. 309–10 and 387–88; *Hong Kong News,* 18 February and 14 March 1943; Robert S. Ward, *Asia for the Asiatics? The Techniques of Japanese Occupation* (Chicago: University of Chicago Press, 1945), pp. 78–79; and Snow, *The Fall of Hong Kong,* pp. 139 and 391.

33 "Third Nationals", in Letters, Memoranda, Reports, Diary Extracts, and Other Narratives Written by Hong Kong Residents Relating Their Experiences and Observations during the Battle for Hong Kong, the Japanese Occupation and Surrender, Hong Kong Manuscript Series (hereafter cited as HKMS)

100-1-6, pp. 1–2, Hong Kong Public Records Office (hereafter cited as HKPRO), Government Records Service, The Government of the Hong Kong Special Administrative Region; and Snow, *The Fall of Hong Kong*, p. 139.

34 Vaughn F. Meisling, intelligence report on Hong Kong, 13 January 1944, RG 226, Box 720, 59686, p. 14, Records of the Office of Strategic Services, U.S. National Archives and Records Administration, Washington, DC.

35 Ibid.

36 Ward, *Asia for the Asiatics?*, p. 102.

37 In his article, d'Almada e Castro sardonically added that "those pseudo-Portuguese have successfully eliminated all trace of the sardine from their systems. The others have gone back to their former pretence and have resumed their false colours". See d'Almada e Castro, "Some Notes on the Portuguese", pp. 274–75.

38 "Further Notes on Conditions in Hong Kong from Material Gathered at the Calcutta Censor Station Up to 12 May 1942", 13 May 1942, War and Colonial Department and Colonial Office: Hong Kong, Original Correspondence/ Situation in Hong Kong, 1942, CO 129/590/24, p. 3, Public Record Office, The National Archives (hereafter cited as PRO/TNA), London. Francis Silva was employed by the Roads and Drainage Office of the Japanese Government Civil Division. His job provided him with a monthly allowance of "35 catties of rice, 80 yen and one beer bottle of peanut oil." See Francis Silva statement, 22 December 1968, in Letters, HKMS 100-1-6.

39 Correa interview, p. 7; and testimony, Maria Leigh, at trial of Joseph Richards, Supreme Court Case Files, 1946–1976, HKRS 245-2-150, HKPRO.

40 Emily Hahn, *Hong Kong Holiday* (New York: Doubleday, 1946), p. 202.

41 John Braga to Viscount Samuel, 19 June 1943, Special Operations Executive: Far East/Registered Files, Hong Kong: General Intelligence, Volunteers, 1943–45, HS 1/171, p. 5, PRO/TNA.

42 Ibid., and John Braga to Mary, 24 June 1943, Special Operations Executive: Far East/Registered Files, Hong Kong: General Intelligence, Volunteers, 1943–45, HS 1/171, p. 5, PRO/TNA.

43 Albert Rodrigues, "A Hong Kong Doctor in War and Peace", in *Dispersal and Renewal: Hong Kong University during the War Years*, edited by Clifford Matthews and Oswald Cheung (Hong Kong: Hong Kong University Press, 1998), pp. 203–8; and Wordie, "The Hong Kong Portuguese Community", p. 170.

44 Eduardo (Eddie) Gosano was born in Hong Kong in 1914. He received an Inês Soares Scholarship and a Sir Paul Chater Memorial Scholarship and graduated from the Hong Kong University Faculty of Medicine in 1937. See Gosano, *Hong Kong Farewell*; and Wordie, "The Hong Kong Portuguese Community", p. 170. At Shamshuipo, a Portuguese prisoner of war by the name of Sonny Castro gained a measure of fame (and some notoriety) among the camp's inmates for his skills as a female impersonator in camp concerts. See Lewis Bush, *The Road to Inamura* (London: Robert Hale, 1961), p. 171.

45 Gomes interview, reels 4 and 5.

46 Ibid.; and John Stericker, "Captive Colony: The Story of Stanley Camp, Hong Kong", mss. 940.547252 S8, chap. 4, p. 1, Special Collections, The University of Hong Kong Libraries, Hong Kong.

47 Snow, *The Fall of Hong Kong*, pp. 121–22; and Hahn, *China to Me*, pp. 360 and 392.

48 Meisling intelligence report, p. 14; J.P. Fehily, interview by L. Ride, 18 December 1942, War and Colonial Department and Colonial Office: Hong Kong, Original Correspondence/Situation in Enemy Occupied Hong Kong, 19 January–20 November 1943, CO 129/590/22, p. 161, PRO/TNA. A Lieutenant H.J. Silva was reported to have worked for the Japanese secret service in Macao, while Johnny Gomes was said to have a Japanese wife and worked in the Japanese Harbour office after the hostilities. One V.F. Souza was even reputed to have had "daily interviews with the Japanese Chief Censor for a year". See "H.K.V.D.C. Personnel Security Check", H.K.V.D.C.: Question of the Entitlement of Those Who for Various Reasons Were Interned in Stanley and Not in P.O.W. Camps, 4 September 1946–9 December 1948, HKRS 163-1-174, pp. 1–4, HKPRO.

49 Sta Maria, *My People, My Country*, pp. 182–83.

50 Manuel Joaquim Pintado, *Survival through Human Values* (Malacca, 1974), pp. 25 and 29; and Daus, *Portuguese Eurasian Communities*, pp. 21–22.

51 Quoted in John Luff, *The Hidden Years* (Hong Kong: South China Morning Post, 1967), p. 170.

52 Ruth Yvonne Gunderson, "My Personal Experiences in Hong Kong during the Japanese Occupation, December 8th 1941 to August 15th 1945", 8 December 1967, HKPRO, HKMS 100-1-6, p. 2; Alan Birch and Martin Cole, *Captive Years: The Occupation of Hong Kong, 1941–45* (Hong Kong: Heinemann Asia, 1982), p. 101; Luff, *The Hidden Years,* p. 175; and Ellen Field, *Twilight in Hong Kong* (London: F. Muller, 1960), p. 214.

53 Rodrigues, "A Hong Kong Doctor", p. 207.

54 Cordeiro interview, p. 3.

55 Ibid., pp. 2–3.

56 Snow, *The Fall of Hong Kong*, p. 197.

57 Arnaldo de Oliveira Sales, "A Gentle War", in *Macao Remembers*, edited by Jill McGivering (Oxford: Oxford University Press, 1999), p. 65.

58 Roger Lobo, "Wartime Resistance", in McGivering, *Macao Remembers,* p. 74.

59 Cordeiro interview, p. 3; and Mary Erwin Martin report, War and Colonial Department and Colonial Office: Hong Kong, Original Correspondence/Situation in Hong Kong, 1942, CO 129/590/24, pp. 97–98, PRO/TNA.

60 Snow, *The Fall of Hong Kong*, pp. 179–80.

61 Barnes was born in Hong Kong in 1904 and graduated from the Hong Kong University Faculty of Medicine in 1931. Despite his Anglo-Saxon sounding name, Barnes was a descendant of a long-established Portuguese family. He died

in Saigon in 1949. See Wordie, "The Hong Kong Portuguese Community", p. 169.

62 Telegram, Foreign Office to Chungking, 12 July 1945, War Office: Directorate of Military Operations and Intelligence, and Directorate of Military Intelligence, Ministry of Defence, Defence Intelligence Staff, Files/Relations with Macao: Conditions in Macao and Japanese Blockage, December 1941–August 1946, WO 208/730, PRO/TNA; and Wordie, "The Hong Kong Portuguese Community", p. 172.

63 Wordie, "The Hong Kong Portuguese Commuity", p. 170.

64 Snow, *The Fall of Hong Kong*, 181; Endacott and Birch, *Hong Kong Eclipse*, pp. 225–26.

65 Lobo interview, pp. 5–6.

66 Braga to Samuel, p. 2. Lobo's passage to Kweilin in Free China was facilitated by operatives of the British Army Aid Group. See Lobo interview, pp. 5–6 and 12–14. Refugee Jorge Sequeira testified that there were "hardly any jobs" in Macao during the period. See Jorge Sequeira, interview by Amelia Allsop, 4 April 2007, transcript, p. 11, HKHP.

67 Bernard Felix Xavier, interview by Imperial War Museum, 21 December 1999, interview 19226, reel 2, transcript, IWM.

68 Charles M. Knaggs, "Information about Macau and the Macau Area", 11 June 1942, Foreign Office: Political Departments: General Correspondence from 1906–1966/Situation in Macao, Code 10 File 65, 1942, FO 371/31630, p. 3, PRO/TNA.

69 Lobo, "Wartime Resistance", pp. 75–76.

70 Luff, *The Hidden Years*, pp. 208–9; and Wordie, "The Hong Kong Portuguese Community", p. 169.

71 The father of this Portuguese family was a prisoner of war himself. See S. Selwyn-Clarke, report, 20 October 1945, Stanley Camp, HKRS 163-1-104, p. 6, HKPRO.

72 G.A. Leiper, *A Yen for My Thoughts* (Hong Kong: South China Morning Post, 1982), pp. 137–38; Frank H.H. King, *The History of the Hongkong and Shanghai Banking Corporation*, vol. 3, *The Hongkong Bank between the Wars and the Bank Interned, 1919–1945: Return from Grandeur* (Cambridge: Cambridge University Press, 1988), pp. 571–72, 613 and 621; and Birch and Cole, *Captive Years*, pp. 22, 103–5 and 107.

73 "Blue" (L. Ride) to "Phoenix", memorandum, 22 October 1943, Documents of Mr. Y.C. Liang, CBE, Concerning Wartime Activities in Hong Kong and Macao in Which He Was Involved, 1943–1946, HKMS 30-1-1, HKPRO; and Leiper, *A Yen for My Thoughts*, p. 135.

74 Leiper, *A Yen for My Thoughts*, p. 171. Writing after his escape to England in late 1942, the British banker J.A.D. Morrison stated: "I would like to place on record now that the Local Staff, both Portuguese and Chinese, behaved in a most exemplary manner during hostilities and that the heads of both sections,

F.X. Soares and Ho Wing, gave them a fine lead ... and I hope that recognition of this will be made when conditions permit." See Morrison, quoted in King, *The History of the Hongkong and Shanghai Banking Corporation,* 3: 573.

75 "Extracts from Weekly Intelligence Report No. 4 from Staff Officer (Intelligence) Hong Kong", 24 September 1945, War and Colonial Department and Colonial Office: Hong Kong, Original Correspondence/Reports on Current Situation: Including Weekly Intelligence Reports, 18 September–20 December 1945, p. 12, CO 129/592/6, PRO/TNA.

76 As G.A. Leiper noted, this "series of records, covering as they did the entire occupation period, were recovered intact after the war and were invaluable in the tremendous task of reconstruction". See G.A. Leiper, "Some Recollections of Duress Banking (4)", *Curry and Rice* 18 (1968) (Chartered Bank Staff Magazine), p. 10; and Leiper, *A Yen for My Thoughts,* p. 208. The Japanese investigations eventually led on to the bankers at Stanley: in January 1944, four British bankers were hauled in for questioning by the Kempeitai. They were accused of keeping secret records of bank transactions and of smuggling supplies into the prison camps. After weeks of torture and solitary confinement, the bankers were eventually detained in a prison in Canton and were only liberated at the end of the war. See Leiper, *A Yen for My Thoughts,* pp. 190–220.

77 Charles McCormac, *You'll Die in Singapore* (London: Hale, 1954), pp. 54–56.

78 The Portuguese Volunteers arrested by the Japanese included Roy de Vries, Andrew Pinto, E.A. Rodrigues and Allen Sta Maria. Two priests were also detained (A.V. Corado and Francisco Manuel) and charged for possessing a radio without a permit. See Sta Maria, *My People, My Country,* pp. 178–79.

79 d'Almada e Castro, "Some Portuguese in Hong Kong", p. 275.

80 Oliveira Sales, "A Gentle War", p. 67. Cordeiro returned from Macao and took up initial work as a warder at Stanley Prison, and then as a clerk in the Hongkong and Shanghai Bank. He eventually became a Hong Kong media personality and was awarded an MBE for his work in the media. See Cordeiro interview, pp. 4–5.

81 George Elliot, interview by Amelia Allsop, 19 September 2007, transcript, pp. 6–7, HKHP.

82 This decline in Hong Kong Portuguese numbers may have even begun before the war. A wartime report prepared by a British internee at the Stanley Camp records that "census figures showed a progressive decline in the Eurasian and Portuguese population of the Colony, and it seems likely that the present war, and the policy of the Portuguese government, will accelerate this". See "Suggestions for Re-organisation: Primary and Pre-Primary Education in Hong Kong", K.M. Anderson Papers, mss. Ind.Ocn.s.110, p. 3, Bodleian Library of Commonwealth and African Studies at Rhodes House, Oxford.

83 Wordie, "The Hong Kong Portuguese Community", p. 173.

84 Cyril Neeves, "The Portuguese in Hong Kong", *Voz dos Macaenses de Vancouver (Newsletter of the Casa de Macau [Vancouver])* 4, no. 4 (November 2002).

[85] Cecil Harcourt to George Hall, Secretary of State for the Colonies, 29 January 1946, in Cecil Harcourt, *Private Papers of Admiral Cecil Harcourt Relating to the British Military Administration of Hong Kong, 1945–1946*, HKPRO Library, 951.2504 HAR.

[86] Ibid., p. 2.

[87] Cordeiro interview, p. 14; and Steve Tsang, *A Modern History of Hong Kong* (London: I.B. Tauris, 2007), pp. 185–86.

[88] Correa interview, pp. 29–30. A description of the Hong Kong Portuguese diaspora is found in Frederic A. Silva, *Todo o Nosso Passado: All Our Yesterdays* (Macao: Livros do Oriente, 1996).

[89] Rodrigues, "A Hong Kong Doctor", pp. 203 and 208; and Wordie, "The Hong Kong Portuguese Community", pp. 170 and 172. Arnaldo de Oliveira Sales was elected chairman of Hong Kong's Urban Council from 1973 to 1981, and chairman of the Commonwealth Games Federation from 1990 to 1994. See de Oliveira Sales, "A Gentle War", p. 63.

[90] Lobo, "Wartime Resistance", p. 71.

10

INDO-PORTUGUESE LITERATURE AND THE GOA OF ITS WRITERS[1]

Everton V. Machado

There is no better introduction to the Goa of its Indo-Portuguese writers than an excerpt from the novel *O Último Olhar de Manú Miranda* (The Last Look of Manú Miranda) by Orlando da Costa (1929–2006), published by Âncora in 2000. It can be said that this work is a *Bildungsroman*, the coming-of-age novel of the Brahmin Catholic Manuel João da Piedade Miranda, entering the world some decades before the end of the Portuguese colonial period with two possible paths open to him: either the route of the Metropolis like those disillusioned with their native land, or becoming a *batcar* (landowner) like his ancestors. This novel, in the words of Orlando da Costa himself,[2] accompanies the life experiences of the Goa of its author, who was born in Mozambique and died in Portugal, but whose childhood and adolescence were profoundly Goan. In the book, Manú's mother gives birth to him in the same moment as another was born who was to become his best friend in childhood, a Hindu boy named Xricanta. These two little creatures were "destined to be twins",[3] even to the point that their physical transformations into adolescence happened for both of them "on the same day and at the same time".[4] Only one thing separated them irrevocably: religion, with its baggage of precepts and customs.

This study is a reflection on the complexities of the Indo-Portuguese culture of Goa as revealed in its literature from the late nineteenth century — when nativist voices began to emerge in the fiction and the poetry — to the present early twenty-first century — a half-century into the postcolonial era. The authors treated herein — including Orlando da Costa, Vimala Devi (Teresa da Piedade de Baptista Almeida), Francisco Luís Gomes, Leopoldo da Rocha and Gip (Francisco João da Costa) — are Goan natives raised in a Catholic and Portuguese-like environment amid the forces of the Indian caste system and the Hindu ancestral universe. Behind the supposed "communion of monasteries and pagodas", religious and socio-economic differences feed an identifiable but thus far irreconcilable "confusion" of personal identity and being. This essay explores the nature and challenges of this irreconcilability, both for the culture itself and for its literary chroniclers.

THE NEXUS OF RUPTURE: SOCIORELIGIOUS DIFFERENCES

It is worth asking if it were not Orlando da Costa's intent in *O Último Olhar de Manú Miranda* to produce a work that has a little touch of the celebrated novel *Midnight's Children* (1981) by another Indian (albeit from a Muslim family and a writer in the English language), Salman Rushdie. Manú and Xricanta were not switched at birth like Saleem Sinai and Shiva, nor did they become sworn enemies like these latter two, but if in the Indo-British author's book, the same socioreligious divergences which brought about the partition of India and Pakistan in 1947 are in play and embody the two personages, in the Indo-Portuguese book the nature of the barrier between Manú and Xricanta, of equal weight, is no less relevant. To the contrary: it is the awareness of this barrier, from early on, that will induce many of the protagonist's existential doubts. With regard to this, Orlando da Costa's narrator does not fail to underscore at any given moment that "it was not customary, for Christians and Hindus, to get along so well, in the sense of getting to know each other at one's place or in the intimacy of their families".[5] Manú and Xricanta can converse in Konkani, the native language of Goa, but upon returning home, the former would alternate Konkani with Portuguese and the latter with Marata, the language of the Maharasta (who are found widely throughout Goa), that is especially used by Hindus with religious training.

The excerpt to which I referred at the outset conveys well that which Eufemiano de Jesus Miranda designates as "the sign of a rupture"[6] found among Indo-Portuguese writers, a rupture that is explained, naturally, by the delicate relations of Goans raised in a Christian and European environment — providing the literature treated herein — with the Hindu ancestral universe. Here is that excerpt that, without lacking its own logic relative to the actantial scheme of the narrative, I suspect summarizes the *Bildungsroman* of all Goan Catholics:

> The truth is ... that, on the other side of the world that [Manú Miranda] inhabited, common to all, now, the world that he inhabited, hidden and whispering like a spring of subterranean waters, extended itself to other questions more appropriate to the growing emotional and mental tides of his personality. A personality being formed, in search of some feeling for its familial and social roots, a tangle of green leaves and dried leaves attached to the same branch of the same tree long since forgotten, an orphan in a jungle lost to human sight, at the foot of the Ghats mountain range since the most ancient of times in which the god Brahma will have created a world and a time already passed in which Parsurama threw the legendary spear of fertility onto the lands of Goa,[7] later coveted and invaded by successive conquerors. The Ghats! Might it be there that the border between Krishna and Christ was to be found? He lost himself in the search for his true and hesitant past in the presence of the future, he felt unprotected and alone, by chance guilty of intolerance of faith and of his religion, that used to set brothers of blood and of language in flight, carrying with them sacred idols, their own divinities, and the stones with which later the dignity of the strong and the pride of the persecuted re-erected their temples anew in the south in clearings protected by the branches of the mango trees and in the peace suspended in the very tall trunks of the palm trees. What would his friend Xricanta, almost a brother born on the same day and at the same hour, think of the wise retreat of his hermitage?[8]

This excerpt from the novel *O Último Olhar de Manú Miranda* reveals a theme that traverses, in a general way, the most relevant works in Goan literature written in the Portuguese language, offering us a representation of Goa through the eyes of native men and women raised in a Catholic and Portuguese-like environment. The societal division between Catholics and Hindus and a common ancestral origin, so traced in Goan works written in the Portuguese language, give the overly pragmatic reader a confused and at times very uncomfortable sensation of the opacity of reality in the face of the existence of two universes at the same time so close and so distant in the Goa formerly colonized by the Portuguese.[9]

The factual separation of these worlds is even represented materially, so to speak, in the book of short stories *Monção* (1963), by Vimala Devi (born 1932), in which the narratives about both worlds, written separately, almost to the point of alternating some of the stories with others in the texts, do not impede Hindu and Catholic personages from coexisting in the same story. Note that the author herself even embodies such a split since, after all, Vimala Devi (a Hindu name that signifies something like "goddess of purity"[10]) is a pseudonym adopted by Teresa da Piedade de Baptista Almeida, a Catholic raised in Portuguese culture. It is worth pointing out in this regard that, like no other Goan Catholic writer in the Portuguese language, Vimala Devi is capable of treating Hindu Goa properly. Orlando da Costa himself affirmed how curious it is to see her, "a woman of a Christian family raised in the moulds of Europeanized Goan social behaviour able to recreate personages as much of Catholic formation as of the Hindu community, moving about in a real world".[11] Also a poet, she comes to observe, in a poem entitled "Goa", from the work *Súria* (1962), that in her thinking Goa will always be "a communion of monasteries and pagodas" and that as a poet, by virtue of feeling "an appeal / painful and ancestral",[12] she sets a task for herself to be "the voice of the conscience: / the voice of two worlds!"[13]

The awareness of this divide is without a doubt much greater in the writers of the postcolonial period (such as Orlando and Vimala themselves), initiated in 1961 with the departure of the Portuguese from Goa, even though within the so-called "nativist" wave (that runs from the end of the nineteenth century to the first decades of the following one) the feeling of rupture had already been exacerbated. A poet like Adeodato Barreto (1905–37) appears to have resolved — in the 1930s, no less — the question for himself with the poems in *O Livro da Vida: Cânticos Indianos* (The Book of Life: Indian Hymns) (published posthumously in 1940), in which Goa appears illuminated by Hindu poetic and philosophic tradition. In all ways, the awareness referred to above as well as the strategies for resolving, circumventing or eliminating the problem function like a backdrop for diverse themes or motives that comprise the image of Goa proposed by Goan authors writing in Portuguese. Hence, we have the representation of a multifaceted but historically and ethnographically delimited Goa.

Within these themes, there is, *et pour cause*, the Indian caste system, maintained within the Catholic medium as a result of the conversion of large segments of the Hindu population, albeit with important differences relative to the original system, whether in their constitution or in their social implications. It is, above all, through the stories related to the common arranged marriages that this literature will insist on painting the force of the castes, notwithstanding the existence of abundant references to them and how they stigmatize or stigmatized the most varied types of socio-human relations in Goa.

Indo-Portuguese literature does not only deal with this, however. After unsuccessful literary attempts in the nineteenth century in which Goa was overlooked as a source of inspiration (most writers did nothing but copy themes and motives from Portuguese literature), colonial Goa came to its fullest expression in the work of local writers. There we find repressed animosity or a discrete love on the part of the *paclé* (the Portuguese), the upsets and intrigues of the colonial and military environment, the leisurely life and arrogance of the aristocratic rural families (with special attention towards the sister spinsters, and the histrionic *genros-comensais*),[14] the opportunism and the lethargy of public service, the difficult readaptation of the emigrants, the "traditional" or Hindu India with its inevitable high dose of idealization, the veiled struggle between the Portuguese language and the vernaculars, without mentioning the difficult existence of the "subordinates"[15] of colonial and postcolonial Goa, of which the award-winning and censured novel *O Signo da Ira* (The Sign of Ira) (1961) by Orlando da Costa constitutes one of the best examples, with its depiction of the life of the *curumbins*, a Christian caste of rural workers. Another important example of this phenomenon are the short stories of Epitácio Pais (1928–2010) in *Os Javalis de Codval* (The Wild Boars of Codval) (1973), which reveal an author "extremely preoccupied with the life around him, and the ore fever, that attacked Goa … with a resulting deterioration in the traditional kind of human relations".[16]

The constant clash between modern convictions of the elite raised in a Christian environment and the popular beliefs among the lower social strata of Goa must be re-emphasized within the set of Indo-Portuguese themes, as is very clearly illustrated in the novel *Bodki* (1962) by Agostinho Fernandes (1932). In it, a young physician from the capital finds himself confronting the superstitions of the people of a village, especially those who marginalize the *bodki*, a Hindu widow, considered to be responsible for all the bad happenings that took place there.

THE EVOLUTION OF GOAN LITERATURE

Born in the Catholic convents of Goa, Indo-Portuguese literature was limited, from the sixteenth to the eighteenth centuries, to texts of a religious and pedagogic character, or to those that discussed problems associated with the castes, in addition to justifying this hierarchical system in the bosom of a religion reputed to embrace the principle of fraternal equality. It was only in the nineteenth century, with the introduction of romanticism and liberalism in Goa, that the first works of imagination began to arise in this literature, notably in the field of romance, of short story and of poetry, where these thematic elements, little by little, moved forward to earn the *droit de cité*.

Curiously, the first Indo-Portuguese novel, without taking place in Goa itself and almost without mentioning it, constitutes one of its most powerful representations, although not uncommon, even though today many see the old Govapuri as such. This novel, *Os Brahamanes*, was published in Lisbon in 1866 by a deputy representing Goa in the Portuguese parliament, an author of works of an historiographic and economic nature, Francisco Luís Gomes (1829–69). I have argued that this novel, at once theoretical and exotic, could be considered not only the first work of fiction to frontally attack the system of Hindu castes, but also the first of an anti-colonialist nature in modern literature. It is in a treatment of this latter point — or in the ambiguity that it envelops — that Goa appears. The novel of Francisco Luís Gomes is, in fact, a critique of an inhumane colonialism found in the British regime (the action unfolds in what is today the region of Uttar Pradesh, then governed by the British) by way of defending the humanist values supposedly embodied in the Christian-centric dimension of Portuguese expansion, an idea that flows later through the Lusotropicalism of the Brazilian Gilberto Freyre and in Salazarist propaganda in defence of the "overseas provinces" of Portugal. Goa is mentioned directly in the novel only two times (once without actually being named), but the attentive reader notices it — since for the author Goa is proof of the realization of that Portuguese destiny — from which it serves as a counterpoint to British India, which is not spared ferocious criticism in the work.

The representation of Goa as a repository of noble Christian and Portuguese ideas can be found, naturally, in later authors, some with more and some with less critical distancing. In spite of the differences between the period when Francisco Luís Gomes lived (marked most strongly by the traps of colonial mimicry) and the time of Orlando da Costa, one can see that the latter always remembers in his novel, as if he wanted to provoke the existential doubts of his character Manú Miranda, the "confusion" lived by "peoples forced, one day, to change their creed and altar".[17] In the latest novel, for the time being, to be written in Portuguese and published by a Goan, *Casa Grande e Outras Recordações de um Velho Goês* (The Big House and Other Memories of an Old Goan) (2008), by none other than the author of a well-known study about the religious orders of Goa, Leopoldo da Rocha (1932), one also comes to lament the Christianization of Goa as a "confusion" in the life of the natives, albeit in terms of sexual matters. Leopoldo da Rocha, in a narrative that is supposed to be autobiographical, uses terms like "Manichaeism" and "brain washing" to define the process of Christianization in Goa, the first of which in the end "contaminated the Christian community of Goa, with its notions of sin (always related to sex)",[18] in contrast with the "natural way" in which sex was assumed among the Hindus.[19]

These observations by the narrator of *Casa Grande* send us more than one hundred years into the past, to the moment when nativism appeared in Goan letters. Despite the belief by the authors of that vein that they will achieve something viscerally Indian, it is almost impossible for the reader of their works not to take into consideration the unlucky sign of exoticism and of the religious upbringing that they received. In the attempt to utilize customs, myths and local legends, the majority of these poets, like Floriano Barreto (1877–1905), Eucaristino Mendonça (dates unknown), Mariano Gracias (1871–1931) and Paulino Dias (1874–1919), were completely subjugated by the dancers of the Hindu temples, either reproaching them or pitying them their fate, but always succumbing to the charm of these stigmatized figures in Hindu culture, which led Orlando da Costa to ask himself one day if the reason the dancers appeared "so repeatedly like the inspired muse of so many Christian poets" was not in the fact of the "transformation of the stigma into a source of an erotic imaginary in spite of the Judaeo-Christian puritanism of sexual repression and only occasionally as a reason for social criticism".[20] The Goa that one glimpses in this nativist space, even though the authors did not have this intention, reveals itself to be totally incompatible with the Christian and Western upbringing that they received. In a general way, these Oriental people remained limited by the use of innumerable stereotypes recurring in Europe, digging a deeper trench between the two halves of the same identity.

If the poetry of the period was preoccupied with reasserting the native part of the identity of its writers in a desperate effort to correct the errors of Portuguese colonization in obliterating Hindu culture completely, the prose (short story and novel), upon taking its first steps, tried to focus on the Christian society itself that resulted from the symbiosis between the Western and Eastern worlds in a way tendentially naturalistic. The key to what would come is found in the novel that has had the greatest repercussions in Goa. The reference here is to *Jacob e Dulce* (Jacob and Dulce) (1896) by Gip (the pseudonym of Francisco João da Costa), a satire about the middling bourgeoisie of Catholic and Portuguese Goa who are definitely subservient to Europe, bringing to light social types that every so often will be dissected again later in Indo-Portuguese literature. As Joana Passos reminds us, "in Gip's narrative, from one chapter to another we accompany the negotiations that lead to Jacob and Dulce's marriage. They illustrate aspects of Goan social life that are ridiculed, especially by virtue of what they reveal about a pattern of superficiality, a lack of upbringing and purpose in life, in addition to the highly criticized subservience to European culture."[21]

Gip in essence created a school, probably inspiring the short stories of José da Silva Coelho (1889–1944) that appeared regularly in the local newspapers, without sparing public functionaries and marriageable young ladies. The contemporary Carmo de Noronha (1915–99), direct heir of Gip in his criticism of cultural dependency, did not cause fewer sorrows in Goa, after describing the Goan of a Catholic background as a cheap imitator. In a polemical speech in 1969 at the Clube Vasco da Gama about the balance of the legacy of European colonization after the winds had changed in the recently initiated postcolonial era, Carmo accused the strongly protected "Goan personality" of "not going beyond being a patchwork quilt, in which we are Europeans in dress, English in language, Portuguese in the softness of habits and sentimentality, French in cooking, Italians in music, medievals in religion, Asians in treachery, cunning, and fatalismo, and Goans only by virtue of the civil registry".[22]

Perceptions of the Christian community of Goa such as this one are inseparable from the very literary choices made by the Indo-Portuguese writers. As Manuel de Seabra has observed in the preface to the short stories by Epitácio Pais,

> every time that one wants to assume a tragic or heroic attitude, the Goan writer has to abandon the petit bourgoisie (to which, in general, he belongs) and has to deal with the underprivileged castes. When one turns to the middle classes, the Goan writer sees himself forced to take one of two attitudes: either take his characters seriously (like Alberto de Meneses Rodrigues and at times Maria Elsa da Rocha do), risking looking ridiculous one's self; or assume a critical, objective, alienating stance.[23]

CONCLUSION

Through these ways of seeing Goa, Indo-Portuguese writers end up creating their own "imagined community", to use Benedict Anderson's expression, without managing to constitute in fact a nation apart from either India or Portugal, as many have wished, in the wake of Goa's so-called cultural specificity. Anderson's definition of imagined communities assumes, among other features, a "deep, horizontal comradeship", despite actual inequalities or exploitation.[24] Does such a "deep, horizontal comradeship" exist in fact among Goans but is it not being captured adequately by its writers, because of the depth of the historical inequalities and exploitation of the colonial legacy? Must more time pass in the postcolonial era before Goans will be able to reconcile their own confused identities enough to capture the uniqueness and essence of Goa's culture? After almost half a millennium of Indo-Portuguese interactions and in spite of efforts of innumerable theoreticians and critics to seize the colonial and postcolonial reality around the world, we are far from having satisfactory answers for those questions.

Notes

1 The author extends his thanks to Professor Laura Jarnagin (Pang) for translating this chapter from Portuguese into English.

2 From the dedication Orlando da Costa wrote in the copy of his book that he gave to me in Lousã, District of Coimbra, Portugal, on 1 November 2003.

3 Orlando da Costa, *O Último Olhar de Manú Miranda* (Lisbon: Âncora, 2000), p. 52.

4 Ibid., p. 98.

5 Ibid., p. 58.

6 Eufemiano de Jesus Miranda, "Literatura Indo-Portuguesa dos Séculos XIX e XX: Um Estudo de Temas Principais no Contexto Sócio-Histórico" (Ph.D. dissertation, University of Goa, 1995), p. 247.

7 This is an allusion to a creation myth for Goa. The poet Adeodato Barreto has also explored the theme in a nationalistic song. See the poem "Apoteose", in *Civilização Hindu Seguido de* O Livro da Vida*: Cânticos Indianos* (Lisbon: Hugin Editores, 2000), pp. 267–74.

8 Costa, *O Último Olhar*, pp. 104–5.

9 The Muslim world of Goa receives very little attention, its characters being relegated to secondary roles.

10 From the Sanskrit *Vimalā* ("pure", "immaculate", "transparent") and *devī* ("goddess", "queen"). See *Sanskrit Heritage Dictionary*, The Sanskrit Heritage Site <http://sanskrit.inria. fr/sanskrit.html> (accessed 19 August 2010).

11 Orlando da Costa, "Uma abordagem à literatura Indo-portuguesa contemporânea no roteiro da colonização", *AprenderJuntos* 4–5 (January 2005): 127.

12 Vimala Devi, *Súria* (Lisbon: Agência Geral do Ultramar, 1962), p. 27.

13 Ibid., p. 28.

14 The term *genro-comensal* (*genros-comensais* in the plural) means a son-in-law who is the head of a family in which there are only female siblings.

15 In the Gramscian sense of subaltern studies.

16 Manuel de Seabra, preface to *Os Javalis de Codval*, by Epitácio Pais (Lisbon: Futura, 1973), p. 9.

17 Costa, *O Último Olhar*, p. 175.

18 Leopoldo da Rocha, *Casa Grande e Outras Recordações de um Velho Goês* (Lisbon: Vega, 2008), p. 45.

19 Ibid., p. 79.

20 Orlando da Costa, "A literatura indo-portuguesa contemporânea: Antecedentes e percurso", paper presented at the Fundação Calouste Gulbenkian's Colóquio Internacional Vasco da Gama e a Índia, Paris, May 1998.

21 Joana Passos, "A ambivalência de Goa como imagem do império português e as

representações da sociedade colonial na literatura luso-indiana", *e-cadernos ces* 1 (2008): 50 <http://www.ces.uc.pt/e-cadernos> (accessed 20 August 2010).

22 Carmo de Noronha, *Contracorrente* (Panaji, Goa: privately printed by the author, 1991), p. 7.

23 Seabra, preface to *Os Javalis*, p. 8.

24 Benedict Anderson, *Imagined Communities: Reflections on the Origin and Spread of Nationalism*, rev. ed. (London: Verso, 1991), pp. 5–7.

11

BINDING TIES OF MISCEGENATION AND IDENTITY: THE NARRATIVES OF HENRIQUE SENNA FERNANDES (MACAO) AND REX SHELLEY (SINGAPORE)

Isabel Maria da Costa Morais

> Vários "pequenos" portugueses fizeram sentir a sua presença na "imensa Asia", uns quase como reis, alguns como escravos, o maior número simplesmente como portugueses capazes de amar mulheres orientais e ser por elas amados. Capazes de fecundar mulheres de cor e fazer sair dos seus ventres portugueses também de cor.
> (Several "small" Portuguese made felt their presence in the "enormous Asia", some as almost kings, others as slaves, the great majority just as Portuguese [who were] able to love oriental women and be loved by them. [They were] able to inseminate women of colour and to make their wombs produce other Portuguese also of colour.)[1]
>
> Gilberto Freyre, *Aventura e Rotina*

Despite the dynamics of globalization and rapid economic and political development, it is still noticeable nowadays that several Portuguese creolized communities in postcolonial societies have resisted cultural homogenization, particularly those scattered throughout the detached, peripheral regions of East and Southeast Asia that were under the Estado da Índia's sovereignty and influence (Goa, Daman, Diu, Sri Lanka, Malacca, Macao and Timor) and that the Portuguese created alongside the local political authorities (Indonesia and today's Singapore).

By the beginning of the seventeenth century, the official population in the colonies of several territories in Asia that proudly claimed Portuguese ancestry had reached nearly one-and-a-half million individuals, as a legacy of colonial (dis)encounters. Centuries later, the Portuguese descendants of this "shadow empire" forged through trading, matrimonial alliances and cultural networks — notwithstanding a pragmatic adaptation to times of unprecedented political, economic and cultural upheaval — persist in a quest for identity and cultural reaffirmation of "Portuguese" cultural differentiation, which continues to be faithfully perpetuated and transmitted, centuries after the earlier Portuguese contacts ceased.[2] These communities show distinctive aspects of what could be called a certain "Luso-Eurasianness", exhibited in oral literature, religious practices, family surnames, ceremonies, cuisine, public structures, ways of speaking and, above all, in identity-making religious and cultural reinterpretation of lived and shared commonalities.

This study argues that, even if relatively scant attention has been paid to the literary production of the communities considered here, in particular in Anglophone postcolonial studies, they have influenced and continue to exercise seminal influence on most postcolonial imaginaries, either in their respective societies or in the contemporary fiction of the Luso diaspora. In fact, as forms of marginal discourses in the colonial and postcolonial societies, their narratives have addressed issues such as a quest for identity, hybridity and (dis)encounters between the colonized and the colonizers, which noticeably influenced colonial and postcolonial imaginaries through their local language by consolidating what can be designated as "Lusophone Asian literature".

These representations, narratives and celebrations of a mythologized Portuguese miscegenated ethnicity, reproduced even in official local languages such as English, testify that from the early nineteenth century until nowadays, some members of the local elite — artists and writers who identified themselves as descendants of the earlier Portuguese settlers and forged solid links with the Catholic Church, colonial and military administrations, and trading networks — have been committed to reinventing themselves through novels and newspapers. These media "provided the technical means for 'representing' the kind of imagined community that is the nation", in consonance with Benedict Anderson's argument in his influential study *Imagined Communities*.[3] In the chapter "Creole Pioneers", Anderson remarks that the invention of the printing press and the rise of print media contributed to a textual representation of a "popular" print culture, which was also crucial in its contribution to a global exchange that would have reinforced the idea of an "imagined community".[4] Anderson further explains that, before the eighteenth century, the concept of nation was extensive, as Latin was the language of a vast imagined community called Christendom. However, as changes occurred in the religious communities, such a concept began to be replaced by French and English as vernacular languages of administrative centralization.

Thus, print capitalism — allied to the book market, supported by the improvement of communications and the emergence of new and diverse forms of national languages — established the creation of clusters of small creole "imagined political communities". They were eager to promote new forms of national and cultural consciousness, aimed at attaining widespread literacy through lines of kinship, fraternity and power loyalties. "Long-standing" narratives of those emerging communities thus played an important role in depicting the history of Portuguese colonial expansion, contributing to a constant reformulation of a sense of belonging to a distant, epic, European nation, perpetuated even in the more recent postcolonial imaginary.

In fact, the Portuguese Eurasians, either on the Malay Peninsula or in Singapore, as well as the Macanese, either in Macao, Hong Kong or in China's treaty ports, were involved in the organization of a wide range of initiatives through the creation of and participation in pioneer institutions of print and society — scientific societies, social clubs, spaces of recreation and congregation, brotherhoods and fraternities. Historical commemorations, cultural and religious festivities, performances and sporting events would help their communities to imagine themselves united to a national Portuguese community, as well as committed to reinventing and perpetuating its historical origins together with their social and religious values. Paramount to all these cultural, festive and spectacular manifestations were all the efforts of folklorists, historians, poets, novelists and musicians in resurrecting the glorious pasts of the empire, to consolidate identities as well as to maintain and promote local creoles and literature among themselves and through ethnic associations, in a steady trend that has lasted until the present day.

This chapter aims to present a reflection upon and rethinking of the literary works of two of the most interesting contemporary authors by constructing the contemporary textualization of a Eurasian identity through a Luso-Asian cultural legacy: Henrique Senna Fernandes (1923–2010) of Macao and Rex Shelley (1930–2009) of Singapore. Focusing on their writings, this paper examines the history of their singular communities, the Eurasians of the Malay Peninsula and the Macanese of Macao. A comparison of the literary tropes of their novels reveals their interrelatedness and shows that these novelists have closely documented the destinies of those communities that became Lusitanized and referred to themselves as Portuguese, in search of a reaffirmation of specific identities and realities.

Although the novels adopt different narrative techniques and literary postures, they reveal noticeable similarities, in both thematic and discursive terms, as a way of recovering past memories and lost identity in order to (re)construct and redefine a positive Lusophone ancestry and identity. In fact, they have formulated the basis upon which to build a unique literature, using the past to reaffirm the present and consolidate the future in terms of the historical continuity of their singular communities.

Bringing the discussion to how cultural representations are perpetuated in the post-Luso-Asian colonial imaginary, specifically, this study identifies important foci that frequently surface in the works of these two novelists that they recover and reconstruct for the reaffirmation of their identities. This chapter will investigate how these two contemporary Luso-Asian writers have (re)formulated some long-lasting nationalist Portuguese myths. Above all, what is important to underscore and argue is that their fiction is intertwined with Gilberto Freyre's master discourse of Lusotropicalism that Vale de Almeida designates as "a type of cultural exceptionalism", which is also coincident in many aspects with the nineteenth-century colonial rhetoric on the representation of the Portuguese empire.[5] In particular, as some critics have remarked, unlike in Anglophone literature, what distinguishes miscegenation or hybridity in the Lusophone context is "the historic association" with the female body.[6]

In fact, what also contributes to the originality of Senna Fernandes and Shelley is that the eulogy of a peculiar miscegenated tropical identity (in this particular case, the mythical origins of the Eurasian communities) is associated with a "Lusotropical love narrative", and to the representation of an archetypal Eurasian female evocative of Freyre's prevalent figure of the native woman.[7] In fact, as Phillip Rothwell notes, while the authors of the former colonies in Portuguese-speaking Africa still use Portugal's twentieth-century imperial mythologies in their literary productions as a form of critique, the Eurasian writers discussed here instead draw on Lusotropicalist mythical discourse to reinforce their distinctive identities within newly reconfigured global sociopolitical contexts.[8] Moreover, these Eurasian writers use language — in their particular cases either English or Portuguese — not "simply as a repository of cultural contents but as a tool or weapon" to allow their identity self-representation and (re)construction to prevail in terms of permanence and future at a local level.[9]

Senna Fernandes and Rex Shelley bequeathed us the worlds of the Creole "sons-of-the-soil" — Macanese, Serani or Geragok — and their female counterparts, the *nonas* (daughters of a European man by a Chinese woman) and *nhonhas* (married women), descendants of the first Luso-Catholic communities who created hybrid tropical paradises located in Macao, Malaysia and Singapore — which, despite their heterogeneous regional or national particularities, reveal similar historical, cultural and textual hybridities yet to be explored and which invite comparisons on many points.[10] Despite the fact that their novels differ significantly from each other in several aspects, mainly due to the longer residence of the Portuguese in Macao compared to their remote and short presence on the Malay Peninsula, both authors construct their fictional world on historical and legendary facts, using the past to question issues of cultural identity that they constantly revisit and project in terms of permanence in the future. Their novels portray the plight of the Eurasian communities of Portuguese ancestry in their respective homelands during the most crucial decades of the first half of the twentieth century, under British and Portuguese colonial rule in Southeast Asia. Senna Fernandes positions himself between a tradition of romantic and neorealist writing, but he also adopts a colonial stance as his narratives depict and expose the cultural and social contradictions and ambivalences in Macanese society during the second half of the twentieth century, and later when Macao was about to conclude its colonial cycle before its transference of sovereignty to China in 1999.

Shelley's novels, on the other hand, although spanning a longer period, take place mostly in the times prior to the independence of the Malay Peninsula in 1957, and conclude in the post-independence period of Singapore and Malaysia. Consequently, Shelley's writings clearly possess the markers of postmodern narratives as they portray Malacca's Portuguese descendants in Singapore and Malaysia, which had already fully assumed their status as postcolonial nations.

REX SHELLEY AND SENNA FERNANDES: PARALLELS, DIFFERENCES AND INTERCONNECTIONS

> "Somos os Portugueses do Oriente." (We are the Portuguese of the East.)[11]
>
> Carlos Montalto de Jesus

> Here, Malacca and Portugal …
> — Portugal?
> — Yes, my son, Portugal is your country, too …
> — My country too?
> — Yes, the land of your grandfather, Augustine …. It is the greatest country, the most splendid land in the whole world …[12]
>
> Rex Shelley, *The People of the Pear Tree*

Rex Shelley and Henrique Senna Fernandes's novels contain unexpected and similar references to Portuguese culture and history, myths, cuisine, linguistic hybridity and shared Portuguese heritage legacies associated with the old and emblematic cities of Macao and Malacca, from where their rich reminiscences and action constantly flow and reflow. Both authors were born in Asian colonies in the 1920s and 1930s to parents of Portuguese ancestry. Both undertook their university studies in Europe and returned to their birthplaces, where they became eyewitnesses to radical sociopolitical changes. They both started their literary careers later in life and passed away in the twenty-first century, coincidentally within a short period of time of each other. Yet over the last decades, long before ethnic literature or studies of the representation of miscegenated communities in literatures became a matter of interest both inside and outside academia, Shelley and Senna Fernandes were the first Eurasian authors to have written about a sense of belonging to a wilfully self-contained and distinctive community, with a long-standing history of shared language, proud identity and an inalterable religious faith of Lusophone roots. Furthermore, the novels discussed here have another aspect in common in that they expose the realities and dilemmas faced by their Eurasian female subjects, either as victims of the threads of colonialism or as patriotic fighters of sociopolitical and wartime upheavals. Another aspect worthy of note in their narratives is the vital function that both writers place on the use of linguistic hybridity, as Creole language is always present and is recovered as a missing link for remembering and making sense of a bygone era. This fundamental importance of Creole in the redefinition of identity becomes immediately evident in the constant references to Macao's Patuá and Malacca's Papia Kristang, and to Portuguese, Chinese (Hokkien), Malay or "Singlish" (colloquial Singaporean English). Although Portuguese was the language of Senna Fernandes's mother, Patuá, English and Cantonese interfere many times in the writer's discourse through expressions that evoke joy, praise, devotions and secular memory. In the case of Shelley, although he writes in English, he uses references in Portuguese, Malay, Chinese and Kristang with corresponding translations or explanations in English.

Rex Anthony Shelley (1930–2009) was a Portuguese Eurasian of Malacca-Portuguese ancestry and the author of eight books. Four of Shelley's novels are dedicated to the stories of generations of Portuguese Eurasian families with a plethora of Portuguese-related surnames like Rosario or Perera. Shelley clearly assumes a postcolonial stance after Malaysia's and Singapore's respective independences. His novels are generally set against the Pacific War — the Japanese invasion and occupation of Malaya and Singapore during

World War II from 1942 to 1945 — but also include other major and minor political events in which the Eurasians actively participated or were targets: the Konfrontasi (the conflict between Indonesia and Malaysia from 1962 to 1966), the Chinatown riots in Singapore in 1927, and the pro-independence rallies during the Malayan emergency in the mid-1950s, among other periods of unrest. They include detailed, real and fictional references to the Merdeka and to the Bandung conference of 1955, a postcolonial moment of solidarity for Asian and African peoples. The novels also shift to more recent periods and to the Luso diaspora. For instance, Shelley's *The Shrimp People* features the reunion of Eurasians in Perth, Australia, and their early recollections of community members and events.

Five of Rex Shelley's books, including his novel *The Shrimp People* (1991) and *The People of the Pear Tree* (1993), received Singapore's Top Fiction Award. Both of these works were also awarded first prize by the National Book Development Council of Singapore, in 1993 and 1994, respectively. Shelley also published *Island in the Centre* (1995), winner of the National Book Development Council's Highly Commended Awards in 1996, and *A River of Roses* (1998) that won the Singapore Literature Prize in 2000. Some of the main characters and their life stories in Shelley's novels reappear or are evoked in each of the books of the saga, reinforcing the strong family and community ties of the Portuguese Eurasians across the Malay Peninsula and elsewhere in the Luso diaspora. Shelley's other works are on Japan and the Japanese (*Cultures of the World: Japan and Culture Shock* and *Island in the Centre*), and on a variety of English peculiar to Eurasians in Singapore entitled *Sounds and Sins of Singlish, and Other Nonsense*. His last book, *Dr. Paglar: Everyman's Hero*, a biography of his uncle, a Eurasian gynaecologist (1894–1954), was published posthumously in 2010. Shelley was a multifaceted personality who passed away in 2009 after probably witnessing many of the events he narrated in his novels. Shelley received his degree in chemistry from the University of Malaya and held degrees in engineering and economics from Cambridge. He worked as an engineer in Malaysia and Singapore, and for a trading company. He served on the boards of several scientific research centres and on public service commissions. He was awarded Singapore's Public Service Star in 1978 and Public Service Star (Bar) in 1989.

His counterpart, the Macanese novelist Henrique Senna Fernandes (1923–2010), has long been recognized as the foremost chronicler of Lusophone Macanese literature, and was a well-known figure with several books published in Portuguese since the 1980s which won literary awards: a collection of short stories, *Nam Van* in 1978; the novels *Amor e Dedinhos de*

Pé (Love and Little Toes) in 1986; *Trança Feiticeira* (The Bewitching Braid) in 1992; *Mong Há* in 1998; and the unfinished book, *A Noite Caíu em Dezembro* (The Night Fell in December) in 2004.[13] Two of his novels were adapted for cinema in 1996 with great success in Portugal and in China, sponsored by both the governments of Macao and the People's Republic of China shortly before the transference of Macao's sovereignty to China. Some of his works have appeared in Chinese and English translations.

Born in Macao in 1923, Senna Fernandes and his family, like the majority of the Macanese community in Macao, Hong Kong and the port cities of China, experienced the consequences of the Japanese invasion of China and Hong Kong in 1942, the Second Sino-Japanese War (1937–45), and the tumultuous period of the implantation of the Republic of China (1912–49).

Senna Fernandes studied at the University of Coimbra in Portugal, where he graduated in law. He later returned to Macao in the 1950s where he also served and held senior positions in a diverse range of areas in Macao under the Portuguese administration, including in education and in the local parliament, while also maintaining his private law practice. In addition, he chaired numerous professional associations, sports, cultural and civic organizations, and he collaborated in theatre plays in Patuá.[14]

Both authors' works rely largely on forms of a broad range of recollections of emotional events, and their stories employ the literary device of constant shifts and a series of flashbacks to supplement more faithfully the narratives of their communities. Yet Senna Fernandes's earlier fiction reveals stronger autobiographical nuances, mainly related to his experiences as a university student in Portugal and more constrained in their depiction of Portugal and Macao in a period of both personal and political turmoil. His characterization of the war climate is radically different from Shelley's. Instead, Senna Fernandes also depicts the saga of his own family, whose ancestors had an aristocratic and wealthy background but who remained in Macao and were affected by the city's decline, the war and the political instability of the region. He offers a nostalgic portrayal of Macao and his close-knit community in the first half of the twentieth century during the pre-war period, before the Japanese occupation of Hong Kong and Macao's neutrality of the 1930s. In that period, Macao was a safe city for refugees, and remained largely immune to the political instability of the region during the 1940s, 1950s and 1960s caused by the Japanese presence, the revolution of 1949 and the influence of the Chinese Communist regime. In Senna Fernandes's novels set during the war and the Japanese occupation of Hong Kong, there are only sparse and indirect references to their presence. He is more concerned about describing the hunger and the high incidence of illness and difficulties suffered by his family and his community, as well as all the sorts of refugees coming from mainland China and Hong Kong.[15] Above all, his works reflect the values of a patriarchal society on the verge of disintegration due to rapid sociopolitical changes. As one of the characters explains, the Japanese attack on China during the Pacific War put an end to the "segurança da era patriarcal" (security of the patriarchal era) in the Macanese community.[16] He describes what led many Macanese to migrate in successive diasporas to China's treaty ports, Hong Kong, Portugal, Brazil, the United States and Canada from the mid-1800s throughout the twentieth century. In both *Amor e Dedinhos de Pé* and *Trança Feiticeira,* several male characters leave Macao in search of better fortune in mainland China, while in the short story "Candy", the main female character leaves for Hong Kong where she meets her former lover who had migrated to Brazil in the 1970s.

On the other hand, issues related to nationalism, independence, racial discrimination, clandestine armed struggle and espionage are openly evoked in Rex Shelley's works, to the point that some authors consider his novellas as examples of Singapore's spy novels or thrillers.[17] In fact, they are in sharp contrast with Senna Fernandes's novels both in narrative strategy and political effects. Shelley's novels are more ideological and politically structured, with obvious references to espionage and to racial riots that targeted the Eurasians in Singapore. Political riots held in Macao as a consequence of China's Cultural Revolution are absent in Senna Fernandes's novels. Written during the dictatorship and before Portugal's democratic revolution in 1974, Senna Fernandes's novels contain only scattered political references; his main characters are nearly all very apolitical and even condemn those who dare to take political positions, as if they have internalized colonially driven stereotypes of race and class.[18] Exceptionally, such as in *Amor e Dedinhos de Pé*, there are occasional references to the clashes that occurred between the Portuguese or Macanese monarchists or republicans, and even references to the presence of Freemasons in Macao as a reflection of Portugal's political atmosphere before the implementation of the Republic in 1910. During World War II, the Japanese did not formally occupy Macao due to Portugal's ambiguous status of neutrality, but their presence was notoriously influential and visible in Macao at various levels. The Macanese in Hong Kong and the so-called Portuguese Eurasians in the Malay Peninsula showed their loyalty towards the British by conspiring against the Japanese. During the war, many Eurasians of Portuguese ancestry enlisted in the companies of volunteers, either in Hong

Kong or in Singapore, in order to fight and resist the Japanese. In 1945, many were made prisoners and were sent to Japanese internment camps, where many perished. Others dared to escape the Japanese army's surveillance in Macao, like Maurício in Senna Fernandes's short story "Chá com Essência de Cereja" (Tea with Essence of Cherry), who manages to succeed in smuggling goods with the Chinese from the Free China movement. Yet, it is worth mentioning that Senna Fernandes's works have the undeniable merit of denouncing the market of female sexual slavery in China and the related exploitation of services and practices.

Shelley's narratives highlight the contradictions and dilemmas several characters face during wartime upheavals and changes in political affiliations. For instance, in the *People of the Pear Tree*, the Eurasian family Perera is forced to abandon Singapore and take refuge in Bahau, a poor and malaria-infested area in the countryside on the Malay Peninsula. There, in Negeri Sembilan, they become vegetable farmers due to the shortage of food, while some members of the community join the nationalist fight against the Japanese and supply them with food. Gus Perera becomes involved in the guerrilla fighting after joining the Chinese nationalists of the Malayan People's Anti-Japanese Army in the mangrove swamps, before the ignominious surrender impelled by a sort of pan-Eurasian political motivation, and also participates in ambushes targeting the Japanese. In Shelley's novels *People of the Pear Tree* and *Island in the Centre*, Japanese are also some of the main characters who play an active role in the plot, like in the case of Anna Perera who becomes romantically involved with a Japanese army officer (Major Takanashi Junichiro), who kills a Communist woman fighter (Ah Lan) but helps to save the Perera family during the occupation. Despite the anti-Japanese atmosphere in the post-war period, Anna dares to marry him even if she has to choose between him and a Chinese guerrilla fighter.

Despite the apparent fragility of the Macanese characters and their Eurasian counterparts in the Malay Peninsula — who sometimes feel lost and confused in their constant search for their identity amidst hardships, doubts and apprehension, and above all because the majority of them were unprepared for independence and integration into their new countries — their vision of the postcolonial world and reaffirmation of collective identities remains unaltered. They seem to know how to find adequate ways to fit in by remaining optimistic and confident about their future roles in their respective countries. They never lose their resilience and faith as they manage to destabilize the narratives through ample use of irony and by concluding their narratives with conciliatory notes.

NONAS, NHONHAS AND SERANIS

The ship's new, the rigging's new,
Sailing suddenly into Malacca
She's new to him; He's new to her,
Yet knowing at once each other.
(Old Malay poem)[19]

Gingli nona, gingli nona,	(Petting damsel, petting damsel,
Eu queré casá,	I want to marry you,
Casa nung teng porta	The house has no door
Qui laia logo passá?[20]	How can I enter?)

(Traditional lyrics to music of Malacca in Kristang)

Nhonha na jinela	(Maiden at the window
Côfula mogarim	With a jasmine flower
Nhonhonha mogarim	Canary Lady
Sua mãi tancaréra	Your mother is a Tanka woman
Sua pai canarim[21]	Your father Konkanin)

(Traditional verse of Macao in Patuá)

For centuries, one of the main characteristics of Macao and Malacca's Christian population was the number of Eurasian females from a great variety of Chinese, Asian and African ethnicities to which the above traditional verses and lyrics in Creole allude.

A remarkable instance of interrelatedness between both Rex Shelley and Senna Fernandes's narratives is that they both contribute to rewriting, transmitting and perpetuating Portugal's myths of colonial "exceptionalism" associated with its maritime and epic legacies, and they often structure their stories around representations of Eurasian female protagonists. Their narratives are made up of heroic Portuguese seamen who distinguish themselves from other Europeans not only because of their courage, but also due to their capacity to freely mix with indigenous societies, accepting interethnic unions and raising their creole progeny. Henceforth, they originated unique and harmonious communities whose prototypical Eurasian men and women were the epitome of empowerment, beauty and courage.

The prologue of Shelley's *The Shrimp People*, for instance, explains metaphorically the origins of *geragok*-people, or the first Portuguese Eurasians from Malacca, merging historical with legendary facts.[22] After the naval battle between the Portuguese and Hindus in the sixteenth century in Malacca, a wounded Portuguese sailor named Rodrigues is found on a beach. A local woman named Bedah, despite her parents' opposition, goes to live with the Portuguese seaman by the seashore, and they survive by catching a special kind of local small shrimp named *geragok*. The legend associated with the earlier fishing community that lives in the Portuguese Settlement in Malacca, created by the British in 1933, resembles Brazil's national myth as it exemplifies what has been lauded as a specifically Portuguese mode of being in the tropics. In fact, Freyre explains that the "misticismo sexual" (sexual mysticism) involving sensuous, dark-skinned women with long hair and dark eyes, personified by the indigenous women whom the first Portuguese colonizers met in Brazil, reminded them of the long contact and sexual attraction they felt towards the legendary "mouras encantadas"(enchanted female Moors or Muslims) on the Iberian Peninsula who shared similar physical attributes.[23]

Regarding the foundations of the Macanese community, Senna Fernandes offers two opposing alternatives to the narrative of miscegenation in the tropics. Although he describes the idyllic world of the Christian city that the Portuguese created in Macao, the ambiguity of the colonial encounters is also expressed through glimpses into Macao's social cleavages that are revealed through the origins of several layers of Macanese society. Significantly, his earlier collection of short stories, *Nam Van*, includes "A Chan, a Tancareira" (Ah Chan, the Tanka Girl), written in the 1950s, which conveys a stereotypically idyllic love encounter in the tropics. Here, a poor and ugly Chinese boat woman from Macao's lower social strata becomes involved with a stereotypically handsome Portuguese sailor. Chinese Tanka boatwomen served as mistresses of Portuguese men, especially those in the lower echelons of the army and navy.[24] Children of these unions formed the beginnings of the lower class of the colony's Eurasian community. In this short story that does not have a happy conclusion, the mother is forced to abdicate custody of her daughter, a mestizo offspring, who is taken to Europe to be nurtured by her European father while she stays behind. Other episodes included in Senna Fernandes's subsequent novels, including *Amor e Dedinhos de Pé*, denounce the complicity of the Macanese elites — Macanese, Portuguese and Chinese — regarding gender stigmatization. They contain open critiques of the negative aspects of Portugal's colonial policies, such as a form of female slavery that existed in the illegal trade of the *mui-tsai*[25] system. In fact, the first-person narrator takes a position in an implicit condemnation revealing the problematic nature of racial mixing that in the majority of cases was intimately associated with prostitution and female concubines. His critique of the hybrid experience in the colonial context, as opposed to the celebrated "Lusotropicalist" rhetoric of multiculturalism, can be considered exceptional.

Eventually, some of these Chinese girls would become "sing-song girls" or prostitutes and concubines of wealthy Chinese like those portrayed in Senna

Fernandes's "Chá com Essência de Cereja". Likewise, in *Amor e Dedinhos de Pé*, the main character, Francisco Frontaria, before being rescued by his soul mate, was an intermediary in the sale of a Chinese girl to a local elderly Chinese man who dreamt of curing his impotence.

But it is Senna Fernandes's last novel, *Trança Feiticeira*, written immediately before Macao's transference of sovereignty to China, that shows the alternative, positive nuance of idyllic inter-ethnic unions. The novel that one critic considers a "politically correct novel" best personifies the eulogy of a successful "tropical love story".[26] The mid-twentieth-century love story between the beau, Macanese Adosindo, and a sensuous Chinese woman, A-Leng, may be regarded as the symbolic assurance of the Portuguese tropical presence in China, which simultaneously and unequivocally supports the discourse of the peaceful integration of Macao with mainland China. Both A-Leng and Francisco Frontaria, as well as their handsome progeny, appear "to live happily ever after" as new, utopian embodiments of a Lusophone Asian imaginary. Macao is converted into a new future, "Tropical China", which embraces racial and cultural differences as "habits and customs from the two cultures blended together without imposition of either side".[27]

Like the Malay woman in Shelley's novels, the Chinese and Macanese women are the archetypal, "coloured" mother figures who, through unions with Portuguese or Macanese, create the matrix of the foundational family, procreating the "legitimate" progeny who then contribute to the construction and reformulation of Portugal's national imaginary in the tropics. Their iconic motherhood status, affirmed as they become symbolic tools in perpetuating a Luso-Asian identity, is a foundational theme for these authors. In *The People of the Pear Tree*, Shelley evokes the policies favouring the intermarriage of Portuguese men with local Indian women implemented in Portugal's occupied Goa in the sixteenth century by the viceroy Afonso de Albuquerque, who also brought them to Malacca when he captured the city. Although the details are not historically accurate, Anna Perera explains to her Japanese suitor, Tanakashi Junichiro, how she and her people are legitimate descendants of Albuquerque, along with his soldiers and sailors who married the women of Malaya 400 years ago.[28] She tells her suitor that although the Portuguese ruled Malacca for only a short period (1511–1641), the Portuguese-native unions led to the emergence of a heroic genealogy of Eurasians in Malaysia who speak Kristang and, against all odds, have survived until today.[29] Anna, Bertha and other Eurasian female characters, whom Shelley traces through the female line to an archetypal Malay native woman, would fit into Freyre's description of the native woman as "well educated" and a "woman endowed with glamour" [in English, in the original text], over the white woman born in Africa.

She is the quintessential Lusotropical woman. The most capable of seducing not only the Rimbauds but also the Burghers."[30]

Shelley's novels trace the impact of the war occupation and independence on the region — especially on women — and highlight their pivotal role. Yet the Eurasian men are also portrayed as brave men who in the early times struggled in battles or on the sea, who during the Pacific War joined the resistance against the Japanese, and who in more modern times dared to migrate to unknown places and succeed. They are also portrayed as having distinctive physical attributes that make them quite handsome to the point of attracting women from different ethnic backgrounds. In *The People of the Pear Tree*, Gus Perera is an excellent guerrilla fighter who is also able to get sexual favours from the Chinese female Communist leader. Similarly, in Senna Fernandes's narratives, the Macanese male characters are handsome heroes and symbolic heirs of the intrepid seafarers of the early fifteenth century.[31] They are represented as colonial subjects who claim noble origins and proudly distinguish themselves as the "legitimate heirs" of a special patriarchal community distinct from other communities, in particular the Chinese.

In *Amor e Dedinhos de Pé*, the ancestors of the main character, Francisco Frontaria, are described as intrepid Macanese who distinguished themselves as captains of the *lorchas* (a hybrid type of sailing vessel common in Macao) under the leadership of the Portuguese *ouvidor* (judge) Arriaga in the fight against the Chinese pirates in the South China Sea.[32] This episode evokes another long-standing myth that the Portuguese got rid of the pirates who threatened the South China Sea, and in return the emperor of China gave the enclave to the Portuguese king as a reward. In the same novel, references are also made to the nineteenth-century Macanese hero Colonel Vicente Nicolau de Mesquita, who bravely repelled the Chinese attacks and siege of Macao under the Portuguese crown.[33]

On the other hand, in Shelley's novels, the Portuguese Eurasians are ultimately shown to be more cosmopolitan, liberal-minded and strong-willed in contrast to the stereotypically portrayed, submissive Asian women. Above all, the female Eurasians are portrayed as heirs of a unique and exceptional cultural blend, which makes them not only incomparable seductresses, but simultaneously zealous guardians of the cultural and religious values of the community. Married or single, Portuguese female Eurasian heroines or *senanis* bear more than a passing resemblance to the Macanese women or *nonas* portrayed in Senna Fernandes's novels.

These women share an exquisite physical beauty, a strong attachment to their families and strict adhesion to their church obligations and sacraments, all the while maintaining a mixed practice of Chinese or Malay superstitions, divination and traditional medicine. Although Senna Fernandes's narratives are centred on domestic themes of family-oriented narratives and the Macanese women in his novels are confined to the sphere of their domesticity and passive femininity, some characters such as Victorina in *Amor e Dedinhos de Pé* defy the prejudices of parochial and heterosexualist patterns of patriarchy. They are an example of what Ann Laura Stoler calls the "racialized economy of sex" prevailing in the colonies: "European women and men won respectability by steering to legitimate paternity and intensive maternal care, to family and conjugal love" while attributing desires for "opulence and sex to Creole and lower-class Europeans".[34] Above all, they are emotionally and economically dependent on the male heroes. On the other hand, however, they are portrayed as the perpetuators of a distinct lineage and of timeless traditions in a strange and sometimes hostile environment.

Shelley's female characters are much more independent, nonconformist and sexually liberated than those of his Macanese counterpart. They work as teachers, secretaries and spies; they practise outdoor sports like hockey, cricket and tennis; they dress and wear make-up stylishly, smoke in public, dance at nightclubs and parties, and are experienced drivers. They also become romantically involved with multiple partners from Europeans to Asians (Malays, Indonesians, Chinese and even Japanese) and even people of the same sex, without fear of being ostracized by their community or condemned by the Catholic Church. For instance, in *A River of Roses*, Philippa Rosario, a Catholic Eurasian, engages in a sexual relationship with Daud bin Ibrahim (a Muslim Malay musician), Duncan Gudgeon (a British agent) and a woman (Vicky).

In the novel *The Shrimp People*, Bertha Rodrigues, tired of her Chinese husband's constant infidelity, joins the Indonesian secret service as a double agent during the period of the Confrontation and becomes involved with another Eurasian secret agent, Andy McKay, whom she later kills as he is a Communist. Above all, she is "committed to doing all she could to prevent the formation of Malaysia and the merger of Singapore and Malaysia".[35] In a similar manner, in the novel *Island in the Centre*, Vicky Viera has a love affair with a Japanese man, Tommy Nakajima, whom she does not hesitate to kill when he threatens to unveil the existence of an anti-Japanese movement. Against all odds, these politically active women do not hesitate to sacrifice love on behalf of their patriotism for their country.[36]

In contrast, Senna Fernandes portrays a Macanese society totally influenced by the values of the traditional Macanese elite families, with their allegedly aristocratic ancestry dating back to the first Portuguese settlers, whose traditions, religion and codes of education were strictly followed and preserved. The Macanese women are shown as totally subalternized and victimized by the patriarchal system that systematically controls all of their social interactions. They are routinely predestined to play the role of *mulher reprodutora* (reproductive woman), responsible for bearing and rearing a reasonable number of virile, courageous and handsome males who will perpetuate their distinct lineage in China. Their only comforts are religion and their culinary traditions.[37] Many of them are subjected to violence and aggression.[38] Other Macanese women are portrayed as *solteironas* (spinsters), as if their only vocation were to find a suitable marriage partner, and as *donzelas sem pergaminhos* (damsels without pedigrees), for those who could not find a husband due to their lack of attractiveness.[39]

On the other hand, the Macanese women in Senna Fernandes's novels who dare to defy or transgress the social and moral norms through adultery or extra-marital liaisons, are generally punished or despised by the community itself. In Senna Fernandes's *Amor e Dedinhos de Pé*, the main character, Victorina, is an exceptional case perhaps because she is a virtuous woman, which might compensate for her lack of physical attributes. In *Nam Van*, Alice, who prefers the company of Portuguese men to Macanese, comes to conceive and bear a "filho atrás da porta" (son behind the door), or an illegitimate son, by her Portuguese lover who returns to Portugal. She is punished by being ostracized by the local society. Only after years of "good behaviour" and penitence does her former lover return to her and recognize his son on Christmas Day, thus contributing to the novel's happy ending.

In sum, there are obvious parallels in the fiction of both Shelley and Senna Fernandes as both authors delve into the lives of Eurasian women, even if the binary opposition between heroic masculinity and effeminate weakness is more visible in Senna Fernandes's novels than in Shelley's. The female characters seem overestimated, disempowered or victimized by the Macanese patriarchal society in Senna Fernandes's novels, but despite this, Macanese women are still shown as empowered because they possess virtuous qualities and play an important role in the education and transmission of the morals and culture of a distinct lineage.

CONCLUSION

This study has investigated the extent to which literary tropes and theoretical concepts associated with Gilberto Freyre's tropicalism influenced Rex Shelley and Henrique Senna Fernandes's fiction in order to disclose interconnectivity and commonalities that have previously been overlooked. The comparison has revealed that Rex Shelley and Henrique Senna Fernandes address a plethora of issues to express how the collective history of Eurasian communities is passed on and preserved from generation to generation, in their multicultural birthplaces and in the Luso diaspora. They corroborate Benedict Anderson's concept of imagined communities as their discourse evokes the diversity of human experience in an imagined or remembered "homeland" around fundamental notions related to self-identity, inclusion and dispersal, yearning and a sense of loss, permanence and change. Nuances of Lusotropicalism shape their narratives about a certain "Luso-Eurasianness" which is constantly reconstructed through the complexity of their responses to new challenges.

Comparative scholarly research on the Portuguese communities' mestizos in Southeast Asia and their continuous development or integration into analogous colonial environments, as well as on their cultural productions (mainly literature) certainly provides much information and insight into their identities and the different types of ethnic evolution. The portrayal of a certain "Creole consciousness" is interlaced with a "Lusotropicalist" discourse, whose revival, in some cases, is still simultaneously representative and surprisingly somehow intertwined with unexpected ramifications. In each case, these communities managed to remain clearly distinguishable from the European, Chinese or Portuguese as well as from other indigenous elements, crystallized into "traditions" and the language of daily use within the community, either Kristang or Macanese Patuá. This was further made possible by the establishment of European outposts in Southeast Asia and the Indian Ocean, mainly in Malacca and Macao, which allowed the emergence of creolized societies that sought to become integrated without disappearing.[40]

Above all, by sharing a utopia of multiculturalism and multiracialism inspired by "Lusotropicalism", the fiction of these authors emphasizes that these Eurasian minority communities managed to face new challenges and preserve a hope for renewal. In particular, they skilfully chose the most appropriate strategies for engaging in new political, social and cultural changes in their beloved countries of birth. They wisely managed to learn how to articulate a pride in the recollections of a distant mythical past with traditions associated with the Portuguese empire in Asia that they still surprisingly and tenaciously preserve, transfigure and transmit incessantly even today, as a reminder of an alleged Portuguese capacity for miscegenation and adaptation.

Notes

1 Gilberto Freyre, *Aventura e Rotina* (Lisbon: Livros do Brasil, 1953), p. 299.

2 George D. Winius, "The Shadow-Empire of Goa in the Bay of Bengal", *Itinerario* 7, no. 2 (1983).

3 Benedict Anderson, *Imagined Communities: Reflections on the Origin and Spread of Nationalism* (London: Verso, 1983), p. 25. See also Benedict Anderson, *Under Three Flags: Anarchism and the Colonial Imagination* (London: Verso, 2005).

4 Anderson, *Imagined Communities*. See also Miguel Vale de Almeida, *An Earth-Colored Sea: "Race", Culture, and the Politics of Identity in the Post-Colonial Portuguese-Speaking World* (Oxford: Berghahn, 2004).

5 Miguel Vale de Almeida, "Portugal's Colonial Complex: From Colonial Lusotropicalism to Postcolonial Lusophony", Queen's Postcolonial Research Forum, Queen's University, Belfast, 28 April 2008, p. 10 <http://site.miguelvaledealmeida.net/wp-content/uploads/portugal-colonial-complex.pdf> (accessed 10 August 2010).

6 Hilary Owen, *Mother Africa, Father Marx: Women's Writing in Mozambique, 1948–2002* (Lewisburg, PA: Bucknell University Press, 2007), p. 31.

7 Phillip Rothwell, "Lusotropical Legacies in Germano Almeida's *Eva*, or Cruelty as a Staged Performance", *Forum for Modern Language Studies* 45, no. 4 (2009): 401–10.

8 Ibid.

9 Bill Ashcroft, *Caliban's Voice: The Transformation of English in Post-Colonial Literatures* (London: Routledge, 2009), p. 4.

10 The Portuguese Eurasians are known as Serani (Nasrani), the followers of Jesus the Nazarene. Rex Shelley, *Shrimp People* (Singapore: Times Books International, 1991), p. 61. *Geragok* is a derogatory term applied to the Eurasians of Portuguese ancestry from Malacca. It is also an abbreviation of the expression *udang gerigau* (a small kind of shrimp) that, after dried, turns into a paste called *belichan*, which is commonly used in the cuisines of both Malacca and Macao. One of the most famous Macanese dishes is *porco balichão*. *Nona* means an unmarried Eurasian girl in Malacca, probably with its origin in the Portuguese *dona* (lady) while *nhonha* in Patuá is used for women of a certain age and position in Macau. António da Silva Rêgo, *Dialecto Português de Malaca: Apontamentos para o Estudo do Português de Malaca* (Lisbon: Agência Geral das Colónias, 1942); and Alan Baxter, "Introdução", in António da Silva Rêgo and Alan N. Baxter, *Dialecto Português de Malaca e Outros Escritos* (Lisbon: Comissão Nacional para os Descobrimentos Portugueses, Imprensa Nacional, 1998), pp. 132–33.

11 The Macanese Carlos Montalto de Jesus (1863–1927) employed this expression for the first time, but it has been widely used by the Macanese themselves and by the Portuguese official rhetoric, especially immediately before the transference of Macao's sovereignty to China.

12 Rex Shelley, *The People of the Pear Tree* (Singapore: Times Books International, 1991), pp. 12–13.

13 Some chapters of the book were published weekly in the daily *Ponto Final* (Macao).

14 In his mid-eighties, Senna Fernandes served on the Advisory Committee of

the Association for Promotion of the Education of the Macanese, one of the member institutions of the Foundation of the Portuguese School in Macao. He received numerous honours, awards and recognition from various institutes and the governments of Macao and Portugal, including the Grand Cross of the Order of Prince Henry, presented by the president of Portugal in 1987, and the Honorary Doctorate Degree of Philosophy from the University of Saint Joseph (Macao) in 2006.

15 Henrique Senna Fernandes, *Nam Van: Contos de Macau* (Póvoa de São Adrião, Portugal: author's edition, 1978; repr., Macao: Instituto Cultural de Macau, 1997), pp. 13–14.

16 Ibid., p. 11.

17 Patricia Wong, "Rex Shelley's *The Shrimp People:* What Manner of Beast Is It?" in *Interlogue: Studies in Singapore Literature*, vol. 1, *Fiction*, edited by Kirpal Singh (Singapore: Ethos Books, 1998), p. 49. See also Peter Wicks, "Eurasian Images of Singapore in the Fiction of Rex Shelley", in *Singaporean Literature in English: A Critical Reader*, edited by Mohammed A. Quayum and Peter Wicks (Serdang, Malaysia: Universiti Putra Malaysia Press, 2002), pp. 377–83.

18 Henrique Senna Fernandes, *Amor e Dedinhos de Pé* (Macao: Instituto Cultural de Macau, 1986; repr. 1994), pp. 333, 362 and 379.

19 Shelley, *The Shrimp People*, p. 8.

20 S. Durai Raja Singam, "Jingli Nona", *Straits Times Annual* (1966), 48–49, quoted by K. David Jackson, "*Singelle Nona/Jinggli Nona*: A Traveling Portuguese Burgher Muse", in *Re-exploring the Links: History and Constructed Histories between Portugal*, edited by Jorge Manuel Flores (Paris: Calouste Gulbenkian Foundation; and Wiesbaden: Harrassowitz, 2007), p. 53. A song generally sung at wedding parties and other festivities in Malaysia and Singapore among the Eurasian communities. António da Silva Rêgo, *Dialecto Português de Malaca: Apontamentos para o seu Estudo* (Lisbon: Agência Geral das Colónias, 1942), pp. 225-27. In Macao, *nona* is the daughter of a European man by a Chinese woman. It is also current in the Portuguese dialects of Malacca, Singapore, Cochin, Diu and Bombay. Sebastião Rodolfo Dalgado and Anthony Xavier Soares, *Portuguese Vocables in Asiatic Languages*, pp. 136–37 <http://www.archive.org/stream/portuguesevocabl033463mbp/portuguesevocabl033463mbp_djvu.txt> (accessed 10 August 2010).

21 A verse collected in the 1960s. The Portuguese and Macanese used the expression *canarin* to designate a person originally from Goa. Graciete Batalha, "Aspectos do folklore de Macau", *Boletim do Instituto Luís de Camões* 2, no. 2 (1968): 5–12. See also João Feliciano Marques Pereira, ed., "Cancioneiro musical crioulo", *Ta-Ssi-Yang-Kuo: Archivos e Annaes do Extremo-Oriente Portuguez*, 1st–2nd ser. (Lisbon: Antiga Livraria Bertrand – José Bastos, 1899–1903), 1: 704. *Nhonha* means a married woman, and it has a diminutive meaning in Macao. Dalgado and Soares, *Portuguese Vocables*, p. 137.

22 Shelley, *The Shrimp People*, p. 10.

[23] Gilberto Freyre, *Casa Grande e Senzala (Formação da Família Brasileira sob o Regime de Economia Patriarcal* (Rio de Janeiro: Schmidt, 1936), pp. 12–13.

[24] Henrique Senna Fernandes, *Nam Van* (Macao: author's edition, 1984).

[25] *Mui-tsai* literally means "little younger sister" in Cantonese. In this case, however, it refers to a system whereby girls were sold to perform household or other work, or to be a prostitute, often for many years or even decades. The system lasted until the twentieth century in South China, mainly in Macao and Hong Kong.

[26] David Brookshaw, "Imperial Diasporas and the Search for Authenticity", in *Lusophonies asiatiques, Asiatiques en Lusophonies* (Paris: Karthala, 2000), p. 279.

[27] Henrique Senna Fernandes, *Trança Feiticeira* (Macao: Instituto Cultural de Macau, 1986; repr., 1993), 141. See also Gilberto Freyre, *China Tropical* (São Paulo: Imprensa Oficial do Estado de São Paulo, 2003).

[28] Shelley, *The People of the Pear Tree*, p. 51.

[29] Ibid.

[30] Freyre, *Aventura*, p. 325.

[31] Senna Fernandes, *Amor e Dedinhos de Pé*, pp. 13–14.

[32] Ibid., pp. 14–15.

[33] Ibid.

[34] Ann Laura Stoler, *Race and the Education of Desire: Foucault's History of Sexuality and the Colonial Order of Things* (Durham, NC: Duke University Press, 1995), p. 183.

[35] Shelley, *The Shrimp People*, p. 370.

[36] Ibid., p. 475.

[37] Senna Fernandes, *Amor e Dedinhos de Pé*, p. 13.

[38] Ibid., pp. 16–17.

[39] Ibid.

[40] Bernard Sta Maria, *My People, My Country: The Story of the Malacca Portuguese Community* (Malacca: Malacca Portuguese Development Centre, 1982).

12

PORTUGUESE PAST, STILL IMPERFECT: REVISITING ASIA IN LUSO-DIASPORIC WRITING

Christopher Larkosh

> The expression "Lusophony" has been gaining increasing currency as a device that helps to regain — in both the "spiritual realm" of the cultural products — (language, with "Lusophony") and the institutional one, with the CPLP [Community of Portuguese-Speaking Countries] — that which has been lost in the political and material one (Empire as such).
>
> Miguel Vale de Almeida, *An Earth-Colored Sea* (2004)

In light of the above epigraph, it is perhaps needless to say that it is with a considerable measure of caution, if not outright ambivalence, that I consider the possibility of a return to Asia for Lusophone literary and cultural studies today. For this reason, perhaps it should first be made clear what is meant by the idea of "commemorating legacies" that is presumably the pretext for our assembly here on the Straits of Malacca for the purposes of this conference. From my point of view, I understand it as an invitation to expand participation in, and thus add what each of us can, to the reworking of a shared (if not always directly inherited) set of memories, however obscured, intermittent and thus continually incomplete they may be: in this case, of a 500-year-long Portuguese presence and subsequent cultural contact in South, Southeast and East Asia. Whatever dates each of us opts to privilege from this long historical narrative in 2011, aside from the presumably foundational date of 1511 — some of us might also wish to highlight under this rubric the fifty years that separate us from the end of Portuguese rule in Goa, or the ten or so that separate us from the vote and eventual independence of East Timor, as well as the return of Macao to China — what remains undeniable is that the dates that mark out our ever-selective memory are politically charged involuntarily. It is with this in mind, that, as in the writings of the Portuguese philosopher Eduardo Lourenço, I too refer to the Portuguese past as "imperfect":[1] that is, a past still recognizably present, one still unfinished and still a "work-in-progress", even if its "darker chapters" simultaneously call into question the very notion of progress.

I also must ask: why is it that the mere mention of the possibility of "darker chapters" continues to provoke such a vehemently defensive reaction from some of us, even those presumably committed to a reading of these historical narratives, ones that remain unavoidably informed by such cultural/political implications? Ultimately, perhaps, any workable ideas as to how we might proceed in this transcultural conversation are not to be found exclusively through historical research as understood in its strictest sense, be it the compilation of exhaustive manuscripts and bibliographies or the recollecting of oral narratives and linguistic details, but in a radical rereading of literary and historical texts in a way that also makes a rethinking of the concept of present or even future possible. This reflection not only on the documented past, but also on possible presents and futures — perhaps that temporal unity that in Sanskrit was called *trikalam* (literally "three times", or past, present and future) — may well prove to be a more enduring and humane contribution, whether made by literary and cultural studies or any other discipline, to this timely or, dare I say, critical discussion of the potential legacy of Luso-Asian encounters today, along with an accompanying set of possibilities for a renewed cultural politics, that stresses respect for difference, even within the context of intensified mutual exchange.

After all, new models of Luso-Asian cultural politics will continue to emerge and circulate, whether academics care to intervene explicitly in them or not: Portuguese-language organizations and authors continue to arrive in Asia to this day, most notably in recent years through a series of creative-writing grants given out by the Lisbon-based Fundação Oriente and publishing house Livros Cotovia, by which they are given the opportunity to spend a few months in Asia writing a fictional work for subsequent publication in Portugal. Granted, in recent years there have been none if any new additions to this particular series, but for the time being, however, we are left with an imperfect example of cultural exchange, of authors in a single European language moving in just one direction, that is, from West to East, more specifically, from the Lusophone world into Asia. A number of crucial questions regarding the series' cultural politics cannot be ignored here, beginning with the monolingual point of departure of the series itself.

This is not to say that such literary collections are not of value to us as academics and cultural theorists; in fact, it is precisely because of the politicized modes of cultural sponsorship inherent to such projects of cultural diffusion and unequal exchange that we should pay close critical attention to what is represented in these texts, and allow the ensuing debate to shape the possible terms of a future for the Portuguese language and Lusophone cultures in their ever-evolving relationship to Asia. Whatever one's cultural point of departure may be, it is perhaps all too hit-or-miss simply to provide authors with a plane ticket and travel grant and send them off to some corner of this massive and impossibly multifaceted continent to write a semi-autobiographical novel or travel narrative of some sort in Portuguese (and the lines between these two genres have perhaps never been so blurred as in this particular collection, to say nothing of the potential for superficiality, if not outright self-indulgence, that these genres can encourage). All the same, such texts nonetheless provide a valuable document that may serve to map out the present possibilities for Luso-Asian intercultural dialogue. For this very reason, we would do well to read closely and critically what practical preconditions make these narratives possible, as well as the cultural and linguistic limitations that predicate them. Do these texts confirm or challenge the preconceptions and commonplaces through which the Portuguese colonial presence in Asia is revisited, and thereby reconstituted and recirculated? And what other currently circulating literary texts might possibly be juxtaposed alongside them, in order to allow for a more nuanced and multidirectional exchange of cultural perspectives and historical interpretations beyond the limitations of an all-too-persistent colonial imaginary?

RETURNING TO GOA, THE LUSOPHONE WAY: AGUALUSA'S *UM ESTRANHO EM GOA*

The well-known, contemporary Lusophone author José Eduardo Agualusa might be said to epitomize a literature written in Portuguese that remains in continual transit, both within and beyond the limits of the Portuguese-speaking world. Born in Angola and now living, as he repeatedly stresses on his book covers, "between Luanda, Rio de Janeiro and Lisbon",[2] he was the beneficiary of a Fundação Oriente/Cotovia creative-writing grant in 1998; from this experience emerged the novel *Um Estranho em Goa*, published in 2000. Beginning with the title, the novel follows the narrative pattern of many of the literary works that revisit Asia, not only in this collection, but of other recent works (with Antonio Tabucchi's 1984 novel *Notturno Indiano* perhaps the most notable of literary precursors).[3] In *Um Estranho em Goa*, the author/narrator arrives in Asia not as a latter-day colonizer, but as a stranger, a putative outsider both to the culture and languages of the foreign space he enters. What all too often stands out against this repeating cultural landscape, then, are those cultural elements which can be most easily interpreted through the lens of his own linguistic familiarity and cultural background, that is to say, Portuguese culture mixed with elements from other Western cultures that can be identified as part of an ongoing process of cultural globalization in Asia and elsewhere.

The result is a more complex vision of contemporary Goa than one might expect at first glance, one that is found only on the west coast of a politically unified, multilingual and multicultural India, but also as part of a broader, global remapping of lingering cultural reference points; one that originates not only in Portugal, but also in other corners of the Portuguese-speaking world. With this all-inclusive approach to Lusophone history, language and culture, one might arrive at the conclusion that Agualusa delivers more than a catalogue of lingering colonial nostalgia: while many of the characters with whom he dialogues and debates in *Um Estranho em Goa* do express more than a small measure of longing for the "good old days" of Portuguese colonial rule, there are other thematic elements presented over the course of the narrative that may, however unwittingly, undermine these discourses, while even providing some alternatives to, and possible exit strategies from, this all-too-recurrent cultural perspective.

While there remain critics who prefer to imagine this work as occupying a sort of "halfway point between different cultures, a kind of in-between place",[4] I am less inclined to see it as an emblematic hybrid or in-between text, but rather one still firmly entrenched on the side of the signs and symbols of the Portuguese colonial world, a world whose institutional authority is by no means neutral. To the reply that, by combining the culturally diverse points of this former global empire, one is also in between cultures, especially in the context of a late-century Goa already integrated into an independent India, I personally still find it difficult to accept that the renewed juxtaposition of these colonial sites is in fact a form of hybridity, and not simply a new form of recognizing and perpetuating colonial geographical configurations under the sign and attendant power of the Portuguese language.

There is already something culturally selective about being a Portuguese-language author in Goa, writing primarily for a Western audience; it would be naïve to assert that cultural and linguistic positionality is not going to continue to attract the confidence of characters aligned with it.

In this novel, such contact begins with the Catholic taxi-driver named Sal (short for Salazar), a *portista* or diehard FC Porto (Futebol Clube de Porto) fan who does not hide his disdain for the Hindu religion: "Olhe bem os deuses deles. Homens com cabeça de elefante, outros com cara de macaco, mulheres com seis braços, como as aranhas, é uma colecção de monstros! Não entendo como alguém pode adorar figuras assim. Agora olhe para a Nossa Senhora, tão linda, veja como a luz se desprende dela."[5] (Take a good look at their gods. Men with the head of an elephant, others with monkey faces, women with six arms, like spiders: a collection of monsters! I don't understand how someone could worship images like that. Now look at Our Lady, see how the light emanates from her.)

While it may well be that such exaggerated characterizations of Hindu deities can only serve to expose the intolerance of the narrator's native informant, what is more important is this representation of what is all too often left unsaid about the lingering misunderstandings of Eastern religions. Instead of the tacit disapproval on the part of the narrator that might be inferred from this caricature of religious intolerance, it could also be argued that a rereading of Hindu religious texts themselves might better serve to introduce the reader to the nuanced understanding of God — that is, as either possessing an identifiable form (*saguna*) or as formless (*nirguna*) — that has engaged Vedic scholars in debate for centuries, even if it is too complex a theological discussion to give due justice here. In the context of the novel, in any case, it would be difficult to argue that religious traditions from outside the Portuguese colonial enclave receive anywhere near as much attention as does Roman Catholicism; a visit to a Hindu temple, for example, is postponed until the end of the narrator's visit and, even then, what stands out is the incorporation of Iberian Baroque elements into its architectural design. To characterize this vision of Goa as somehow "in-between" would entail glossing over the implicit selectivity of any colonizing gaze, to say nothing of the power differentials that determine the valorizing of more readily accessible European cultural images, and the colonial languages (whether Portuguese, English or others) in which they most recognizably appear and can be categorized.

All the more disconcerting in this context, if not strangely encouraging at the same time, is the narrator's mention of the impact that the symbol of the swastika has when encountered by the Western visitor for the first time as part of Eastern religious traditions: "este símbolo, com os braços voltados para a esquerda, representa para os hindus e os budistas a boa sorte, a chave do paraíso .... Um estrangeiro, mesmo sabendo que os Nazis roubaram a cruz gamada e a perverteram, não pode deixar de experimentar um certo incómodo ao vê-la exposta aqui, um pouco por toda a parte."[6] (This symbol, with its arms turned to the left, represents good luck and the key to Paradise for Buddhists and Hindus .... A foreigner, even if he knows that the Nazis stole the swastika and perverted it, cannot but feel a certain discomfort seeing it exhibited here, wherever you happen to look.) What is perhaps most troubling is that in this narrative, this inverted Nazi swastika is to be found on none other than on the box that is said to hold the heart of São Francisco Xavier, the patron saint of the Portuguese colonial presence in Asia. The author's search for the bodily remains of this Portuguese saint, once considered by Salazar and the Portuguese colonists to possess a divine power to extend colonial rule over this corner of Asia, could be said to constitute the narrative thread of the novel, one that, however unwittingly, now draws uncomfortable parallels between the early years of Portuguese exploration and colonization and its eventual dismemberment in a twentieth century marked not only by the totalitarian violence of an inverted swastika but also by the equally persistent slogans and symbols of the Estado Novo and its colonial empire.

This clear separation between the novel's sequence of interlocutors and the general population extends to an Indo-Portuguese widow who tearfully recounts her story as she offers the narrator a serving of *bebinca*, the traditional dessert of Portuguese Asia, found no longer only in Goa, Macao and Timor, but throughout the Portuguese-speaking world and beyond. Almost forty years after Goa's integration into India, she and her family of Portuguese *descendentes* (descendants) are evidently still unable to adapt fully to the new cultural and political reality: her husband "não sobreviveu aos novos tempos: 'Ele bem tentou aprender inglês, coitado, mas burro velho não aprende línguas. Dizia *good morning*, e era tudo'.... Dona Marcelina também não fala inglês e do concanim só aquelas coisas do dia-a-dia: 'o mínimo que preciso saber para me comunicar com os criados'".[7] (He didn't survive to see these times; he tried really hard to learn English, but as the saying goes, an old donkey doesn't learn languages. He could say "good morning," and that was it .... Dona Marcelina doesn't speak English either and can only say everyday things in Konkani: "the minimum that I need to know to communicate with the servants".) Throughout the novel, it becomes all the more clear the important role that linguistic proficiency has in creating the character's sense of cultural identity and social belonging, one reflected also in the theorists that argued either for or against Goan integration into either a unified India or a transoceanic Lusophone world.[8] Ultimately, if it is indeed the case that "old donkeys don't learn languages", we may indeed have to be patient, as I have argued elsewhere, as we await the arrival of not one or two, or even a handful, but a "critical mass" of multilingual, intercultural scholars, whose linguistic experiences extend beyond Portuguese, its Asian creoles and English to allow for a more representative sample of contemporary Luso-Asian voices and traditional texts from across the linguistic, cultural, caste and religious spectra.[9] In this particular case, our narrative may be transformed by a knowledge of South Asian languages from Sanskrit to Konkani; elsewhere, by any Asian language with which Portuguese has come in contact, from Bahasa Malaysia and Bahasa Indonesia to Burmese, Cantonese and Japanese. In the end, only time will tell how this comparative and multilingual turn might change our research focus.

For the time being, however, Goa through the eyes of Agualusa and his interlocutors continues to be shaped by the terms of their shared points of cultural contact and reference, to say nothing of their linguistic limitations, and Agualusa's own set of literary and historical associations. Perhaps to his credit, his perspective is one not only conscious, but unapologetically chosen: from the Cuban music in Spanish that he brings along to listen to — "black music from Latin America harmonizes with excess and languor"[10] — to the fictional literary elements from earlier creative projects that still seem closer to him than his lived experiences here. One of them is a character that he says that he has wanted to develop for some time, and has in his 1999 collection of short stories *Fronteiras Perdidas*: one who goes by the name of Plácido Domingo. He makes clear from the outset that this is not the opera singer of the same name, but a character of his own reinvention, who has arrived in Goa by way of the city of Corumbá on the faraway shores of the Paraguay River in the Brazilian Pantanal, as well as via the Angola of a lengthy anti-colonial struggle and subsequent civil war.[11] As might be expected in a Goa that is inextricably linked to the literary world of Agualusa, we are never far from Lusophone Africa and its historical protagonists, whether the Angolan Agostinho Neto and the Mozambican Eduardo Mondlane on the one hand or those Portuguese colonial officials eventually expelled by the liberation movements these revolutionary figures led on the other.

In the meantime, other Portuguese speakers also continue to arrive here, many with the same literary and historical fascinations at the heart of Agualusa's narrative: one is a young Portuguese researcher whose bachelor's thesis concerns the proper restoration and maintenance of colonial manuscripts: "she argues that the markings left in a book through being handled over the course of centuries make up a part of the book's history":[12] that is, not only the marginalia, but the stains and other traces left by readers. Such a conception of the limits of literary discourse may find itself quite at home in the present critical moment, still in the wake of post-structuralist thought and related unworkings of the text at its margins; if it is possible to carry this understanding forward, one might also place Agualusa's text within the same porous conception of intertextuality, one in which there is no other way to read the text but through the markings left at its margins, between commentary, critique and the continual possibility of effacement and erasure. Writing remains a collective project not only of preservation but also of writing over, even crossing out and beginning again. Agualusa's attempt to initiate a critical encounter with these colonial commonplaces may well be imperfect by its very nature, but it is also, and perhaps precisely for this reason, one that leaves space in its discursive margins for others to add to the discussion, both with historical details, intercultural material or a wider set of possible contemporary interpretations.

After all, the text's frame of reference makes clear that the colonial narrative is by no means over with the formal end of Portuguese colonialism. One moment where this is most evident is in the comparison made between the political situation in Goa and that of the Southeast Asian nation of East Timor, still struggling for independence from Indonesian military occupation and a transition towards democracy at the time of the novel's publication. It does not come as any surprise when the narrator's *portista* taxi-driver Sal calls attention to the possible parallels between Goa and Timor as he argues in favour of an independent Goa: "what we need here is someone like Xanana Gusmão."[13]

Even so, it is all too easy from this culturally bordered perspective to ignore what separates Goa and Timor; most importantly, the fact that, unlike Indonesia under Suharto, India was then, and remains, the world's largest democracy, and that violence on a mass scale was never used against the inhabitants of Goa in the aftermath of Indian occupation. It is in this political context that Goa takes its place as India's smallest state — haltingly perhaps, and no doubt facing many of the same problems of any multicultural democracy, as well as the challenge of a new national and global influx, as represented in the arrival of migrants from other regions of India, or those who come seeking the tail end of Goa's trance music party culture, with its drugs, ravers and other assorted "freaks". But then again, against the broad cultural backdrop of the last five centuries and beyond, how are these arrivals really any more freakish than those Portuguese explorers who arrived 500 years before? We may even do well to turn to them, along with those established authors expressly invited to this continually evolving cultural space, to add their own commentaries in the margins of this narrative as well.

OR PERHAPS: REMAPPING ASIA THROUGH PORTUGUESE-AMERICAN POETRY?

It is from this recurring impulse to revisit former Portuguese colonial spaces as a means of proposing contemporary cultural alternatives that I return, not only to Asia, but also to my own home region of southeastern New England, home not only to North America's oldest and largest Portuguese-speaking diaspora community but also to one of the most prominent Portuguese-American authors, the Provincetown-born poet and novelist Frank X. Gaspar. Over the last twenty-odd years, he has created a body of work that has often lent itself to discussions framed largely, if not entirely, within the context of his ethnicity: indeed, his two novels, *Leaving Pico* (1999), reviewed in the *New York Times Book Review* as "an expert portrait of the Portuguese immigrant experience",[14] and the recently published *Stealing Fatima* (2009),[15] also draw heavily on the familiar reference points of Portuguese-American culture in the region in creating their literary sense of place. Many of his poems, especially from his first collection, *The Holyoke* (1988), could also be said to revisit the memories of a Portuguese-American boyhood in a small Massachusetts coastal town. All the same, his frame of reference extends beyond the boundaries of ethnic identity from the very beginning. Nowhere is this more noticeable than in his two most recent collections of poetry, *Field Guide to the Heavens* (1999)[16] and *Night of a Thousand Blossoms* (2004),[17] where the particularities of his bi-coastal existence, played out between his childhood and his present home in southern California, are supplemented by a series of remembrances and readings that link his work to Asia and beyond.

Gaspar is no stranger to Asia; he was drafted and subsequently stationed on a U.S. naval aircraft carrier during the Vietnam War, and had the opportunity to visit, if briefly, a number of countries while stationed there. Most prominent is his shore leave in the port of Olangapo, Philippines, which provided the material for his poem entitled "Carmelita Raez".[18] Other places I discussed with him in a recent interview — held, ironically enough, in a Thai restaurant in downtown New Bedford, Massachusetts, at the heart of North America's oldest and largest Portuguese-speaking community — were, not surprisingly, quite diverse. They ranged from visits to the Confucian temples and British social clubs of colonial Hong Kong; first reading *The Teachings of Buddha* in a hotel room in Sasebo, a Japanese port city on Kyushu Island, not far from the city of Nagasaki, not only the point of first contact with the Portuguese "southern barbarians" as depicted on Japanese *namban* screens, but also one indelibly marked by this point by the human and structural aftermath of atomic cataclysm; his first visit to a mosque in Malaysia, one that first added Islamic civilization to this collage of cultural discovery; and even his work in the Pacific as part of the recovery team for the 1969 Apollo 11 moon landing, perhaps the most compelling detail that might draw parallels between this both epic and tragic chapter of U.S. history and that of the fifteenth- and sixteenth-century era of Portuguese exploration and discovery.[19] Whatever the specific cultural setting of any of his poems or prose works may be, his multifaceted work nonetheless serves to raise important questions as to what other, less examined spaces might become involved in reimagining a dialogue between the Lusophone world, especially through its less recognized diaspora cultures, and Asia.

In these two collections, what stands out most vividly is the way that the Portuguese-language literary figures from whom he continues to draw inspiration in English translation, such as Fernando Pessoa ("I Am Not a Keeper of Sheep"), João Cabral de Melo Neto, and Eugénio de Andrade ("One Arm and Another Arm") and the equally revered and effaced figures of Western philosophy such as Descartes ("The Work Was Too Easy"), are juxtaposed against texts from a wide range of Eastern religions and cultural traditions: from Buddhism as experienced both in written teachings and in his everyday life experience, to the *Bhagavad Gita* ("One Thousand Blossoms"), the *Tao Te Ching* ("The Way That Can Be Spoken of Is Not the Way"), the Koran ("The Lilies of the Field") and the Sufi poetry of Rumi ("Seven Roses"), all of which come to inform and expand upon the conventional cultural frames of reference that have come to add a uniquely multifaceted Asian dimension to Portuguese-American literature.

Whether the poet is placing a statue of Buddha in his garden ("The Garden Will Come to You") among its lemon trees ("The Lemons") and jasmine flowers ("Last Hymn to Night"), paging through his library late at night, exploring the Cambodian doughnut shops and multiracial neighbourhoods of his multicultural, twenty-first century megacity called Los Angeles, set on the edge of both Latin America and the Pacific ("The Fruit Trees and the Junipers"), or gazing up at the distant celestial bodies in the night sky, his poetry seems to suggest a divergent model for remapping a cultural dialogue between East and West, one in which Portuguese-American culture, for example, is as irreversibly shaped by other points in the universe, whether in Asia or somewhere in the rest of the cosmos, as by Portugal, the U.S. or the Western tradition. As Gaspar affirms in his poem "Don't You Want to Walk Out Among the Lilies?", such cultural elements are in eternal combination with one another: "So when I'm on my knees in the stacks humming to the Buddha, or mumbling to the Prophet, or swaying to the Psalms, don't judge me. When I puzzle over the Sutras, leave me to my defects."[20] This is not simply the narrative of a brief, intercultural encounter, but of one that has, through an in-depth and extended reading and re-reading, permeated profoundly and inextricably into this poet's cultural consciousness.

Numerous poems still maintain the inextricable relationship to the Roman Catholicism of his childhood, but just as many incorporate the Buddhist teachings that became part of his poetic vision after his first visit to Asia. They do not attempt to exoticize this experience, perhaps because they are not without their all-too-unavoidable inherent traumas: one of his most recent poems, "Sanctuaries", was written and recited in the autumn of 2010 as part of a forthcoming collection of poems entitled "Late Rapturous",[21] begun while the poet was living in New Bedford as part of his appointment as a writer-in-residence at the University of Massachusetts Dartmouth. It reconnects his work not only with the Portuguese-American culture and Roman Catholic faith of his youth, but also with one of the most frequently reproduced images of East Asia that continues to shape our historical consciousness: "Thich Quang Duc, sitting calm and resolved, in the consuming holocaust of your own flagrant body, lighting the world in a shudder of orange and the black smudge of your own fat in the dimpled street in old Saigon."[22] After all, this ever-repeating image of a Vietnamese Buddhist monk immolating himself in protest over the ongoing U.S. military presence in his country is one that no government — no matter how hard it may try through an ever-longer list of more recent military engagements — can ever completely erase. As a soldier recruited to fight in this conflict, Gaspar neither attempts to justify his role nor does he point the finger at others, but instead expresses his awareness, in poetic language, of the implications of his own personal connection to this war: what one might identify as his own past imperfect, along with its unavoidable human consequences.

Ultimately, as Gaspar contemplates in his poem "The Bodhidharma Preaches the Wake-Up Sermon", "*To seek nothing is bliss*, said the saint Bodhidharma, but isn't he the one who cut off his eyelids in search of a more perfect meditation?"[23] The possible cultural paradoxes and moral contradictions in this poetic and spiritual quest may well be as endless as those created by any other syncretistic world-view, but isn't that the point? Here one might recognize what is most compelling about Gaspar's cultural journey: either both seeking and not seeking, or letting go, seeking by not seeking, and perhaps allowing oneself in this way to be found and marked indelibly by others in the process. This is perhaps what might be identified and proposed here as the *necessary multidirectionality of future Luso-Asian encounters*: one in which new examples of writing and research are found, discussed and circulated among a broader set of global, cultural and linguistic realities, and in which at times the only thing necessary to make a new set of literary and cultural connections possible is, paradoxically, nothing at all. After all, as described in Gaspar's poem "The Garden Will Come to You", the Buddha has already found a place in his own southern California backyard, and all that is missing at this point is the right frame of mind to recognize it: "Don't despair. Don't lose yourself in these daily vexations. You'll see, if you are still, if you are disciplined, that the garden will come to you."[24]

IN PLACE OF CONCLUSION: ALTERNATIVE FUTURES FOR LUSO-ASIAN CULTURES

In lieu of a definitive conclusion, I would do better to recall the way in which this conference actually included an international border crossing for its participants. As we passed through customs together at the border from the city-state of Singapore into the Malaysian sultanate of Johor en route to the Strait Settlement of Malacca, I could not ignore the fact that others had already crossed this line before: Gaspar in 1969, on yet another shore leave; and Agualusa, as described in a chronicle entitled "A Nossa Pátria na Malásia", included in a collection that also appeared in 2000, the same year as *Um Estranho em Goa*. In it, he narrates the encounter with a border policeman who speaks to him in the Portuguese Creole of Malacca, and their attempt to understand one another by way of a common Portuguese language. The title seems to suggest much more than it might at first glance: Most importantly, who is the one who identifies Portugal as *pátria* in this narrative? An imagined metropolitan Portuguese reader, or perhaps the narrator as well, to say nothing of his Luso-Asian interlocutor? For Agualusa to adopt openly the notion that Portugal could serve as a shared *pátria*, indeed to suggest that this concept of *pátria* was even still operable, seems to create an unsettling paradox in any discussion of postcolonial and diasporic identity. It may be that one must travel, as Agualusa and so many others of us do, to arrive at an awareness of these apparent contradictions; for others, as Gaspar's work so eloquently illustrates, no real voyage is necessary to make these connections, as long as the lines of communication through literature and human contact are left open. As one Portuguese critic has commented: "Lusophone identity is more than an essence, or a politics, it is an emotional and personal discovery that gives meaning to a casual encounter and perhaps only makes sense in that same encounter."[25] It is thus that the ever-imperfect cultural dialogue, between being and non-being becomes one that I too revisit in the here and now; one that continues to reinvent, however imperfectly, the terms of its own continuation, quite often in those people and places furthest, and in terms most different, from those of the original encounter.

Notes

1 Eduardo Lourenço, *A Nau de Ícaro Seguido de Imagem e Miragem da Lusofonia* (Lisbon: Gradiva, 1999).

2 This example of Lusophone cultural politics — in this case, of a Lusophone author positioning himself culturally either between or outside the conventional borders of nation-states and their literary traditions, presumably to link his work thematically and stylistically to a broader corpus of literary texts — is also the point of departure for a series of critiques levelled by Agualusa, often against the very possibility of expanded literary community into which he so insistently inscribes himself. In one 2004 interview given to the Brazilian newsweekly *Época,* few of his contemporaries escape his outright disapproval: from Brazil, which he considers to be still "uma colônia" (a colony), one "ainda moldado pela escravatura," (still shaped by slavery), or contemporary Portuguese authors, whom he qualifies as "todos terrivelmente melancôlicos. Não há personagem de autor português que não se suicide no final. Os portugueses parecem alguns autores paulistas atuais, soturnos e pessimistas. E há aqueles que não escondem a nostalgia do império e inventam um herói, sempre português, que percorre a África e a América, em geral povoadas por coadjuvantes sem importância." (All terribly melancholic. There is no character from a Portuguese author who doesn't commit suicide at the end. The Portuguese are like some of the current authors from São Paulo, maudlin and pessimistic. And there are those who do not hide their nostalgia for empire and invent a protagonist, always Portuguese, who travels through Africa and America, populated by sidekicks of little importance.) José Eduardo Agualusa, interview, "O Brasil é colônia", *Época* 330 (13 September 2004) <http://revistaepoca.globo.com/ Epoca/0,6993,EPT808282-1666-1,00.html> (accessed 20 December 2010). See also José Eduardo Agualusa, *Um Estranho em Goa* (Lisbon: Cotovia/Fundação Oriente, 2000). In the wake of such blanket criticisms, the question becomes to what extent is it only fair that such generalized disapproval, from this or any other contemporary Portuguese author, also be extended towards the author's own fiction, above all in this particular case to a reading of his travel narrative *Um Estranho em Goa*?

3 Antonio Tabucchi, *Notturno Indiano* (Palermo: Sellerio Editore, 1984).

4 Mário Lugarinho, "Trânsito por ruinas: Resistência e subjetividade na era da globalização", paper presented at the VIII Congresso Luso-Afro-Brasileiro de Ciências Sociais, "A Questão Social do Novo Milênio", Coimbra, September 2004, p. 8, Centro de Estudos Sociais <http://www.ces.uc.pt/lab2004/inscricao/pdfs/painel28/MarioLugarinho.pdf> (accessed 20 December 2010).

5 Agualusa, *Um Estranho em Goa*, p. 22.

6 Ibid., pp. 81–82.

7 Ibid., p. 64.

8 Ibid., p. 154.

9 Christopher Larkosh, "Passage to Our Selves: Translating Out of Portuguese

Asia", in *Parts of Asia*, Portuguese Literary & Cultural Studies 17/18, edited by Cristina Bastos (Dartmouth: University of Massachusetts Dartmouth Center for Portuguese Studies and Culture, 2010), pp. 189–206.

10 Agualusa, *Um Estranho em Goa*, p. 23.

11 José Eduardo Agualusa, *Fronteiras Perdidas: Contos para Viajar* (Lisbon: Dom Quixote, 1998).

12 Ibid., p. 31.

13 Ibid., p. 111.

14 Erik Burns, review of *Leaving Pico,* by Frank X. Gaspar, *New York Times Book Review,* 12 September 1999 <http://www.nytimes.com/books/99/09/12/bib/990912.rv133520.html?_r=1> (accessed 20 December 2010).

15 Frank X. Gaspar, *Stealing Fatima* (Berkeley: Counterpoint Books, 2009).

16 Frank X. Gaspar, *A Field Guide to the Heavens* (Madison: University of Wisconsin Press, 1999).

17 Frank X. Gaspar, *Night of a Thousand Blossoms* (Farmington, ME: Alice James Books, 2004).

18 Frank X. Gaspar, *The Holyoke* (Dartmouth: University of Massachusetts Dartmouth, 2007), pp. 63–65.

19 Frank X. Gaspar, interview by author, Spicy Lime Thai Restaurant, New Bedford, Massachusetts, 10 September and 10 December 2010.

20 Gaspar, *Night of a Thousand Blossoms,* p. 57.

21 Frank X. Gaspar, "Late Rapturous" (unpublished MS, 2010).

22 Ibid.

23 Gaspar, *Night of a Thousand Blossoms,* p. 25.

24 Ibid., p. 43.

25 Maria Cristina do N.C. Seixas, "Discursos pós-coloniais sobre a lusofonia: Comparando Agualusa e Saramago", *Cronos* 8, no. 1 (January–June 2007): 144.

BIBLIOGRAPHY

Archival Sources

BRAZIL

Biblioteca Nacional, Rio de Janeiro, Setor de Manuscritos

Curiosidad: Un Libro de Medicina Escrito por los Jesuitas en las Misiones del Paraguay en el Año 1580.

ENGLAND

Bodleian Library of Commonwealth and African Studies at Rhodes House, Oxford

K. M. Anderson Papers.

Imperial War Museum, London

Arthur Ernesto Gomes, interview 21131, 23 Mar. 2001.

Barras Botelho, interview 8409, 1983.

Bernard Felix Xavier, interview 19226, 21 Dec. 1999.

Chris d'Almarda, interview 8410, 1983.

The National Archives, London, Public Records Office

Colonial Office, War and Colonial Department and Colonial Office, Hong Kong, Original Correspondence.

Foreign Office, General Correspondence 1906–1966, Political Correspondence.

Special Operations Executive, Far East, Registered Files, 1940–1947.

War Office, Directorate of Military Operations and Intelligence, and Directorate of Military Intelligence, Ministry of Defence, Defence Intelligence Staff, Files.

FRANCE

Biblioteque National de France, Paris, Département des Manuscrits

Breve Compendio de Varias Receitas de Medicina, 1598, Fonds Portugais No. 59.

HONG KONG

Hong Kong Heritage Project https://www.hongkongheritage.org/Archive/internet/eng/ArchiveBasicSearchForm.aspx

Amalia Sales, interview, 19 May 2008.

Frank Correa, interview, 17 Oct. 2008.

George Elliot, interview, 19 Sept. 2007.

Jorge Sequeira, interview, 4 Apr. 2007.

Margaret Lobo, interview, 25 Aug. 2009.

Ray Cordeiro, interview, 4 Sept. 2008.

Hong Kong Public Records Office, Government Records Service, The Government of the Hong Kong Special Administrative Region

Documents of Mr. Y. C. Liang, C.B.E. Concerning Wartime Activities in Hong Kong and Macao in Which He Was Involved, 1943–1946.

Endacott and Birch Papers Relating to the Publication "Hong Kong Eclipse", Letters, Memoranda, Reports, Diary Extracts, and Other Narratives Written by Hong Kong Residents Relating Their Experiences and Observations during the Battle for Hong Kong, the Japanese Occupation and Surrender, Hong Kong Manuscript Series.

General Correspondence Files (Confidential), Stanley Camp.

General Correspondence Files (Secret), 1943–1961.

Supreme Court Case Files, 1946–1976.

Hong Kong University Library, Hong Kong, Special Collections

John Stericker, "Captive Colony: The Story of Stanley Camp, Hong Kong".

Michael Ferrier, "China Boy".

INDIA

Historical Archives of Goa, Panaji, Goa

Assentos do Conselho da Fazenda, 1631–37.

Botica do Convento do Santo Agostinho.

Cartas Patentes e Alvarás.

Despezas do Convento de São João de Deus.

Doentes do Hospital Real do Baçaim.

Embaixada de China.

HAG 646.

HAG 1736.

HAG 7926.

HAG 8030.

Livro das Posturas.

Livro da Receita e Despeza de Medicamentos do Hospital do Convento de São João de Deus.

Livros das Monções do Reino.

Livros de Reis Vizinhos.

Pessoal do Real Hospital Militar.
Relação de Medicamentos que Vão da Botica do Hospital Real [de Goa] para a Fortaleza de Diu.

Shembaganur Province Archives, Sacred Heart College, Kodaikanal, Tamil Nadu
Annual Jesuit Missionary Letters of the Maduri Province.

West Bengal State Archives, Calcutta
Proceedings of the Board of Customs.
Proceedings of the Board of Revenue.
Proceedings of the Committee of Revenue.
Proceedings of the Provincial Council of Revenue at Calcutta.
Proceedings of the Provincial Council of Revenue at Dacca.

ITALY
Archivum Romanum Societatis Iesu, Rome
Colecção de Varias Receitas e Segredos Particulares das Principais Boticas da Nossa Companhia de Portugal, da India, de Macao e do Brazil, 1766.
Goa 48.
Japonica-Sinica.
Lettere dalla Cina.

MACAO
Arquivo Histórico de Macau
Leal Senado.

NETHERLANDS
Nationaal Archief, The Hague
Dagregister Van Vliet.

PORTUGAL
Arquivo Histórico Ultramarino, Lisbon
Codex 449.
Índia.

Arquivo Nacional da Torre do Tombo, Lisbon
Documentos Remetidos da Índia.
Manuscritos da Livraria.

Biblioteca da Ajuda, Lisbon
Codex 46-13-30 (Goa board of Portuguese India Company to crown).
Codex 51-7-12 (Diary, Miguel de Noronha, fourth Conde de Linhares).

Biblioteca Nacional, Lisbon
Codex 939 (Diary, Miguel de Noronha, fourth Conde de Linhares).
As Novas do Reyno de Sião.

UNITED STATES
U.S. National Archives and Records Administration, Washington, D.C.
Records of the Office of Strategic Services

Secondary Sources

Abley, Mark. *Spoken Here: Travels among Threatened Languages*. New York: Houghton Mifflin Co., 2005.

Abreu, Brás Luís de. *Portugal Médico: Ou Monarchia Médico-Lusitana*. Coimbra: Joam Antunes, 1726.

Aesop. *Aesopi Fabellas vna cvm argvmentis novis: Vobis admodvm conducibiles accipite adolescentuli, nunc demum … solertius ….* Brixiae: Apud héredes Ludouici Britanici, 1563.

———. *Fables of Aesop: Selected, Told Anew, and Their History Traced*, selected by Joseph Jacobs. New York: Macmillan, 1946.

Agualusa, José Eduardo. *Um Estranho em Goa*. Lisbon: Cotovia/Fundação Oriente, 2000.

———. Interview, "O Brasil é colônia". *Época* 330 (13 Sept. 2004). http://revistaepoca.globo.com/Epoca/0,6993,EPT808282-1666-1,00.html.

———. *Fronteiras Perdidas: Contos para Viajar*. Lisbon: Dom Quixote, 1998.

Alden, Dauril. *The Making of an Enterprise: The Society of Jesus in Portugal, Its Empire, and Beyond, 1540–1750*. Stanford: Stanford University Press, 1996.

———. "The Population of Brazil in the Late Eighteenth Century". *Hispanic American Historical Review* 43, no. 2 (1962): 177–80.

Almeida, Miguel Vale de. *An Earth-Colored Sea: "Race", Culture, and the Politics of Identity in the Post-Colonial Portuguese-Speaking World*. Oxford: Berghahn, 2004.

———. "Portugal's Colonial Complex: From Colonial Lusotropicalism to Postcolonial Lusophony". Queen's Postcolonial Research Forum, Queen's University, Belfast, 28 Apr. 2008. http://site.miguelvaledealmeida.net/wp-content/uploads/portugal-colonial-complex.pdf.

Alves, Jorge M. dos Santos and Pierre-Yves Manguin. *O Roteiro das Cousas do Achem de D. João Ribeiro Gaio: Um Olhar Português sobre o Norte de Samatra em Finais do Século XVI*. Lisbon: CNCDP, 1997.

Amaro, Ana Maria. *Filhos da Terra*. Macao: ICM, 1988.

Ames, Glenn Joseph. *Renascent Empire? The House of Braganza and the Quest for Stability in Portuguese Monsoon Asia, c. 1640–1683*. Amsterdam: Amsterdam University Press, 2000.

Amorim, Francisco Gomes de. *O Cedro Vermelho*. Lisbon: Imprensa Nacional, 1874.

Anderson, Benedict. *Imagined Communities: Reflections on the Origin and Spread of Nationalism*. London: Verso, 1983.

———. *Imagined Communities: Reflections on the Origin and Spread of Nationalism*. Rev. ed. London: Verso, 1991.

———. *Three Flags: Anarchism and the Colonial Imagination*. London: Verso, 2005.

Arana-Ward, Marie. "A Synchronic and Diachronic Investigation of Macanese: The Portuguese-Based Creole of Macao". PhD diss., University of Hong Kong, 1977.

Aranha, Paulo. " 'Glocal' Conflicts: Missionary Controversies on the Coromandel Coast between the Seventeenth and the Eighteenth Centuries". In *Evangelizzazione e Globalizzazione: Le Missioni Gesuitiche Nell'età Moderna Tra Storia e Storiografia*, edited by Michela Catto, Guido Mongini, and Silvia Mostaccio, 79–104. Rome: Società editrice Dante Alighieri, 2010.

———. "Malabar Rites: An Eighteenth-Century Conflict on the Catholic Missions in South India". PhD diss., European University Institute, Florence.

———. "Sacramenti o *sāskārā*? L'illusione dell'*accommodatio* nella controversia dei riti malabarici". In *Politiche Sacramentali tra Vecchio e Nuovi Mondi*, edited by Maria Teresa Fattori, 621–46. Monographic issue of *Cristianesimo nella storia* 2, no. 31 (2010).

Arasaratnam, Sinnapah. *Merchants, Companies and Commerce on the Coromandel Coast, 1650–1740*. Delhi: Oxford University Press, 1986.

Araújo, Maria Benedita. "A Medicina Popular e a Magia no Sul de Portugal". PhD diss., Universidade de Lisboa, 1988.

Ashcroft, Bill. *Caliban's Voice: The Transformation of English in Post-Colonial Literatures*. London: Routledge, 2009.

Attlee, Helena. *The Gardens of Portugal*. London: Francis Lincoln, 2008.

Augusto, Sara. "O papagaio ilustrado: Lição e exemplo na ficção barroca". *Máthesis* 14 (2005): 137–48.

Azevedo, Manuel. *Correcçam de Abusos*. Lisbon: Officina de Joam da Costa, a custa Martim Vaz Tagarro, 1680.

Bandyopadhyay, Brajendranath, ed. *Sambadpatre Sekaler Katha*. Vol. 2. Calcutta: Bangiya Sahitya Parisad, 1977.

Barendse, R. J. *Arabian Seas, 1700–1763*. Vol. 1, *The Western Indian Ocean in the Eighteenth Century*. Leiden: Brill, 2009.

Barreto, Adeodato. "Apoteose". In *Civilização Hindu Seguido de* O Livro da Vida: *Cânticos Indianos*, 267–74. Lisbon: Hugin Editores, 2000.

Basak, Gourdas. "Kalighat and Calcutta". *Calcutta Review* 92 (1891): 319–20.

Bask, Bhaskar Jyoti. "The Trading World of Coromandel and the Crisis of the 1730s". In *Proceedings of the Indian History Congress, Forty-Second Session, Magadh University, Bodhgaya, 1981*, 333–39. New Delhi: Indian History Congress, 1982.

Batalha, Graciete. "Aspectos do folklore de Macau". *Boletim do Instituto Luís de Camões* 2, no. 2 (1968): 5–12.

Bate, George and Caetano de Santo António. *Pharmacopea Bateana na quel Se Contem Quasi Oytocentos Medicamentos Tirados de Pratica de Jorge Bateo*. Lisbon: Officina Real Deslandesiana, 1713.

Bauss, Rudy, "A Demographic Study of Portuguese India and Macau as well as Comments on Mozambique and Timor, 1750–1850". *The Indian Economic and Social History Review* 34, no. 2 (1997): 199–216.

Baxter, Alan N. "Introdução". In *Dialecto Português de Malaca e Outros Escritos* by António da Silva Rêgo and Alan N. Baxter, 13–44. Lisbon: Comissão Nacional para os Descobrimentos Portugueses, Imprensa Nacional, 1998.

Bengal. *Historical and Ecclesiastical Sketches of Bengal from the Earliest Settlement until the Virtual Conquest of That Country by the English in 1757*. Calcutta, 1831.

Bengal Gazette, 12 Feb., 26 Feb., and 11 Mar. 1780.

Bethell, Leslie and José Murilo de Carvalho. *Joaquim Nabuco, British Abolitionists and the End of Slavery in Brazil.* London: ISA, 2009.

Bethencourt, Francisco and Diogo Ramada Curto, eds. *Portuguese Oceanic Expansion, 1400–1800*. Cambridge: Cambridge University Press, 2007.

Bèze, Claude de. *Mémoire du Père de Bèze sur la Vie de Constance Phaulkon, Premier Ministre du Roi de Siam, Phra Narai, et Sa Triste Fin: Suivi de Lettres et de Documents*. Tokyo: Presses Salésiennes, 1947.

Biker, Julio Firmino Judice. *Collecção de Tratados e Concertos de Pazes que o Estado da India Portugueza Fez com os Reis e Senhores com Quem Teve Relações nas Partes da Asia e Africa Oriental desde o Principio da Conquista até o Fim do Seculo XVIII*. Vol. 4. Lisbon: Imprensa Nacional, 1884.

———. *Collecção de Tratados e Concertos de Pazes que o Estado da India Portugueza Fez com os Reis e Senhores com Quem Teve Relações nas Partes da Asia e Africa Oriental desde o Principio da Conquista até ao Fim do Seculo XVIII*. Vol. 8. Lisbon: Imprensa Nacional, 1885.

Birch, Alan and Martin Cole. *Captive Years: The Occupation of Hong Kong, 1941–45*. Hong Kong: Heinemann Asia, 1982.

Bocarro, António. *Década 13 da História da India*. Lisbon: Typographia da Academia Real das Sciencias, 1876 [written before 1642].

———. "Livro das plantas de todas as fortalezas, cidades e povoações do Estado da India Oriental". In *Arquivo Português Oriental,* edited by A. B. de Bragança Pereira. New ed., bk. 4, *História Administrativa*. Vol. 2, *1600–1699*, pt. 1. Bastorá, Goa: Typografia Rangel, 1937.

Borschberg, Peter. *Hugo Grotius, the Portuguese and Free Trade in the East Indies*. Singapore: NUS Press, 2011.

———. *The Singapore and Melaka Straits: Violence, Security and Diplomacy in the Seventeenth Century*. Singapore: NUS Press, 2010.

———. "VOC Blockade of the Singapore and Malacca Straits: Diplomacy, Trade and Survival, 1633–1641". In *O Estado da Índia e os Desafios Europeus: Actas do XII Seminário Internacional de História Indo-Portuguesa*, 163–86. Lisbon: CHAM/CEPCEP, 2010.

Bosma, Ulbe and Remco Raben. *Being "Dutch" in the Indies*. Singapore: National University of Singapore Press, 2008.

Boxer, C. R. "The Achinese Attack on Malacca in 1629, as Described in Contemporary Portuguese Sources". In *Malayan and Indonesian Studies: Essays Presented to Sir Richard Winstedt on His Eighty-fifth Birthday*, edited by John Bastin and R. Roolvink, 105–21. Oxford: Clarendon Press, 1964.

———. "A Fidalgo in the Far East: Antonio de Albuquerque Coelho in Macao". *Far Eastern Quarterly* 5, no. 4 (Aug. 1946): 387–410.

———. *Francisco Vieira de Figueiredo: A Portuguese Merchant-Adventurer in South-East Asia, 1624–1667*. The Hague: Martinus Nijhoff, 1967.

———. "The One-Armed Governor". In *Fidalgos in the Far East, 1550–1770*. 2nd rev. ed., reprinted with corrections. Hong Kong: Oxford University Press, 1968.

———. "Portuguese and Spanish Projects for the Conquest of Southeast Asia, 1580–1600". *Journal of Asian Studies* 3 (1969): 118–36.

———. *The Portuguese Seaborne Empire, 1415–1825*. London: Hutchinson, 1969.

———. *The Portuguese Seaborne Empire, 1415–1825*. New York: Knopf, 1975.

———. "Three Historians of Portuguese Asia (Barros, Couto and Bocarro)". *Boletim* (Instituto Português de Hongkong) 1 (1948): 15–44.

Boyajian, James C. *Portuguese Trade in Asia under the Habsburgs, 1580–1640*. Baltimore: Johns Hopkins University Press, 1993.

Braga, José Pedro. *The Portuguese in Hong Kong and China*. Macao: Fundação Macau, 1998.

Braga-Blake, Myrna. *Singapore Eurasians: Memories and Hopes*. Singapore: Times Editions, 1992.

Brah, Avtar and Annie E. Coombes. *Hybridity and Its Discontents: Politics, Science, Culture*. London: Routledge, 2000.

Breazeale, Kennon, ed. and trans. "Memoirs of Pierre Poivre: The Thai Port of Mergui in 1745", *Journal of the Siam Society* 97 (2009): 177–99.

Bressan, Luigi and Michael Smithies. *Siam and the Vatican in the Seventeenth Century*. Bangkok: River Books, 2001.

Briggs, Katharine Mary. *A Dictionary of British Folk-Tales in the English Language*. Bloomington: Indiana University Press, 1971.

Brookshaw, David. "Imperial Diasporas and the Search for Authenticity". In *Lusophonies Asiatiques, Asiatiques en Lusophonies*, 271–82. Paris: Karthala, 2000.

Bruce, Philip. *Second to None: The Story of the Hong Kong Volunteers*. Hong Kong: Oxford University Press, 1991.

Burnay, Jean. "Notes chronologiques sur les missions Jésuites du Siam au XVIIe siècle". *Archivum Historicum Societatis Iesu* 43, no. 22 (1953): 170–202.

Burns, Erik. Review of *Leaving Pico* by Frank X. Gaspar, *New York Times Book*

Review, 12 Sept. 1999, http://www.nytimes.com/books/99/09/12/bib/990912.rv133520.html?_r=1.

Bush, Lewis. *The Road to Inamura*. London: Robert Hale, 1961.

Campos, J. J. A. *History of the Portuguese in Bengal*. New Delhi: Asian Educational Services, 1979. First published 1919.

———. *History of the Portuguese in Bengal*. Patna: Janaki Prakasham, 1998. First published 1919.

Cantigas ne o Lingua de Portuguez. Matre, Ceylon, 23 June 1914.

Caplan, Lionel. *Children of Colonialism: Anglo-Indians in a Postcolonial World*. Oxford: Berg, 2001.

Carita, Heldar. *Palácios de Goa*. 2nd ed. Lisbon: Quetzal Editores, 1996.

Carreira, António. "O primeiro 'censo' de população da Capitania das Ilhas de Cabo Verde (1731)". *Revista de História Económica e Social* 19 (Jan.–Apr. 1987): 33–76.

Carreira, Ernestina. "O Estado Português do Oriente: Aspectos políticos". In *Nova História da Expansão Portuguesa*, edited by Joel Serrão and A. H. de Oliveira Marques. Vol. 5 tomo 1, *O Império Oriental*, coordinated by Maria de Jesus dos Mártires Lopes, 91–96. Lisbon: Estampa, 2006.

"Carta das autoridades de Sião para Manuel Favacho acerca da dívida do Leal Senado para com o dito reino". *Arquivos de Macau*, 3rd ser., 6, no. 1 (Jul. 1966): 15–16.

Carton, Adrian. "Beyond 'Cotton Mary': Anglo-Indian Categories and Reclaiming the Diverse Past". 2009, http://home.alphalink.com.au/~agilbert/carton.html.

Castelo Branco, Camilo. *A Brasileira de Prazins: Scenas do Minho*. Porto: Lello & Irmão, 1882.

Castelo Branco. Miguel. "500 Anos Portugal-Tailandia". http://500anosportugaltailandia.blogspot.com/2009/10/portuguese-minority-in-siam.html.

Castro, Affonso de. *As Possessões Portuguesas na Oceânia*. Lisbon: Imprensa Nacional, 1867.

Castro, Joaquim Magalhães de. *Os Bayingyis do Vale do Mu: Luso-Descendentes na Birmânia*. Santa Maria da Feira, Portugal: Câmara Municipal, 2002.

Castro, Leo d'Almada e. "Some Notes on the Portuguese in Hong Kong". *Boletim* (Instituto Português de Hong Kong), 2 (Sept. 1949): 265–76.

Censo da População do Estado da Índia de 1900. Panaji: Imprensa Nacional de Goa, 1903.

Ceo, Maria do. *Aves Illustradas em Avisos para as Religiosas Servirem os Officios dos Seus Mosteiros*. Lisboa Occidental: Officina de Miguel Rodrigues, 1738.

Cerutti, Pietro. "The Jesuits in Thailand: Part I, 1607–1767". Society of Jesus Thailand. http://www.sjthailand.org/english/historythai1.htm.

Chandler, David P. *A History of Cambodia*. Boulder, CO: Westview Press, 2008.

Chaudhuri, K. N. *The Trading World of Asia and the English East India Company, 1660–1760*. Cambridge: Cambridge University Press, 1978.

Chumsriphan, Surachai. "The Great Role of Jean-Louis Vey, Vicar of Siam (1875–

1909), in The Church History of Thailand during the Reformation Period of King Rama V, the Great (1868–1910)", PhD diss., Pontificiae Universitatis Gregorianae, 1990.
"The City of Macao to Siam, 20 March 1720". *Arquivos de Macau,* 1st ser., 1, no. 3 (Aug. 1929): 151–52.
Coates, Timothy J. *Convicts and Orphans: Forced and State-Sponsored Colonization in the Portuguese Empire, 1550–1755.* Stanford: Stanford University Press, 2002.
Cohen, Rip. *500 Cantigas d'Amigo.* Porto: Campo das Letras, 2003.
"O Comercio desta cidade de Macao com a Cochinchina foy o meyo pello qual a providencia e bondade Divina quiz que se dilatace a nossa Santa Fé". *Arquivos de Macau,* 1st ser. (Dec. 1929).
A Compendius Ecclesiastical, Chronological and Historical Sketches of Bengal: Since the Foundation of Calcutta, Calcutta, 1818.
Concepción, Juan de la. *Historia General de Philipinas.* Vol. 9. Manila: Imprenta del Seminar de San Carlos, 1790.
Cordier, Henri. *Mélanges D'histoire et de Géographie Orientales.* Vol. 4. Paris: Jean Maisonneuve, 1923.
Cortesão, Armando. *The Suma Oriental of Tomé Pires: An Account of the East, from the Red Sea to Japan, Written in Malacca and India in 1512–1515.* London: The Hakluyt Society, 1944.
Costa, Orlando da. "A Literatura indo-portuguesa contemporânea: Antecedentes e percurso". Paper presented at the Fundação Calouste Gulbenkian's Colóquio Internacional Vasco da Gama e a Índia, Paris, May 1998.
———. *O Último Olhar de Manú Miranda.* Lisbon: Âncora, 2000.
———. "Uma abordagem à literatura Indo-portuguesa contemporânea no roteiro da colonização". *AprenderJuntos* 4–5 (Jan. 2005): 115–30.
Coutinho, Miguel. *Goa no Tempo do Marquês de Alorna (1744–1750): Uma Sociedade em Transformação.* Lisbon: Universidade Nova de Lisboa, 2008.
Couto, Diogo do and others. *Décadas na Asia.* Vol. 1, *Décadas IV e V.* Lisboa Occidental: Officina de Domingos Gonsalves, 1736.
Crabbe, C. H. *Malaya's Eurasians: An Opinion.* Singapore: D. Moore, 1960.
Crown to Linhares, 1632, *Boletim da Filmoteca Ultramarina Portuguesa* 9 (1958): 233.
———. 20 Dec. 1632, *Boletim da Filmoteca Ultramarina Portuguesa* 9 (1958): 325–26.
Crystal, David. *Language Death.* Cambridge: Cambridge University Press, 2000.
da Orta, Garcia. *Colóquios dos Simples e Drogas e Cousas Medicianais da Índia.* Goa: Rachol Seminary, 1563. Facsimile edition. Lisbon: Academia das Ciências de Lisboa, 1963.
Dalgado, Sebastião Rodolfo. "Dialecto indo-português de Damão". *Ta-Ssi-Yang-Kuo* 3 (1902): 359–67; and 4 (1903): 515–23.
———. *Dialecto Indo-Português de Damão.* Facsimile edition. Lisbon, 1903.

———. "Dialecto indo-português do Norte". *Revista Lusitana* 9 (1906), 142–66 and 193–228.
———. *Glossário Luso-Asiático*. 2 vols. Coimbra: Imprensa da Universidade, 1919–1921. Reprint. New Delhi: Asian Educational Services, 1988.
———, ed. *Portuguese Vocables in Asiatic Languages*, translated by Anthony Xavier Soares. Baroda, India: Oriental Institute, 1936.
Dalgado, Sebastião Rodolfo and Anthony Xavier Soares. *Portuguese Vocables in Asiatic Languages*. http://www.archive.org/stream/portuguesevocabl033463mbp/portuguesevocabl033463mbp_djvu.txt.
Daus, Ronald. *Portuguese Eurasian Communities in Southeast Asia*. Singapore: Institute of Southeast Asian Studies, 1989.
De Witt, Dennis. *History of the Dutch in Malaysia*. Petaling Jaya, Malaysia: Nutmeg Publishing, 2009.
Delaunoit, Leopold. "Archdiocese of Calcutta". In *The Catholic Encyclopedia*. Vol. 3. New York: Robert Appleton Company, 1908. http://www.newadvent.org/cathen/03152a.htm.
Devi, Vimala. *Súria*. Lisbon: Agência Geral do Ultramar, 1962.
Diário do Terceiro Conde de Linhares. Lisbon: Biblioteca Nacional, 1937.
Disney, Anthony. "A Queda de Ormuz, Malaca e Mombaça". In *Portugal no Mundo*, edited by Luís de Albuquerque. Vol. 5, 42–46. Lisbon: Publicações Alfa, 1989.
———. *A History of Portugal and the Portuguese Empire*. Vol. 2, *The Portuguese Empire*. Cambridge: Cambridge University Press, 2010.
———. "The Portuguese Empire in India c. 1550–1650". In *Indo-Portuguese History: Sources and Problems*, edited by John Correia-Afonso, 148–62. Bombay: Oxford University Press, 1981.
Doyle, James. "Saint Thomas of Mylapur". In *The Catholic Encyclopedia*. Vol. 13. New York: Robert Appleton Company, 1912, http://www.newadvent.org/cathen/13382b.htm.
D'Souza, Bento G. *Goan Society in Transition*. Bombay: Popular Prakashan, 1975.
Endacott, G. B. and Alan Birch. *Hong Kong Eclipse*. Hong Kong: Oxford University Press, 1978.
Fedorowich, Kent. "The Evacuation of Civilians from Hong Kong and Malaya/Singapore, 1939–1942". In *Sixty Years On: The Fall of Singapore Revisited*, edited by Brian Farrell and Sandy Hunter, 122–55. Singapore: Eastern Universities Press, 2002.
Ferdinands, Rodney. *Proud and Prejudiced: The Story of the Burghers of Sri Lanka*. Melbourne: F. R. L. Ferdinands, 1995.
Fernandes, Henrique Senna. *Amor e Dedinhos de Pé*. Macao: Instituto Cultural de Macau, 1986. Reprint. 1994.
———. *Nam Van*. Macao. Author's edition, 1984.
———. *Nam Van: Contos de Macau*. Póvoa de São Adrião, Portugal: author's edition, 1978. Reprint. Macao: Instituto Cultural de Macau, 1997.

———. *Trança Feiticeira*. Macao: Instituto Cultural de Macau, 1986. Reprint. 1993.

Fernandis, Gerard. "*Papia, Relijang e Tradisang*: The Portuguese Eurasians in Malaysia: *Bumiquest*, a Search for Self Identity". *Lusotopie* (2000): 261–68.

———, ed. *Save Our Portuguese Heritage Conference 95 Malacca, Malaysia*. Malacca, 1996.

Ferrão, José E. Mendes. *A Aventura das Plantas e os Descubrimentos Portugueses*. 3rd ed. Lisbon: Instituto de Investigação Científica Tropical and Chaves Ferreira Publicações, 2005.

Field, Ellen. *Twilight in Hong Kong*. London: F. Muller, 1960.

Figredo, Benedict A. *Voices from the Dust: Archeological Finds in San Thome and Mylapore*. Madras: Archdiocese of Madras-Mylapore, 1953.

Flores, Jorge Manuel. "Relic or Springboard? A Note on the 'Rebirth' of Portuguese Hughli, ca. 1632–1820". *Indian Economic and Social History Review* 39, no. 4 (Dec. 2002): 381–95.

Fonseca, José Nicolau da. *An Historical and Archaeological Sketch of the City of Goa*. Bombay: Thacker & Co., 1878. Second reprint. New Delhi: Asia Educational Services, 1994.

Fontaney, Jean de. *Lettres édifiantes et curieuses*. Tome 17. New ed. Paris: J. G. Merigot le Jeune, 1781.

Forjaz, Jorge. *Familias Macaneses*. 3 vols. Macao: Instituto Cultural de Macau, 1996.

Foster, William. *The English Factories in India, 1618–1669: A Calendar of Documents in the India Office, British Museum and Public Record Office*. Vol. 1. Oxford: Clarendon Press, 1906.

"Francisco Telles to the Noble Senate of Macao, 28 June 1721". *Arquivos de Macau*, 1st ser., 1, no. 3 (Aug. 1929): 165.

Fraser, George. *The Golden Bough: A Study in Magic and Religion*. 3rd ed. London: Macmillan, 1906–15. Reprint, abridged edition. New York: Macmillan, 1922.

Frenz, Margret. "Global Goans: Migration Movements and Identity in a Historical Perspective". *Lusotopie* 15, no. 1 (2008): 183–202.

Freyre, Gilberto. *Aventura e Rotina*. Lisbon: Livros do Brasil, 1953.

———. *Casa Grande e Senzala (Formação da Família Brasileira sob o Regime de Economia Patriarcal*. Rio de Janeiro: Schmidt, 1936.

———. *China Tropical*. São Paulo: Imprensa Oficial do Estado de São Paulo, 2003.

Fry, Howard Tyrrell. *Alexander Dalrymple (1737–1808) and the Expansion of British Trade*. London: Routledge, 1970.

Gaspar, Frank X. *A Field Guide to the Heavens*. Madison: University of Wisconsin Press, 1999.

———. *The Holyoke*. Dartmouth, MA: University of Massachusetts Dartmouth, 2007.

———. "Late Rapturous". Unpublished manuscript, 2010.

———. *Night of a Thousand Blossoms*. Farmington, ME: Alice James Books, 2004.

———. *Stealing Fatima*. Berkeley: Counterpoint Books, 2009.

Gist, Noel P. and Anthony Gary Dworkin, eds. *The Blending of Races: Marginality and Identity in World Perspective*. New York: John Wiley & Sons, 1972.

Gittins, Jean. *Eastern Windows, Western Skies*. Hong Kong: South China Morning Post, 1969.

Gomes, Maria Bernadette. "Ethnomedicine and Healing Practices in Goa". PhD diss., University of Goa, India, 1993.

Goonewardena, K. W. *The Foundation of Dutch Power in Ceylon: 1638–1658*. Amsterdam: Djambatan, 1958.

Gosano, Eddie. *Hong Kong Farewell*. Privately printed, n.d.

Gottlieb, Anthony. "My Parrot, My Self". *New York Times*, 12 Oct. 2008.

Gracias, Fátima da Silva. "Goans Away from Goa: Migration to the Middle East". *Lusotopie* (2000): 423–32.

———. *Health and Hygiene in Colonial Goa, 1510–1961*. New Delhi: Concept Publishing, 1994.

Gracias, Ismael. *Dom Antonio José de Noronha Évêque d'Halicarnasse: Les Aventures d'un Pseudo Neveu de Madame Dupleix (1720–1776)*. Pondichéry: Imprimerie Moderne, 1933.

Gracias, J. B. Amancio. *Médicos Europeus em Goa e nas Cortes Indianas nos Séculos XVI a XVIII*. Bastorá, Goa: Tipografia Rangel, 1939.

Gracias, José António Ismael. *Uma Dona Portugueza na Côrte do Grão-Mogol: Documentos de 1710 a 1719 Precedidos d'um Esboço Historico das Relações Politicas e Diplomaticas entre o Estado da India e o Grão-Mogol nos Seculos XVI, XVII*. Nova Goa: Imprensa Nacional, 1907.

Gunn, Geoffrey C. *First Globalization: The Eurasian Exchange, 1500–1800*. Lanham, MD: Rowman & Littlefield, 2003.

Gupta, Pamila. "The Relic State: St. Francis Xavier and the Politics of Ritual in Portuguese India". PhD diss., Columbia University, 2004.

Habib, Irfan. "Population". In *The Cambridge Economic History of India*, edited by Dharma Humar e Tapan Raychaudhuri. Vol. 1, *C. 1200 – c. 1750*. 3rd ed, 163–71. New Delhi: Orient Longam / Cambridge University Press, 2004.

Hahn, Emily. *China to Me*. Philadelphia: Blakiston, 1944.

———. *Hong Kong Holiday*. New York: Doubleday, 1946.

Haig, Wolseley and Richard Burn, eds. *The Cambridge History of India*. Vol. 4, *The Mughal Period*. Cambridge: Cambridge University Press, 1937.

Hamilton, Alexander. *New Account of the East Indies, Being the Observations and Remarks of Capt. Alexander Hamilton, Who Spent His Time There from the Year 1688 to 1723*. Vol. 2. Edinburgh: J. Mosman, 1727.

Han Suyin. *A Many-Splendoured Thing*. London: Jonathan Cape, 1952.

Hancock, Ian. "Field Notes". Personal copy, ca. 1960.

Harcourt, Cecil. *Private Papers of Admiral Cecil Harcourt Relating to the British*

Military Administration of Hong Kong, 1945–1946. London: Imperial War Museum, 1945.

Hayden, Robert M. "Antagonistic Tolerance: Competitive Sharing of Religious Sites in South Asia and the Balkans". *Current Anthropology* 42, no. 2 (April 2002): 205–31.

Heras, Henry. *South India under the Vijayanagara Empire: The Aravidu Dynasty*. Vol. 2. New Delhi: Coso Publications, 1980.

Hill, S. C., comp. *Bengal in 1756–1757: A Selection of Public and Private Papers Dealing with the Affairs of the British in Bengal during the Reign of Siraj-ud-daula*. London: John Murray, 1905.

Holm, John. *Pidgins and Creoles*. Vol. 2, *Reference Survey*. Cambridge: Cambridge University Press, 1989.

Hong Kong News, 18 Feb. and 14 Mar. 1943.

Humboldt, Alexander von, Aimé Bonpland, and Helen Maria Williams. *Personal Narrative of Travels to the Equinoctial Regions of America during the Years 1799–1804*. Vol. 5. London: Longman, Hurst, Rees, Orme, and Brown, 1821.

Hutchinson, E. W., ed. "Four French State Manuscripts". *Journal of the Siam Society* 27, no. 2 (1935): 220.

Hutchinson, Edward. *Adventurers in Siam in the Seventeenth Century*. London: Royal Asiatic Society, 1940.

Jackson, K. David. "Indo-Portuguese *Cantigas*: Oral Traditions in Ceylon Portuguese Verse". *Hispania* 74, no. 3 (Sept. 1991): 618–26.

———. *Sing without Shame: Oral Traditions in Indo-Portuguese Creole Verse*. Amsterdam: John Benjamins; and Macao: Instituto Cultural de Macau, 1990.

———. "*Singelle Nona/Jinggli Nona*: A Traveling Portuguese Burgher Muse". In *Re-exploring the Links: History and Constructed Histories between Portugal and Sri Lanka*, edited by Jorge Manuel Flores, 299–323. Paris: Calouste Gulbenkian Foundation; and Wiesbaden: Harrassowitz, 2007.

Jacobs, E. M. *Merchant in Asia: The Trade of the Dutch East India Company during the Eighteenth Century*. Leiden: CNWS Publications, 2006.

Jain, S. K. *Medicinal Plants*. New Delhi: National Book Trust, India, 1999.

Jumsai, M. L. Manich. *A History of Anglo-Thai Relations*. Bangkok: Chalermnit, 1970.

Kaplan, Robert D. "CNAS – RSIS [Center for a New American Security — S. Rajaratnam School of International Studies] Panel Discussion on 'The United States and Asia: Prospects and Challenges in 2010'". Remarks, Four Seasons Hotel, Singapore, 20 Jan. 2010.

———. "Obama Takes Asia by Sea". *New York Times*, 11 Nov. 2010. http://www.nytimes.com/2010/11/12/opinion/12kaplan.html?pagewanted=all.

King, Frank H. H. *History of the Hongkong and Shanghai Banking Corporation*. Vol. 3, *The Hongkong Bank between the Wars and the Bank Interned, 1919–1945: Return from Grandeur*. Cambridge: Cambridge University Press, 1988.

———. *History of the Hongkong and Shanghai Banking Corporation*. Vol. 4, *The Hong*

Kong Bank in the Period of Development and Nationalism, 1941–84: From Regional Bank to Multinational Group. Cambridge: Cambridge University Press, 1991.

Kleczewski, Stanisław. *Kalendarz Seraficzny Zamykaiący w Sobie Zywoty Wielebnych Sług Boskich Zakonu S.O. Franciszka Reformatów Polskich Osobliwą Swiątobliwoscią Znamienitych. Przez X. Stanisława Kleczewskiego, Tegoż Zakonu Kapłana Zebrany, Dla Pożytku Wiernych, y Nasladowania Cnoty Do Druku Podany*. Lwow: I. K. M. y Bractwa Swętej Troycy, 1760.

Koo Hon Mun, Barnabas. "The Survival of an Endangered Species: The Macanese in Contemporary Macau". PhD diss., University of Western Sydney, 2004.

Koop, John Clement. *The Eurasian Population in Burma*. New Haven: Yale University Press, 1960.

Kraan, Alfons van der. "On Company Business: The Rijckloff van Goens Mission to Siam, 1650". *Itinerario*, 22, pt. 2 (1998): 42–84.

Larkosh, Christopher. "Passage to Our Selves: Translating Out of Portuguese Asia". In *Parts of Asia*, Portuguese Literary & Cultural Studies 17/18, edited by Cristina Bastos, 189–206. Dartmouth, MA: University of Massachusetts Dartmouth Center for Portuguese Studies and Culture, 2010.

Launay, Adrien. *Histoire de la Mission de Cochinchine, 1658–1823: Documents Historiques*. Vol. 2: *1728–1771*. Paris: Charles Douniol et Réteaux, Tequi successeurs, 1924.

Lee, Vicky. *Being Eurasian: Memories across Racial Divides*. Hong Kong: Hong Kong University Press, 2004.

Leiper, G. A. "Some Recollections of Duress Banking (4)". *Curry and Rice* 18 (1968) (Chartered Bank staff magazine): 9–13.

———. *A Yen for My Thoughts*. Hong Kong: South China Morning Post, 1982.

Leow Bee Geok. *Census of Population 2000: Education, Language and Religion, Statistical Release 2*. Singapore: Department of Statistics, Ministry of Trade and Industry, 2001.

L'Estra, François. *Relation ou Journal d'un Voyage Fait aux Indes Orientales: Contenant l'Etat des Affaires du Païs, & les Établissemens de Plusieuss Nations, qui s'y sont faits dépuis quelques années. Avec la description des principales Villes, les mœurs, coûtumes & Religions des Indiens*. Paris: E. Michallet, 1677.

Lethbridge, Henry J. "Caste, Class and Race in Hong Kong before the Japanese Occupation". In *Hong Kong: Stability and Change: A Collection of Essays*, 77–128. Hong Kong: Oxford University Press, 1978.

———. "Hong Kong under Japanese Occupation: Changes in Social Stucture". In *Hong Kong: A Society in Transition*, edited by I. C. Jarvie and Joseph Agassi, 77–127. London: Routledge, 1969.

Li, Lillian M. *China's Silk Trade: Traditional Industry in the Modern World, 1842–1937*. Cambridge, MA: Council on East Asian Studies, Harvard University, 1981.

Li, Tana. *Nguyên Cochinchina: Southern Vietnam in the Seventeenth and Eighteenth Centuries*. Ithaca, NY: Southeast Asia Program Publications, 1998.

Liberman, Victor. "Local Integration and Eurasian Analogies: Structuring Southeast

Asian History, c. 1350–c. 1830". *Modern Asian Studies* 27, no. 3 (1993): 475–572.

Ljungstedt, Anders [Andrew]. *An Historical Sketch of the Portuguese Settlements in China and of the Roman Catholic Church and Mission in China.* Boston: John Munroe, 1836. Reprint. Boston: Elibron Classics, 2006.

Llanes, Ferdinand. "Food Crisis of 1718: Siam Rice, Diplomacy and Reforms". *Philippine Daily Inquirer,* 10 May 2008.

———. "New Knowledge in an Old Account: The Bustamante Diplomatic Mission to Ayudhya, 1718". PhD diss., University of the Philippines, 2005.

Lobato, Manuel. "Malaca". In *História dos Portugueses no Extremo Oriente,* edited by A. H. de Oliveira Marques. Vol. 1, tomo 2, *De Macau à Perifeira,* 11–76. Lisbon: Fundação Oriente, 2000.

Lobo, Roger. "Wartime Resistance". In *Macao Remembers,* edited by Jill McGivering, 71–78. Oxford: Oxford University Press, 1999.

Lopes, Maria de Jesus dos Mártires. *Goa Setecentista: Tradição e Modernidade (1750–1800).* 2nd ed. Lisbon: Universidade Católica Portuguesa, 1999.

———. *Tradition and Modernity in Eighteenth-Century Goa.* Delhi: Manohar / CHAM, 2006.

Lopes, Maria de Jesus dos M. and Paulo Teodoro de Matos. "Naturais, reinóis e luso-descendentes: A socialização conseguida". In *Nova História da Expansão Portuguesa,* coordinated by Maria de Jesus dos M. Lopes. Vol. 5, *O Império Oriental (1660–1820),* 15–70. Lisbon: Presença, 2006.

Loubère, Simon de la. *A New Historical Relation of the Kingdom of Siam.* London: Printed by F. L. for Tho. Horne ... Francis Saunders ... and Tho. Bennet, 1693.

Lourenço, Eduardo. *A Nau de Ícaro Seguido de Imagem e Miragem da Lusofonia.* Lisbon: Gradiva, 1999.

Love, Davison Henry. *Vestiges of Old Madras, 1640–1800: Traced from the East India Company's Records Preserved at Fort St. George and the India Office, and from Other Sources.* London: John Murray, 1913.

Luff, John. *The Hidden Years.* Hong Kong: South China Morning Post, 1967.

Lugarinho, Mário. "Trânsito por ruinas: Resistência e subjetividade na era da globalização". Paper presented at the VIII Congresso Luso-Afro-Brasileiro de Ciências Sociais: "A Questão Social do Novo Milênio". Coimbra, Centro de Estudos Sociais, Sept. 2004. http://www.ces.uc.pt/lab2004/inscricao/pdfs/painel28/MarioLugarinho.pdf.

Machado, Ana Maria. *Filhos da Terra.* Macao: ICM, 1988.

Machado, Elza Paxeco and José Pedro Machado. *Cancioneiro da Biblioteca Nacional.* Vol. 3, *Cantigas 446 a 675.* Lisbon: Edição da *Revista de Portugal,* 1952.

Marbeck, Joan. *Ungua Adanza: An Inheritance,* translated by Celine J. Ting. Malacca: Loh Printing Press, 1995.

Martin, Rafe. "The Steadfast Parrot". In *The Hungry Tigress: Buddhist Legends and Jataka Tales,* 60–61. Berkeley: Parallax Press, 1999.

Martínez de Zúñiga, Joaquin. *História de las Islas Philipinas*. Manila: Impreso en Sampoloc, 1803.

Martins, Paulo Miguel. *Percorrendo o Oriente: A Vida de António de Albuquerque Coelho (1682–1745)*. Lisbon: Livros Horizonte, 1998.

Mathews, Robert Henry. *Chinese-English Dictionary*. Rev. ed. Cambridge, MA: Harvard University Press, 1943.

Matos, Paulo Teodoro de. "Grupos populacionais e dinâmicas demográficas nas Ilhas de Goa (1720–1830)". In *O Estado da Índia e os Desafios Europeus: Actas do XII Seminário Internacional de História Indo-Portuguesa*, 615–32. Lisbon: CHAM / CEPCEP, 2010).

———. "O numeramento de Goa de 1720". In *Anais de História de Além-Mar*. Vol. 8, 241–324. Lisbon: CHAM, 2007.

McAuley, Ian. *Guide to Ethnic London*. London: Immel Publishing, 1999.

McCormac, Charles. *You'll Die in Singapore*. London: Hale, 1954.

McGilvray, Dennis B. *Crucible of Conflict: Tamil and Muslim Society on the East Coast of Sri Lanka*. Durham, NC: Duke University Press, 2008.

———. "The Portuguese Burghers of Eastern Sri Lanka in the Wake of Civil War and Tsunami". In *Re-exploring the Links: History and Constructed Histories between Portugal and Sri Lanka*, edited by Jorge Manuel Flores, 325–47. Paris: Calouste Gulbenkian Foundation; and Wiesbaden: Harrassowitz, 2007.

McPherson, Kenneth. "Anglo-Portuguese Commercial Relations in the Eastern Indian Ocean from the Seventeenth to the Eighteenth Centuries". *South Asia: Journal of South Asian Studies* 19, supp. 1, Special Issue: Asia and Europe: Commerce, Colonialism and Cultures (1996): 41–57.

Meersman, Achilles. *The Franciscans in Taminad*. Schöneck, Germany: Nouvelle Revue de Science Missionnaire, 1962.

Meilink-Roelofsz, M. A. P. *Asian Trade and European Influence in the Indonesian Archipelago between 1500 and about 1630*. The Hague: Martinus Nijhoff, 1962.

Mellow, Melville de. "Anglo-Indians". *The Illustrated Weekly of India*, 19 July 1970.

Melo, João Vicente. "The Sagoate: Diplomacy and Gift Exchange in the Eighteenth-Century Estado da Índia". Paper presented at the 13th International Seminar on Indo-Portuguese History, Aix-en-Provence, France, 24 Mar. 2010.

Mendes, António Lopes. *A India Portuguesa: Breve Descripção das Possessões Portuguezas na Asia*. Lisbon: Imprensa Nacional, 1886.

Mendoza Cortes, Rosario. *Pangasinan, 1572–1800*. Quezon City: University of the Philippines Press, 1974.

Miranda, Eufemiano de Jesus. "Literatura Indo-Portuguesa dos Séculos XIX e XX: Um Estudo de Temas Principais no Contexto Sócio-Histórico". PhD diss., University of Goa, 1995.

Molà, Luca. *The Silk Industry of Renaissance Venice*. Baltimore: Johns Hopkins University Press, 2000.

Moore, Gloria Jean. *The Anglo-Indian Vision*. Melbourne: AE Press, 1986.

Moslund, Sten Pultz. *Migration Literature and Hybridity: The Different Speeds of Transcultural Change*. Basingstoke: Palgrave Macmillan, 2010.

Mukund, Kanakalatha. *The Trading World of the Tamil Merchant: Evolution of Merchant Capitalism in the Coromandel*. Chennai: Orient Longman Limited, 1999.

Mundadan, Antony Mathias. *History of Christianity in India*. Vol. 1, *From the Beginning Up to the Middle of the Sixteenth Century (Up to 1542)*. Bangalore: Theological Publications in India for the Church History Association of India, 1943. Reprint. Bangalore: Bangalore Church History Association of India, 1989.

———. "History of Christianity in Madras and Mylapore from the Beginning Up until the End of the Seventeenth Century". *Indian Church History Review* 39, no. 1 (2005): 21–46.

———. "The Portuguese Settlement in Mylapore". *Indian Church History Review* 3, no. 2 (1969): 103–14.

Mundadan, Anthony Mathias, Joseph Thekkedath, and Hugald Grafe. *History of Christianity in India*. Vol. 2, *From the Middle of the Sixteenth to the End of the Seventeenth Century (1542–1700)*. Bangalore: Church History Association of India, 1988.

Mundy, Peter. *The Travels of Peter Mundy in Europe and Asia, 1608–1687*, edited by Richard Carnac Temple and Lavinia Mary Antsey. London: Hakluyt Society, 1919.

Neeves, Cyril. "The Portuguese in Hong Kong". *Voz dos Macaenses de Vancouver (Newsletter of the Casa de Macau [Vancouver])* 4, no. 4 (Nov. 2002). http://www.casademacau.org/Newsletters/2002/1102news.htm.

Newbold, T. J. *Political and Statistical Account of British Settlements in the Straits of Malacca*. Vol. 1. London: John Murray, 1839.

Newitt, Malyn. *A History of Portuguese Overseas Expansion, 1400–1668*. London: Routledge, 2005.

Noronha, Carmo de. *Contracorrente*. Panaji, Goa: Privately printed by the author, 1991.

Olearius, Adam and Johann Albrecht von Mandelslo. *The Voyages and Travels of J. Albert de Mandelslo*. London: Starkey, 1669.

Owen, Hilary. *Mother Africa, Father Marx: Women's Writing in Mozambique, 1948–2002*. Lewisburg, PA: Bucknell University Press, 2007.

Pallegoix, Jean Baptiste. *Description du Royaume Thai ou Siam: Comprenant la Topographie, Histoire Naturelle, Moeurs et Coutumes, Legislation, Commerce, Industrie, Langue, Littérature, Religion, Annales des Thai et Précis Historique de la Mission: Avec Cartes et Gravures*. Paris, 1854. Reprint. Farnborough: Gregg International Publishers, 1969.

Pandit, Heta. *Hidden Hands: Master Builders of Goa*. Porvorim, Goa: Heritage Network, 2003.

Parker, H., comp. and trans. *Village Folk-Tales of Ceylon*. 2nd ed. London: Luzac & Co., 1910–1914. Reprint. Dehiwala, Sri Lanka: Tisara Prakasakayo, 1971.

Passos, Joana. "A Ambivalência de Goa como imagem do império português e as representações da sociedade colonial na literatura luso-indiana". *e-cadernos ces* 1 (2008): 50, http://www.ces.uc.pt/e-cadernos.

Pearson, Michael N. *The Indian Ocean*. London: Routledge, 2007.

———. "Markets and Merchant Communities in the Indian Ocean: Locating the Portuguese". In *Portuguese Oceanic Expansion, 1400–1800*, edited by Francisco Bethencourt and Diogo Ramada Curto, 88–108. New York: Cambridge University Press, 2007.

———. *The Portuguese in India*. New York: Cambridge University Press, 1987.

———. "The Thin End of the Wedge: Medical Relativities as a Paradigm of Early Modern Indian-European Relations". *Modern Asian Studies* 29, no. 1 (1995): 141–70.

Pereira, Alexius A. "No Longer 'Other': The Emergence of the Eurasian Community in Singapore". In *Race, Ethnicity, and the State in Malaysia and Singapore*, edited by Lian Kwen Fee, 5–32. Leiden: Brill, 2006.

Pereira, João Feliciano Marques, comp. "Cancioneiro musical crioulo", *Ta-Ssi-Yang-Kuo: Archivos e Annaes do Extremo-Oriente Portuguez*, 1st ser., 1: 239–43 and 2: 703–07. Lisbon: Antiga Livraria Bertrand – José Bastos, 1899–1903.

———. "Uma resurreição histórica (paginas ineditas d'um visitador dos jesuitas, 1665-1671)". In *Ta-Ssi-Yang-Kuo: Archivos e Annaes do Extremo-Oriente Portuguez*, 1st ser., 1: 305–10, 2: 693–702, and 2: 747–63. Lisbon: Antiga Livraria Bertrand – José Bastos, 1899-1901.

Pessoa, Fernando. *Quadras*, edited by Luísa Freire. Lisbon: Assírio & Alvim, 2002.

Pessoa, Fernando and Philip Krummrich. *A Critical, Dual-Language Edition of Quadras ao Gosta Popular / Quatrains in the Popular Style*, translated by Philip Krummrich. Lewiston, N.Y.: E. Mellen Press, 2003.

Phelan, John Leddy. *Hispanization of the Philippines*. Madison: University of Wisconsin Press, 1967.

The Philippine Chronicles of Fray San Antonio: A Translation from the Spanish, edited by Pedro Picornell. Manila: Casalinda, 1977.

"The Phrakhlang of Siam to the Noble Senate of Macao, June 1721". *Arquivos de Macau*, 1st ser., 1, no. 3 (Aug. 1929): 163–64.

Pintado, Manuel Joaquim. *Survival through Human Values*. Malacca, 1974.

Pinto, Fernão de Mendes. *Peregrinacam de Fernam Mendez Pinto, em que Da Conta de Muytas et Muyto Estranhas Cousas que Vio et Ouvio no Reyno da China, no da Tartaria, no do Sornau*. Lisbon: P. Crasbeeck, 1614.

Pinto, Paulo Jorge de Sousa. *Portugueses e Malaios: Malaca e os Sultanatos de Johor e Achém, 1575–1619*. Lisbon: Sociedade Histórica da Independência de Portugal, 1997.

Pissurlencar, Panduronga S.S., ed. *Assentos do Conselho de Estado*, vol. 4, *1659–1695*. Bastorá, Goa: Tipografia Rangel, 1956.

———. *Assentos do Conselho de Estado*, vol. 5, *1696–1750*. Bastorá, Goa: Tipografia Rangel, 1957.

Pissurlencar, Panduronga S.S. and Vithal Trimbak Gune, eds. *Assentos do Conselho de Estado, 1618–1643*. 2 vols. Bastorá, Goa: Tipografia Rangel, 1953.

Pombejra, Dhiravat na. "Ayutthaya at the End of the Seventeenth Century: Was There a Shift to Isolation?" In *Southeast Asia in the Early Modern Era: Trade, Power and Belief*, edited by Anthony Reid, 250–72. Ithaca, NY: Cornell University Press, 1993.

———. "Princes, Pretenders and the Chinese Phrakhlang". In *On the Eighteenth Century as a Category of Asian History: Van Leur in Retrospect*, edited by Leonard Blussé and Femme Gaastra, 107–30. Aldershot: Ashgate, 1998.

———. "VOC Employees and Their Relationships with Mon and Siamese Women". In *Other Pasts: Women, Gender and History in Early Modern Southeast Asia*, edited by Barbara Watson Andaya, 195–215. Honolulu: Center for Southeast Asian Studies, 2000.

Price, Charles A. *Immigration and Ethnicity*. Canberra: Commonwealth Department of Immigration and Multicultural Affairs, 1996.

Pye, Maung Maung. "Shin-Mway-Loon and Min-Nanda". In *Tales of Burma*. New York: Macmillan, 1952.

Pyrard, François, Pierre de Bergeron, and Jérôme Bignon. *The Voyage of François Pyrard of Laval to the East Indies, the Maldives, the Moluccas and Brazil*. London: Printed for the Hakluyt Society, 1887. Reprint. New Delhi: Asia Educational Services, 2000.

Quadros, Jeronymo. *Diu: Apontamentos para sua História e Chorographia*. Nova Goa: Tipographia Fontainhas, 1899.

Raychaudhuri, Tapan. *Jan Company in Coromandel, 1605–1690*. The Hague: Martinus Nijhoff, 1962.

"Regimento do Hospital Real da Cidade de Goa", 23 Aug. 1583, doc. 838. In *Archivo Portuguez-Oriental: Fasc. 5*, edited by J. H. da Cunha Rivara. Vol. 3, 1006–67. Nova Goa: Imprensa Nacional, 1865. Reprint. New Delhi: Asia Educational Services, 1992.

———. "28 May 1584". In *Documenta Indica*, edited by Joseph Wicki. Vol. 13, *1583–1585*, 867–73. Rome: Institutum Historicum Societus Jesu, 1975.

Rego, António da Silva, ed. *As Gavetas da Torre do Tombo*. 3 vols. Lisbon: Centro de Estudos Históricos Ultramarinos, 1960–1963.

———. *Dialecto Português de Malaca: Apontamentos para o seu Estudo*. Lisbon: Agência Geral das Colónias, 1942.

———. *O Ultramar Português no Século XVIII (1700–1833)*. Lisbon: Agência Geral do Ultramar, 1967.

———. *Portuguese Colonization in the Sixteenth Century: A Study of the Royal Ordinances (Regimentos)*. Johannesburg: Witwatersrand University Press, 1959.

Rêgo, António da Silva and Alan N. Baxter. *Dialecto Português de Malaca e Outros Escritos*, Lisbon: Comissão Nacional para os Descobrimentos Portugueses, Imprensa Nacional, 1998.

Reid, Anthony. "Changing Perceptions of the 'Hermit Kingdoms' of Asia". In *Charting the Shape of Early Modern Southeast Asia*, 235–45. Chiang Mai: Silkworm Books, 1999.

———. *Southeast Asia in the Age of Commerce 1450–1680*. Vol. 2, *Expansion and Crisis*. New Haven: Yale University Press, 1993.

Reinecke, J. E. "Marginal Languages: A Sociological Survey of the Creole Languages and Trade Jargons". PhD diss., Yale University, 1937.

Ribeiro, Madalena. "The Japanese Diaspora in the Seventeenth Century According to Jesuit Sources". *Bulletin of Portuguese/Japanese Studies* 3 (Dec. 2001): 53–83.

Rivara, J. H. da Cunha. *A Jurisdicção Diocesana do Bispado de S. Thome de Meliapor nas Possessões Inglezas e Francezas*. Nova Goa: Imprensa Nacional, 1867.

Rocha, Leopoldo da. *Casa Grande e Outras Recordações de um Velho Goês*. Lisbon: Vega, 2008.

Rodrigues, Albert. "A Hong Kong Doctor in War and Peace". In *Dispersal and Renewal: Hong Kong University during the War Years*, edited by Clifford Matthews and Oswald Cheung, 203–08. Hong Kong: Hong Kong University Press, 1998.

Rodrigues, L. A. "Portuguese-Blood Communities in India". *Boletim do Instituto Menezes Bragança* 108 (1973).

Romero, Sílvio. *Contos Populares do Brasil*, edited by Luís da Câmara Cascudo, illustrated by Santa Rosa. Rio de Janeiro: José Olympio, 1954.

Roque, Ricardo. *Headhunting and Colonialism: Anthropology and the Circulation of Human Skulls in the Portuguese Empire, 1870–1930*. Basingstoke: Palgrave Macmillan, 2010.

Rothwell, Phillip. "Lusotropical Legacies in Germano Almeida's *Eva*, or Cruelty as a Staged Performance". *Forum for Modern Language Studies* 45, no. 4 (2009): 401–10.

"A Royal Reception of Spaniards from the Philippines". In *Descriptions of Old Siam*, edited by Michael Smithies, 102–04. Kuala Lumpur: Oxford University Press, 1995.

Rozario, M. de. *The Complete Monumental Registers Containing all the Epitaphs, Inscriptions, etc. etc. in the Different Churches and Burial-Grounds, in and about Calcutta etc.* Calcutta, 1815.

Ruangsilp, Bhawan. *Dutch East India Company Merchants at the Court of Ayutthaya: Dutch Perceptions of the Thai Kingdom, c. 1604–1765*. Leiden: Brill, 2007.

Sá, Luís Andrade. *The Boys from Macau: Portugueses em Hong Kong*. Macao: Instituto Cultural de Macau, 1999.

Saldanha, António Vasconcelos. *De Kangxi para o Papa, pela Via de Portugal: Memória e Documentos Relativos à Intervenção de Portugal e da Companhia de Jesus na Questão dos Ritos Chineses e nas Relações entre o Imperador Kangxi e a Santa Sé*. Macao: Instituto Português do Oriente, 2002.

Saldanha, M. J. Gabriel de. *História de Goa (Política e Arqueológica)*. Bastorá, Goa, 1925–1926. Reprint. New Delhi: Asia Educational Services, 2002.

Sales, Arnaldo de Oliveira. "A Gentle War". In *Macao Remembers*, edited by Jill McGivering, 63–70. Oxford: Oxford University Press, 1999.

San Antonio, Juan Francisco de. *Cronicas de la Provincia de San Gregorio Magno*. 1738–1744.

Sanskrit Heritage Dictionary. The Sanskrit Heritage Site, http://sanskrit.inria.fr/sanskrit.html.

Santa Maria, Agostinho de. *História da Fundação do Real Convento de Santa Mónica*. Lisbon: Antonio Pedrozo Galram, 1699.

Santos Filho, Lycurgo de Castro. *História de Medicina no Brasil, do Século XVI ao Século XIX*. São Paulo: Editora Brasiliense, 1947.

Santos Hernández, Ángel. *Jesuitas y Obispados*. Vol. 2, *Los Jesuitas Obispos Misioneros y los Obispos Jesuitas de la Extinción*. Madrid: Universidad Pontificia de Comillas, 2000.

Sarkissian, Margaret. "Being Portuguese in Malacca: The Politics of Folk Culture in Malaysia". *Ethnografica* 9, no. 1 (2005): 196–220.

———. *D'Albuquerque's Children: Performing Tradition in Malaysia's Portuguese Settlement*. Chicago: University of Chicago Press, 2000.

Schuchardt, Hugo. "Kreolische Studien III: Über das Indoportugiesische von Diu". *Sitzungsberichte der Kaiserlichen Akademie der Wissenschaften zu Wien (philosophisch-historische Klasse)* 103 (1883): 3–18.

———. "Kreolische Studien VI: Über das Indoportugiesischen von Mangalore". *Sitzungsberichte der Kaiserlichen Akademie der Wissenschaften zu Wien (philosophisch-historische Klasse)* 105 (1883b): 881–904.

Seabra, Leonor de. *The Embassy of Pero Vaz de Siqueira to Siam (1684–1686)*, translated by Custódio Cavaco Martins, Mário Pinharanda Nunes, and Alan N. Baxter. Macao: University of Macau, 2005.

———. Preface to *Os Javalis de Codval* by Epitácio Pais. Lisbon: Futura, 1973.

Sedaris, David. *Squirrel Seeks Chipmunk*. New York: Little Brown, 2010.

Seixas, Maria Cristina do N. C. "Discursos pós-coloniais sobre a lusofonia: Comparando Agualusa e Saramago". *Cronos* 8, no. 1 (Jan.–Jun. 2007): 131–55.

Sena, Jorge de. "Homenagem ao Papagaio Verde". In *Os Grão-Capitães: Uma Sequência de Contos*, 23–52. Lisbon: Edições 70, 1976.

Serrão, José Vicente. "Macau". In *Nova História da Expansão Portuguesa*, edited by Joel Serrão and A. H. de Oliveira Marques. Vol. 10, *O Império Africano, 1825–1890*, coordinated by Valentim Alexandre, 719–65. Lisbon, Estampa, 1998.

Shelley, Rex. *The People of the Pear Tree*. Singapore: Times Books International, 1991.

———. *Shrimp People*. Singapore: Times Books International, 1991.

Shelton, Flora Beal, ed. *Tibetan Folk Tales*, translated by A. L. Shelton. New York: George H. Doran Co., 1925.

Sibin, Phillip. *Brieff Defz Ehrw. Paters Philippus Sibin Aufs der Gesellschafft JESU, An Ihro Churfürstl. Durchl. zu Cöllen &c. &c.*, Cölln, 1737.

Silva, Frederic A. *Todo o Nosso Passado: All Our Yesterdays*. Macao: Livros do Oriente, 1996.
Simpson, John and Edmund Weiner, eds. *Oxford English Dictionary*. 2nd ed. Oxford: Oxford University Press, 1989.
Singam, S. Durai Raja. "Jingli Nona". *Straits Times Annual*, 1966.
Singh, Anjana. *Fort Cochin in Kerala, 1750–1830: The Social Condition of a Dutch Community in an Indian Milieu*. Leiden: Brill, 1976.
Sitsayamkan, Luang. *The Greek Favourite of the King of Siam*. Singapore: Donald Moore Press, 1967.
Sivarajan, V. V. and Indira Balachandran. *Ayurvedic Drugs and Their Plant Sources*. New Delhi: Oxford & IBH Publishing Co., 1994.
Smith, Stefan Halikowski. *Creolization and Diaspora in the Portuguese Indies, 1640–1720: The Social World of Ayutthaya*. Leiden: Brill, 2011.
———. " 'The Friendship of Kings Was in the Ambassadors': Portuguese Diplomatic Embassies in Asia and Africa during the Sixteenth and Seventeenth Centuries". *Portuguese Studies* 22, no. 1 (15 Mar. 2006): 101–34.
———. "Seventeenth Century Population Displacements in the Portuguese Indies and the Creation of a Portuguese 'Tribe' ". In *Christians and Spices: Sri Lanka and the Portuguese Orient*, edited by Gaston Pereira, 196–220. Sri Lanka: ICESKY, 2010.
Smithies, Michael, ed. *Alexander Hamilton: A Scottish Sea Captain in South-East Asia, 1689–1723*. Chiang Mai: Silkworm Books, 1997.
———, ed. *Aspects of the Embassy to Siam, 1685: The Chevalier de Chaumont and the Abbé de Choisy*. Chiang Mai: Silkworm Books, 1997.
Snow, Philip. *The Fall of Hong Kong: Britain, China and the Japanese Occupation*. New Haven: Yale University Press, 2003.
Soares, Padre António. "Company of Jesus, to the Noble Senate [of Macao], 20 June 1721". *Arquivos de Macau*, 1st ser., 1, no. 3 (Aug. 1929): 157–61.
Sousa, A. Botelho de, ed. *Nuno Álvares Botelho: Capitão Geral das Armadas de Alto Bordo e Governador da Índia*. Lisbon: Agência Geral das Colónias, 1940.
Sta Maria, Bernard. *My People, My Country: The Story of the Malacca Portuguese Community*. Malacca: Malacca Portuguese Development Centre, 1982.
Stocqueler, J. H. *The Hand-book of India: A Guide to the Stranger and the Traveller, and a Companion to the Resident*. London: W. H. Allen, 1844.
Stoler, Ann Laura. *Race and the Education of Desire: Foucault's History of Sexuality and the Colonial Order of Things*. Durham, NC: Duke University Press, 1995.
Subrahmanyam, Sanjay. "Asian Trade and European Affluence? Coromandel, 1650–1740". *Modern Asian Studies* 22, no. 1 (1988): 179-88.
———. *Improvising Empire: Portuguese Trade and Settlement in the Bay of Bengal, 1500–1700*. Delhi: Oxford University Press, 1990.
———. "Manila, Melaka, Mylapore: A Dominican Voyage through the Indies ca. 1600". *Archipel* 57 (1999): 223–42.
———. "Written on Water: Designs and Dynamics in the Portuguese Estado da

Índia". In *Empires: Perspectives from Archaeology and History*, edited by Susan E. Alcock, 42–69. New York: Cambridge University Press, 2001.

Svoboda, Robert E. *Ayurveda: Life, Health and Longevity*. New Delhi: Penguin Books, 1993.

Tabucchi, Antonio. *Notturno Indiano*. Palermo: Sellerio Editore, 1984.

"The Tale of the Husband and the Parrot". In *The Book of the Thousand Nights and a Night*, translated by Richard F. Burton. Vol. 1, 62–64. New York: Heritage Press, 1934.

Tavan, Gwenda. *The Long, Slow Death of White Australia*. Melborne: Scribe Publications, 2005.

Taylor, Jean Gelman. *The Social World of Batavia: European and Eurasian in Dutch Asia*. Madison: University of Wisconsin Press, 1983.

Teixeira, Manuel. *The Portuguese Missions in Malacca and Singapore (1511–1958)*. Vol. 1, *Malacca*. Lisbon: Agência Geral do Ultramar, 1961.

"Termo do Conselho Geral do Leal Senado sobre uma carta que o capitão-geral de Macau escreveu à Mesa da Câmara acerca do requerimento que lhe foi feito pelos capitães das naus do rei de Sião para se recolherem nesta cidade". *Arquivos de Macau*, 2nd ser., 1, no. 3 (Apr.–May 1941): 157–58.

Thomaz, Luís Filipe. "Goa: Uma sociedade Luso-Indiana". In *De Ceuta a Timor*. 2nd ed., 244–89. Lisbon: Difel, 1998.

Thomaz, Luís Filipe Ferreira Reis. *Early Portuguese Malacca*. Macao: CTMCDP, 2000.

Thompson, Stith. *Motif-Index of Folk-Literature: A Classification of Narrative Elements in Folktales, Ballads, Myths, Fables, Mediaeval Romances, Exempla, Fabliaux, Jest-Books, and Local Legends*. 6 vols. Rev. enl. ed. Bloomington: Indiana University Press, 1955–1958.

Tomás, Isabel. "Makista Creole". *Review of Culture* 5 (1988): 33–46.

Tsang, Steve. *A Modern History of Hong Kong*. London: I. B. Tauris, 2007.

United Nations Statistics Division, Department of Economic and Social Affairs. *Demographic Yearbook*. Special Census Topics. Vol. 2b, "Social Characteristics: Ethnocultural Characteristics". http://unstats.un.org/unsd/demographic/products/dyb/DYBcensus/NotesTabSpecial2_4.pdf.

Vale, António M.M. do. "A População de Macau na segunda metade do século XVIII". *Povos e Culturas* 5, *Portugal e o Oriente Passado e Presente* (1996): 241–54.

———. "Macau: Os eventos políticos 2". In *História dos Portugueses no Extremo Oriente*, edited by A. H. de Oliveira Marques. Vol. 2: *Macau e Timor: O Declínio do Império*, 159–227. Lisbon: Fundação Oriente, 2001.

Vasconcellos, J. Leite de, comp. *Cancioneiro Popular Português*. Vol. 1, edited by Maria Arminda Zaluar Nunes. Coimbra: Universidade de Coimbra, 1975.

Velho, Álvaro. *Roteiro da Primeira Viagem de Vasco da Gama*. Lisboa: Agência Geral do Ultramar, 1960.

Venezia, Pietro Antonio da. *Giardino Serafico Istorico fecondo di Fiori e Frutti di Virtù di Zelo e di Santità nelli trè Ordini Instituiti da S. Francesco*. Venice: Lovisa, 1710.

Wagner, Ana Paula. *População no Império Português: Recenseamentos na África Oriental Portuguesa na Segunda Metade do Século XVIII*. Curitiba: Universidade Federal do Paraná, 2009.

Walker, Timothy. "Abolishing the Slave Trade in Portuguese India: Documentary Evidence of Popular and Official Resistance to Crown Policy, 1842–1860". *Slavery & Abolition* 25, no. 2 (Aug. 2004): 63–79.

———. "Acquisition and Circulation of Medical Knowledge within the Portuguese Colonial Empire during the Early Modern Period". In *Science, Power and the Order of Nature in the Spanish and Portuguese Empires*, edited by Daniela Bleichmar, Kristin Huffine, and Paula De Vos, 247–56. Stanford: Stanford University Press, 2008.

———. "Evidence of the Use of Ayurvedic Medicine in the Medical Institutions of Portuguese India, 1680–1830". In *Ayurveda at the Crossroads of Care and Cure*, edited by A. Salema, 74–104. Lisbon: Centro de História de Além-Mar, Universidade Nova de Lisboa, 2002.

Ward, Robert S. *Asia for the Asiatics? The Techniques of Japanese Occupation*. Chicago: University of Chicago Press, 1945.

Weatherbee, Donald E. "Portuguese Timor: An Indonesian Dilemma". *Asian Survey* 6, no. 2 (1966): 683–95.

Webster, Anthony. "British Export Interests in Bengal and Imperial Expansion into South-East Asia, 1780–1824: Origins of the Straits Settlements". In *Development Studies and Colonial Policy*, edited by Barbara Ingham and Colin Simmons, 138–74. London: F. Cass, 1987.

———. *Gentlemen Capitalists: British Imperialism in South East Asia, 1770–1890*. London: Tauris Academic Studies, 1998.

Wheeler, James Talboys. *Madras in the Olden Time: Being a History of the Presidency from the First Foundation to the Governorship of Thomas Pitt, Grandfather of the Earl of Chatham, 1639–1702. Compiled from Official Records*. Madras: Printed for J. Higginbotham by Graves and Co., Scottish Press, 1861.

Whinnom, Keith. *Spanish Contact Vernaculars in the Philippine Islands*. Hong Kong: Hong Kong University Press, 1956.

Wicki, Joseph, ed. *Documenta Indica*. Vol. 5, *1561–1563*. Rome: Monumenta Historica Soc. Iesu, 1958.

Wicks, Peter. "Eurasian Images of Singapore in the Fiction of Rex Shelley". In *Singaporean Literature in English: A Critical Reader*, edited by Mohammed A. Quayum and Peter Wicks, 377–83. Serdang, Malaysia: Universiti Putra Malaysia Press, 2002.

Wills, John Jr. *Embassies and Illusions: Dutch and Portuguese Envoys to K'ang-hsi 1666–1687*. Cambridge, MA: Harvard University Press, 1984.

Winius, George D. "Early Portuguese Travel and Influence at the Corner of Asia". In *Studies on Portuguese Asia, 1495–1689*, 213–28. Aldershot: Ashgate, 2001.

———. "Embassies from Melaka and the 'Shadow Empire'". In *Proceedings of the International Colloquium on the Portuguese and the Pacific*, edited by Francis A. Dutra and João Camilo dos Santos, 170-78. Santa Barbara: Center for Portuguese Studies, 1995.

———. "The Shadow-Empire of Goa in the Bay of Bengal", *Itinerario* 7, no. 2 (1983): 83–101.

———. "A Tale of Two Coromandel Towns: Madraspatam (Fort St. George) and São Thomé de Meliapur". *Itinerario* 18, no. 1 (1994): 51–64.

Wong, Patricia. "Rex Shelley's *The Shrimp People:* What Manner of Beast Is It?" In *Interlogue: Studies in Singapore Literature*, edited by Kirpal Singh. Vol. 1, *Fiction*, 45–54. Singapore: Ethos Books, 1998.

Wordie, Jason. "The Hong Kong Portuguese Community and Its Connections with Hong Kong University, 1914–1941". In *An Impossible Dream: Hong Kong University from Foundation to Re-establishment, 1910–1950*, edited by Chan Lau Kit-ching and Peter Cunich, 163–74. New York: Oxford University Press, 2002.

Wright, Arnold and H. A. Cartwright, eds. *Twentieth Century Impressions of Hong Kong: History, People, Commerce, Industry and Resources*. Singapore: Graham Brash, 1990.

Wyatt, David. *Thailand: A Short History*. New Haven: Yale University Press, 1984.

Yeo, George. "Foreword". In *The Most Comprehensive Eurasian Heritage Dictionary: Kristang-English, English-Kristang*. Singapore: SNP Reference, 2004.

Yolen, Jane, ed. "The Waiting Maid's Parrot (China)". In *Favorite Folktales from around the World*. New York: Pantheon, 1986.

Young, Robert. *Colonial Desire: Hybridity in Theory, Culture and Race*. 2nd ed. updated. London: Routledge, 2010.

Yule, Henry, Arthur Coke Burnell, and William Crooke, eds. *Hobson-Jobson: A Glossary of Colloquial Anglo-Indian Words and Phrases, and of Kindred Terms, Etymological, Historical, Geographical and Discursive*. New edition. London: John Murray, 1903. Fourth reprint. New Delhi: Rupa & Co., 2002.

Županov, Ines G. "A Reliquary Town: São Tomé de Meliapor: The Political and the Sacred in Portuguese India". In *Missionary Tropics: The Catholic Frontier in India (Sixteenth–Seventeenth Centuries)*, 87–110. Ann Arbor: University of Michigan Press, 2005.

INDEX